THE COMPLETE PROJECT MANAGER

Other publications by Van Haren Publishing

Van Haren Publishing (VHP) specializes in titles on Best Practices, methods and standards within four domains:
- IT and IT Management
- Architecture (Enterprise and IT)
- Business Management and
- Project Management

Van Haren Publishing is also publishing on behalf of leading organizations and companies: ASLBiSL Foundation, BRMI, CA, Centre Henri Tudor, Gaming Works, IACCM, IAOP, IFDC, Innovation Value Institute, IPMA-NL, ITSqc, NAF, KNVI, PMI-NL, PON, The Open Group, The SOX Institute.

Topics are (per domain):

IT and IT Management	Enterprise Architecture	Project Management
ABC of ICT	ArchiMate®	A4-Projectmanagement
ASL®	GEA®	DSDM/Atern
CATS CM®	Novius Architectuur	ICB / NCB
CMMI®	Methode	ISO 21500
COBIT®	TOGAF®	MINCE®
e-CF		M_o_R®
ISO/IEC 20000	**Business Management**	MSP®
ISO/IEC 27001/27002	*BABOK® Guide*	P3O®
ISPL	BiSL® and BiSL® Next	*PMBOK® Guide*
IT4IT®	BRMBOK™	Praxis®
IT-CMF™	BTF	PRINCE2®
IT Service CMM	EFQM	
ITIL®	eSCM	
MOF	IACCM	
MSF	ISA-95	
SABSA	ISO 9000/9001	
SAF	OPBOK	
SIAM™	SixSigma	
TRIM	SOX	
VeriSM™	SqEME®	

For the latest information on VHP publications, visit our website: www.vanharen.net.

The complete project manager

The essence and application of project management and Agile leadership

Roel Wessels

Colophon

Title:	The complete project manager
Subtitle:	The essence and application of project management and Agile leadership
Author:	Roel Wessels
English translation:	Luc Munnekom (WordVision)
Reviewers:	Ben Bolland (BEVON Gilde)
	Alexander Celie (Traction10)
	Hans Fredriksz (IPMA-NL, Haax)
	Bas Könemann (You Improve)
	Ben van de Laar (Randstad Groep IT)
	Ruud Merks (ASML)
	Henny Portman (Hedeman Consulting)
	Dieter van der Put (DAF Trucks)
	Ron Schipper (Van Aetsveld)
	John Verstrepen (former director of IPMA-NL)
Text editor:	Dutch edition: Nienke van Oeveren (Boekredactie)
	English translation: Steve Newton
Publisher:	Van Haren Publishing, 's-Hertogenbosch, www.vanharen.net
ISBN Hard copy:	978 94 018 0400 4
ISBN eBook pdf:	978 94 018 0401 1
ISBN eBook EPUB:	978 94 018 0402 8
Editions:	Dutch edition: First edition, first impression, August 2016
	English translation: First edition, first impression, July 2019
Layout and DTP:	Coco Bookmedia, Amersfoort – NL
Copyright:	© Van Haren Publishing, 2016, 2019

PRINCE2® is a registered trademark of AXELOS Limited.

Preface

The only thing I know is that I know nothing.
Socrates

What is a complete project manager? I cannot answer that question; only you can.

This book covers the enormous playing field of the project manager. The emphasis is on the ***how*** of project management and how adopting a proactive attitude allows you to stay in control, even during ***difficult situations***. The book covers several themes that are made as explicit and clear as possible with the help of examples and anecdotes. These do not illustrate the only correct method; instead, they are intended to touch and inspire you. I am not for or against anything. Rather, I want you to think and make your own choices!

Even though I am interested in anything to do with project management and leadership, I have a background in product development and manufacturing. That is a world of product and service development, multidisciplinary teams, a strong emphasis on lead times, quality and costs, a focus on innovation, and collaboration with a global network of suppliers and clients. Nevertheless, this book was written first and foremost for ***general project managers***. I received support from a group of reviewers from various fields.

Complete project managers are best characterized by the fact that they do not know everything, yet they are curious and eager to develop themselves further. The reading guide on the next page can help with that. The chapters of this book form a coherent story, yet they can also be read on their own. You can even jump straight to the section on project execution in chapter 10, because that chapter begins with a summary of the preceding chapters.

Choose your theme, dare to go your own way and become an even more complete project manager!

Reading guide

The complete project manager

	&-&-&-paradox	The TomTom	V-model	Factor 10	Plan: the breakdown	Plan: detailed plan	Project motivator	Heartbeat	The blind check	Final Countdown
	Ch1	Ch2	Ch3	Ch4	Ch5	Ch6	Ch7	Ch8	Ch9	Ch10
For novice project managers who want to gain an overview of the field of project management	*Use the book as a textbook*									
For experienced project managers who want to become even more complete	*Choose your subjects and learn how to become even more effective*									
For people who want to learn how to combine the hard and soft aspects of project management	*Experience how methods and behavior lead to 1+1=3*									
For practicing project managers who want to know more about the *how* and day-to-day application					■		■			■
For people who want to learn how to stay in control at all times, even when dealing with less-than-perfect clients and environments		■		■			■			■
For people who want to learn to go their own way and become less reliant on methods		■		■						
For people who want to become more effective and flexible		■							■	
For people who want to learn how to structure and gain an overview of complex projects		■	■		■					
For project managers working in the field of product development who want to learn how to integrate hardware and software development	■		■		■	■				
For project managers in other fields who want to learn more about the methods used in product development		■			■	■				
For people who want to get an overview of project management and leadership literature by reading a novel-like text	*Become inspired and experience the story as if you were attending a seminar*									
For people who want to gain a quick understanding of what it means to be a complete project manager	*Flip through the book and only read the 'tiles' on the pages*									

Contents

Introduction

The title of this book, *The complete project manager*, might appear a bit pretentious. Nevertheless, it comes straight from my heart. This book is for you. An enormous amount has been written about project management, yet most texts do not focus on the experiences and perception of the project manager: you.

There are countless books that tell you exactly *what* to do to successfully execute projects. They cover the ins and outs of stakeholder analysis, risk management, the importance of plan-do-check-act and what is expected of you when managing your team. However, most people are still left to find out for themselves *how* to apply these techniques in practice, how to be successful *even* in less-than-perfect conditions, how to integrate the methods in their *own* work processes and how to make sure they *actually* do so.

In this book I cover everything I have learned in the past two decades about project management and leadership in as comprehensive and practical a manner as possible. I looked for the essence, because understanding that will help you apply and integrate the methods in your own behavior. In other words, this book can teach you how to abandon your reactive behavior and become proactive and influential instead and, in particular, how to make project management fun (again) for yourself, your team and your environment.

The project manager of the 21st century

Over the past decades a lot has changed in the world of project management. The environment has become more dynamic and the expectations made of project managers have grown. They are expected to deliver results regardless of the circumstances, offer commitment despite major uncertainties, manage highly educated knowledge workers while also coaching them to act more autonomously, deal with stakeholders with different interests and encourage creative breakthroughs without taking excessive risks. In other words: project management can sometimes be a balancing act of Herculean proportions!

Managing all of this requires expertise and the ability to stay in control in any situation. It is like sailing a boat during a storm: there is no time to think and try different approaches to see what works best. You have to manage your project with conviction and decisiveness, and be optimally effective and efficient. How can you do all that?

On top of that, you will probably have noticed that the problems you struggle with and the obstacles that seem insurmountable to you are sometimes dealt with by others without them breaking a sweat. The reverse is also true. It would appear that *how* you manage a project is an all-important factor: applying the right methods in the right situations and demonstrating the right behavior. How can you learn to do that? Where can you find examples to follow? There are countless inspirational management and motivation techniques, but what is the best way to combine them all?

Can you still see the wood for the trees or are you caught up in the theory and do you keep promising yourself over and over again *that you will do better next time*?

Physicist and musician

To answer the aforementioned questions, I went in search of the essence of successful project management. I was able to make use of my years of experience as a project manager, program manager and director of product development, as well as my experience as both a physicist and a musician. The physicist in me is reflected in the focus on structuring projects, the urge to uncover the similarities between methods and the desire to simplify complicated matters. In other words, managing complexity. The musician is felt when I talk about combining constant high-level performance with letting go to facilitate the creative process, the belief that project managers should always take the initiative and therefore need to bring out the performer in themselves, and the emphasis on the importance of rhythm in projects and change processes.

I am passionate about bringing people, methods and philosophies together. The whole is greater than the sum of its parts. As you will see, the aim of this book is not to refute other methods and promise the umpteenth new path to success. Instead, I want to illustrate how methods such as PRINCE2, Agile, DSDM Atern, *PMBOK Guide*, PRINCE2 Agile, the ICB competence framework by IPMA and a multitude of leadership techniques can be effectively deployed together. True experts are not limited by their tools; instead, the tools enrich them. I love to combine modern Agile techniques with more traditional methods. After all, this combination of dynamics is quite common in the real world as well. That is why I prefer to talk about Agile *leadership*: the Agile attitude is more important than the Agile processes.

Over the past seven years, in addition to applying the methods myself, I have taught the contents of this book to more than six hundred professionals during four-day master classes. These people came from a variety of backgrounds: the high-tech sector, the public sector, the medical world, education, construction, IT and other fields. In short, this book was written for anyone who wants to hone their project management skills.

What will this book bring you?

This book contains a complete overview of how to apply project management and Agile leadership to product, service and organizational development. It is accessible for someone who wants to gain an initial understanding of the ins and outs of project management, yet its primary audience consists of advanced project leaders who are eager to take their knowledge and skills to the next level. An in-depth understanding of project management is not required, because this book covers all you need to know. Nevertheless, your existing knowledge and experience will definitely come in handy as you work through it. The book offers plenty of substantive depth, but its focus is on the interaction between the theory and your own behavior and methods. After all, it is all about the *how* and about actually *doing it*, even under less-than-perfect conditions. You will, therefore, also learn how to successfully implement the knowledge found in this book in your day-to-day work processes.

The book consists of three parts. Part 1 (chapters 1 to 4) describes how to set up and manage a project. The focus is on the basic principles, the essence of taking control, creating structure and using Agile behavior. Part 2 (chapters 5 and 6) explains how to draw up a plan and schedule in small steps, which results in improved completeness, coordination and support. Finally, part 3 (chapters 7 to 10) covers how to manage the project execution: how to realize the path to the final goal with a strict PDCA rhythm, how to evaluate the quality of interim results and how to keep your team and environment motivated.

I have sought to make this book as practical as possible by combining theory with practical application and anecdotes. Let this be a source of inspiration to you. It is important to combine the essence of what you learn with your own style and personality. Do things your way, otherwise, your chances of success will be slim and, more importantly, *people will not believe you!*

I hope you enjoy reading this book and putting what you learn into practice.

Project management is a lot of fun!

Roel Wessels

1 The &-&-&-paradox[1]

- How the growing demand for and-and-and turns a project manager's life on its head.
- Why focusing on control and focusing on results and processes are two different things.
- The importance of being able to deal with uncertainty.
- Explaining what Agile is and how it ties into traditional methods.
- The central theme of this book: from reactive to proactive to influencing.

The first time I went skiing I was nearly thirty. I was the only novice in our group of friends, which meant that I was taught the basic principles together with the other rookies, while the rest of my buddies were still eating breakfast. The class was scheduled in the morning and I did not leave the beginner's slope at all that first day. However, I caved to peer pressure on the second day and joined my friends on their run in the afternoon. They had promised to keep my lack of experience in mind.

It all went quite well at first and although I felt a bit awkward about always being the last one to come down, my positive attitude showed me that the others seemed to appreciate the little breaks I afforded them, because it gave them a chance to enjoy a smoke. However, after an hour, the group paused and some people started grumbling a bit. We had missed a turn and ended up at an expert slope. In my naivety, I looked for a way back. There wasn't one; the only way forward was down...

My friends told me that, although the slope was steep, the snow was excellent and that I could get down the steepest sections by sliding sideways. After some hesitation, I started my descent and I did quite well, despite sweating like a pig the entire time. I slowly grew more confident and after I got past the steepest section, I actually started to feel a bit elated.

Before I knew it, I had reached the bottom. I often think back on the things I do and reflect that it wasn't that hard after all. Looking up from below, however, a slope looks even steeper than it actually is. I felt like a king after coming down that mountain unscathed – until a far more experienced skier came racing down as if it were nothing. It made me realize that, despite everything, *I still had plenty left to learn.*

I often begin my lectures with this anecdote, before asking the audience the following question: "Who among you has received feedback from a professional during or after a difficult project about how to improve the project execution?" More often than not, people

---

1 This chapter ties into the following competences from IPMA's ICB4: Strategy, Governance, structures and processes, Resourcefulness, Project design, Change and transformation.

do not raise their hand. Instead, most people are used to hearing something along the lines of "Projects are always difficult here, better get used to it" or "Our environment is so complex that standard project management methods are no use."

 Do you receive feedback during or after a project about how to improve things?

Project managers and their environment have apparently accepted that projects do not go the way they want. They lack experts in the organization to analyze the problem and show them how to improve the situation. Worse, they may not even realize that there is room for improvement; they fail to realize that experienced skiers actually enjoy going down the expert slope and that difficult projects, e.g. those with a lot of uncertain factors or difficult stakeholders, can actually be undertaken successfully. If people have accepted that there is no need to improve matters, they often also lack the ability to learn *how* to improve. This in turn leads to a lack of project managers in the organization who actively look for difficult projects because they enjoy the challenge and are eager to develop themselves further.

Good project managers do not avoid difficult projects, but look for them instead.

I call these apparent contradictions that have to be overcome the *&-&-&-paradox*: allowing for uncertainty *and* being flexible *and* completing the project successfully *and* enjoying the process! Project managers who strive to improve themselves in order to tackle more and more difficult circumstances are professionals who want to break through the &-&-&-paradox.

1.1   More with less

After this anecdote, you may recognize other forms of the &-&-&-paradox in project management. I describe three of them in this chapter. Note that for now I will only focus on the challenges that they present; the solutions are covered later on in this book.

1. **More with less**: the project must be completed as soon as possible *and* it must be possible to make changes along the way *and* the costs have to be reduced *and* the functionality has to improve *and…*
2. **Monitoring things closely** *and* giving your team **plenty of space**.
3. **Recognizing uncertainty** *and* **making a commitment** with regards to the project's completion date and costs.

I will cover the first challenge, more with less, in this section. The other two are covered in sections 1.2 and 1.3. By looking at more than just the project manager, it is possible to gain an insight into the environment in which the modern project manager operates. This illustrates the ways in which a project manager has to develop in order to stay successful.

Goodbye to trade-offs

The &-&-&-paradox describes situations in which choosing is not good enough. To illustrate this, I will use the example of three well-known car brands, Alfa Romeo, Volvo and Mercedes, and compare the situation of thirty years ago with that of today. A Volvo was a safe car and drivers took the boring design for granted. If you wanted design, you had to get an Alfa Romeo, although that design came at the cost of reliability. Mercedes, meanwhile, produced high-quality cars that combined reliability and design, yet customers had to pay a premium price to get one.

These days, this classic *or-or-or trade-off* is accepted less and less. As a result of technological developments, increased competition, globalization and collaboration between corporations, the bar is raised higher and higher. A lot of product characteristics have become standard. We are no longer willing to pay extra for quality. The same goes for extra features, safety, service level, etc. Similarly, the lead times for product development are becoming shorter and development costs have to be reduced. In other words, we have to do more with less. If you cannot meet these demands, you will fall behind: *we want it all*.

 Do you recognize this growing demand for and-and-and?

Expertise and creativity in leadership

We also want and-and-and in projects. One might say that, in this modern day and age, a project has to overcome the *devil's triangle*, which states that money, quality and time are all interconnected. Technologically speaking, that is certainly possible. Raymond Kurzweil, for example, describes an exponential pattern of technological progress that is changing our world at a breakneck pace. Ultimately, this will lead to *singularity* (figure 1.1). Singularity refers to the moment when technology exceeds the capacities of the human brain (Kurzweil,

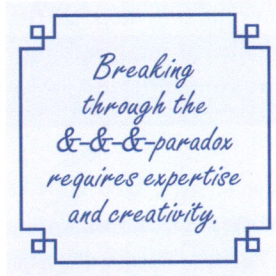

Breaking through the &-&-&-paradox requires expertise and creativity.

1999). Focusing on the present, we see that projects and organizations have become more complex as a result of the growing demands, but also due to inherent complexity. The &-&-&-paradox therefore creates challenges for, and imposes limitations on, the project team. Is that a bad thing? A football player who manages to score despite being marked by several other players is considered a hero. Cyclists want their races to be difficult, so only the best remain at the head of the pack during the final stages of the race. When you realize that everyone faces the limitations of the &-&-&-paradox, you could also say that the person who possesses the most expertise has the highest chance of success. Expertise pays off.

Imposing limitations stimulates one's creativity. Resolving the &-&-&-paradox calls for creative conceptual breakthroughs, because normal design improvements during product development result in a proportional increase in costs, components, etc. Smart solutions

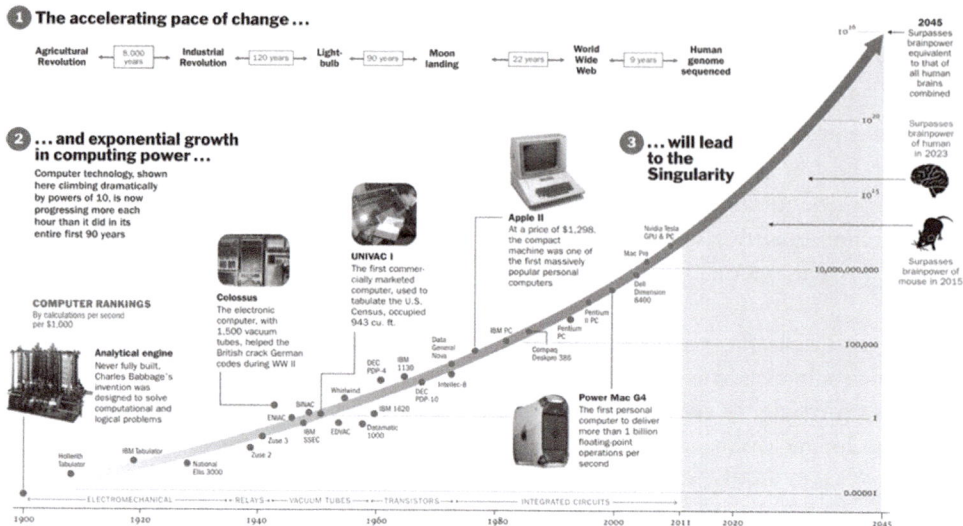

Figure 1.1   The exponential growth of technological progress according to Raymond Kurzweil

are needed, such as setting up faster systems by leaving certain aspects out, or making organizations more efficient by simplifying their structure.

Expertise has to be combined with plenty of creativity. This imposes certain requirements on employees and the (project) manager's leadership style. The latter will have to let things go and still meet the deadlines, create structure and give the team plenty of space, and challenge employees substantively without prescribing every single detail. To do all that at the same time, the project manager has to exercise plenty of leadership.

1.2   Monitoring things closely *and* giving plenty of space

At the start of the financial crisis in 2007, I was leading projects as a program director at Assembléon, a high-tech company with a development department comprising more than 200 full time equivalent (FTE) employees. The financial crisis had a major impact on our sales, reducing them by more than 50%.

The company's CEO faced the challenge of saving money however he could. This process is all about micromanagement. The CFO and he had to sign off on all expenses, regardless of the authorization rules – even those under 100 euros. The company stopped hiring new employees and every contract renewal was also vetted by him first. As a result, the company quickly got its financial situation largely under control. This was because not a single step was taken without the CEO's knowledge, he knew exactly what was going on at all times. A real crisis calls for real measures. Even though they may impede many processes, most employees will actually want and expect such measures during difficult times.

What I remember most is that the CEO made it abundantly clear that this was a *temporary* state of affairs. He excelled at dealing with the second example of the &-&-&-paradox: monitoring things closely while also giving the team plenty of space. That made it easier for employees to participate and hang in there. The CEO was not micromanaging because he was a *control freak*; he had a clear message and wanted his staff to *follow his example* of critically evaluating all expenses. His motto was: "We are a mom-and-pop store once again," which was his way of saying that everyone had to treat every source of income and every expense as if their own money was at stake. The old philosophy of "that is how we have always done things" was no longer good enough. You could only spend money you actually had and you had to know what value it would bring for the company. This measure was applied at every level of the organization.

This demonstrates the power of having a clear message, repeating it often and setting the right example yourself. As the American politician Benjamin Franklin once said: "*Tell me and I forget, teach me and I may remember, involve me and I learn.*"

During a real crisis, temporary measures are needed to increase control. This is a deliberate choice. Every project manager should be able to carry out crisis management. However, things go wrong if crisis management is applied when there is no actual crisis. In that case, it becomes a self-fulfilling prophesy. The crisis is caused by an excessive focus on control and accountability, in other words *micromanagement*.

You might say that the &-&-&-paradox of "monitoring things closely *and* giving plenty of space" is handled incorrectly in those situations. The focus on maintaining control becomes too strong and monitoring employees and understanding every detail becomes an obsession. This is often driven by a lack of faith in the intentions or abilities of others, or a lack of self-confidence.

Is attention to detail necessarily a bad thing? No! On the contrary, it is essential to maintain control over your project. *The devil is in the detail.* However, things can go wrong when it becomes an obsession and management claims an important role in all of the everyday processes. When that happens, decisions cannot be made until the (micro)manager has approved them and, if that were not enough, the manager also tends to prescribe every detail of the project execution. In other words, focusing on details is not the problem, but the micromanager who decides *which* details to focus on is.

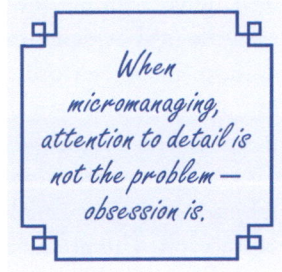

When micromanaging, attention to detail is not the problem — obsession is.

The result is that employees stop taking the initiative and start performing at an average level, instead of at the top of their game. After all, they are monitored and instructed to do just that. Additionally, this obsession causes the micromanager to lose sight of the real goal, actualy achieving the project result! It is no wonder that the term "management" often has negative connotations in our society; we are simply talking about the *wrong kind of management*.

Focusing on control

We see evidence of the excessive focus on control and the lack of focus on results and processes in our society as well. Recent problems, such as the financial crisis and the misuse of power within major organizations, have impacted our faith and trigger our neurotic reflex to add more control measures. New *Key Performance Indicators* (KPIs) are being introduced left and right. We should ask ourselves whether these are intended to improve the process or monitor the executors. KPIs are indicators, yet they are often misused as targets. As a result, employees chase after KPIs instead of doing what needs to be done. In doing so, the solution actually becomes worse than the problem itself.

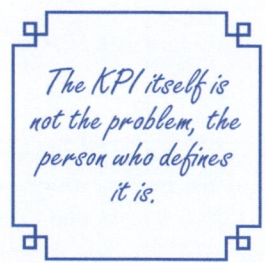

The KPI itself is not the problem, the person who defines it is.

Here is an example from the Dutch healthcare sector. After healthcare insurance providers were criticized for a lack of benchmarking regarding the quality of healthcare organizations, they got to work to improve their processes. They opted to use a system of "practice variation," for which the declarations of GPs and other healthcare providers is statistically compared to data from similar providers. The goal is to filter out outliers without having to consult patients' medical information (which is prohibited under the General Data Protection Regulation). It is only after this initial filter process that healthcare providers with outliers are subjected to a more detailed study and asked to explain these deviations.

Used in that manner, this method is a means of control. Although it is possible to conduct all kinds of additional analyses with the help of data mining, it does not appear to result in better healthcare for patients. Healthcare providers are not thrilled about the measure either. They feel accused and their professional pride is hurt when they are asked to explain deviations regarding the practice variation KPI. Who can blame them? After all, there are many logical explanations other than fraud for a medical practice's deviations from the average. In other words, it creates mistrust among the parties involved. In addition, the use of this method unsurprisingly causes healthcare providers to adapt to the monitoring method. This means the party being monitored will also focus on control instead of results, for example by planning patient care in such a way that it falls neatly within the averages. It would be better to tailor the process to the patients' wishes in order to maximize patient satisfaction. This all but eliminates healthcare providers' ability to innovate.

A focus on control instead of on results and processes is quite common in the public sector. It is often driven by the desire to focus on accountability. Of course, public sector organizations should be able to prove that they are spending their budget wisely, since they are using taxpayers' money. Nevertheless, this is still a backwards perspective. It would be better to focus on finding the optimal path to the goal. That would truly be in the taxpayers' best interest.

Defining KPIs is therefore a job that calls for systematic thinking. The creators of the *Business Balanced Scorecard (BBSC)*, Robert Kaplan and David Norton, already warned us that choosing KPIs requires care and attention with their use of the word "balanced" (Kaplan and Norton, 1996). First, a *connection* has to be established between the indicators of the various perspectives (for the BBSC, those are the financial, customer, internal business processes and learning & growth perspectives) to make sure that individual KPIs actually lead to results that benefit the organization. Furthermore, KPIs must be accompanied by a *complementary* KPI to prevent the process from shifting too far to one side. A well-known example is the call center, for which the "first call resolution rate" is a major KPI. It indicates what percentage of incoming questions are resolved right away. However, measuring just this KPI tells you nothing about how efficiently the organization resolves its customers' questions. Adding a complementary KPI, e.g. "call duration," will provide valuable insight into the company's efficiency.

Defining balanced KPIs, combined with the fact that the substantiation of KPIs can make or break people's confidence, makes clear that compiling a good set of measuring instruments is not easy and calls for the right kind of expertise!

Diminishers and multipliers

Many people spend their entire professional life trying to find the right balance between monitoring things closely and giving the team plenty of space. There is no shame in that. The American growth guru Verne Harnish has been studying the basic principles of organizational growth for years. In his book *The Rockefeller strategy* (Harnish, 2002), he explains – and this should not come as a surprise – that the only way to scale up is by delegating. He adds that 96% of all businesses have fewer than ten employees, with the vast majority of these having fewer than three. The reason for this, he claims, is the fact that most entrepreneurs fail to start delegating responsibilities.

The American leadership expert Liz Wiseman presents a different perspective on this &-&-&-paradox in her book *Multipliers - How the best leaders make everyone smarter* (Wiseman, 2010). She describes how to bring out the genius in others and get more than twice the results. Although we will strive for a *factor 10* in chapter 4, this is a great start. Based on her analysis of 150 managers, Wiseman states that organizations do not necessarily have a shortage of employees or other assets, but rather the inability to properly utilize the most valuable assets they already possess. In practice, most managers, whom she refers to as *diminishers*, fail to bring out the best in their employees. They exhibit behavior that curbs rather than stimulates their employees' intelligence and creativity. On the other hand, *multipliers* manage to get more out of their people. Employees are willing to go to great lengths for this type of manager. Multipliers are able to uncover their employees' hidden talents and have faith in their staff.

Do you ever display diminisher behavior?

Even if you believe you are doing the right thing, everyone will – consciously or subconsciously – display diminisher behavior from time to time. For example, managers who have a strong

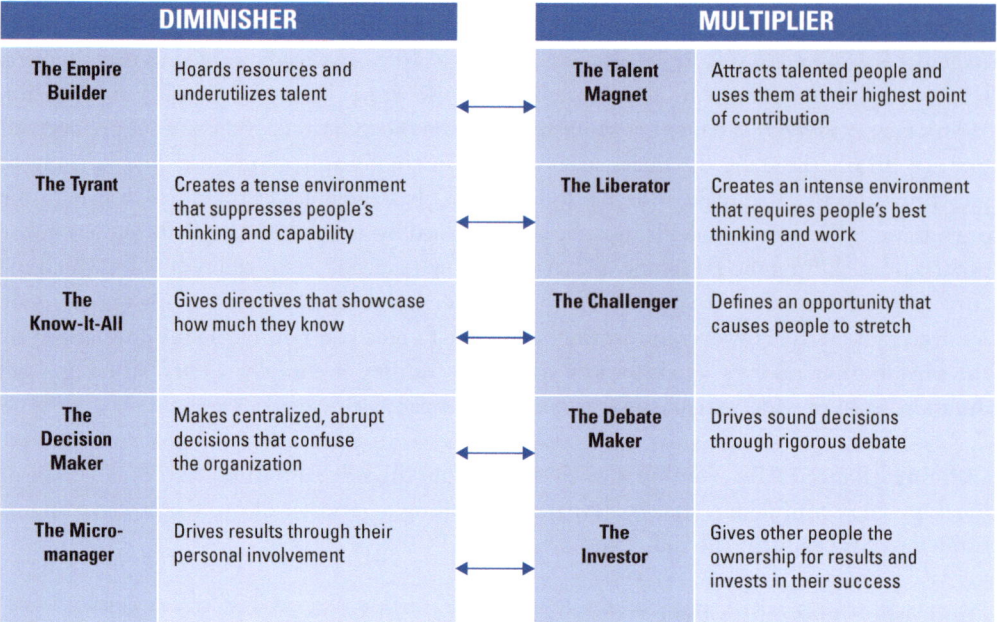

DIMINISHER		MULTIPLIER	
The Empire Builder	Hoards resources and underutilizes talent	**The Talent Magnet**	Attracts talented people and uses them at their highest point of contribution
The Tyrant	Creates a tense environment that suppresses people's thinking and capability	**The Liberator**	Creates an intense environment that requires people's best thinking and work
The Know-It-All	Gives directives that showcase how much they know	**The Challenger**	Defines an opportunity that causes people to stretch
The Decision Maker	Makes centralized, abrupt decisions that confuse the organization	**The Debate Maker**	Drives sound decisions through rigorous debate
The Micro-manager	Drives results through their personal involvement	**The Investor**	Gives other people the ownership for results and invests in their success

Figure 1.2   The five distinguishing disciplines of multiplier and diminisher behavior

drive to achieve results together might unintentionally keep others from taking charge because of their own abundant energy and enthusiasm. Wiseman calls these people *accidental diminishers*. Even though you may not consider her insights to be particularly ground-breaking, the five disciplines with which multipliers distinguish themselves from diminishers can certainly help you discover blind spots in your own behavior (figure 1.2). Furthermore, Wiseman states that everyone can learn to adopt multiplier behavior. There is still hope.

1.3   Recognizing uncertainty *and* making a commitment

Who has ever turned down an assignment because it was too unclear? Whenever I pose this question to project managers, I get a range of different responses. Some are quite firm and claim that an unclear assignment is a poor foundation for a successful project. Others shrug and say that an unclear scope at the start of a project is to be expected in their organization. They have accepted this fact and are used to it. The third &-&-&-paradox of recognizing uncertainty *and* making a commitment affects many project managers. Commitment is about moving forward despite any uncertainties (while risking your personal integrity) and creating the right expectations by doing so.

 Have you ever returned a project to a client?

An organization's culture appears to be an important factor when answering this question. The response that "returning an assignment would not be appreciated" is quite common.

For many organizations, returning projects is not considered to be a good thing. Nevertheless, I wonder if this is truly the case, or if people simply assume it is and therefore never try. Later in this book, we will see that nothing is ever black and white and there are ways to control these situations and exert your influence. It is all about *how* you return an assignment. The results are often surprising. Regardless of your own approach, it also depends on whether your client is a diminisher or a multiplier. A diminisher will view the returning of the assignment as a refusal to do the work, while a multiplier will appreciate your honesty. *Know your audience!*

I recall that, to me, the option to return an assignment was a true revelation. I was about to start a new project for one of my first employers. At the time, they were working hard to improve their organization's project and quality management. One of the company's Quality Assurance Officers, tasked with supporting project leaders with regards to quality, said: "If the client did not send you a User Requirements Specification, it makes sense to return the assignment, because you have no idea what you are supposed to do!" Although I did not return the assignment that time, I did work with the client to clearly define the project scope. Fortunately, that client responded well to my request and helped me make the assignment sufficiently concrete. Being critical and firm and not simply starting my work with an unclear project description paid off in the end. I am still thankful to that Quality Officer for the valuable life lesson he taught me.

I should note that I did eventually return a different assignment at that same company. Instead of making any changes, they simply assigned the project to someone else who accepted it without hesitation. Although this project manager showed guts, he ended up having to work very hard to keep the unfocused project execution on track. Another valuable lesson: there is no optimal way to deal with the paradox of "recognizing uncertainty and making a commitment."

Expectations are created immediately
I believe that most project management methods have more similarities than differences. Depending on the specific field and vision, they may emphasize different aspects, but, with a little effort, they can fit together quite well. That is good, because although organizations often use different project management methodologies, this should not impede their collaboration and the management of the project as a whole.

Most project management guidelines also agree about the moment at which a project manager officially makes a commitment with regards to the required time, budget, resources, etc. Although IPMA's International Competence Baseline is not that explicit, the global ICB4 standard states, under the plan and control competence, that this moment occurs at the conclusion of the project initiation phase, as part of the *decision to fund* milestone. When using PRINCE2, you make a formal commitment upon delivery of the *Project Initiation Documentation* at the conclusion of the initiation stage. At that moment, the project management plan is delivered and approved as if it were a contract of sorts, the project definition phase is completed and the execution phase can begin. The client and the contractor formally accept their respective obligations and responsibilities.

Traditional project management methods therefore assume that, as a result of the activities conducted during the definition phase, any uncertainties have been cleared up to such an extent that there is no more confusion about the project's budget, lead time, etc. The project management plan has been finalized and stabilized, and it is now time to stop thinking and start doing. However, we all know that things are never that simple in practice. At the conclusion of the definition phase, there are often still significant uncertainties. These may be caused by, for example:

- The project goal is unclear or it changes during the project.
- There is not enough knowledge about the desired solution to plan ahead. People learn as they go during the execution phase.
- The organization does not take the time to go through the definition process and jumps directly to the execution phase instead.
- There is a lack of decisiveness to make choices regarding the project scope, the desired solution or the use of resources.

A project manager often has to make a commitment when it is really too early to do so. It can help to extend the definition phase, but it is likely there will still be some uncertainties left – if the client is even willing to give you this extra time to begin with. There could be a practical reason for this: the project's end date is set, so extending the definition phase will automatically leave less time for the execution phase. If that is the case, waiting to make a commitment can seriously test the client's patience. There may also be a political reason, for example the clients know that what they want is impossible, yet they are unwilling to admit it. That presents you with an even greater dilemma - do you play along or not?

You can time your commitment, but not the expectations you raise.

Perhaps the importance of *when* you make your commitment is relative anyway; you may be able to time your commitment, but not the expectations you raise. I often talk to project managers who are upset about the fact that their client starts drawing conclusions about lead times and budgets during the definition phase, before any formal communication has taken place. That makes sense and they are technically right to feel this way. However, even though an official commitment has not been made yet, expectations are raised – consciously or subconsciously – from the very start. Although these expectations are informal, clients are not likely to care about or even realize this. If their expectations are not met, they are disappointed. Disappointed clients are less flexible and cooperative, which results in a downward spiral before the project is even underway. Surely, that is not what you want as a project manager?

A project manager, therefore, has to start managing expectations from the get-go. By definition, there will still be many uncertainties at that stage. For that reason it is crucial that

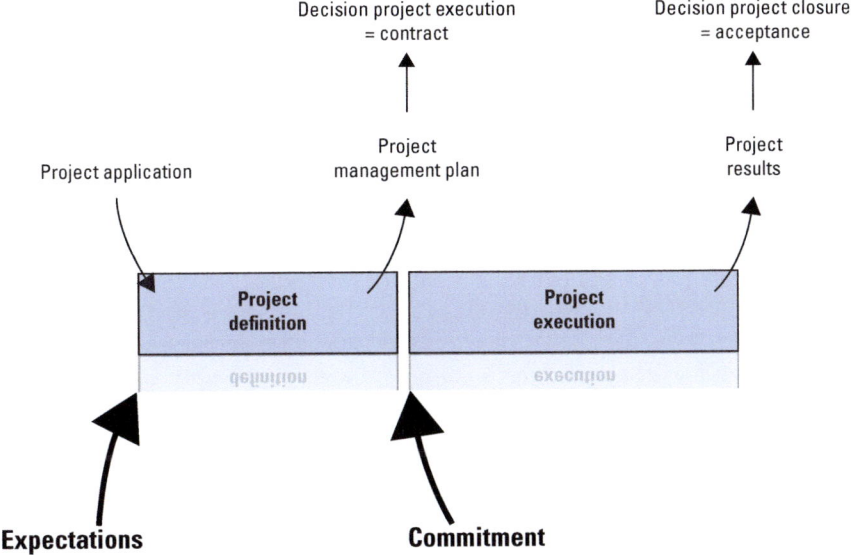

Figure 1.3   Expectations are raised long before a commitment is made

project managers are able to clarify the project scope and the expected delivery moments despite all the uncertainties that still exist, regardless of whether they are formally making a commitment or informally raising expectations.

Cynefin

Uncertainties concerning your project make it difficult to make a commitment. You probably know this to be true, even though it can be quite subjective. How complex is your project, really? Is the degree of uncertainty truly so great that it is impossible to make a stable plan, or is that simply due to your own inability? How do you keep the client satisfied in the meantime? What approach is best, taking into account the complexity of your project?

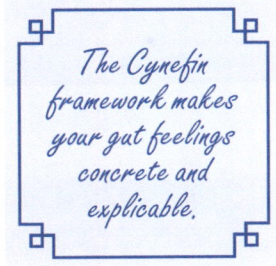

The Cynefin framework makes your gut feelings concrete and explicable.

You can use the *Cynefin framework* (Snowden, 2007) to define how complex your project is. This framework was developed by Professor Dave Snowden. Cynefin (phonetically: kih-neh-vin) is a Welsh word that means something like "multiple factors in our environment and in our experiences affect us in a way we can never fully understand." The Cynefin framework helps to determine the degree of complexity and uncertainty of the project. Furthermore, it answers the question of which actions and types of solutions are appropriate and which are not. It is therefore also a *decision-making instrument* that helps you choose the optimal project approach.

Snowden divides situations and problems into four quadrants (figure 1.4). Each quadrant has its own specific steps:

1. **Simple** (*sense* ⇨ *categorize* ⇨ *respond*): the solution is known in advance and easy to plan for.
2. **Complicated** (*sense* ⇨ *analyze* ⇨ *respond*): an expert is needed to determine the right solution.
3. **Complex** (*probe* ⇨ *sense* ⇨ *respond*): earlier solutions are not applicable. The solution and the plan are drawn up after conducting experiments.
4. **Chaotic** (*act* ⇨ *sense* ⇨ *respond*): drawing up a plan is not a top priority. First, it is important to take action and get the crisis under control. Only then will it be possible to identify the solution and make a plan.

It is interesting that Dave Snowden distinguishes between simple and complicated situations on the one hand and complex and chaotic situations on the other. For *simple* and *complicated* situations, the solution is known in advance – although simple situations can be resolved by anyone and complicated problems require an expert. In other words, the situation is predictable enough to draw up a plan and start the project execution.

This is not the case for *complex* and *chaotic* situations, because too many factors are unpredictable or changeable. Complex situations call for experiments that you can learn from; routine actions and standard solutions will not work. Rather, these situations require innovative and creative methods: try first, plan later. Chaotic situations, on the other hand, demand immediate action. There is an ongoing crisis that must be dealt with as soon as possible to restore order. Only then can work begin to determine the correct follow-up measures. Act first, before starting the definition phase.

Complex

Probe – sense – respond

The correlation between cause and effect is only obvious in hindsight and existing solutions are ineffective. We learn through experimentation.

Emergent practice

Complicated

Sense – analyze – respond

An expert is needed to discover the link between cause and effect based on existing solutions, to make choices and a plan.

Good practice

Disorder

Novel practice

There is no correlation between cause and effect at system level. First take action to stabilize, then determine the right follow-up measure.

Act – sense – respond

Chaotic

Best practice

There is a clear relationship between cause and effect. The solution is known in advance and easy to plan for.

Sense – categorize – respond

Simple

Figure 1.4   Dave Snowden's Cynefin framework

Personally, what I love about Snowden's model is that it ties in seamlessly with my common sense as I make choices concerning the project approach. Simple and complicated projects are predictable and therefore plannable from the start. You should, therefore, focus on gathering the right information or the right experts, rather than on brainstorming, experimentation or other needless distractions. It is also important to develop a unified vision with the rest of the team. There are as many suppositions as there are persons involved, even for predictable projects. The definition phase is about moving ahead, communicating, making choices and not allowing yourself to be distracted until a plan has been drawn up. Just do it!

This is not the case for complex projects. As you have probably guessed, most projects that involve the development of new products or services fall into this category, as do projects that involve many people and interests, such as reorganizations and work process improvements. At the start of these projects, not enough is yet known about the right approach and solution. Depending on the degree of complexity, it may be possible to resolve some of these uncertainties during the definition phase. If the amount of uncertainty is limited and if a feasibility study

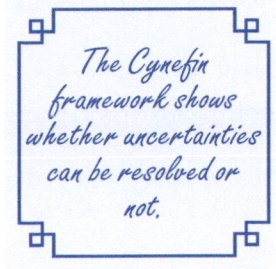
The Cynefin framework shows whether uncertainties can be resolved or not.

(using the principle of probe, sense, respond) can provide more clarity quickly, you can bring the project down from complex to complicated before making a commitment. In other words, you make a commitment with a plan for the execution phase based on a predictable project course. However, this is not possible for projects with a higher degree of uncertainty or changeability. For these projects, the execution phase begins when a significant amount of uncertainty and changeability is still to be expected. Complex projects require more expertise and creativity from project managers, who have to deal with the &-&-&-paradox of recognizing uncertainty and making a commitment. It goes without saying that all this is especially true for projects that fall into the chaotic category.

 What types of projects from the Cynefin framework have you managed in the past?

To conclude, I want to address two special circumstances that Dave Snowden touches upon with his model. Firstly, the model actually features a fifth domain: *disorder*. A situation is classified as disorderly when it is unclear to which of the aforementioned four quadrants it belongs. This makes for an exceptionally dangerous situation. It may be caused by, for example, a project manager who fails to seize enough control over the project. The project members will revert to their personal comfort zones and make wrong decisions because they do not tailor their methods to the problem at hand. Disorder can be recognized by remarks such as "this is how we always do things." In this type of situation, it is important to take action immediately and leave the domain as soon as possible.

The other element is the remarkable transition from simple to chaotic. Organizations that systematically underestimate situations or changes (i.e. simplify them when they really shouldn't) can fall into chaos. This is known as a *catastrophic failure*. As Snowden says: "complacency leads to failure."

1.4   A project model as a support tool

In this and the subsequent section, I will focus on two topics that are important for what comes next in this book: a *model of the project* and *Agile project management*. The model of the project will serve as an orientation tool and mnemonic device as we introduce new concepts. Agile project management is an iterative project management approach that helps with the execution of projects that contain many uncertainties and changing objectives. I will not present Agile as the counterpart of traditional project management; instead – you've guessed it! – we will go for the and-and approach: Agile thinking and acting combined with traditional project management methods. You will also encounter this combination in multidisciplinary projects when mechanical (waterfall) development is combined with (Agile) software development.

The phasing of the project model

Figure 1.5 shows the project management elements that can be used to model most projects. This model is primarily intended to support the IPMA Individual Competence Baseline, but it can also be used for PRINCE2 and PMI's *PMBOK Guide*. The basic goal is to provide support for understanding, rather than impose choices and push for a certain method. The model focuses on the *definition phase* and the *execution phase*. Together, these phases are often seen as "the project." Of course, it is possible to split these phases into subphases for your own project. Because this book is mainly focused on the development of new products and services, I have coined three subphases for the execution phase: the *design phase*, the *realization phase* and the *test phase*.

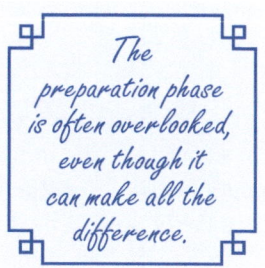

The preparation phase is often overlooked, even though it can make all the difference.

The project model consists of two additional phases, which are usually not viewed as formal parts of the project. Firstly, there is the *exploitation phase*, during which the client uses the project results. This phase is generally not part of the project itself, because the project is commonly closed after the execution phase. Nevertheless, project managers should not forget about this phase, because this is the time when the client starts to use the project results and expects to realize the project goals. Furthermore, it is good to remember that most projects only become profitable from the exploitation phase onwards. The second additional phase is the *preparation phase* (known as the Starting Up process in PRINCE2), which we will be coming back to often in this book. The preparation phase has been deliberately separated from the definition phase. This was done because the transition to the definition phase is so important and because the activities from the preparation phase are often overlooked – even though a successful project manager can make all the difference during this important time!

The definition and execution phases, together with the preparation and exploitation phases, are known as "the project in the broadest sense." Note that many of the parties involved will only experience the "project in the strictest sense" (the execution phase), because they are only part of the project execution or experience the effects of this phase. The project model includes three major *decision-making moments*:

■ **Decision to justify**: decide whether an idea or application can be turned into a project.
■ **Decision to fund**: decide whether the execution phase can begin. This marks an important go/no-go moment in any project.
■ **Acceptance**: accept the project results, decide whether the project can be closed and the project team dissolved.

For your own project, you may of course add additional milestones and decision-making moments to your plan and leave out certain other elements. The project model is not a strict guideline, but rather a useful tool and frame of reference for your project.

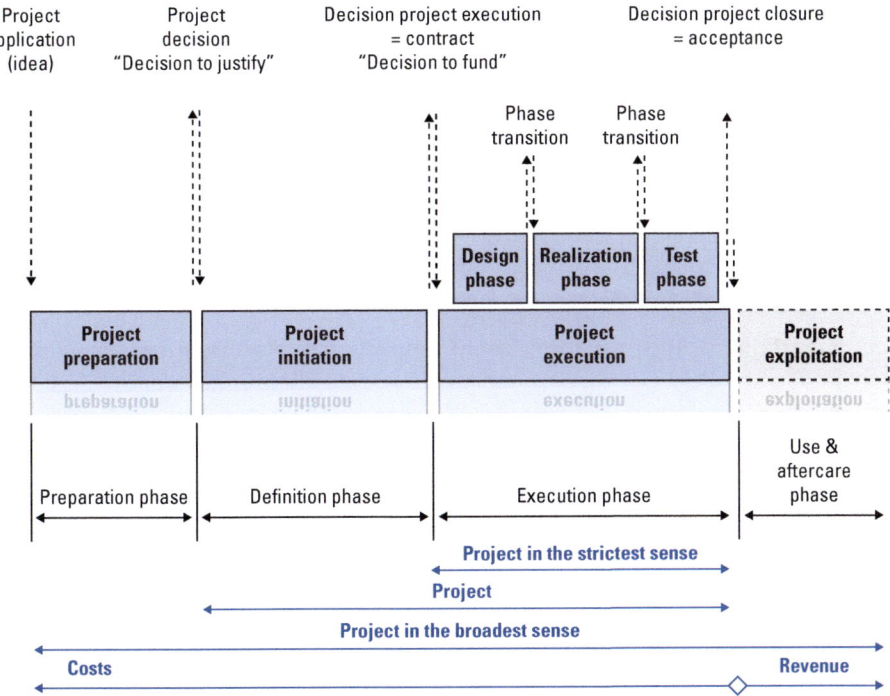

Figure 1.5   A model of a project with phases and key decision points

The deliverables of the project model

The project model also features a number of elementary *project management deliverables* or (interim) results. These deliverables have been added to their respective phases in figure 1.6. A downward-facing arrow means a deliverable serves as input for its phase, while an upward-facing arrow indicates a phase's delivered results. We will return to the deliverables many times throughout this book; for now, I will only cover the essentials needed to understand the model and the cohesion.

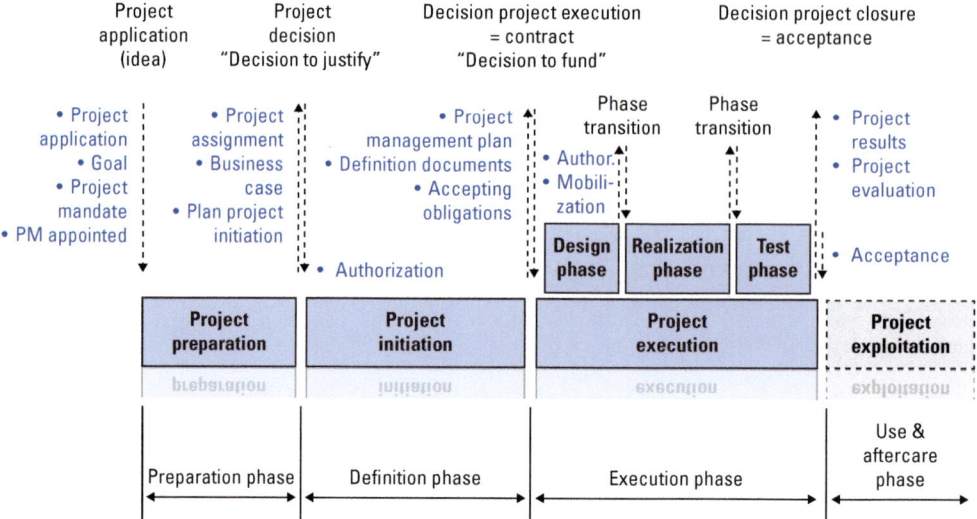

Figure 1.6   The project management deliverables of the project model

Preparation phase

Let's begin with the start of the project; the moment at which the client has an idea for a project and submits a project application in order to realize the associated goals. Part of the intention of starting a project is appointing a project manager and giving him or her the appropriate mandate. Of course, the reality is not always that simple, but we will come back to that later.

Project managers in this situation could immediately start working on the project management plan, although they would miss out on an important opportunity by doing so, namely the (one-time) chance to critically evaluate the project assignment and go over it with the client. In other words, this is their chance to affect the course of the project. We will reveal how to do this in chapter 4. For now, it is important to understand that, despite its usual brevity, the project preparation phase is the perfect time to build a solid foundation for future success.

Project managers translate the project application into a project assignment (which records the initial scope) and draw up a plan of action for the definition phase. Furthermore, they critically examine the business case (which the client has often drawn up during an earlier stage) and present any improvement suggestions they may have. The project preparation phase results in a conscious decision regarding whether it is useful to turn the idea into a real project: the *decision to justify*. In a sales process, this moment is known as the bid/no-bid moment - will we submit an offer to the client or not? The initiation phase will begin following a positive decision.

Initiation phase

The goal of the initiation phase is to draw up a realistic project management plan that the organization supports, based on which obligations can be accepted and a commitment can be made. The information needed for this plan (e.g. specifications and feasibility studies) falls under the umbrella term of "Definition documents" in the model. We will come back to these documents in chapter 3, the V-model. The process of drawing up the plan is covered in chapters 5 and 6. The initiation phase ends with the *decision to fund*, which marks the start of the execution phase. We have already mentioned that the initiation phase also includes the creation of the project management plan. This means we deliberately make no distinction between an initiation phase and a planning phase as, for instance, PMI's *PMBOK Guide* does. The planning activities take place during the entire initiation phase and possibly even in the execution phase, as we will learn later in this book. By not talking about a separate planning phase, integration with the Agile approach will also become more logical.

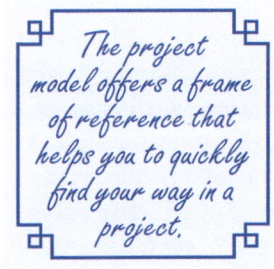

The project model offers a frame of reference that helps you to quickly find your way in a project.

Execution phase
For the execution phase, the project model only lists generic project management deliverables for the start and completion of the phase, namely the mobilization of the team, the delivery of the project results, the client's acceptance of the results and the project evaluation. As you know, most deliverables of the project execution phase are specific to each project. They are not part of the project model, rather they are identified when drawing up the project management plan.

Deliverable or intake	Result or input	Owner
Project preparation phase		
Project application	Input	Client
Goal	Input	Client
Project mandate	Input	Client
Project manager appointed	Input	Client
Project assignment	Result	Project manager
Business case	Result	Client
Plan project initiation	Result	Project manager
Project initiation phase		
Authorization project initiation	Input	Client
Project management plan	Result	Project manager
Definition documents	Result	Project manager
Accepting obligations	Result	Project manager
Project execution phase		
Authorization project execution	Input	Client
Mobilization	Input	Project manager
Design deliverables	Result	Project manager
Realization deliverables	Result	Project manager
Test deliverables	Result	Project manager
Project results	Result	Project manager
Acceptance of project results	Result	Client
Project evaluation	Result	Project manager

Figure 1.7   Summary of the project model's deliverables

Although this book focuses primarily on projects that result in new products or services, the project model is universally applicable – even for personal projects such as remodeling your home or hosting a party. The model shows you which type of questions you need to answer during which phase of the project, as well as what needs to be done before you take on any obligations (decision to fund). Appendix 1 contains applications of the project model for the following examples:

- Project "developing a new website" (Cynefin complicated);
- Project "raising the productivity of an operational process up to a predefined performance level" (Cynefin complex);
- Project "merger of two organizations" (Cynefin complex);
- Project "increasing employee satisfaction" (Cynefin complicated).

Finally, figure 1.7 presents a summary of all deliverables included in the project model and lists whether ownership lies mainly with the project manager or the client. Note that the owner and the executor are not necessarily the same. For example, a project manager may choose to draw up the business case for the client. In fact, doing so often presents useful opportunities to influence the project scope. However, it is important to ensure that the client feels ownership over the final business case, otherwise the project manager will be on thin ice.

1.5   Agile thinking and working

Will the project model also work in situations that are rife with uncertainties (Cynefin complex)? Yes and no. *Yes*, because at the client level the commonly used pattern follows the structure of the project model:

request ⇨ plan/offer ⇨ contract ⇨ execution ⇨ acceptance

This more or less forces you to think and communicate in a similar manner yourself.

No, because the project model is based primarily on the *waterfall model*. This means that the phases are tackled one at a time, a new phase can only begin once the preceding phase has been completed entirely, and it is not encouraged to go back to a previous phase later on. That is why we will expand the project model using Agile in this section. Instead of focusing on either the waterfall model or the Agile approach, I will show you how to combine the two (Agile for one part of the project, the waterfall model for the other). After all, that is what most projects are like in practice.

The waterfall model
When following the waterfall model, you do not start working on the design until all requirements are known and you only move on to the test phase once the design has been fully realized. If you discover an error or want to make a change, you revert to the phase

in question and go through the processes all over again from there. That can be troublesome in situations with a lot of uncertainties where nothing is 100% clear. Furthermore, there is a significant chance that some aspect of the specifications will change anyway, even though you have already moved on to the design phase. *Waterfall in Cynefin complex projects is about waiting for clarity while you know that changes still have to be made later on...*

Waterfall in Cynefin complex: waiting for clarity while you know corrections are still coming.

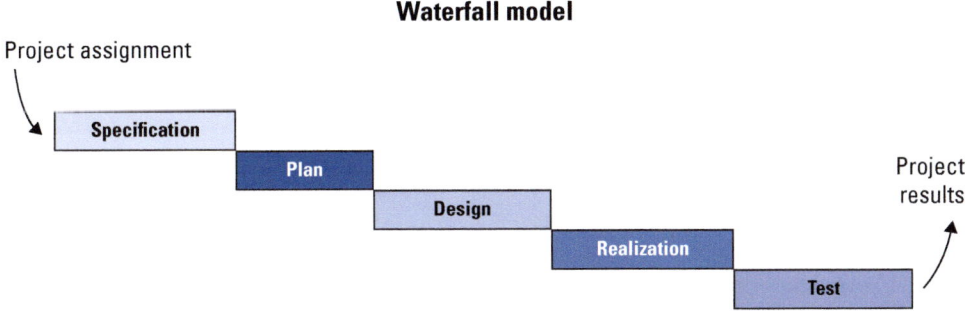

Figure 1.8   The waterfall model

Concurrent engineering

To ease the pain, you can make use of *concurrent engineering* or parallel development. Concurrent engineering allows different project phases to be carried out at the same time. That means it is possible, for example, to work on the design, even though the specifications have not yet been finalized. It gives a project team the ability to make progress even in the face of uncertainties.

Truth be told, the real reason to use concurrent engineering is often to shorten the project's lead time. The project is compressed, as it were. Although there is nothing wrong with this method, it does make the project execution more complex. After all, concurrently working on activities that should really take place one after the other requires a lot of expertise from the team members, as well as insight into each other's activities and excellent communication.

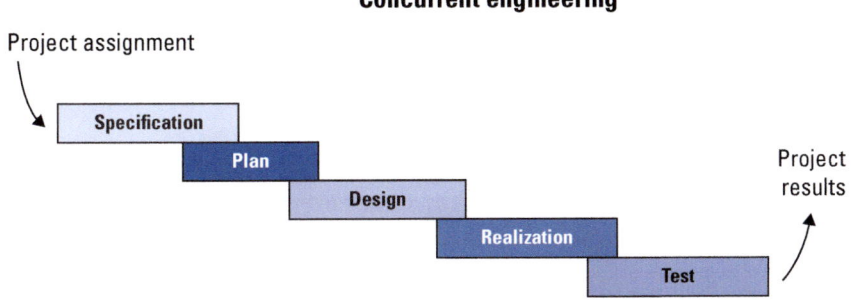

Figure 1.9   Concurrent engineering

Agile: uncertainties are a given

Although concurrent engineering is a step in the right direction, the additional flexibility of working in parallel leads to an increase of the complexity of the project execution. Furthermore, this method – like the waterfall model – also assumes that phases have to be completed entirely and that uncertainties can be eliminated. What if this is not the case?

The *Agile* approach (the Italian musical term "agile" means fast, flexible) turns things around. Agile views uncertainties as a given, rather than as something undesirable. The world cannot be controlled and projects carried out in an uncertain and dynamic environment are, by their nature, unpredictable. Furthermore, Agile working creates an environment in which team members' taking responsibility is explicitly stimulated and facilitated. This allows the project manager to adopt more of a coaching and facilitating attitude, instead of being controlling and directive. The Agile approach stems from the world of software development, although with some skill it can also be applied to other environments, e.g. the mechatronics, construction and public sectors.

Although PRINCE2 and other methods have already integrated the Agile approach, the waterfall and Agile models are often seen as opposites. That is too bad, because this emphasizes their differences, even though it would be impossible to make everyone adopt either the Agile or the waterfall way of working. The two models coexist and this should not impede a project's execution. Nevertheless, many organizations struggle with combining (waterfall) mechanical product development and (Agile) software development. The teams speak different languages and view the other group's processes as an incomprehensible black box. Even within one and the same organization, this can create different spheres of people who fail to understand each other properly or work together effectively.

 How are waterfall and Agile used in your organization?

Viewing the Agile and waterfall models as polar opposites can, therefore, be counterproductive. In this book, I will illustrate how both can be combined, e.g. by using the waterfall model for mechanical development and the Agile approach for the related software development. Furthermore, I will not only discuss Agile as a method, but also as a form of behavior. Even during traditionally structured (waterfall) projects, Agile behavior will allow you to improve your team members' flexibility, their focus on interim results and their autonomy.

Short iterations

An important difference between Agile and the traditional project approach has to do with the method of *project control*. In a traditional project, the project scope is usually seen as being set in stone. If there are setbacks or changes, this will automatically lead to delays and higher costs. This pressure on time and budget results in a need to modify the plan during the project. Consequently, it is not unusual to compromise the quality of the product or service being developed: for example, less time is spent on the execution of tasks, reviews are cancelled, there is a reduced focus on risk management, the test program is cut short, etc. In other words, the pressure is mainly on the project's final phase.

In Agile projects, on the other hand, *time*, *money* and *quality* are viewed as immutable factors. The scope is also important, but it is negotiable during Agile projects. It is, therefore, recorded as an overview of functions to be delivered, ordered by priority. These functions are then realized insofar as the available timeframe and budget allow. If there are setbacks along the way, the least essential or optional functions are cut first. Time, money and the quality of the execution are non-negotiable, but functionality is. This results in a markedly different management climate compared to traditional project control methods.

Are the cut functions dropped entirely from the project scope? Usually not, since Agile development makes use of *multiple short iterations* instead of a single execution phase. Functions cut during one iteration are generally included as part of the subsequent iteration. If the final few iterations allow for a large enough buffer (or contain optional functionalities), the final result of the project will include the functions originally outlined in the project scope. If said buffer is not available, you will at least know that the *most important* functions have been realized without compromising the project's timeframe, budget or quality.

Creating value

The focus on quality is increased because iterations must produce functioning interim results that the (end) user can evaluate. This means that although iterations only implement part of the project functionality, they do consist of the *entire* development cycle of design, realization and testing. In other words: *you do not do everything, but you finish what you do completely*. Agile working therefore allows the user to give feedback and creates value while the project is still ongoing. Figure 1.10 presents a schematic overview of Agile development.

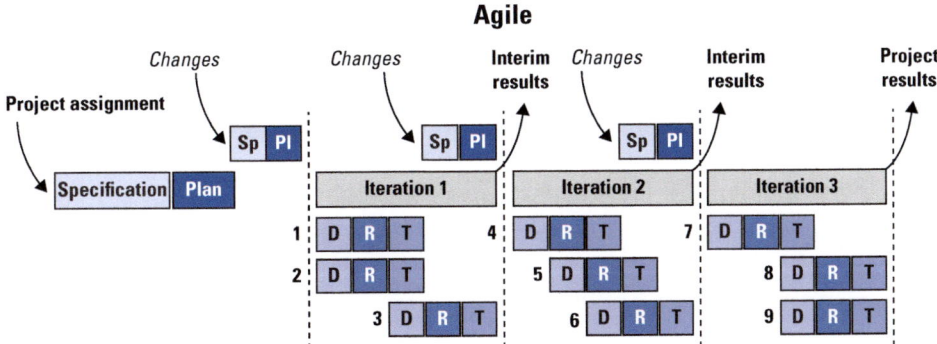

Figure 1.10   Agile development. The nine functions are incrementally designed (D), realized (R) and tested (T)

Working in iterations offers another advantage. The client has the option of making changes prior to the start of a new iteration. After all, Agile expects changes to be made along the way. One rule does apply: *once an iteration has begun, the team members can no longer be interrupted and changes cannot be made until the start of the next iteration*. This combines the best of both worlds, flexibility for the client and efficiency for the team. Since iterations

Feedback from the client while the project is still ongoing.

have a lead time of several weeks at most, this ban on making changes during an iteration is usually not seen as a problem by clients. In other words, Agile working makes for a perfect combination of optimal flexibility and efficiency.

In addition to the rhythm of the iterations, Agile also has a *daily* rhythm: the team meeting. This is a daily meeting during which all team members *stand up* and effectiveness and efficiency are paramount. People's attitudes during this meeting are active and focused, because that is the only way to ensure the meeting is both effective and brief. The team members take turns explaining what they have achieved, what they will be doing next and what problems they expect to encounter. Everyone gets a chance to talk, but they all have to be brief and concise. It is therefore essential to prepare properly for this meeting. If discussions run too long and are no longer relevant for the entire group, they are continued as one-on-one conversations after the team meeting.

With the daily team meeting, together with the clear priorities regarding the functionality to be delivered and the immediate evaluation of interim results at the end of each iteration, it is possible to give the development team a lot of autonomy. In this manner, Agile offers important preconditions to allow the team to be *self-organizing*. This means that the team members take responsibility for the planning and realization of the products they have to deliver, as well as the collaboration and coordination this requires. In traditional projects, this responsibility lies mainly in the hands of the project manager.

The role of the project manager
What role does the project manager play in an Agile project? To ensure the answer to this question is as clear as possible, I will be referring to *Scrum* throughout the rest of this book. Scrum is an Agile framework that calls iterations *sprints*, the prioritized overview of functionalities the *product backlog*, the assigned scope per sprint the *sprint backlog* and the daily team meeting the *daily stand-up meeting*. The planning meeting at the start of every sprint is called the *sprint planning meeting* (Pl in figure 1.10). Scrum also describes two main roles which the project manager has no part in: that of *product owner* and *scrum master*. Note that this is not a bad thing for the project manager. Indeed, it presents a number of opportunities.

Product owners manage and prioritize the product backlog. In doing so, they serve the interests of the customer and will therefore require the right mandate from the client. The daily stand-up meeting is the perfect time for the product owner to coordinate with the team members about the interim results and the reasons behind the client's wishes. The product owner is an explicit part of the team, which ensures that the voice of the customer is clearly heard during the daily coordination meetings. With traditional project management methods, the "business role" is usually not part of the team itself. Therefore, the challenge of making sure the client's voice is heard by the team mainly falls to the project manager.

The team and the product owner are supported by the *scrum master*. This role is different from that of the project manager, because a scrum master does not actually direct the team. Instead, a scrum master acts in a coaching and facilitating manner, since a development team must be self-organizing in an Agile environment in order to efficiently realize its assigned goals.

The added roles of product owner and scrum master therefore result in preconditions that allow for an explicit focus on the business and facilitate the teams' self-organizing capacity. That is good news for project managers. It allows them to focus on the primary activities, e.g. leading the project as a whole, synchronizing subprojects (including the Scrum teams and other subprojects), managing external interfaces, providing the necessary resources, coordinating with external stakeholders and managing the budget.

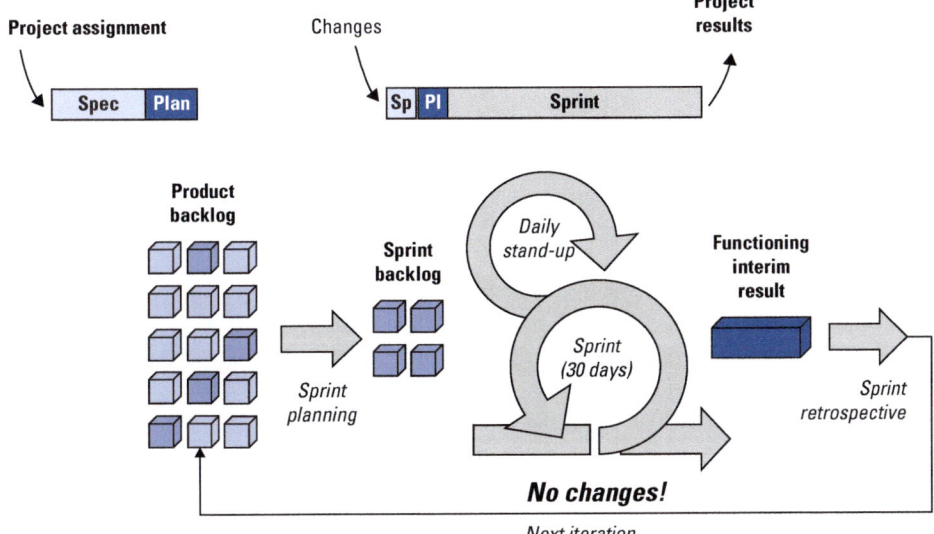

Figure 1.11   The Scrum process (with a thirty-day sprint period)

In an environment of *unpredictability*, Agile creates a *predictable* rhythm of interim results. Brief iterations in fixed timeboxes and self-organizing multidisciplinary teams form the foundation of this rhythm. Agile has a markedly different view on project control than traditional project management methods, but you will surely have noticed that the various Agile elements are based on little more than common sense. Nothing therefore keeps you from applying them in a traditional project organization.

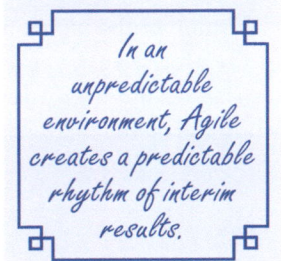

In an unpredictable environment, Agile creates a predictable rhythm of interim results.

Agile and the project model

Agile fits well within the project model. A notable difference is that the project execution phase no longer consists of *just one* sequence of design, realization and testing. Instead, a number of functionalities go through the entire development life cycle during each iteration. At the end of the iteration, they are delivered as tested interim results (see figure 1.12). That also means the exploitation phase will start sooner.

In addition, the project initiation phase will look quite different. After all, because changes are expected to be made during the execution phase, it is not convenient to work out all the details in advance. Detail only has to be created at the start of an iteration. The focus during the project initiation phase is therefore on drawing up a clear list of functionalities (the product backlog), an architecture that facilitates iterative development, an estimate of the size of the functionalities on the product backlog and a plan that outlines which functionality is to be realized during which iteration.

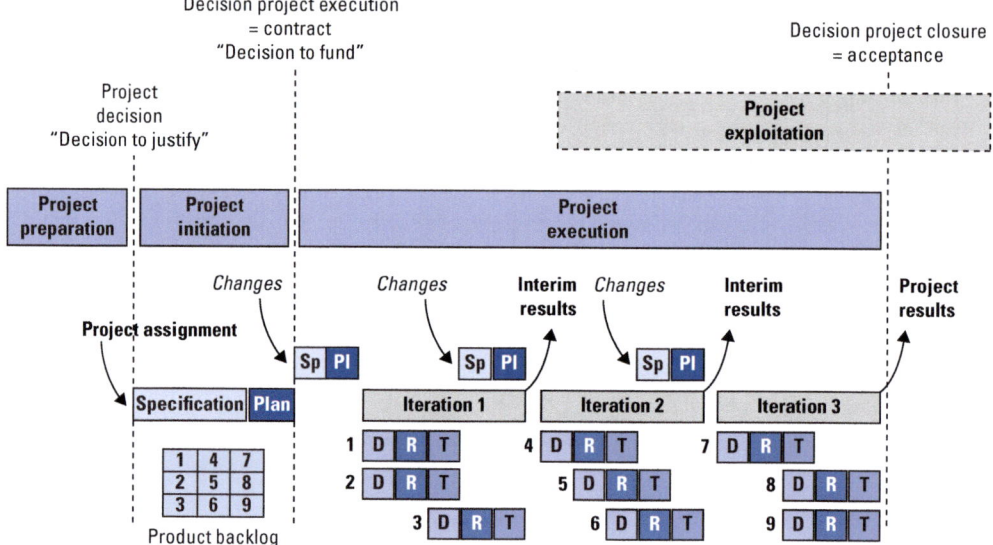

Figure 1.12 Agile development and the project model

1.6   What does the &-&-&-paradox mean for project managers?

After briefly exploring Agile, I would like to conclude by summarizing what the &-&-&-paradox means for project managers. The position of project managers has changed rapidly over the past twenty years. It used to be mainly about coordinating the planning and execution of activities, but today's project managers are explicitly responsible for the realization of the project result – regardless of the assignment's complexity and the maturity of the project environment. The challenges of the &-&-&-paradox are a daily factor: you have to do more with less, you must maintain control over your team members' progress while also giving them more autonomy and you have to make a commitment regarding time and budget despite the many uncertainties that plague the project.

This means project managers also have to perform during difficult "expert slope" projects and under less-than-perfect conditions. That can feel quite unfair at times. Everything is fine as long as the project proceeds as planned, but you are made the scapegoat as soon as something goes wrong – sometimes even by clients or project board members who are themselves unable to figure out where the problem lies, because they lack the necessary competences to do so. The realization that the business of project management can be quite unfair and that others feel the same way can be a huge relief. It makes it easier to shrug off the criticism and take appropriate measures with renewed vigor to get the project back on track.

It can be an unfair business at times.

Performing in an environment with micromanagers

You are probably not a micromanager yourself, but chances are that you will frequently work in a micromanaged environment throughout your career. You will have to learn to deal with this and avoid the many pitfalls along the way.

For example, it took me a long time to realize that most project management instruments are not tools to be used for the benefit of the project manager, but rather a means to control the project manager. Think of, for instance, financial analyses that only show accomplished results, instead of information that can be used to make proactive adjustments. This was an important trigger for me to truly understand which tooling I needed to effectively execute planning, tracking and control. Since then, I have become less reliant on what is and is not available to me, I only use the things that benefit my project, and I no longer allow myself to be distracted. This topic will be covered extensively later on in this book. In a micromanaged environment, you will have to be quicker on your feet and more (politically) savvy than your environment!

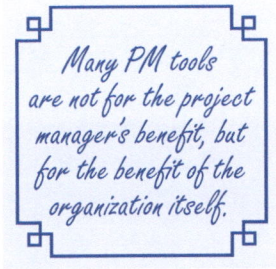

Many PM tools are not for the project manager's benefit, but for the benefit of the organization itself.

Have you noticed that offering transparency in a controlling organization can actually be counterproductive? We have all been there: you are in a project board meeting and everyone avoids the difficult issues until you show that, as a result of different factors and with the current plan and staffing, there is a three-week delay. "That is not good, project manager. How are you planning to solve *your* problem?" Later on, you notice that other project managers do not give an up-to-date prediction of the completion date at all, yet they are not criticized for it either. I am a big fan of transparency, but it is all about how you use it. It seems giving out information invokes a response; the reverse is also true. If you want to make positive use of transparency, you need to replace your naivety by expertise pertaining to leadership and influencing skills. You also have to develop a thick skin, for example by getting to know your own fears and defense mechanisms. Chapter 2 (Your Agile inspirator) and chapter 4 (The factor 10) will teach you all you need to know.

Anticipating what you already knew

I did not call the business of project management unfair to instill a feeling of self-pity or indifference in you. On the contrary, I mention it because we often feel self-pity without even realizing it. This gets in the way of our willingness to learn and grow. When that happens, you do exactly what many methods inadvertently advise: *blame others*. The project did not go as planned because the organization was not ready, because the necessary instruments and systems were not implemented, because the team members did not apply the methods correctly, because the client kept changing the goals, etc.

Of course, others are at fault, but… you already knew that.
Of course, there are many uncertainties, but… you already knew that.
Of course, you have to meet the deadline while not being given enough resources, but… you already knew that.
Of course, you start implementing additional functionality at your own expense and you will still be blamed when you miss the deadline, but… you already knew that.
Of course, suppliers claim to be on schedule until their delivery is late, but… you already knew that.

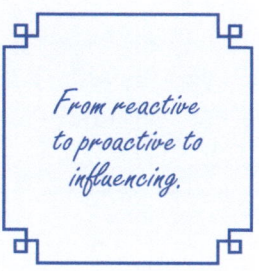

From reactive to proactive to influencing.

Stop blaming others and start taking the initiative in order to become less dependent on things that never go as planned anyway. Make use of the things you already know, anticipate them and do not allow yourself to be surprised again. As hockey coach Marc Lammers puts it in his book *Yes! a crisis* (Lammers, 2010): "Winners have a plan, losers have an excuse!"

This brings us to the central theme of this book: *from reactive to proactive to influencing.*

Summary

- Today's project manager has to deal with the various forms of the &-&-&-paradox:
  - Doing more with less;
  - Monitoring things closely while also giving the team sufficient autonomy;
  - Recognizing uncertainty and making a commitment.
- A focus on control is not the same as a focus on results and processes. KPIs are a refined tool that can make or break people's trust.
- You can time your commitment, but expectations are raised from the very start of a project. By definition, there are still many uncertainties at that point. It is therefore important to learn to deal with uncertainty in projects. View it as a positive, rather than a negative.
- The Agile approach has the following characteristics:
  - Time, money and quality are set in stone, while functionality can be prioritized and negotiated about;
  - Functioning interim results are regularly delivered in iterations and evaluated by the (end) user;
  - It is possible to adjust the scope prior to the start of an iteration, but the project team is not to be disturbed once an iteration begins;
  - The multidisciplinary team must be self-organizing in order to realize its assigned goals in an efficient manner. The daily stand-up meetings, the product owner's clearly prioritized product backlog and the scrum master's support all help with this;
  - The project manager's main tasks are creating the right preconditions for the team and managing the project's external interfaces.
- Agile project management and the classic waterfall model can be used in conjunction. You should know how to use them together, because that is what you will encounter in practice.
- A project's success starts with you. Stop blaming others and make use of what you know and expect in advance. Take the initiative to become less dependent on things that never go as planned anyway; instead, choose to influence the course of the project.

2 Your Agile inspirator, the TomTom

> ➤ Why is the TomTom such an effective project manager?
> ➤ How goal-oriented working is tested every single day.
> ➤ Why you should start conducting stakeholder management at an early stage.
> ➤ As a *scenario creator,* always showing a single up-to-date route brings peace of mind, clarity, feedback, decisions and action.

What or who is your biggest inspirator? That is a very personal question. However, I would like to recommend one that all project managers are sure to be familiar with: the TomTom (or any other modern GPS car navigation system). That answer might well surprise you, but after you have completed this chapter, the chances are that you will feel inspired by its remarkably effective behavior or be a little embarrassed about opportunities you have missed in the past.[2]

2.1 What you can learn from your TomTom GPS navigation system

Let's say you want to take your car to visit a friend in his new home in a different city. You are supposed to arrive there by ten o'clock, because you and a few other people have agreed to help your friend around the house. You know how to get to the city itself, but you will need some help once you reach the city center. You decide to trust in the directions of your GPS navigator and leave a little after nine o'clock. In this scenario, you are the client, while your navigation system – which we shall assume is a TomTom – is the project manager.

The TomTom GPS navigation system is off to a great start. As long as you have not entered a destination yet, it does not create false expectations by suggesting random directions. The TomTom also does not offer an unfounded indication of the likely arrival time. Lastly, it does not freak out when you decide to drive the first part of the journey on your own because you are sufficiently familiar with the route. Instead, it stays professional and, brimming with confidence, presents you with the information it can offer: your (changing) location on a clear map.

After fifteen minutes or so, you – the client – start to feel a bit uneasy. What road are you supposed to take into the city? Will you get there by ten o'clock? Time to start using the TomTom. Something wonderful happens after you enter your friend's address, although you fail to notice it because you are so used to it. You are immediately told that the plan

---

2 This chapter ties into the following competences from IPMA's ICB4: Strategy, Power and interest, Self-reflection and self-management, Personal communication, Relations and engagement, Leadership, Conflict and crisis, Negotiation, Results orientation, Requirements and objectives, Stakeholders.

(the route) is known, as well as what your expected arrival time is and what to do next. In other words, you get all the information you need without having to ask for any missing information. Good news, your projected arrival time is 09:48. You're going to be on time.

You continue your drive and think about the challenges you will face today as you do various chores around your buddy's home. Your mind is not focused on the route at all. Along the way, you reap the benefits of your TomTom's risk management activities: you are notified about an upcoming speed trap and the fact that you are going slightly over the limit. The TomTom's communication is perfectly client-oriented. It soon proves its usefulness in other ways: even before you spot the traffic jam yourself, you are notified about the possible delay. "Great, it looks ahead and continues to actively monitor the remaining route," you think. You have complete faith in your navigator. The delay on your current route will be ten minutes, but the TomTom suggests an alternate path using an earlier exit that will put your arrival time at 09:51. Subconsciously, you rejoice about the time you saved. You would not even consider blaming the TomTom for the delay.

Things do go wrong for a while inside the city limits. You are told to turn right down the wrong side of a one-way street. Perhaps this is an error in the TomTom's map data? You take initiative and continue straight, while the TomTom recalculates the remaining route. New arrival time: 09:53. You're fine! With ten minutes left to go, the TomTom once again tells you to turn right. However, you believe you know the city well enough and want to stay on your current road for a bit. Isn't there a bakery somewhere down the road where you can buy some cookies? You deviate from the prescribed path and continue straight.

For the TomTom, replanning is a useful routine activity.

What does the TomTom do? Does it become annoyed? Of course not! It recalculates the route and shows your arrival time to be 09:54. That is not too bad, you think. You are told to turn right again at the next intersection. Instead, you ignore the advice three more times. The TomTom stays professional and quietly recalculates the remaining route. It says you will now arrive at 09:56. The bakery appears ahead. You have just enough time.

You ring the bell at your friend's new house at 10:03. Without apologizing for being a bit late, complaining about traffic jams or the error on your navigator's data, you happily tell him that you stopped along the way to buy some delicious cookies.

With every step they take, project managers should ask themselves: "What would the TomTom do in this situation?" Doing so can result in some interesting revelations:
1. The path to the goal is all that matters, the rest is history;
2. Replanning is a part of life;
3. The client lives in the world of the final destination.

The path to the goal

The TomTom's first point of attention is focusing on the client's project goal. Successful project management is ultimately about only one thing: realizing the goals. That does not mean that the path you choose doesn't matter at all. The process that leads to the result is an important factor in the project's success (think of, for example, stakeholder satisfaction or the motivation of your team members). However, when making these choices, you should never lose sight of the project goal. Reaching the goal is more important than how you get there and the road ahead is all that matters; the road behind is history.

The TomTom metaphor helps us to stay focused as we encounter operational issues left and right. Amid all this craziness, our focus might unintentionally begin to shift to the issues of the day. Although we cannot ignore these problems, we should ask ourselves whenever we do anything: "What does this action mean for the remaining path to the final goal?" Focusing first and foremost on the path to the goal is a combination of behavior and the ability to quickly map out the road ahead. The TomTom is perfectly equipped to do just that. By measuring its position with GPS, it tells you about your current status, while a detailed map and advanced optimization algorithms help it determine the optimal path to the final destination.

 How good are you at determining the path to the goal?

Replanning is a part of life

How do you react when things don't go as planned? Do you stay focused or become annoyed? When I tell people the TomTom story, I sometimes get the response that "the TomTom has it easy, it's an emotionless computer." That is absolutely true, its lack of emotion is a definite advantage in this case. Luckily, as we will see later on in this book, having emotions can also be beneficial. If that is true, why not learn from what the TomTom does so well: *instead of making futile protests, just start replanning right away.*

If you assume that the path to the goal is dynamic, i.e. when you use Agile thinking, there is no need to react in an annoyed way; "Too bad, I have to change my plan." You expect there to be changes along the way and you employ constant forward thinking in order to choose the optimal path to the goal. This makes you both goal-oriented and flexible. This behavior not only offers the advantage of making you flexible in the event of unexpected changes. By constantly keeping an eye on the path ahead, you can also spot risks and opportunities earlier. A forward-thinking attitude creates the opportunity to anticipate what is coming.

 Do you change your plan when you absolutely must, or all the time because you are curious about the optimal path to the goal?

The message is only heard if you show what it means for the final goal.

The client lives in the world of the final destination

The third aspect is the one I personally realized last, even though its impact may be bigger than that of the first two aspects. What was the driver thinking about in my story about the TomTom? Was he focused on the path ahead or on what he would be doing after he arrived? In fact it was the latter, which is often the case in practice. The journey is commonly seen as a "necessary evil," something to endure before you can start doing what you really want. We are not interested in the TomTom's exact route or calculation methods. Regardless of whether the path is difficult or easy for it, all we want is to reach our destination.

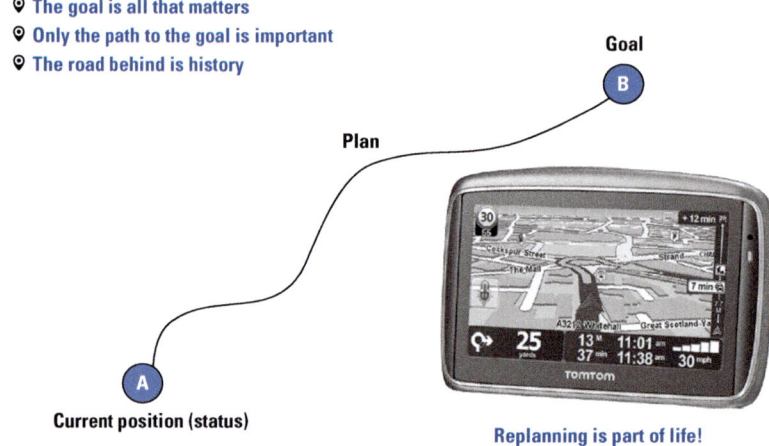

Figure 2.1   The TomTom as inspirator: always looking for the optimal path to the goal

The same is true for projects. *Many clients will not be able – or willing – to understand your plan.* Their focus is on what they are going to do with the results that you, the project manager, will deliver at the end of the project. That is why they will often fail to understand that the budget is insufficient if you tell them, midway through the project, that more money has been spent than expected. Similarly, they will not count on the project taking longer to complete when you inform them that an essential team member is off sick for a month. Your message will only be heard if you tell the stakeholder in question exactly what it means for the project's (final) result whenever you have anything to report.

This is what the TomTom excels at, no matter how simple its approach may sound. With the help of a clever user interface, it gives us no choice but to understand its message. How? By always displaying the *current* expected *arrival time*, whether we want to know this piece of information or not:

Initial commitment TomTom: Arrival time 09:48
TomTom predicts traffic jam: Arrival time 09:58
TomTom suggests alternate route: Arrival time 09:51

TomTom has to restore incorrect route: Arrival time 09:53
Driver ignores instruction: Arrival time 09:54
Driver ignores instruction three more times: Arrival time 09:56
Driver stops at bakery: Arrival time 10:03

Do you see what is going on? The TomTom, i.e. the project manager, creates peace of mind and stability at six different moments of change by always having the optimal path to the goal at the ready and communicating it in the client's own language as a predicted arrival time. Instead of having a dynamic project, the plan and expected results are clear at all times, the environment will experience peace of mind and clarity, and the client always knows what to expect. Most importantly, *cause and effect* are automatically clear because of the TomTom's high refresh rate. As a result, a project manager has far less explaining to do and is pushed into a defensive role less often.

Moreover... *clients no longer have a conflict with you, but instead with the facts.* In my example they even take responsibility for their own late arrival. That is not surprising, because when they chose to ignore the TomTom's instructions, they knew they were cutting it close. Every time they chose their own path, they received immediate feedback about the effects of that change. However, they had a good reason for doing what they did, because being able to buy some cookies would more than make up for the lost time. Given that the TomTom knew nothing about the clients' motivation, it did what it had to do: not make a fuss and keep suggesting alternate paths to the final goal!

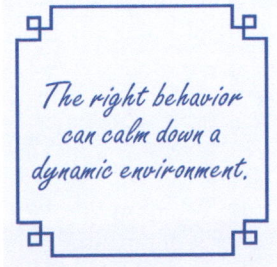

The right behavior can calm down a dynamic environment.

What might have happened if the TomTom had not presented the up-to-date arrival times during all those moments of change? Chances are that the driver would have subconsciously overlooked all those changes, only to be surprised by the late arrival time at the end of the journey. That would probably have upset him. *"Why is it after ten o'clock? Didn't we have twelve extra minutes when we began?"* As you might expect, the project manager TomTom would have been held responsible for the fifteen minutes' delay, including the changes that the driver himself had caused. Who could blame the driver? Surely, those did not add up to fifteen minutes? Similarly, there is no way the driver would understand the TomTom's smart intervention to avoid the future traffic jam.

On top of that, the project manager TomTom would have missed out on its opportunity to influence the client and pressure him or her for the sake of the project. On the contrary, it gave the client the impression of having plenty of time at the start of the journey. This expectation was not updated along the way: there was some time left, but not enough to take a detour and stop at the bakery. *The project manager would have failed to make the journey into a shared challenge.*

? *Do you consistently take the initiative to communicate a project's current status, translated into consequences for the client, even if the client does not ask for these updates?*

2.2   The TomTom and Agile leadership

Our navigator accurately illustrates several essential basic principles of project management. However, it should be clear to you that a real project gives you more freedom in terms of how you communicate with your client, what you choose to report and in which manner. We are not computers and this gives us more ways in which to act. More on that later. For now, the TomTom has taught us the following points about Agile leadership:

■ The goal is all that matters;
■ Only the path towards the goal is important, the road behind is history;
■ Replanning is a fact of life and you should always actively look for the optimal path to the goal;
■ Make sure the client understands the project's current status and how this affects the final goal at all times.

Summed up in this way, it looks like mere common sense. Nevertheless, do you do all this yourself in practice? Do you always know what the optimal path to the final goal is during a project? Do you inform stakeholders in such a way that they truly understand the situation at hand and act in the best interests of the project?

As is often the case, the challenge lies in the execution and in finding the discipline to stick with it. In other words, it is about integrating the TomTom's logic in our own behavior. In this book, we constantly strive to reduce the principles of project management to their essence, which makes it easier to integrate them into your personal style and your daily work processes.

Acting instead of reacting
Until now, we have mostly talked about the realization process. If the execution does not go as planned, our first impulse will be to resist the changes. Of course, there is nothing wrong with fighting for your cause, especially if the current plan is the most optimal one. However, things tend to get out of hand when we lose sight of our goal and only fight to get our way – especially if we stubbornly neglect to update the plan and lose our direction. The TomTom would never do that… That is why we can aptly apply the TomTom metaphor to leadership and behavior in a general sense. We call this "acting instead of reacting."

We have all been there. We react subconsciously to stimuli and situations. In other words, we react without thinking about what the most constructive response would be. Think of, for instance, getting angry, becoming distracted by unimportant issues or refusing to consider an excellent suggestion because the person who came up with it once slighted you.

These are all examples of situations in which we lose sight of our goal. The TomTom stimulates us to firstly let the situation sink in and then deliberately choose our response, rather than reflexively reacting in the heat of the moment. Although the latter might feel good at first, it is usually not very productive in the long run. Just think of the difference between functional and emotional anger.

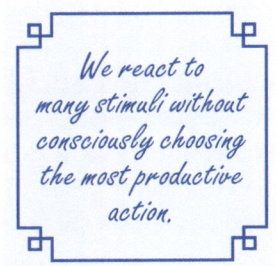

We react to many stimuli without consciously choosing the most productive action.

So, take a time-out, count to ten ... and then ask yourself: "Which action brings me closer to my goal?" You can use this method when making plans, reporting, during conversations, while communicating and in countless other situations. It keeps you from acting out of ingrained patterns, fear or unwanted behavior.

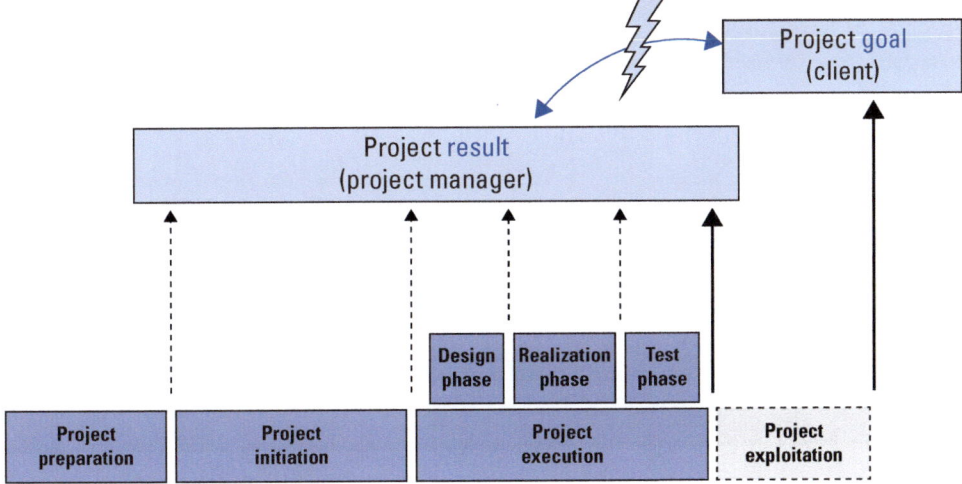

Figure 2.2   Project goal and project result

Project goal and project result

Now that we are making frequent use of the term "project goal," it is a good idea to go over the differences between a project goal and a project result. This is an important theme that can help clarify the role division between a project manager and a client.

The *project goal* is whatever the client wishes to achieve with the project result. The desired project result and the project requirements are derived from this goal. The responsibility for the realization of the project goal is primarily in the hands of the *client*.

The *project result* is the product or service to be delivered with the project. The responsibility for the realization of the project result is primarily in the hands of the *project manager* (the contractor). If we use the example of the TomTom once more, the project goal was "help out at the friend's house," while the project result was "arrive at 10:00." Other examples include:

- Product development. Goal = profit, result = product;
- Website development. Goal = more visitors, result = website;
- Book a trip. Goal = enjoying a nice holiday, result = a choice of destination.

The project result is delivered by the project manager at the end of the project. During the exploitation phase, the client will use this result to realize the project goal. This often happens after the project has already been concluded. As a project manager, it is important to understand that clients have a different goal in mind than the project result they ask for. This distinction is sometimes clear right away, but it usually requires a degree of coordination and alignment during the project preparation phase. At the end of this phase, the project goal and project result are recorded in the project assignment (see figure 1.6).

Understanding the underlying goal helps you to better understand the desired project result. If the project goal and the project result do not tie in well together, you can count on more changes during the project. You may also receive negative feedback afterwards because the goal was not achieved with the project result you delivered. During a project, experienced project managers will therefore not only evaluate whether the project result will be realized (the official assignment); they will also make sure whether the interim results offer the client sufficient opportunity to realize the project goal. Consequently, it is important to regularly update the business case during a project, so you can actively check with the client whether it is still valid.

Look ahead

I will not claim that talking about activities conducted during the past period is entirely pointless. However, it is strange that many progress meetings are mainly used to sum up what people have done over the past week, instead of talking about what they still need to do to finish the project. Looking back is a good way to test results, coach team members, evaluate projects and learn from them, but it is important to primarily focus on the path ahead. There are specific KPIs for this, e.g. *time-to-go, costs-to-go* and *issues-to-solve*. In other words, what needs to be done to complete the project?

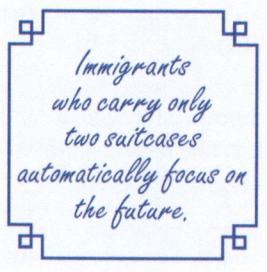

Immigrants who carry only two suitcases automatically focus on the future.

Allowing ourselves to be distracted by past concerns makes us less productive and goal-oriented. As strategic coach Dan Sullivan says about the high degree of entrepreneurship among immigrants in the United States: "Immigrants only get to bring two suitcases. Their focus is on the future, the rest is left behind." Let yourself be inspired by the TomTom and focus mainly on the path ahead, both in the way you manage your projects and in terms of how you structure your personal life.

2.3   The TomTom and stakeholder management

You may not realize it when you are working on your project, but most projects lead to some form of change. In order to retain support during such a change process, stakeholder management and communication are essential.

Effective stakeholder management is one of the biggest success factors for project managers. *Stakeholders* are the people who have an interest in the project's performance and success (or lack thereof…) or who can influence the project execution to a greater or lesser extent. These stakeholders can be found both within the organization (e.g. internal clients, members of the project board, team members and other executors) and outside it (clients, end users, suppliers, supervisors, etc.). It is important to note that the client is not the only stakeholder in a project.

Together with the other external factors that affect the project, stakeholders form the *environment* of the project. Keeping the stakeholders involved is an essential task for a project manager. After all, the stakeholders decide whether to accept the project's result and, consequently, whether the project manager is successful. Stakeholder management is carried out in three steps: by analyzing the stakeholders, by deciding on your method of approach and by keeping the stakeholders involved (see figure 2.3).

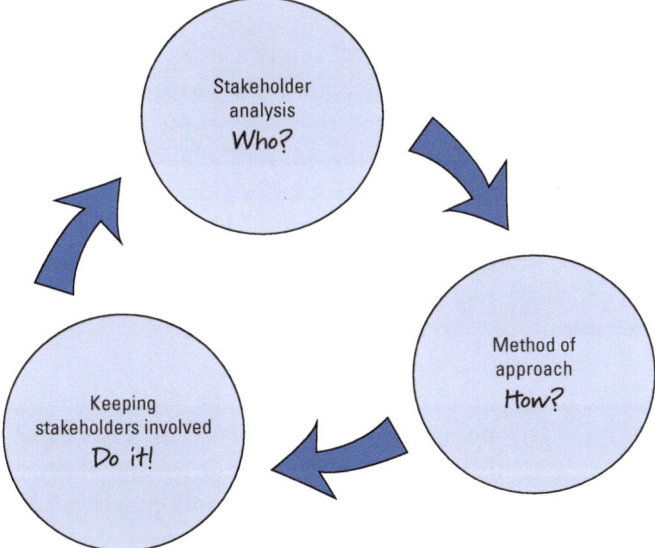

Figure 2.3   The stakeholder management process

Stakeholder analysis
Stakeholder management is a challenge that demands a great deal of attention from a project manager throughout the entire project. It is not a one-time task, but rather a recurring activity that is recorded in the project management plan (or separately, in a communication plan).

Before you can draw up this plan, you must first identify the persons who can influence the project and learn what their interests are. I have little to add to everything that has already been written about stakeholder analyses in management books, though I do have something to say about how it is commonly used. I am referring to the reactive way of using stakeholder management, mainly to fix problems that have already occurred. That is too bad. Just like expectation management, stakeholder management should really be conducted from the very start of a project. At that point, the stakeholders are still flexible, which gives a project manager more ways to influence the project's course. This is why I focus extensively on *how* to integrate proactive stakeholder management into your own behavior and make it a positive force for both parties. This helps to turn the management *of* stakeholders into management *for* stakeholders.

 Do you start conducting stakeholder management right away or only when you have to?

Figure 2.4 shows the various steps of a stakeholder analysis. These help you answer the question of *who your stakeholders are and how they feel about your project*. The steps are as follows:
1. Identify stakeholders;
2. Analyze the power and interests of each stakeholder;
3. Analyze the position of each stakeholder.

The first step, the identification, looks easy enough. It is a simple question: who are the people that can positively or negatively influence the success of your project? The answer is not that easy, though. I frequently find that I don't ask myself this question enough, which means that I am surprised during the project by influences that I did not take into consideration. Added to this is the fact that, with this reactive approach, usually only stakeholders that present a problem are added to the list. Stakeholder management is then limited to fixing existing relationship problems and all attention goes to the difficult cases. It is often far more beneficial in terms of the project to prevent problems and focus more on the positive relationships.

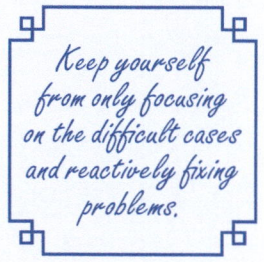
Keep yourself from only focusing on the difficult cases and reactively fixing problems.

To conduct proactive stakeholder management, you can use figure 2.5 as a checklist for stakeholder identification. It distinguishes between four groups of stakeholders: decision makers, users, suppliers, and executors. If your focus is on more than just the difficult cases, your list will soon contain more than twenty names. Furthermore, this checklist helps to ensure that you don't lose sight of the end user, e.g. because you focus all your attention on the project board members (who ultimately decide if you are doing your work well enough). This, in turn, helps to prevent you from focusing too much on control and not enough on results. After all, the TomTom would never make that mistake…

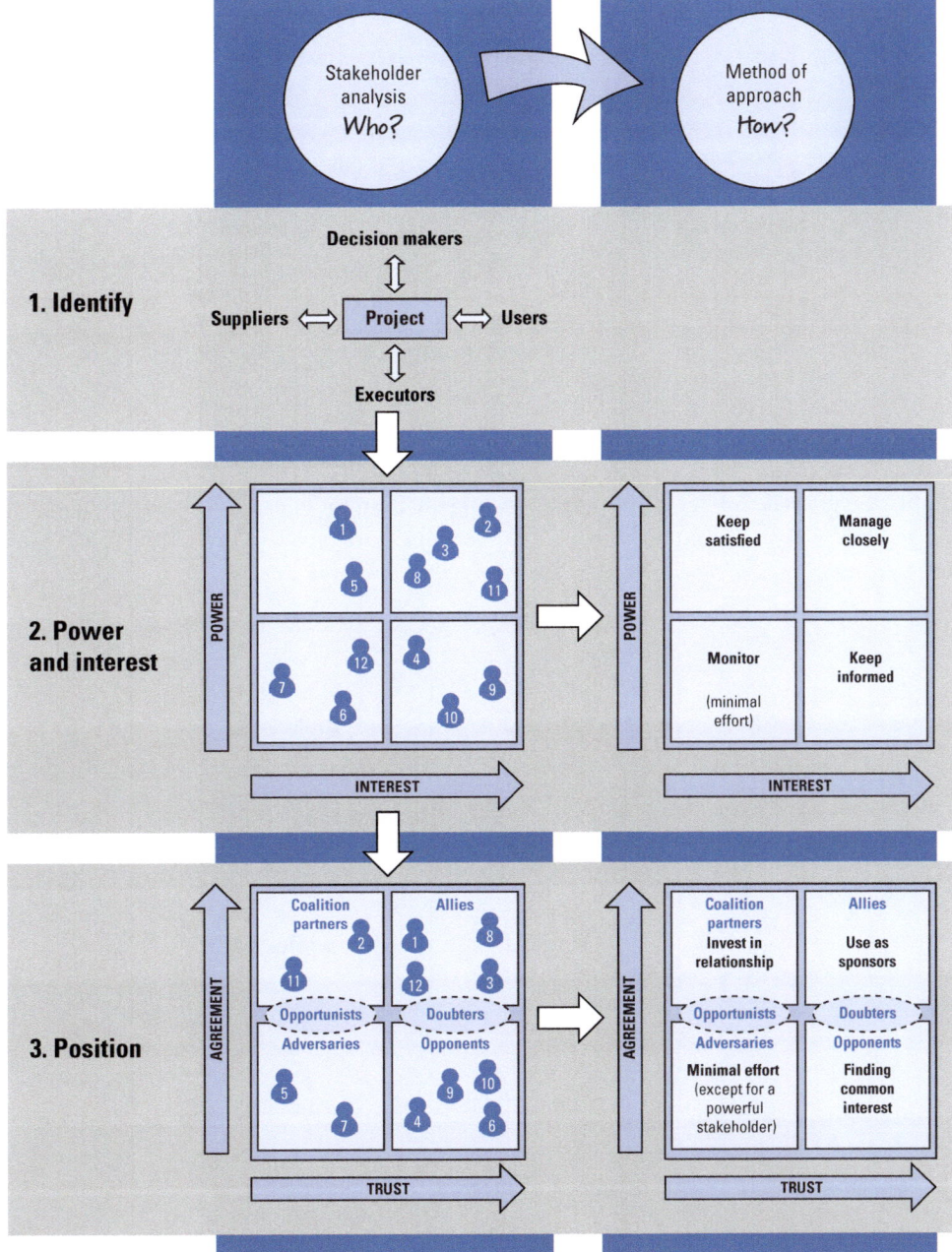

Figure 2.4   The steps of a stakeholder analysis

After identifying the stakeholders, you can determine their position in relation to the project. It is common to use the *power/interest grid* (Mendelow, 1991) for this:

- **Power**: how does the stakeholder influence the decision-making process?
- **Interest**: how much interest does the stakeholder have in the project results?

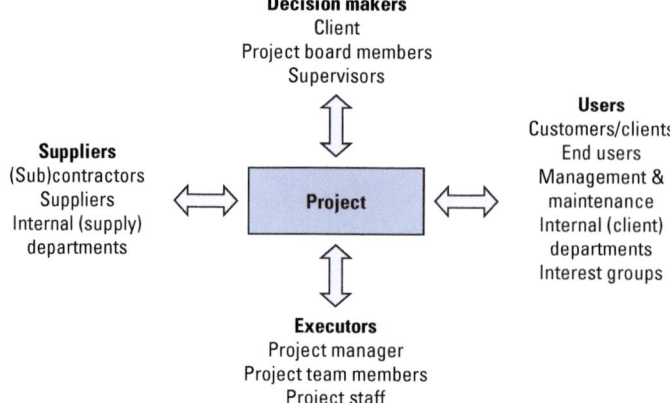

Figure 2.5   Checklist for stakeholder identification

You place every stakeholder in the corresponding quadrant of figure 2.6. By mapping out the stakeholders' power and interests, you can determine how each of them should be involved in the project: *manage closely, keep satisfied, keep informed* and *monitor*.

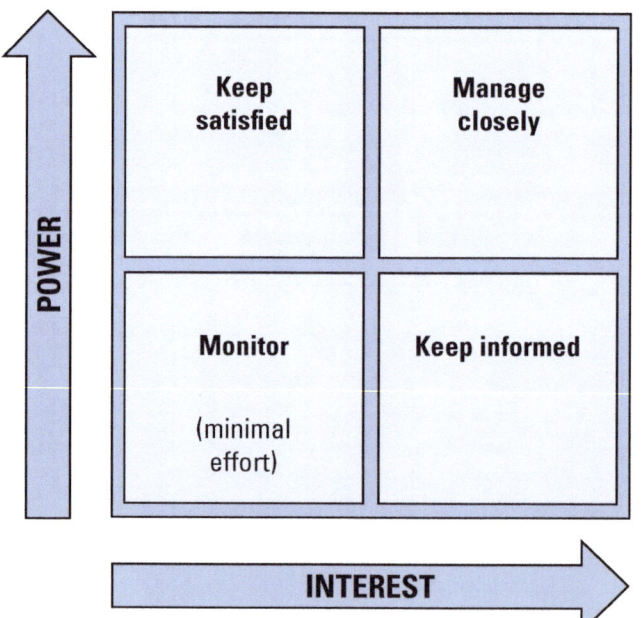

Figure 2.6   Approaching stakeholders based on their power and interest

Finally, you can determine the position of each stakeholder in relation to the project content and yourself as a project manager, an assessment derived from Peter Block's *trust/agreement matrix* (Block, 1986):

- **Agreement**: to what extent does the stakeholder support the project's content?
- **Trust**: how much trust does the stakeholder have in the project manager (and the project team)?

This once again results in a useful matrix that can help you decide on the optimal approach (figure 2.7):

1. *Allies* want the same things as you. Be sure to work together closely with these people and protect your good relationship. You can use them as project sponsors or to approach an adversary.
2. *Coalition partners* have the same interests as the project, but they still lack sufficient trust in their relationship with you. As a result their behavior is unpredictable. Changing interests can put an end to the coalition. You can invest in this relationship by communicating clearly about everyone's expectations and making explicit agreements. Building trust takes time, so be sure to communicate clearly about any positive results.
3. *Opponents* have a different view on the project, but they do have trust. This makes their behavior predictable. You can negotiate about shared and conflicting interests with them. These conversations can even bring you new insights that turn opponents into allies. This generally takes less time than the transition from coalition partner into ally, because the necessary trust already exists.
4. Spending any time at all on *adversaries* is basically a waste of your energy. You should limit your communication to professional discussions and be clear about your own beliefs. Acting instead of reacting definitely applies here. It can only be useful to build a relationship of trust through intensive contact if adversaries hold an important position (in this case, Mendelow's power/interest grid advises you to at least keep them satisfied). Allies may be able to help you approach the adversary, if they have a better relationship with said person.

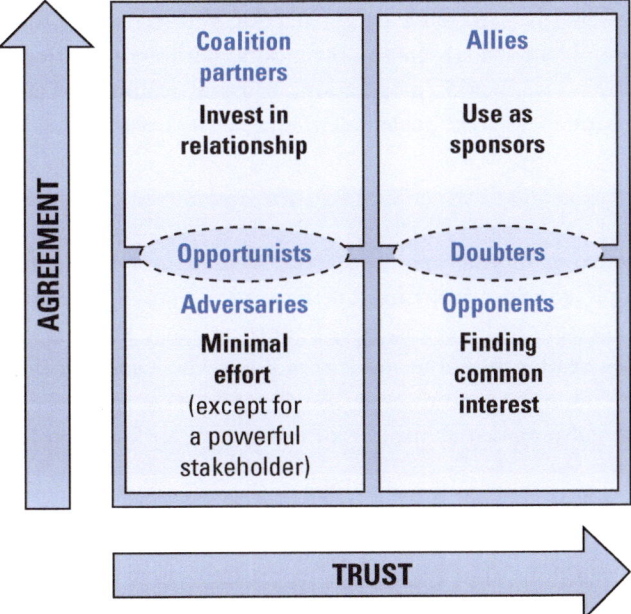

Figure 2.7   Approaching stakeholders based on their position

The doubters and the opportunists are positioned between the quadrants. They have not yet adopted a clear position based on their interests. The *doubters* are easy to communicate with because of the good relationship that exists between you. You should involve them in your project and make sure to give them enough information. The *opportunists* are deliberately waiting to see which way the wind will blow. That makes their behavior highly unpredictable. Because no good relationship exists yet, it is best to adopt a professional approach and try to find common interests.

Note that a stakeholder can fall into several categories at the same time. A logistical manager can, for example, be the client (with a goal of faster delivery times), the supplier of project employees (for the project execution) and the user of the project result (an updated logistical system). A properly executed stakeholder analysis will provide valuable insight in this regard. It is also important to take into account the fact that the stakeholder analysis is not set in stone; it may change as the project goes on. By now, your Agile TomTom voice probably says: "If the situation does not change because of outside factors, I will change it myself through the right interventions with the right people!"

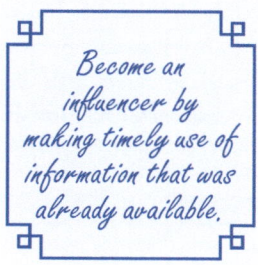

Become an influencer by making timely use of information that was already available.

By conducting the stakeholder analysis in a timely manner, you can put yourself in an influencing position, rather than a reactive one – all by simply using information that was already there! You can influence who is given which position in the project organization and you will often have a head start during conversations in the project initiation phase. Be sure to relish the satisfaction you feel as you watch your discussion partners fumble around without a clear tactic because of their poor preparation. You will realize that you are well on your way to exhibiting much smarter behavior. In chapter 4, we will refer to this as *Factor 10 behavior*.

Always inform

Do you enjoy reporting? If your answer is "No," take comfort in the fact that you are not alone. Many people consider reporting on the project status an annoying administrative chore. That is understandable to a degree. Reporting can take up a lot of valuable time, especially if you are dealing with multiple stakeholders who each have their own preferences. Such thoughts as "Things are going well, so what do I have to report about?" and "Don't they trust me?" can also make the business of reporting a lot less appealing.

However, the TomTom has shown us that passive behavior can be counterproductive. Failing to clearly communicate the consequences of a detour for the expected arrival time made the driver feel uneasy. The belief that "reporting is done for the benefit of the client" holds us back. By turning it around – "reporting is done for my benefit" – you open up a whole range of natural influencing opportunities. *Each reporting moment presents a chance to share your successes and influence the stakeholders.*

You should, however, make sure that the way you inform your stakeholders is appropriate for the situation. From time to time, people tell me that their clients want their concerns alleviated and are not interested in all that information. Although I understand their point that is no reason to sell yourself short! Be creative and remember that informing others does not have to be a whole song and dance. Keep it short, clear and goal-oriented. You can even do it as you are waiting for your coffee at the machine. Furthermore, you appear more professional when you discuss your proposal for communication from the stakeholder analysis with the stakeholders themselves. This keeps you from raising the wrong expectations.

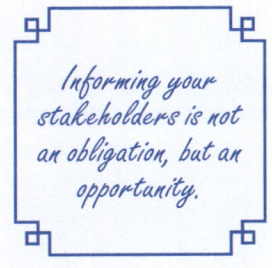

Informing your stakeholders is not an obligation, but an opportunity.

When you look at informing others as something that benefits *you*, you can start doing it your own way. For example, you can forward an email from an end user who is happy with a new application to your client, along with the text "they love it." It would be even better to change the subject line from "FW: feedback new application" to "SUCCESS: feedback new application" (figure 2.8). Your client does not even have to read the email to get the message. After sending emails back and forth for a while to discuss a problem, I usually put "RESOLVED:…" in the subject line of my final message on the matter.

In summary, you should make sure that the stakeholders possess all the information you feel they should have. This information increases their trust in you and makes them act in the best interests of the project. By properly informing them, they start thinking in terms of *us* instead of *me* and *you*. You could, for example, send your client a message from

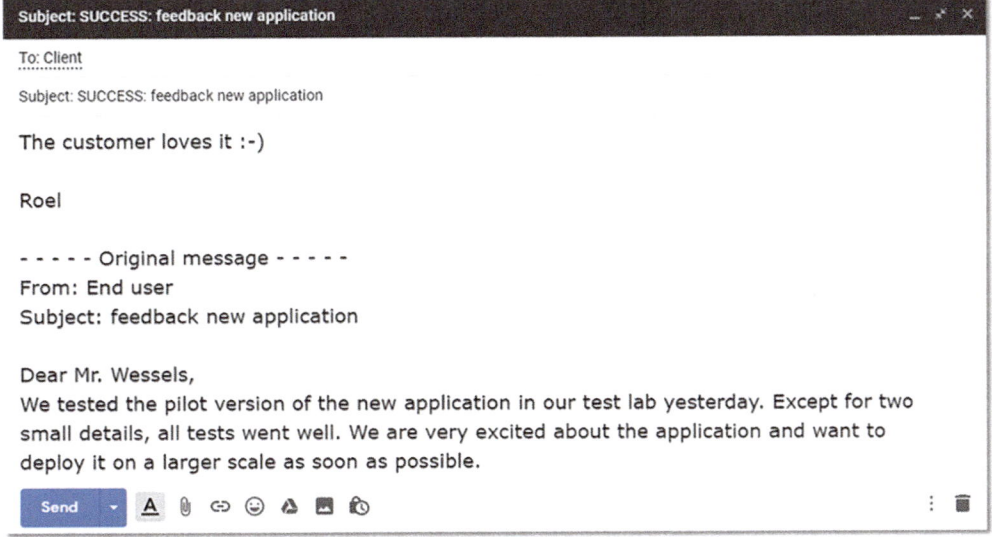

Figure 2.8   Celebrating success with small, deliberate actions

the location of a supplier where you are conducting a risk analysis, so the client knows you are doing good work. While having lunch with stakeholders, casually mention that their colleague is messing around with the specifications, which is not in the project's best interests, and reassure them that you have everything under control. These stakeholders are almost guaranteed to start helping you without you needing to ask. Inform your client that you can deliver tomorrow if the client responds today, because you will be gone for the next three days to work on a different project. This information creates a natural sense of urgency in your client and you also make it clear that you have plenty of other work to do. If a change is made that only just fits within the available budget, explain to the client that there is no more budget room now and that, next time they want to add something, they should also figure out what can be left out. This shows that you know exactly what the budget allows for and that you do not like exceeding the limit either, giving the client time to think things through.

You will find that deliberately informing and reporting to stakeholders will help you influence the project's course. If you believe doing so will be counterproductive in a micromanaged organization that already calls for constant reports and updates, you should understand that your rhythm of information moments can actually reduce the organization's urge to control everything and make your clients trust you more. I will discuss this rhythm in more detail in chapter 8 when we talk about heartbeat.

Communicate before problems arise
You learn a lot by messing up first. A point of attention for me was that I sometimes relied too much on the strength of the project and did not do enough to keep some stakeholders involved. I believed that if all of the coordination took a lot of time and if my story was good enough, I could surely update the stakeholders in question "at the last second?" It is true that this approach often works well – until the projects become so complex that they do not go entirely smoothly, or until there are so many stakeholders with conflicting interests and unrealistic wishes that a good story is no longer good enough. In those situations, it was unhelpful that I, as the project manager, waited too long to smooth things over with the uninformed stakeholders. Especially because the people I had ignored were usually those with little interest in the project or with whom I did not have much of a personal connection. In other words, exactly the kinds of people for whom the power/interest grid and trust/agreement matrix of the stakeholder analysis call for action. Ouch!

A meeting with the CFO

At the start of a new project, a friend and I were going over the list of candidates for a strategic introduction. Luckily for me, he was critical and noted that the CFO was on my list of stakeholders, but without an assigned action. "When are you going to visit him?" he asked. I told him that the CFO of an organization with 1,200 employees would not be interested in a meeting with a program manager who was not even in charge of any key programs. "So, you are already choosing the easy way out?" he said. I realized he was right. You can learn everything there is to know about stakeholder management, but the most important thing is to actually DO IT.

To illustrate the usefulness of developing a relationship with stakeholders before any problems arise, I will tell you how the conversation went. I went to see the CFO on my second day and this visit proved invaluable later on!

Firstly, how do you set up such a meeting? We have already discussed that informing someone does not have to be a complicated affair. If you go through the CFO's secretary to schedule an official appointment, that is exactly what it will become and you can expect to wait around for weeks before the CFO has time to see you. Furthermore, I was not looking for an hour-long conversation, because I did not feel comfortable about keeping a board member from his work for so long. Instead of setting an appointment, I therefore simply knocked on his door. I had planned to do little more than introduce myself and shake the CFO's hand.

I should tell you that this CFO, as is often the case, had his office on the top floor, next to the CEO. A little out of breath from walking up the stairs, I walked in with nothing prepared apart from my opening line: "Good morning, my name is Roel Wessels. I was hired as a program manager, so I am mostly here to spend your money. It seemed only fair that I should introduce myself in person." The CFO looked up from his desk and I believed I could read the surprise in his eyes that any employee dared to enter this floor. His reply was: "Great, have a seat." Our conversation ended up lasting for more than an hour. After he asked me about what program I was managing, he explained what he believed were the challenges for the organization. We talked about that for quite a while. When we were done talking about substantive matters, I spotted four paintings of jazz musicians behind his desk. That was a great icebreaker to start talking informally.

In hindsight, this was a clear case of "don't overthink it, just act." Everyone will appreciate it if you come up to them to shake their hand and introduce yourself. Try to keep things from getting so big that they get out of control. However, I was really surprised by what happened during subsquent meetings that the CFO attended. I saw him as an ally whom I no longer had to prove myself to, because during our very first meeting I had already demonstrated my attention to detail pertaining to budgeting and sticking to the project finances during the project execution. I could only have done that during the personal meeting we had, because no one is interested in those details during a project report session.

Whenever I reported to the board, I knew that the CFO understood the numbers and figures I mentioned were not made up. During my presentations, he made remarks that gave the other board members more trust in me. Furthermore, when the project encountered some financial difficulties later on, I was able to discuss possible solutions with him beforehand. It is remarkable to note how much is possible during a preliminary one-on-one meeting that cannot be done during a joint review session. We all know that the real decisions are often made in advance, but you do have to create a position for yourself that will allow you to discuss issues with the right people.

Start communicating
while the project is
still fun.

As Stephen Covey calls it, that initial visit was a successful opening of the *emotional bank account*. We will come back to this in chapter 4. It also earns you some valuable initial credit that is far more difficult to acquire later when the heat is on. Remember to conduct a proper stakeholder analysis (figure 2.9) at the start of your projects and incorporate your approach in your communication plan. Most importantly, however, you should come up with an initial proactive action for each stakeholder and begin filling up your emotional bank account while the project is still fun. Doing so ensures you are well on your way from reactive to proactive to influencing!

No.	Name	Wishes	Analysis power & interest			Analysis position			Stakeholder management	
			Power (low 1, high 5)	Interest (low 1, high 5)	Method of approach	Agreement (low 1, high 5)	Trust (low 1, high 5)	Method of approach	Communication during execution phase	Initial proactive action
Decision makers										
1										
2										
3										
...										
Users										
4										
5										
6										
...										
Suppliers										
7										
8										
9										
...										
Executors										
10										
11										
12										
...										

Figure 2.9   Table for all stakeholder analysis data and the final communication approach including the initial proactive actions

2.4   Scenario creator

In this chapter, we have seen that the TomTom effectively focuses our attention on achieving the path to the goal. It also inspires us when it comes to leadership and behavior. Is that Agile enough though? For a TomTom, the goal and the final destination are known and stable, while the challenge of complex and chaotic projects (according to the Cynefin framework) usually lies in the fact that it is not immediately possible to plot a detailed path to the final goal, e.g. because experiments have to be conducted first, or because the goal has not even been set yet. This is where the comparison with a TomTom starts to break down.

The TomTom is Agile because it prefers to go along with changes, instead of sticking to the original plan. The navigator *expects changes* and therefore continuously tests its assumptions and uses new information to find the optimal path to the current final goal. The TomTom prefers to *act* and hit the road to realize interim results, which are then verified against the measured GPS position. It opts for direct contact and strives to collaborate with the driver by constantly communicating the consequences of certain actions for the final result. Value creation and collaboration are more important than contractual and formal scope management, which is an important basic principle of the Agile philosophy.

What about the rigidity when it comes to prescribing the desired result? It is true that the TomTom is less tolerant in this regard; if the driver does not enter a destination, it will not plot a route. We will have to help the driver (client) a bit, which also happens in the real world. One example is going on vacation and looking for a sunny destination rather than a specific place. The plan is then to drive south until the weather improves. You start out by selecting a location in a given direction, e.g. France or Austria. During the trip, you decide where to stop and where to go next. The various locations are the (interim) results, while good weather is the goal. In other words, we are going through iterations that are not known in advance, but only become clear as we go along. This is also what happens during the iterations of an Agile project. You learn by doing.

Always a plan

The TomTom not only teaches us to always have an up-to-date plan, but to have one *immediately* at the start of a project. This might sound like naïve idealism. Besides, why should you do this – for the client's benefit?

It is for *your* benefit. Just imagine what would happen if a TomTom took fifteen minutes to calculate a route. Drivers would lose their trust in it and decide to come up with something on their own. The same happens during real projects. Being able to quickly present an up-to-date path results in peace of mind and clarity, even in a highly dynamic environment rife with uncertainty. It also inspires stakeholders to offer feedback and make decisions. Vice versa, lacking a clear plan leads to changing goals, incorrect assumptions, reactive

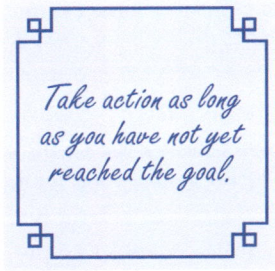

Take action as long as you have not yet reached the goal.

behavior from your team, or a wasted budget because everyone was working on the wrong things. *Taking action as long as the goal has not yet been reached is an essential characteristic of a project manager.* That goes for all activities: making a plan, leading a meeting, coordinating the approach, etc. It improves stakeholders' trust in you and the results of the actions will boost your confidence.

How soon after the start of a project can you present the initial outlines of the plan and the required budget?

Start with a sketch

Developing a good plan and having it available quickly appear to be mutually exclusive. However, if you can pull it off, your life as a project manager will be a lot easier. In chapter 6, we will call this initial plan the "sketch with the team" and I will explain everything in more detail. For now, think of the project sketch as being similar to the initial sketch a designer makes at the start of a new construction project.

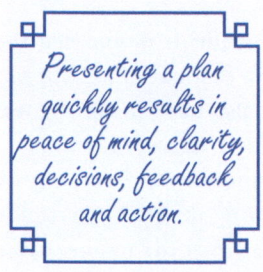

Presenting a plan quickly results in peace of mind, clarity, decisions, feedback and action.

Of course, it is very Agile to accept that drawing up a 100% complete plan will take a long time because of the uncertainties that have to be dealt with and to, therefore, opt for starting early with a quick sketch of the path to the final goal (a path that may change as the project goes on). However, being able to, and daring to, make such a sketch are also important characteristics of project managers who use more traditional methods. Even though these methods are not formally limited to the waterfall model at all, they are often interpreted as primarily focusing on having a complete, detailed plan by the end of the definition phase. Remember that it is about your behavior and not just the agreed-upon process. By presenting a quick sketch, you can take the lead at *the very start* of the definition phase and:

- Create clarity and peace of mind about the direction and the goal;
- Receive quick feedback from the client;
- Receive trust from the client, because the client sees actions are being taken;
- Make choices and decisions;
- Take appropriate action when stakeholders keep changing their mind;
- Create a sense of urgency in the environment;
- Ensure your team takes the right actions.

Is every sketch a good sketch? No, making a good sketch requires a degree of expertise. To avoid raising the wrong expectations, you must be able to show "every aspect" of the path, even the things you do not know yet! Why? Because that is what the client will rely on. Note that showing every aspect does not mean showing every detail. Just look at how contractors handle a remodeling project. Suppose their client has not yet chosen a type of radiator. The contractor will put together a quote, including a detailed summary of all materials and hours, of €28,500. Does that include the radiators? Yes, if you look carefully, you will see an item on the list called "provisional sum 5 radiators: €3,500." The contractor delineates the costs without having all the information to hand. Many project managers would present their initial plan with a cost estimate of €25,000, not including the radiators, and a note for the client that the plan is not entirely complete because some information is missing. However, the client lives in the world of the final goal and is unable or unwilling to understand this distinction. By mentioning a cost of €25,000, you subconsciously create the expectation that the entire project will cost that much. You also fail to pressure the client into choosing a type of radiator. It is better to be creative and always include the entire path in your plan, including a delineation of any missing information, uncertain factors, risk management or expected changes. We will come back to this later.

Think in scenarios

In other words, project managers are akin to *scenario creators*. By continuously looking forward and exploring possible paths that lead to the goal, you stay in control and create the ability to anticipate changes and obstacles.

Thinking in scenarios can also help you stay calm in situations where you lose sight of the solution for a moment, e.g. because you cannot realize the goal both on time and on budget. You might be tempted to avoid any contact with stakeholders, because you do not have a solution and therefore nothing to talk about. Avoid that situation by coming up with two paths that are possible (even though they do not meet both requirements): one path that stays on budget yet slightly exceeds the available timeframe and one path that ensures the project will be done on time, yet which will exceed the budget. Explain the situation and the actions needed to resolve the issue. Instead of postponing, you turn the problem into a shared challenge. Who knows? You might be surprised and see the client modify the requirements because of the valuable insight you have provided. We will cover this mechanism, the *10% confrontation rule*, in more detail in chapter 5.

Remember to stay in control and keep taking action as long as the goal has not yet been reached, even (or especially) when things are not going your way! That is what an influencer does.

Summary

⦿ This is what the TomTom GPS navigation system teaches us about Agile leadership:
  - The goal is all that matters;
  - It is only the path to the goal that is important, the path behind is history;
  - Replanning is a fact of life, you should always actively look for the optimal path to the goal;
  - Instead of (reflexively) reacting, you should be acting (in a goal-oriented manner);
  - Take action as long as you have not yet reached the goal. It makes stakeholders trust you and increases your self-confidence;
  - Make sure the client understands the project's current status and how it affects the final goal at all times. Reporting is not an obligation, but rather an opportunity;
  - Start communicating at the beginning of a project, before any problems arise;
  - Act in line with the agreed-upon path, but think in terms of different scenarios;
  - Present your initial plan at the earliest opportunity to create peace of mind, clarity, feedback, decisiveness and action;
  - Make sure your plan contains the path to, and the consequences for, the final goal, despite any uncertainties along the way.
⦿ The stakeholder analysis should:
  1. Identify stakeholders;
  2. Analyze the power and interest of each stakeholder;
  3. Analyze the position of each stakeholder in relation to the project and yourself.
⦿ Make proactive use of stakeholder management. Do not focus solely on the difficult cases, instead surprise each stakeholder at the start of the project with a communication and influencing moment.

3   First time right: The V-model and the critical parameter

➤ What the V-model teaches us about the development process.
➤ Why mistakes made early on in the project have more impact than those made later.
➤ How Design for X and Agile help you in confronting at an early stage.
➤ Focus during the entire project through consideration of the critical parameter.
➤ How the V-model can help improve your own behavior.

Now that your attention is focused on the path to the goal, it is important to give more structure to this path. Most projects, especially those concerned with product and service development, are based on a change process (development life cycle). Results are achieved by creating a design, implementing it and then evaluating the results. The V-model (figure 3.1) is a perfect tool to gain insight into the structure of such projects.[3]

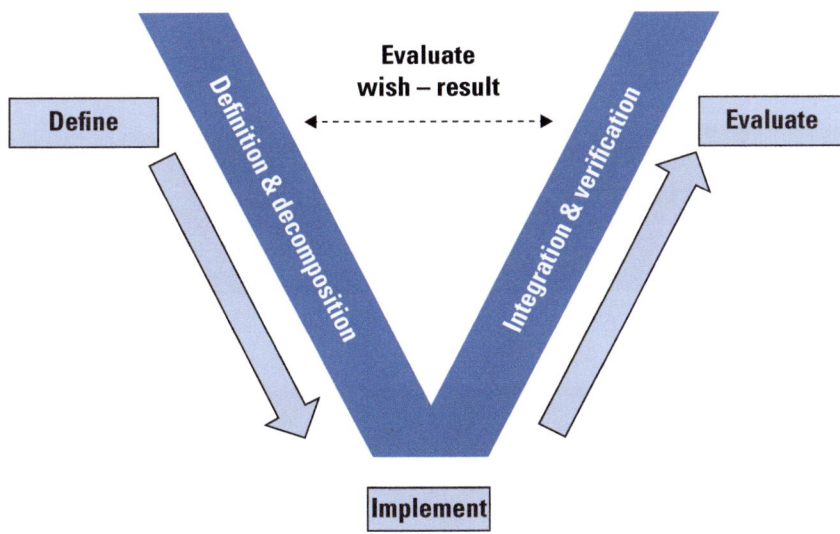

Figure 3.1   The V-model: define – implement – evaluate

Paul Rook's V-model comes from the world of software development and was originally derived from the waterfall model. It clarifies the relationship between associated design and testing activities. This makes the V-model a great tool to help you move towards *right first time project management*, i.e. delivering the desired project result in one go, without any unplanned corrections along the way.

---

3   This chapter ties into the following competences from IPMA's ICB4: Strategy, Governance, structures and processes, Leadership, Resourcefulness, Results orientation, Project design, Requirements and objectives, Quality.

3.1   Introduction to the V-model: design, realization, verification

The V-model (Rook, 1986) is really nothing more than a different representation of the phases we have already covered in chapter 1. The model is created by moving the integration and testing activities up to form the right side of a large V-shape. The left side contains the activities of the definition and design process (the definition), the bottom point details the activities of the realization process (the implementation) and the right side shows the integration and verification process (the evaluation).

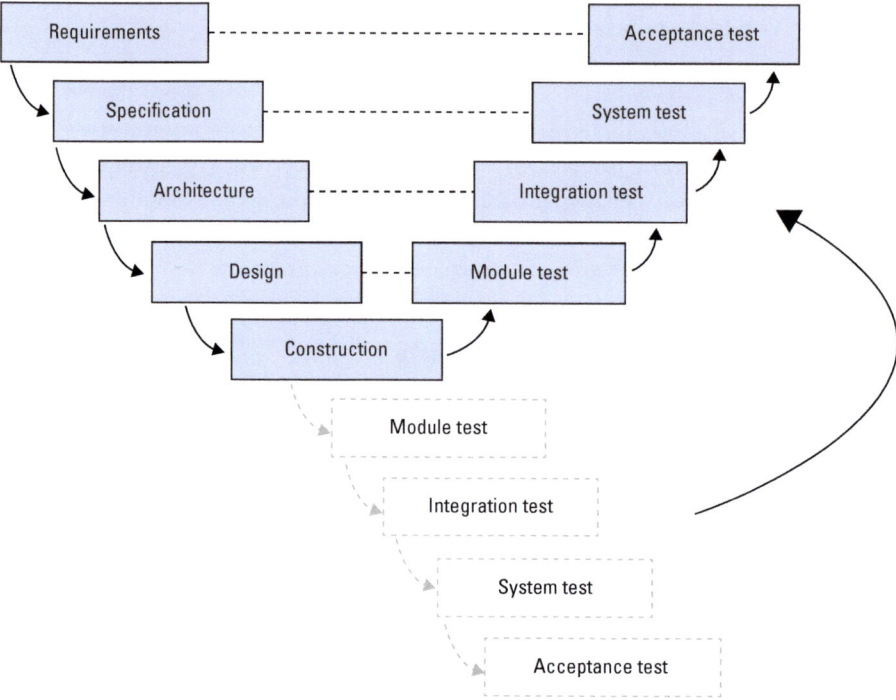

Figure 3.2   Creating the V-model by moving the integration and testing activities up

Of course, the V-model is a simplified representation of your actual project. That is exactly where its strength lies. Being able to quickly project the V-model onto your own project helps you create structure and define proactive actions, as we will see in section 3.2.

Horizontal relationships
The relationship between the left and right sides of the V-model involves more than simply distinguishing between design and testing. For *every* specification or design phase on the left-hand side of the V-model, there is a *corresponding* testing phase on the right side of the model. The client's requirements, for example, are tested with the acceptance test, the system specification with a system test and the designed components with specific module tests. In other words, a large number of horizontal relationships exist between wish and result. As you move down the V, these relationships concern increasingly smaller aspects of the project.

In figure 3.3, the V-model is shown in relation to the project model. Both follow the same horizontal time axis. Compared to the project model, the V-model adds deliverables for technical design, implementation and verification. These substantive interim results are not included in the project model (figure 1.6), because they are not project management deliverables. The project model only contains the specification and architecture deliverables from the initiation phase under the shared denominator of "definition documents," because these are necessary in order to draw up the project management plan.

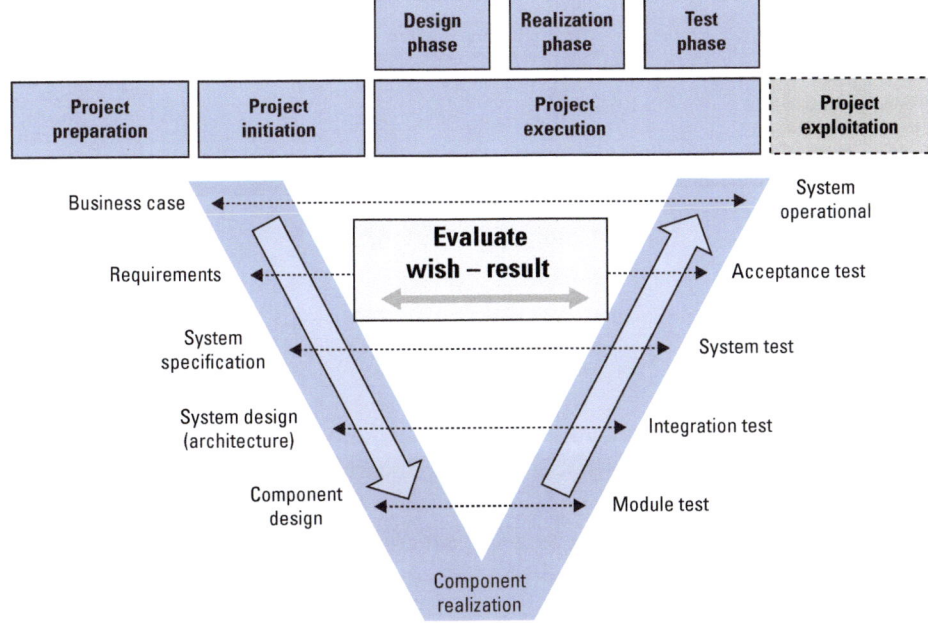

Figure 3.3   The relationship between the V-model and the project model

The terminology in figure 3.3 covers the majority of projects in the technical product development, IT, construction and infrastructure sectors. However, the V-model can also be used for projects in other sectors, as long as they are based on a process of design, realization and verification.

Integration level

The vertical axis of the V-model represents the *integration level* of your project. Along this axis, on the left, the system is *decomposed* into subsystems that themselves consist of components. Along the right side of the model, these components are then *integrated* to form a functioning final product. Figure 3.4 shows how this works for a car. Thinking in terms of systems and decomposing complex systems into an architecture are aspects of Systems Engineering. I am in favor of the close integration between project management

Project management = creating structure + influencing.

and Systems Engineering, which is why the latter will be frequently mentioned in chapters 5 and 6 when we discuss the planning process. It is like the link between project management and leadership, which I also believe to be of the utmost importance: *project management = creating structure + influencing.*

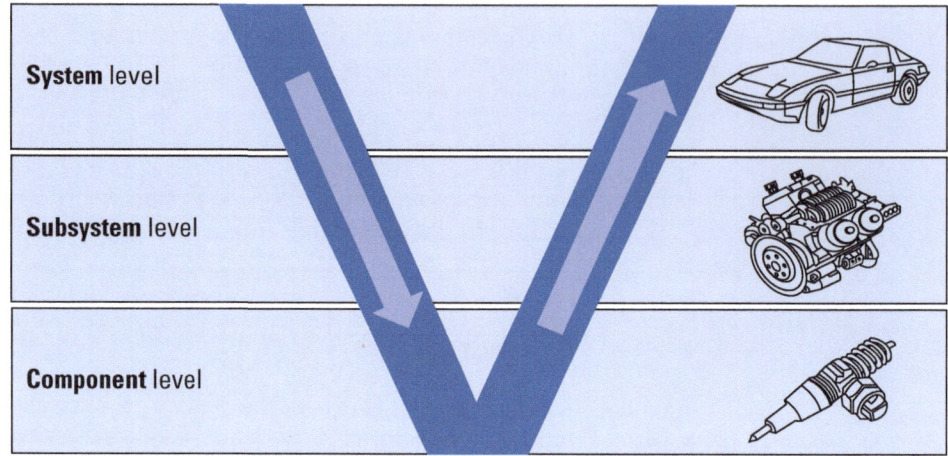

Figure 3.4   Decomposition of system to subsystem to component

Creating a good decomposition requires expertise. Only if a project has been properly divided using clear and stable interfaces can components be delegated to other departments or outsourced to suppliers and then integrated into a final product. That is why I do not believe in the dogmatic separation of management and substance, which is sometimes recommended. Although you can divide systems into components that contain less management or (technical) substance, *you cannot do so without proper knowledge of both aspects.*

3.2   Understanding the impact of issues

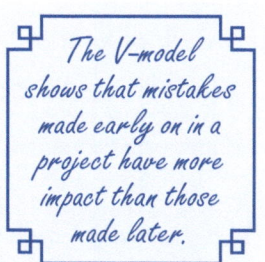

The V-model shows that mistakes made early on in a project have more impact than those made later.

Which mistake will have a bigger impact: one made while drawing up the *business case* or one made while *designing a component* of the system? Without the right context it is difficult to answer this question with complete certainty. However, if you look at the V-model and assume that any mistakes are spotted during testing, you will quickly realize that the risk of a major impact increases for mistakes made early on in a project. Why is that? Because a mistake in the business case (e.g. developing a product for the wrong target audience) will only be discovered after the product's release, when sales figures are not up to par. A mistake concerning the design, manufacturing or ordering of a component is discovered immediately upon its reception or testing, which will lead to corrective measures that are much faster and easier to implement (see figure 3.5).

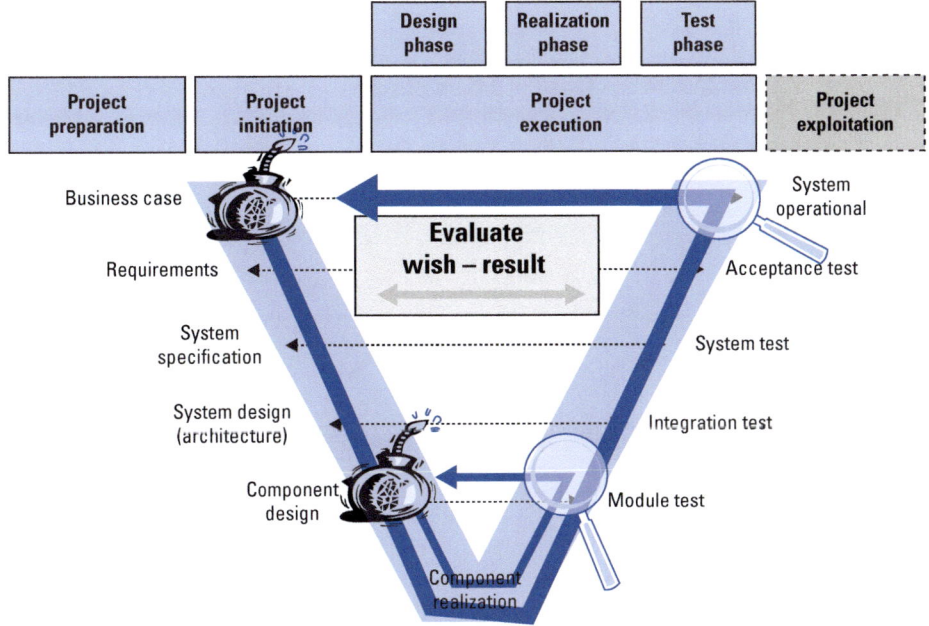

Figure 3.5   The V-model and the impact of issues

Risk reduction in the V-model

The V-model shows that executing a project using a linear waterfall approach is risky, because you may go through the entire process from idea to completion before discovering a problem during testing. The risks involved in the project are only reduced at a late stage, which is the exact opposite of what project managers want. Instead, they want to gain insight into key problems early on and actively work to reduce the project risks at that point (figure 3.6).

The late reduction of risks is even more problematic for projects that consist of multiple integration levels of subprojects. It is only when all of the system components have been developed and integrated that system tests can show whether the final result meets the original wishes. In other words, you will only get feedback after a large part of the project budget has already been spent.

The V-model shows that "waiting" for test results leads to late feedback and a significant chance of having to implement unplanned corrective measures. To avoid this, you need feedback as early as the specification and design phase on the left side of the V-model.

 Do you wait for the test phase or do you acquire feedback earlier on in a project?

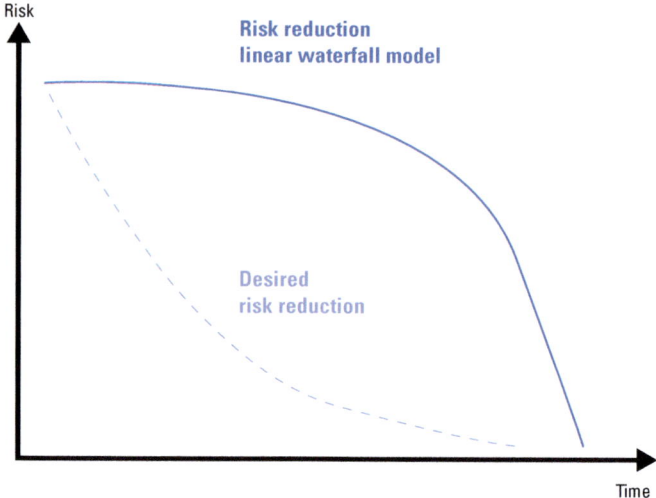

Figure 3.6   Risk reduction in the linear waterfall model

Early confrontation

In addition to focusing on the path to the final goal, it is therefore important to consider *the structure of the path* as well. This structure determines the point at which you can receive feedback concerning the direction and execution of the project. I call evaluating a project's current status in relation to the final goal *confronting*. This is easy for a TomTom, because all it has to do is measure its position with GPS. It is harder for project managers since acquiring feedback early on calls for a proactive attitude. You can do this by, for example, conducting measurements, asking the end user relevant questions, conducting additional studies or testing prototypes. Confronting reveals the true status of the product to be developed and what value you have created so far. Note that this is not the same as evaluating a project's status based on activities completed or budget spent.

Confronting on the left side of the V will result in the following:
1) ***Build the right product***: do not wait for the result to be delivered to the client, instead test the business case and the requirements early on in the project.
2) ***Build the product right***: test the specifications before all components are designed and verify the design of components as far as possible before the manufacturing process begins.

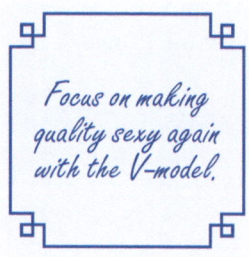

Focus on making quality sexy again with the V-model.

As you will see, I propose a shift of attention to the left side of the V-model. This will involve a cultural change. It means that you have to stop assuming that all problems will be caught during testing (which, by the way, is not true). Instead, you continuously ask yourself what you can do early in the project to make the tests later on a mere formality. The right side of the V-model, the test side, is there to prove the product's quality, not to add missing quality as you conduct your tests.

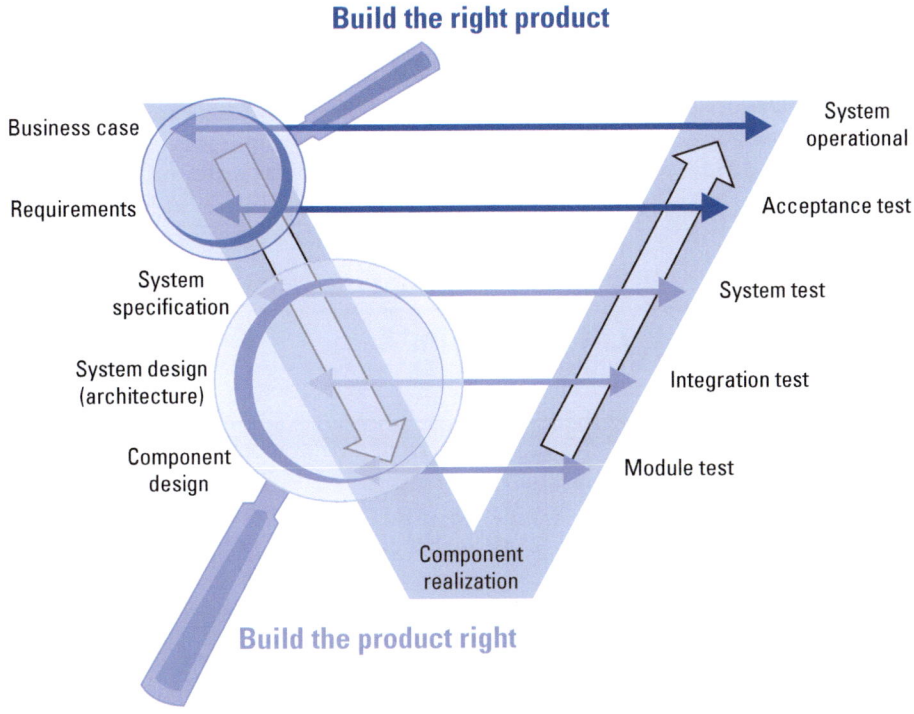

Build the right product

Business case

Requirements

System
specification

System design
(architecture)

Component
design

Component
realization

Build the product right

System
operational

Acceptance test

System test

Integration test

Module test

Figure 3.7   Risk reduction by acquiring feedback from the end user on the left side of the V

The great thing about the V-model is that it clarifies the *how* and *why* of activities that result in higher quality. This is good in a world in which working on quality is often seen as simply checking off items on a list. The V-model allows you to place the focus on quality in a different light, because it illustrates what you do and why you do it. Every problem that you resolve on the left side of the V will be one less problem that may lead to unplanned extra activities during the official tests. Furthermore, early feedback from the end user provides insight into the status in relation to the final goal. This allows you to make timely adjustments if necessary and it offers another communication opportunity with the stakeholders.

Early confrontation in the V can be done by:
1. Adding evaluation moments to the specification and design phase on the left side of the V-model. We will cover this in more detail as part of Design for X (section 3.3)
2. Developing subfunctionalities in iterations. This is covered as part of Agile project management (section 3.4).

These methods are complementary and can be applied to your project together. They expand the V-model into a framework in which early confrontation results in active risk reduction, based on the following themes:
■ Proactive behavior instead of reactive behavior;
■ Forcing the client/end user to provide feedback early on, which helps to make choices and monitor progress;

- Risk reduction during the entire project, instead of only during the concluding test phase;
- Gaining experience in the customer environment early on by having the end user test interim results;
- Testing the design, in addition to testing the implementation;
- The "horizontal linking" of design and verification before starting the process of realization and integration. For example, think of inspections, analyses, model calculations and simulations.

3.3 Early feedback with Design for X

You might think that early confrontation is complicated. Fortunately, that is not the case. In fact, you will have often used this method yourself – consciously or subconsciously. Here are some examples:

- Creating a scale model when designing a new building;
- Drawing up a test protocol during the design phase (instead of at the start of the test phase);
- Creating a model of the system and making calculations;
- Creating a prototype with a 3D printer to check whether everything fits;
- Evaluating the end user's opinion with a survey;
- Testing the political waters by deliberately leaking some information;
- Discussing the implementation plan with an organization that has experience with similar realization processes;
- Conducting a feasibility study with a sample product;
- Conducting your own on-site measurements instead of relying on the client's input;
- Reviewing a proposal with knowledgeable parties.

Although it is not rocket science that does not mean it is easy to apply early confrontation consistently. Furthermore, what should you look out for during the specification, design and realization phases? You can create focus with the *critical parameter*.

Critical parameters are the essential elements of the product, service or organization to be developed, which must be realized at the end of the project or which determine if results can be achieved during the project.

Examples include technical aspects such as production output, system accuracy, energy consumption, cost price or delivery time, as well as non-technical aspects such as customer satisfaction, the competence level of project staff, the client's reaction speed, how fast the HRM department can fill vacancies or the number of change requests made. Professionals know *which critical parameters* to focus on during the project's definition and execution. They also make sure that these parameters are actively monitored throughout the entire project, instead of only during the final test phase. Finally, they make sure that corrective measures are taken *immediately* if any deviations are detected.

The driveway constructor

A decade ago, I wanted to build a driveway in front of my new home. The preparations were made and a half-meter layer of sand had been deposited. Everything was ready for the driveway constructor. We had scheduled an appointment with one that very afternoon. Like a good academic engineer should, I came prepared. I had drawn the entire driveway on 5 mm2 graph paper and included every possible detail. I felt like the best client in the world.

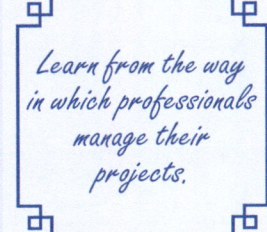

Learn from the way in which professionals manage their projects.

The driveway constructor turned out to be exactly what I expected: not particularly focused on communication and with an air that paving a driveway was no big deal. That's when I pulled out my sketch. I quickly noticed that my detailed instructions were going in one ear and out the other. He asked me three questions after I was done: "How many square meters?", "Is the layer of sand thick enough?" and "What stone?"

I was still excited, because that was all included in my design. Well, I had to calculate the area by counting the squares on my piece of paper and we had not yet decided what type of stone we wanted.

Figure 3.8   Do you know the critical parameters of the definition and execution phases?

"I have to know what type of stone you want," he said. "Otherwise, I cannot put together a quote." I started explaining what our selection process consisted of and that the stones would definitely be delivered on time. He interrupted me: "If I do not know what type of stone you want, I do not know how many times I have to cut it, and that means I cannot give you a quote!"

Point taken. As a client, I had walked right into a common trap. Providing a lot of information is not necessarily the same as providing the right information. I was talking to a professional who was not distracted by irrelevant information and knew exactly what the *critical parameters* were to provide a quote: *the number of square meters, the correct thickness of the layer of sand and the type of stone.*

 Do you know the critical parameters of your project during the definition phase?

Three days before the work was scheduled to begin, my phone rang. Even before I got a name, I heard a voice say: "We cannot work like this, there are weeds all over." He was right; there was plenty of sand on the path behind the gate, but it was covered in weeds by now. I explained that I was planning to remove it all that weekend. In a reflex, I said: "It's good of you to check, but how could you see over our high gate?" He said that he always came by to make sure everything was in order and that he had climbed over our wall. This professional did not like assumptions...

 Do you take your project's critical parameters seriously enough to check them yourself, instead of relying on assumptions?

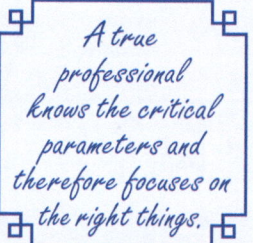

A true professional knows the critical parameters and therefore focuses on the right things.

That Monday, work was scheduled to begin. When I came over to bring the men some coffee and cookies, they had made serious progress. The driveway constructor was on his knees laying the stones down quickly. His colleague refilled the pile of stones with a wheelbarrow. The way he dumped the stones out of the wheelbarrow was so haphazard that a few kept hitting the driveway constructor's right shoe. There will be trouble, I thought and I decided to stay and watch for a bit.

Sure enough, there was trouble – although the cause was the complete opposite of what I had expected. The driveway constructor lost his temper when the stones had *not* hit his shoe a few times. After thirty years, he apparently expected the stones to be dropped so close to him that they hit his shoe, since that was the only way for him to lay them down quickly enough. If no stones hit his shoe, they were dropped too far away, which meant he had to reach for them and that would slow him down too much. It was clear to me: this professional also knew the critical parameters of the execution phase!

 You probably know what is coming: do you know the critical parameters of your project during the execution phase?

The critical parameters direct your focus to *the things that matter*. In this way, they help you act rather than react to all project stimuli. Focusing on the critical parameters (often *leading indicators*) is therefore much more than just focusing on time and money (which are often *lagging indicators*). Knowing a project's critical parameters helps you maintain an overview and creates (team) focus during complex situations. Along with situational leadership, I consider focusing on critical parameters as the best way to monitor things closely

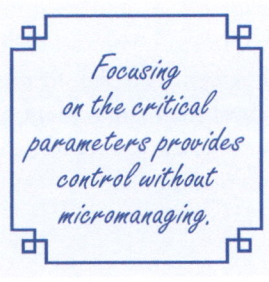

Focusing on the critical parameters provides control without micromanaging.

without micromanaging, e.g. when drawing up the plan, during project execution and when reporting status. Critical parameters should be *measurable* and later in this book we will see that it is important to know both the desired value of the final situation and the desired value of the interim results (e.g. a prototype).

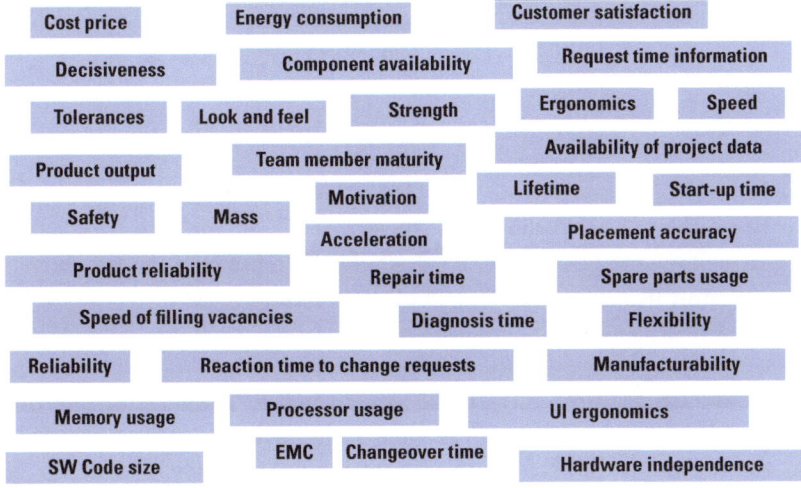

Figure 3.9   Examples of critical parameters

Note that there are many similarities between the critical parameters of the project and the *CTQ (Critical to Quality)* parameter used in Six Sigma (a methodology that focuses on reducing the variation in processes). In Six Sigma, CTQs are quality characteristics that are important to the process and therefore decisive for the project team's success. Six Sigma also uses the *CTC (Critical to Customer)* metric, which indicates which characteristics are important to customers. A well-known example is the fact that the sound of a closing car door is a CTC for the end user, while the dimensional tolerances and the damping characteristics of the door are CTQs for the car manufacturer (see figure 3.10). When using Six Sigma, you usually make a decomposition (CTQ breakdown), for which you relate the end result to measurable and controllable properties of the interim results.

The critical parameters of projects are often CTQs, but it is important to stay practical. Creating focus in your plan, approach, and behavior of your team is more important for a project manager than covering all details with a validated measuring process (which is of course very important for a Six Sigma Black Belt). When determining your project's critical parameters, you can definitely use the CTQ breakdown if you have one. First and foremost, however, you should use your common sense and focus primarily on those elements that affect the management of your project. These may include elements that are less obvious as CTQs: e.g. the response time for change requests or the team's motivation after an impactful reorganization.

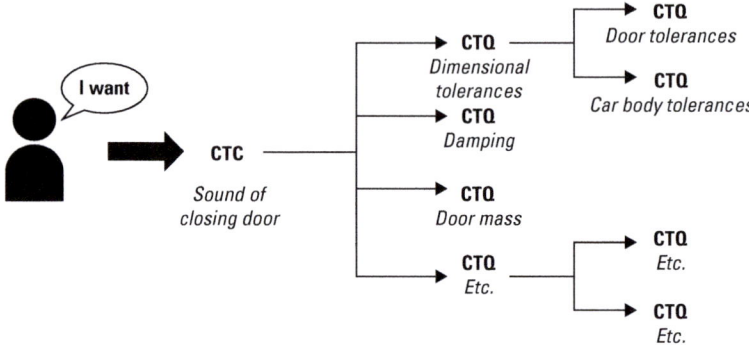

Figure 3.10   Translating the client's needs (CTC) into quality parameters for the product (CTQs)

Design for X

When you know the critical parameters, you can focus on them on the left side of the V-model. This is known as *Design for X* (DfX). The X represents the property (or critical parameter) that must be realized by the end of the project.

Examples:
- Design for Manufacturing (DfM): make sure during the specification and design phase that the products can be easily produced and assembled later on in the project.
- Design for Reliability (DfR): ensure during the specification and design phase that expectations pertaining to the reliability and maintenance costs will be realized later on in the product's life cycle.
- Design for Testability (DfT): ensure during the specification and design phase that the product can be tested easily and effectively.
- Design for Six Sigma (DfSS): ensure during the specification phase that the product or service meets the client's wishes and ensure during the design phase that the variation in the critical properties of the service or produced products falls within the specified limits.

In other words, you realize Design for X by focusing on the critical parameters from the very start of the project. For a project manager, that means constantly asking yourself the following question while conducting the activities on the left side of the V: "How can I receive feedback now about the status in relation to the desired end result?" That means moving away from the tendency to view the specification, design and realization phase as a substantive *black box* and go through these stages "with blinders on," while only evaluating the actual project status during the test phase. DfX turns the activities on the left side of the V into a kind of *white box* (you create insight into the substantive quality as early as the

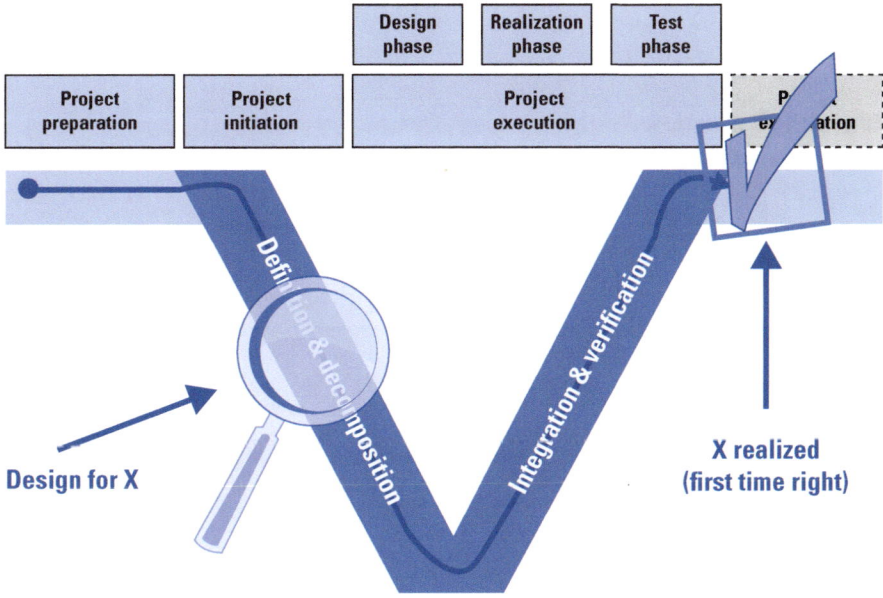

Figure 3.11 Design for X: ensuring that X will be realized during the design phase

design phase), in which you make immediate adjustments based on the critical parameters you measure. When we discuss the planning process in chapter 5, we will cover how to integrate DfX into the project management plan in more detail.

With the critical parameter, DfX brings the proactive element within reach. This ties in perfectly with the central theme of this book: moving from reactive to proactive to influencing. I should tell you that I call proactive project management *Design for Execution*. You do this by establishing such a solid foundation for the project's execution during the initiation phase that the execution phase itself proceeds virtually without a hitch. Of course, there may be bumps in the road from time to time, but those will have to do with issues that could not

have been foreseen or which have changed due to certain circumstances. You will agree that solving problems that could not have been prevented is better than solving problems that could have been avoided!

3.4 Early feedback with Agile development

In addition to DfX, there is another way to acquire feedback early on in the project: the Agile approach. If there are many uncertainties or changes, it is advisable to go through the V not just once, but multiple times during several iterations. For DfX, we focus on the left side of the V-model; with Agile development, we go through the entire V-model many times during the various sprints. Agile development and focusing on the critical parameters with DfX can easily be used in conjunction. When you do so, the two approaches actually improve each other's effectiveness.

A V during each iteration

Figure 3.12 shows what Agile development means for the V-model. The top of the V remains unchanged. The process up to and including the system design will also have to be conducted during an Agile project in order to draw up the architecture, define the product backlog, and plan the sprints. Similarly, the top of the right side of the V-model will not change either – although the system tests will be briefer because the sprint results have already been tested at the system level.

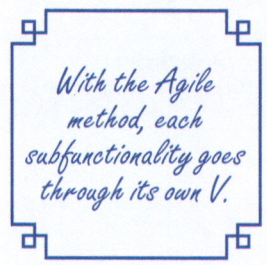

With the Agile method, each subfunctionality goes through its own V.

The differences are therefore found along the bottom of the V. In an Agile project, the process of design-realization-testing is conducted as a separate V for each subfunctionality from the product backlog. At the end of a sprint, the results are tested at the system level because Agile requires the end user to be able to evaluate the sprint results. These are precisely the early feedback moments we are after. For the sake of clarity, figure 3.12 shows the many small Vs during a single sprint as one large V. In reality, however, the subfunctionalities each go through their own V during a sprint, only to be integrated into a single sprint result at the end (see also figure 1.10).

In chapter 1, we learned that it is possible to modify the scope at the start of a sprint. These changes then have to go through the specification and planning process at the top-left side of the V all over again. That is why the V for the sprints starts at the specification level.

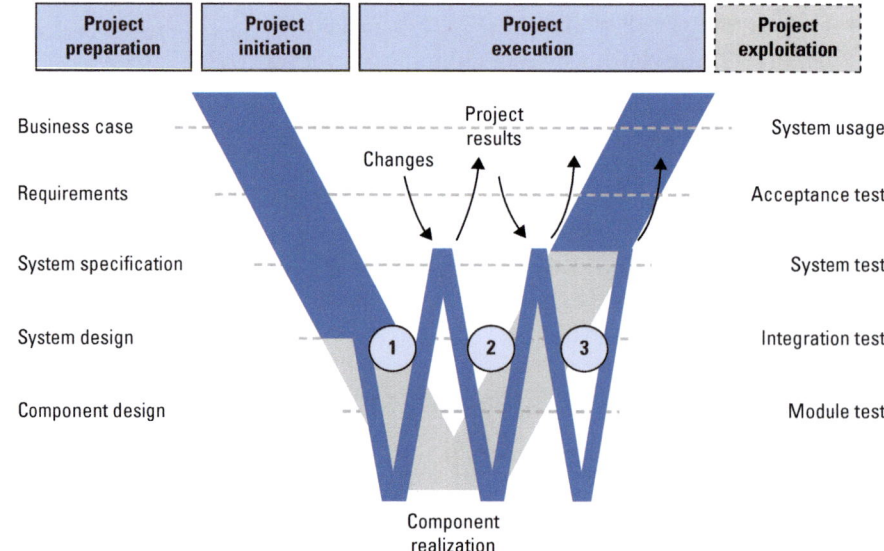

Figure 3.12   The V-model and the Agile process with three sprints

Effects

The benefits of acquiring early feedback with DfX and Agile will be clear to you by now. We will now learn how these two methods compare to the waterfall model in terms of factors such as risk reduction, adaptability, visibility and value creation.

Figure 3.13 shows this comparison, as well as the effects of combining Agile with DfX. Remember that even though incremental development (Agile) and focusing on critical parameters (DfX) are perfectly compatible, it is not advisable to use the Agile approach for every type of project, for example some construction or hardware-oriented projects. On the other hand, DfX can be used for virtually all types of projects.

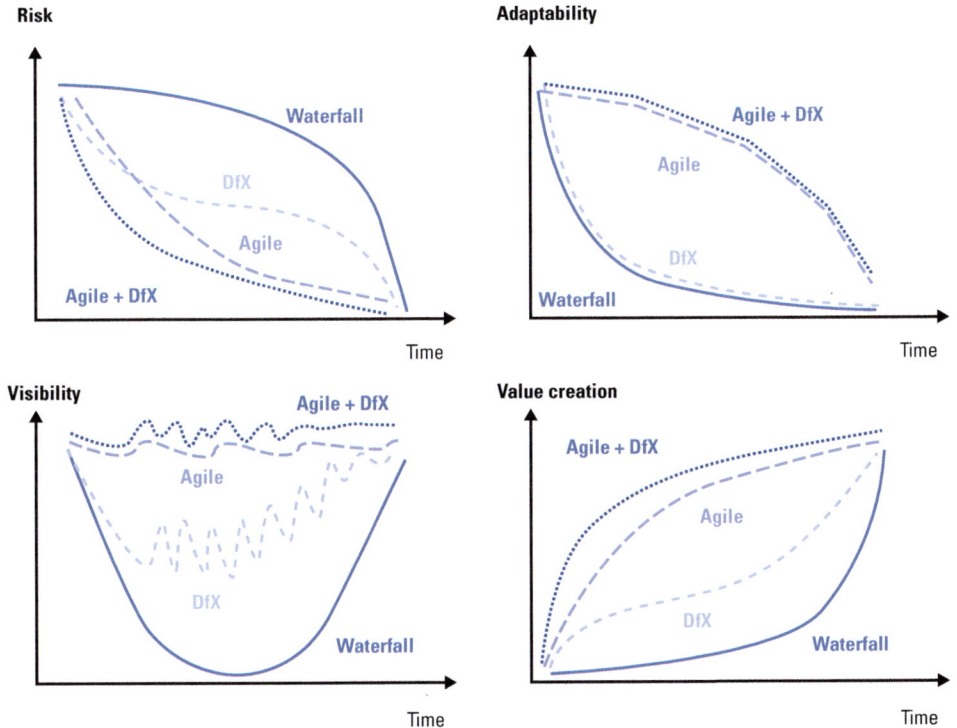

Figure 3.13   The effects of Design for X and Agile compared to the waterfall model

The comparison between waterfall, DfX and Agile can be explained as follows:

- **Risk reduction**: development using the waterfall model will only offer risk reduction during the concluding tests. DfX offers a significant reduction early on with the evaluation moments on the left of the V-model. With Agile, interim products are delivered, which results in the swiftest risk reduction. The combination with DfX results in an additional reduction, particularly during the definition phase (before the start of the first sprint).
- **Adaptability**: this is low for the waterfall model, because changes mean you have to go "backwards" along the V. DfX does not change this. However, Agile does since modifications can be made before each sprint. The more sprints that remain and the shorter each sprint is, the more flexible you will be.

- **Visibility**: once again, the waterfall model performs relatively poorly. At the start of the project, you "dive under water with your submarine" and you only show results during the integration and test phase. DfX improves the visibility because evaluation moments are also communication moments. Agile offers the highest visibility, since each sprint ends with at least a demonstration for the client and possibly even a commercial interim product. The combination with DfX improves the visibility a bit more, because the status of the critical parameters is shown alongside the sprint results.
- **Value creation**: the waterfall model will only offer results – and therefore value for the client – after the concluding test phase. DfX creates value sooner because the confrontation moments prove that the product or service performs well in terms of the critical parameters. Agile is once again the best option, since each iteration results in a finished interim product. DfX amplifies this effect with the additional validation of the activities on the left side of the V.

3.5   The V-model and your own behavior

Leading up to the next chapter, in which we look at factor 10 in some detail, we will now cover another factor 10 element. The proactive actions from the V-model can also be applied to your own behavior. By not viewing an important activity as *a moment*, but rather as *a small V with a result in the top-right corner*, this creates confrontation moments on the left side of the V that ensure the activity is conducted in a more effective manner. By doing so, you increase your chance of achieving the desired result and consciously create (healthy) pressure to make decisions and choices.

The meeting
I'll use a recognizable example. You are tasked with organizing a meeting because the desired solution for a problem is unclear. You are surely familiar with the many tips for effective meetings but you are busy right now, so the first thing you do is send out an invitation via Outlook.

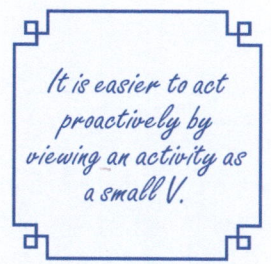

It is easier to act proactively by viewing an activity as a small V.

Chances are that you will be subconsciously stuck in "reactive mode" from then until the start of the meeting. You react to absent colleagues, to questions about what the meeting will cover, to concerns that you forgot to invite someone important and to your stress the night before that tells you it might be a good idea to create some presentation slides to start off the meeting. Even when the meeting begins, you are still reacting. You are annoyed by latecomers and by people who are on time, only to lean back and say: "I wonder what we will talk about for a full hour." During the meeting, your annoyance remains a factor. It does not go as planned, there are discussions about information that should have been available beforehand and it turns out an essential person will not be attending after all. At the end of the meeting, you do your best to make some concrete agreements, but you are left feeling dissatisfied: this was not an effective meeting.

 How often do you get the feeling that you were not in control and were overtaken by events?

You can prevent all this by using the V-model. Try to look at the meeting not as a moment, but as a brief V process. Next, think of things you can do prior to the meeting to ensure it will be a guaranteed success. *Confront and create action before the meeting starts* (see figure 3.14), for example with these initiatives:

1. When inviting people, make sure you have a clear goal, a good title for the meeting and, preferably, an agenda. When people accept the invitation, they must be *substantively triggered*, instead of only attending because they have nothing else planned. Consciously choose whom to invite and make the reason to participate as clear as possible.

2. Well before the meeting, send out an email to inform invitees about the decisions that have to be made. Also clarify which actions are needed beforehand, for example to acquire the information necessary to make decisions together. This raises the bar and shows participants that the available time will be used efficiently. Furthermore, this action kicks off the *warming-up* for the meeting, which ensures everyone will come prepared and eager to start.

3. Before the meeting, make sure that key individuals will actually be attending – preferably through personal contact. If some people have doubts, tell them why their attendance is so important. If there are any problems, suggest that they attend for, say, twenty minutes and explain what you expect from them during that time. If they are absolutely unable to attend, ask them to send their vision or analysis to the other attendees before the meeting.

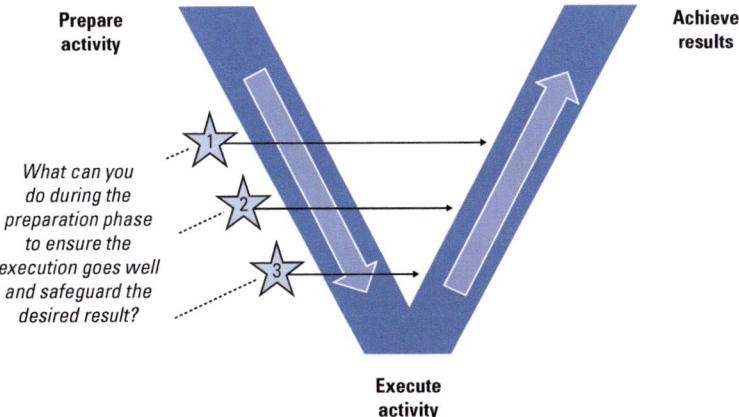

Figure 3.14   Preparing the environment with the V-model prior to the activity

You can probably imagine the effects these initiatives will have on your meeting. Participants will come in with an active and motivated attitude, ready to get to work quickly. Your conversational partners are prepared, both substantively and mentally, because everyone has been working towards this moment for several days now and they received important information beforehand. Finally, all participants understand why their attendance is required. That motivates them and ensures they will do whatever they can to be there.

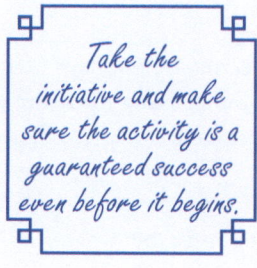

Take the initiative and make sure the activity is a guaranteed success even before it begins.

If someone is late despite these preparations, you do not have to sit around waiting for him or her, or opt to start right away despite knowing that you will have to repeat everything that has been said when the latecomer finally arrives. Because of your investment beforehand, you can now act confidently: "We will not start without Carl. He knows that his attendance is required in order for us to perform together. I will call him right away." You know that Carl will answer immediately, because he told you the meeting is important to him. Five minutes later, he rushes in: "Sorry, sorry, I got delayed. Let's get started immediately!"

I call this *money-for-nothing-behavior*: you are not doing anything extra; instead, you are simply doing things sooner and with the right focus. You invest in the preparation and, in doing so, create the conditions that allow the team to perform optimally. That is how easy it can be to take control. Experience the power of action and create confrontation moments on the left side of the V for important activities, e.g. meetings, drawing up an offer, giving a presentation, conducting negotiations, making a difficult decision or preparing a celebration. This method of taking action will be integrated into the personal planning process in chapter 5 as the *10% confrontation rule*.

Preventing procrastination

In addition to creating a warming-up before important activities, confrontation is also a good way to create pressure. This pressure can help you as a:
- Weapon against the student syndrome;
- Way to make choices and decisions.

The *student syndrome*, i.e. procrastination, is a constant risk. I would be lying if I told you I never do this myself. I procrastinate too from time to time and I sometimes realize that I should have started certain tasks sooner. This is often because the path to a deadline is unclear. In other words, the deadline lies beyond your personal horizon. When you postpone your work, there is no signal telling you there is now less time remaining. The time you have left feels infinite.

A solution is to schedule interim goals that fall within your personal horizon. View the path to the deadline as a small V and create several confrontation moments before the deadline. By doing so, you chop the unclear path up into several short sprints, which creates a healthy sense of pressure. The interim goals also serve as communicating and influencing moments. This example of taking action will be discussed in more detail when we talk about the planning process.

We also see the student syndrome occur when we have to make *decisions*. Why make a choice today when you have two weeks left to do so? To look at it from a different perspective: how often do you wait to make a decision, only to find that two weeks have passed and you still have no information? *All you did was waste two weeks*. This is a dangerous path, because as the saying goes: *if you do not make a decision, it will be made for you*. Procrastination usually leads to a decision in the end – just not one made by you.

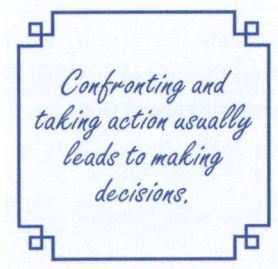

Confronting and taking action usually leads to making decisions.

I believe that many decisions feel further away than they really are because there is no confrontation. Put the right people in a room together, make sure they know their options and explain the benefits of making a decision today. You will find that the sky is suddenly the limit. If you want to stay in control, it helps to plan the decision moments yourself. Compare it to going on holiday by car: deciding beforehand whether everything will fit in the car and whether you really have to bring everything will only lead to endless discussions. If you simply start loading up the car instead, a sense of urgency will arise automatically as space begins to run out. *Confronting usually leads to making decisions.*

A useful tool to enforce decision-making is my *decision enforcement matrix*, shown in figure 3.15. It bothered me that a decision table often turns out to be a procrastination table. The more extensive the table, the clearer it is that certain information is still missing. That makes people feel like a decision cannot be made yet. The decision enforcement matrix is a table like any other decision table, but with one essential addition: people are forced to either fill out a decision or an action that will result in the right information to make that decision.

Decisions that have to be made	Options to choose from	Criteria score (e.g. critical parameters)			Decision or action that results in the right information to make a decision	
		Criterion 1	Criterion 2	Criterion 3	Decision	Action
Subject 1	Option 1: ...					
	Option 2: ...					
	Option 3: ...					
Subject 2	Option 1: ...					
	Option 2: ...					
Subject 3	Option 1: ...					
	Option 2: ...					
	Option 3: ...					
	Option 4: ...					

Figure 3.15   Stimulating decision-making with the decision enforcement matrix

I have often used the decision enforcement matrix in teams, but also for my own personal use. Consciously thinking about an action results in an interesting psychological process that eliminates procrastination. After a heated discussion about everything people don't know yet and are still waiting for, they often come to the same conclusion: "If we wait, we will know more, but it will not bring the decision any closer. We might as well decide now." On the other hand, if the action does result in useful information, it will reveal a clear path to the decision. In this manner, you combine speed and quality and prevent "idle waiting."

Of course, this only applies when it is necessary to make a decision. There are also situations in which this is not the case yet, or in which you deliberately choose to make a decision as late as possible, e.g. to utilize the advantage of having multiple scenarios or to avoid unnecessary repair work resulting from incorrect assumptions. Note that you can still use the decision enforcement matrix for this, simply write down in the action column how long you want to wait before making a decision.

Summary

- The V-model shows the horizontal relationships between definition activities and the corresponding test activities.
- Waiting for the test phase results in late feedback and necessitates extensive corrective measures. To avoid this, ask for feedback during the specification, design and implementation phases.
- Use Design for X and Agile project management to confront at an early stage. These methods can be used together.
- You realize Design for X by focusing on the critical parameter X from the very beginning of a project.
- With Agile development, you go through the V-model for each individual subfunctionality. During the sprint, these subfunctionalities are then integrated into one sprint result for the client.
- Focusing on the critical parameters during a project provides control without micro-management.
- Keep yourself and your team focused by viewing activities as small Vs. This method also helps to prevent procrastination and enforce decision-making. Enjoy the power of action!

4 The factor 10

- ◀ Discover the power of factor 10 behavior.
- ◀ How flip-thinking allows you to take control even during difficult times.
- ◀ Understand Stephen Covey's path to independence and interdependence.
- ◀ Your employee's task maturity determines which leadership style to use.

You can take the step from reactive to proactive to influencing in one of several ways. If you are open to it, you will quickly realize that there are opportunities to be seized everywhere around you. That is what I call the factor 10. It is important that your method of influencing ties into your own style and your sense of integrity. Otherwise, you will not exert your influence at all, you will not stick with it and others will not believe you.[4]

4.1 Smart leadership and behavior is the factor 10

You have probably heard this before at a party: "I work seventy hours a week!" What do you think when someone says that? "He sure works hard," "Wow, his new business is really taking off" or "Rather him than me." There is nothing wrong with working long hours from time to time. We have all felt it when a deadline approaches: the focus, the excitement, the drive to keep going and the euphoria once you are done. However, things go wrong when this becomes a structural situation and you have to work such long hours because that is the only way you can finish your work. This will have a negative impact on your career, hobbies, friendships, relationships and physical and mental health.

It is quite normal to work more during peak times, but there are limits. After all, there are only twenty-four hours in a day. On top of that, it is virtually impossible to perform at the top of your game if you cannot strike the right balance between work and downtime. I call *working hard* the *factor 2*. The annoying thing about this factor 2 is that there is no factor 3, because there are no more hours in a day. When the situation calls for hard workers to go the extra mile, there will be nothing left for them to give.

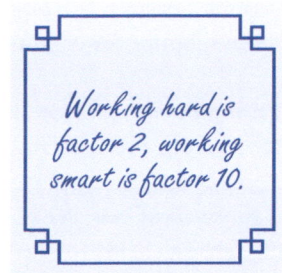

Working hard is factor 2, working smart is factor 10.

Instead, I am a firm believer in the factor 10: *working smart*. Is this exactly a factor 10? Not really, I have chosen that number because it looks good. Besides, I have found from time to time that working smart can offer a factor 17 or even a factor 40 advantage. I do not want

---

4 This chapter ties into the following competences from IPMA's ICB4: Power and interest, Culture and values, Self-reflection and self-management, Personal integrity and reliability, Personal communication, Relations and engagement, Leadership, Teamwork, Conflict and crisis, Resourcefulness, Negotiation, Risk and opportunity, Stakeholders, Change and transformation.

to turn this into an exact science, however. The important thing to remember is that working smart makes it much easier to scale up than working hard. Only using the factor 2 is not enough for (project) managers. It will not allow them to keep performing consistently, it will get in the way of their private life and it will definitely prevent them from developing.

> *The factor 2 alone is not enough for a project manager.*

What is this factor 10? I call something *factor 10 behavior* when you consciously do your work in a smarter manner and complete the task at hand faster, better or with less energy than you normally would. It is all about consciously making smart choices, acting consciously, influencing consciously, being critical, making good use of your own experience, making the right analyses, etc. The factor 10 is about utilizing the right leadership and behavior. This leadership is essential during the project preparation phase, when conducting stakeholder management, when motivating and directing your team, etc. In other words, it is a vital component for project managers who want to realize goals together with their team and exert a positive influence on the project course.

We will frequently come back to the factor 10 after this chapter. You will see that an integral approach to leadership and behavior (the *soft skills*) together with the methods and techniques (the *hard skills*) can result in a powerful and versatile toolkit for project managers.

Examples of factor 10 behavior
Here are some examples of factor 10 behavior. Note that this list is nowhere near exhaustive, there are many more examples. However, it does serve to illustrate what factor 10 behavior is and that it is certainly not rocket science. I have also included the time that, in my experience, can be saved with this behavior. It is important to understand that saving time is often not even the biggest benefit of factor 10 behavior; it can also lead to better results, more support, fewer (unwanted) changes or more motivated employees.

Examples of the factor 10 include:
- Making the specialist with the right competences available for an activity, instead of choosing an employee who happens to have time available: a lead time of four hours instead of two weeks.
- Giving clients the feeling that it was their idea, instead of forcing the idea upon them as your own: convincing them for ten minutes instead of two days.
- Giving team members freedom and coaching them by clearly putting your trust in them and making them responsible for the end result: thirty minutes of supervision per week, instead of an hour every day.
- When submitting a proposal, enforcing a decision at the outset to limit the number of variants that have to be described: working on the proposal for three days instead of two weeks.

- At the start of a project, actively outlining the scope and the goals, instead of waiting for discussions that necessitate modification of the plan: a time investment of two days, instead of spending three weeks modifying the plan later on.
- Preparing for a meeting by viewing it as a V (section 3.5): a preparation time of one hour, instead of four hours of aftercare and corrections.
- During the annual budget allocation, instead of asking for 20 FTEs and then replanning because you only got 16, drawing up a plan and targets for different numbers of allocated FTEs (16-18-20-22 FTEs). This way, you can immediately indicate what you can deliver and you only have to draw up a plan once: working on the plan for four days, instead of spending twenty days on the plan and its modifications.
- Getting your way by exercising effective stakeholder management, instead of only being right by adding more substantive detail to your proposal: three thirty-minute meetings, instead of working on a proposal for three days.

These examples also include topics that were covered in the preceding chapters. The TomTom's characteristics of acting instead of reacting, communicating before problems arise and displaying proactive behavior inspired by the V-model are all examples of factor 10 behavior. Consciously acting and taking the initiative will give your results a serious boost.

Leadership	Management
Doing the right things	Doing things right
Goal	Path
What and why	How and when
Effectiveness	Efficiency
Change	Stability
Future	Present
Working on the project	Working in the project
Inspire	Coordinate
Motivate	Instruct
Focus on organizing	Focus on organization
Support	Enforce
Create	Implement
Realize goals	Achieve results
Innovate	Resolve problems
New opportunities	Standardize
Policy	Procedures
Challenge	Reduce risks
Focus on trust	Focus on control
Followers	Employees

Figure 4.1   The differences and balance between leadership and management

Leadership versus management

Have you ever said the following about someone: "That is a manager and clearly not a leader?" You probably have. Nevertheless, before moving on to the competence of leadership, I want to show my support for managers everywhere. The American leadership expert Warren Bennis once said: "Leadership is about 'doing the right things,' whereas management is about 'doing things right.'" Leadership and management are complementary and you need both. As seen in figure 4.1, one focuses mainly on growth and development, while the other focuses on direction and control.

Leadership is about doing the right things; management is about doing things right.

As a project manager, you will need both leadership and management competences to successfully complete a project. You may know some examples of situations where this balance was missing. Some people can present a wonderful vision, yet they lack the ability to properly direct its execution. Others, meanwhile, get their team to complete tasks on time, yet they completely overlook such aspects as ownership or motivation. Finding the right balance between leadership and management can sometimes feel like an impossible &-&-&-paradox.

4.2   Flip-thinking and the power of action

To apply factor 10 behavior, I often employ the useful cognitive technique of *flip-thinking*, developed by the Dutchman Berthold Gunster (Gunster, 2016). Flip-thinking is about thinking in terms of opportunities rather than problems and accepting reality as it comes. Note that this is not the same as failing to acknowledge the problem! When using flip-thinking you do not resist the problem, instead you use the situation at hand to create something new. Rather than offering resistance and saying "Yes, but… ," you open yourself up entirely to the possibilities by saying "Yes, and…" This helps you to stay in control and come up with new, creative solutions.

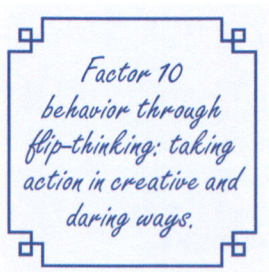
Factor 10 behavior through flip-thinking: taking action in creative and daring ways.

In difficult situations it is tempting to stop taking the initiative. This prevents you from taking advantage of more effective options. Your fear may even exacerbate the problem. Compare it to riding a mountain bike. If you get scared, you squeeze the brakes to slow down. However, by going more slowly, steering becomes more difficult. When managing projects, you can also get stuck in reactive patterns that only make your problems worse – often without you even realizing it. You might call this *factor ½ behavior*. In those situations, flip-thinking can be surprisingly effective and lead to the factor 10 instead. I will give you four examples:

1. Taking the initiative when you are called out for failing.
2. Safeguarding the scope by provoking changes.
3. Creating opportunities through risk management.
4. Presenting yourself as the requesting party at the start of a project.

1. Taking the initiative when you are called out for failing

The first example is about flip-thinking when you are called out on problems with your project. The standard behavior would be to resist or react in a guilty manner, instead of taking the lead. The advantage of factor 10 behavior is that competition becomes collaboration.

I was working as a program manager for a new production system, of which the first series had been delivered to several customers in Asia. After a week of hard work and dotting some i's on Saturday, I could finally relax on Sunday and spend some time with my family. We had planned to go on a trip and leave at 11 am. However, around 09:30 I "accidentally" noticed an escalation email on my smartphone. Using a lot of capital letters, the sales manager from Asia told me that everything had gone wrong with the machine of one of our customers, that this customer had lost faith in us and that we had to come up with a plan to resolve the situation by noon on Wednesday. The sales manager was furious, as was evident from the fact that the email had been sent to many people besides myself.

I was bummed out and upset because my team had its back against the wall. I also dreaded having to make plans with my team members while their schedules were already full. However, if I did not take control right now, the problem would continue to bother me for the rest of the day. Everything had already been blown out of proportion, which made me realize that resistance was futile. That helped me flip my thinking - I had no choice. If I did not take action immediately, someone else would, which would only make the problem worse.

The sales manager was upset. So was I, because we were put in a difficult position. I decided to act instead of react: get over my frustration, drop my defense and reply to the email right away. In my message, I would acknowledge the sales manager's anger and propose actions that would satisfy him *and benefit my team.*

Furthermore, I wanted to surprise the sales manager by going along with him immediately and taking the initiative right away. I suggested that waiting until Wednesday was not in the client's best interest. Instead, I proposed that we should come up with a plan by *Monday morning,* so we could surprise the customer (the sales manager did not need to know that all kinds of other meetings had been scheduled for Monday morning, so my people would not be working on the project anyway). I asked the sales manager to exert his influence and ensure the right people were available to work on this task on Monday morning.

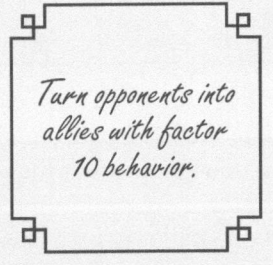

Turn opponents into allies with factor 10 behavior.

You probably know what happened next. From then on, everything went smoothly. The sales manager's reaction was one of surprise. He was glad to be taken seriously from the off and that he was not alone that Sunday. He also started doing everything in his power to support the team. In less than fifteen minutes I had turned an opponent into an ally!

On Monday morning we discussed the problem at hand without using up any project time. Because we had our solution ready on Monday, the customer was also pleasantly surprised and willing to go along with us. Flip-thinking had allowed us to solve a problem together, instead of fighting each other.

?   *Have you ever got your way by initially going along with the other party and giving them their way?*

2. Safeguarding the scope by provoking changes

Prevent changes? Standard behavior would be to carefully safeguard the scope and apply change management when necessary. It is common to either say *no* or charge the client extra. There is nothing wrong with that approach, but I would like to show you how much more you can achieve by flip-thinking. Instead of resisting, because changes are to be expected, try flexibly going along with them and saying "yes" twice before saying "no." The factor 10 effect: you develop your relationship and safeguard the scope *together*.

This flip-thinking is based on my observation that while a project's scope is usually clear to the project manager, clients tend to be oblivious in this regard. Often, they fail to realize that asking for more will take more time or stray away from the contract. Flip-thinking can be used in two ways in this example.

Only say "no" after first saying "yes" twice.

The first way is by taking advantage of the available flexibility instead of acting in a rigid manner. When drawing up a contract, try writing a list of elements that can change and the dates until which these changes can be made. Of course, you should only choose elements that will not pose any problems for you. By doing so, you show flexibility and options that were already available. Next, ask the client for a response. This is often a good way to trigger the process of thinking ahead about what might change. You come across as flexible and make the other party think. More often than not, clients will conclude on their own that the other elements of the project are not open to change, which is exactly what you wanted.

The second way goes like this. Suppose that a client asks you to do something differently two days after the start of the project execution. The change would have quite an impact and you have plenty of reasons to say "no." However, even if the client understands your point, you will still come across as inflexible and afraid of taking risks. That will not do your image any good, nor will it benefit the rest of the project when this is your client's first impression of you. It would be better to start out by playing along twice. Say that what the client asks for will result in a lot of extra work, but that you will consider the request nonetheless. Next, surprise the client by agreeing – preferably without charging anything extra. The result is that the client feels like they got a good deal and now has a better understanding of the project scope. Repeat this process when the next change request comes in, but change your stance the third time. That is when you explain how it would not be very professional to be flexible again without thinking of your own interests. Clients will now accept your story about more work and extra costs, because they have seen both sides of you. From now on, you safeguard the project scope together.

Whenever I tell this story, people often remark that a lot depends on what those two initial changes entail. My answer is that exhibiting factor 10 behavior naturally means that you influence those first two changes and perhaps even provoke them. It is essential to take the initiative! Just look at car salesmen: they know exactly what extra options (i.e. changes) you will ask for and what they can offer you for free. Also remember that it is important to genuinely act in the client's best interest (they must not feel cheated afterwards). For more on this, read about Covey's win-win later on in this chapter.

3. Creating opportunities through risk management
For many of us, it takes a conscious effort to realize that a crisis also offers opportunities. A crisis often results in decisions that would not otherwise have been made. Everything becomes fluid under pressure. Furthermore, most crises result in a revival, the development of new technology, the building of something new or other breakthroughs.

This means you can not only use the risk management process to identify risks, but also to spot opportunities. Several project management methods already incorporate this approach and that helps, but it is also largely a mental process. Keep your faith when things do not go the way they should and always try to recognize the positive effects. In a way, risk management is about managing uncertainties. Instead of only asking yourself what might go wrong, also consider what opportunities there are to achieve more. Flip your thinking and do some opportunity management instead!

4. Presenting yourself as the requesting party at the start of a project
The final form of flip-thinking may not always be comfortable, yet it can lead to a major change in your behavior and it has a ton of factor 10 potential. I am talking about your attitude during the first moment of a project, the project preparation phase.

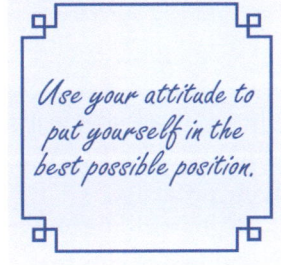

Use your attitude to put yourself in the best possible position.

When you receive a new project assignment, you will probably be thrilled. Gratitude and a critical attitude do not appear to mix. However, as we have seen before, the very first moment of a project is when you have the most opportunities to influence the project course. An interesting form of flip-thinking is not only acting as a project manager who has received a gift, but also as one who evaluates the new project with a professional and critical outlook.

You should therefore tell yourself that there are other options and that it is only useful to start a project if it can be completed successfully. This will put you in a more powerful position, make you ask different questions and lead the conversation in a new direction. Returning a project, as discussed in chapter 1, fits well within this form of flip-thinking. Note that you do not literally have to return the project; it is all about your attitude towards it.

Of course, you can apply this method in other situations as well, e.g. when applying for a job. Instead of thinking "I hope they want me," ask yourself if *you* even want this position. You will become more independent, it will lead to different discussions and the requesting party is more likely to view you as a worthy conversational partner.

Of course, your success will depend on your actual position. Flip-thinking requires a measure of independence and guts. You will not be able to pull it off if you come across as desperately needing the job. Market forces will still apply, whether you use flip-thinking or not. In this case, it is about the principle of *scarcity*, one of the six universal principles described by the persuasion scientist Robert Cialdini (Cialdini, 1984). When a product, in this case you as the project manager, is scarce, its perceived value increases and you can use the other party's fear of losing it. Another useful principle developed by Cialdini is that of *reciprocity*: when you do something for people, they will feel obligated to return the favor. You can combine this principle with that of "Saying 'yes' twice before saying 'no'" when safeguarding the project scope. We will come back to this in the next section when we talk about Covey's emotional bank account.

4.3 Stephen Covey's treasury

Work on your independence and your ability to create a sense of interdependence.

When we talk about the factor 10, we cannot ignore the philosophy of Stephen R. Covey. First of all, that is because his book *The Seven Habits of Highly Effective People* (Covey, 1989) changed the professional and personal lives of millions of people. Secondly, because those seven habits form the foundation for any project managers who want to become more effective at realizing their goals. During my master classes I often find that Covey's principles are not yet fully ingrained in everyone's mind. Because his seven habits are so important and so wonderful, I will discuss each of them briefly and explain how they relate to the world of project management:

1. **Be proactive.**
2. **Begin with the end in mind.**
3. **Put first things first.**
4. **Think win-win.**
5. **Seek first to understand, then to be understood.**
6. **Synergize.**
7. **Sharpen the saw.**

Although these habits impart many valuable lessons on their own, their true strength lies in their combination and correlation. The first three habits have to do with achieving *independence*. Independent people are effective because they choose their own goal, act on their own beliefs and do not allow themselves to be distracted by the actions of others. They take responsibility for their own course and they do not seek to blame external factors when they fail. The fourth, fifth and sixth habits are about acknowledging *interdependence*: the understanding that you need other people to be successful and that you can contribute to the success of others. Believing in the power of collaboration leads to better performances. However, you can only achieve interdependence by being independent yourself. Independence and interdependence are completed by the seventh habit, maintaining and continuously improving yourself and your ability to inspire others.

1. Be proactive

Covey says that we are all responsible for our own lives: "I am not a product of my circumstances. I am a product of my decisions." Reactive people like to avoid their responsibilities and place the blame of failure on others or external events. Proactive people, on the other hand, focus mainly on their own behavior and realize that this behavior depends on their own decisions, not their circumstances.

Covey makes proactive behavior applicable with his *circles of influence and concern* (figure 4.2). The circle of concern contains the things we cannot control, such as the outside world, our origin, the way we were raised and our past. There is no point in worrying about those things. We should focus entirely on the circle of influence. Proactive people focus on the things they can control.

Covey has something else of interest to say about the outer circle. You cannot influence the circle of concern, but you can influence your response to it; i.e. action instead of reaction, just like the TomTom showed us earlier. You should, therefore, devote your energy to useful initiatives and choose your actions from your circle of influence. Doing this and sticking with it is hard enough, but your circle of influence will grow if you can pull it off! That means you are doubly rewarded. The stakeholder analysis from chapter 2 also offered behavioral

Actions in the circle of influence expand it.

advice that ties into the circles of influence and concern. For example, not wasting any energy on your adversaries (circle of concern) but approaching them through an ally (circle of influence). It is a powerful tool that helps you focus your energy on the things you can influence.

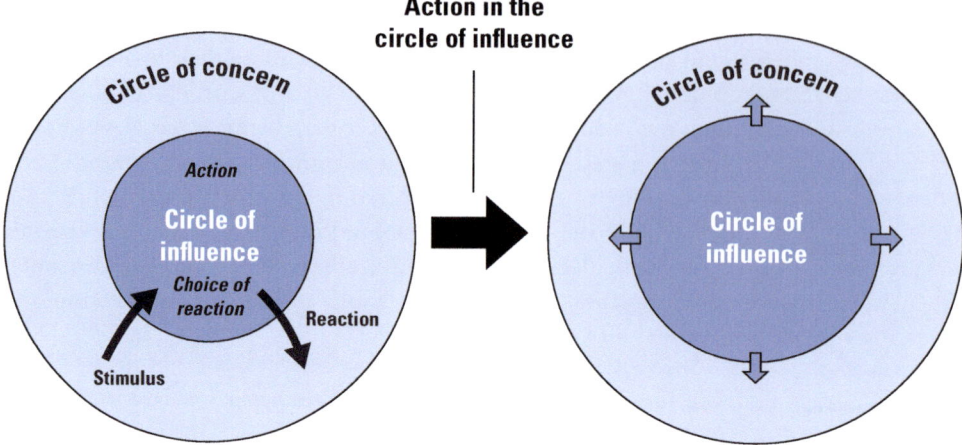

Figure 4.2   Actions in the circle of influence have effects and expand it

 Have you ever wasted energy by choosing an action in the circle of concern?
What action from the circle of influence should you have chosen instead?

The circles of influence and concern can also help you perform better in a micromanaged environment, as we discussed in the section on the &-&-&-paradox (chapter 1). You have probably heard this one before: "At work, all *they* focus on are measurements and KPIs. There is no room left for anything else!" It is true that working in a strict, controlling environment can be highly demotivating. At the same time, however, this reaction itself is a waste of energy, because you are struggling with the circle of concern. The use of the word "they" says it all: you are trying to blame others. It is a harsh truth, but by allowing yourself to be controlled, you are more passive than the person doing the controlling. It is better to take the initiative, conduct your own measurements, show your results and make choices that help you make better use of your time. Look around you and see that other people in similar situations do manage to have time left for other things. They have probably already expanded their circle of influence, which took time, expertise and creativity. No matter how simple the diagram is, dealing well with the circles of influence and concern requires a great deal of determination and perseverance.

2. Begin with the end in mind
Covey says: "You can work hard to climb the ladder, only to realize at the end of your life that the ladder was leaning against the wrong wall." Effective people know where they want to go and always strive towards reaching their goal. They are able to put their day-to-day actions in the broader context of their higher goals and maintain a strong focus.

Covey talks about the importance of having a compass in your personal life, although this habit also ties in perfectly with the business of project management. Start with the end – the *why* – and the goal will follow. Effective people work "from back to front," they start with the final goal and work backwards through time to the present, e.g. when making a plan. Later in this book we will apply this concept to the execution of a project by looking at the end of a project as a "landing strip." The trick is to make this landing strip visible *from the very first moment* of a project, so everyone can focus on the path leading to the final goal. When reporting on the project, this results in communication in terms of time-to-go, costs-to-go, hours-to-go, etc.

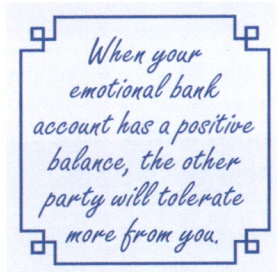

Make the landing strip visible from the very start of the project.

3. Put first things first

Whereas the first two habits were mostly about what you want to achieve and do, the final habit pertaining to the individual is about how to realize your goals. It is about setting *priorities*, which offers an interesting perspective on time management. Covey's method, which he calls *the time management matrix*, is based on Dwight D. Eisenhower's *decision matrix*. Eisenhower said: "Urgent matters are rarely important and important matters are rarely urgent."

Covey's four quadrants are based on two opposites: important versus not important and urgent versus not urgent (figure 4.3). By dividing your activities across these quadrants, you gain an insight into your priorities:

1. **Important & urgent:** tasks that require immediate attention (reactive behavior).
2. **Important & not urgent:** tasks that have to do with reaching your goals (proactive behavior).
3. **Not important & urgent:** unnecessary interruptions (distraction).
4. **Not important & not urgent:** pleasant activities that offer little tangible benefit (waste of time).

In addition to the time management aspect, the quadrants indicate what you should focus on to realize your goals: the second quadrant with its *proactive* activities. It is, therefore, important to *spend as much time as possible in the second quadrant: do important things before they become urgent.* That means taking charge and making choices, because otherwise urgent reactive activities will always come first. It is advisable to consciously schedule time for the second quadrant, for example by blocking off time in your agenda. Isn't that how you would plan a holiday? If we return to the V-model for a moment, we will see that the activities on the left side of the V mostly fall in the second quadrant. Be warned, if you do not deliberately schedule these activities, you will struggle to find the time to do them…

4. Think win-win

Acting on the basis of win-win is the first habit that concerns the state of interdependence. Interdependence is all about developing long-term relationships based on mutual *trust*. Covey has developed a wonderful metaphor to describe the amount of trust between parties: the *emotional bank account*. This bank account, which we already briefly discussed when we talked about stakeholder management in chapter 2, lets you make deposits and withdrawals, just like a real bank account. If you have a high balance, there is ample trust between you and

When your emotional bank account has a positive balance, the other party will tolerate more from you.

the other party and your communication will be easy and effective. You can even afford to make some mistakes. The reverse may also happen; if your balance is low or even negative, the relationship will be inflexible and delicate. You can invest in your relationship by making deposits into the other party's bank account, e.g. by keeping your promises, being polite and honest, showing genuine interest in the other party, expressing your expectations and acting in a professional manner. You withdraw from the account by doing the opposite, e.g. acting in a rude or dishonest manner, ignoring the other party, making mistakes or not living up to expectations.

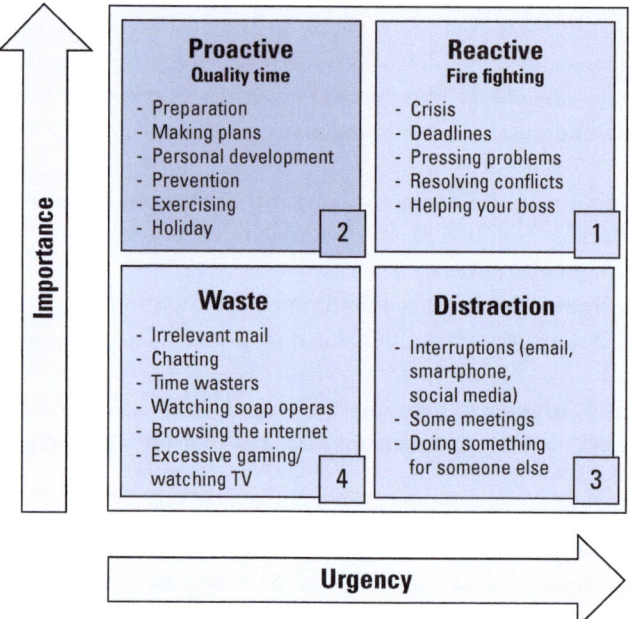

Figure 4.3   Covey's time management matrix and the distinction between important and urgent

 Do you actively work to build trust between you and your stakeholders? Try playing with the emotional bank account by deliberately making deposits and withdrawals and experience the effects of having a positive balance.

Working on win-win is important when building relationships. Many people tend to act on a win-lose mentality: if the other person loses, you win. In the long run, however, win-lose will lead to lose-lose, because you are constantly withdrawing from the other person's emotional bank account without making any deposits. To achieve effective collaboration, you must not think in terms of competition, but in terms of win-win. I should note that Covey actually calls this variant "win-win or no deal." That means you only make agreements that benefit both parties. If that is not possible, there will be no deal. This ensures you do not jeopardize your relationship for the benefit of future plans.

Thinking in terms of win-win is an attitude that calls for leadership. It means constantly looking for ways to make both parties benefit from an interaction. You must be willing to do something for the other person, learn from and influence each other. For a project manager, it requires wisdom, self-awareness, empathy, conscience, an independent will, creativity and strength. For example, do not devote all your energy to eliminating any and all risks from a contract. Instead, it might be better to invest this energy in increasing the project result for both parties. In other words, rather than focusing on dividing the cookie, you strive to make it larger.

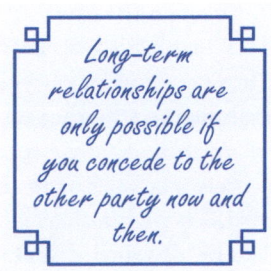

Long-term relationships are only possible if you concede to the other party now and then.

5. Seek first to understand, then to be understood

Like win-win, Covey's fifth habit is an important one for project managers who want to develop their relationships with others. Covey states that most people do not listen with the intent to understand, but with the intent to reply. We hear the other person, but we filter his or her story through our own frame of reference and mostly hear what we want to hear. That is why it is important to listen with the intent to truly understand the other person. Covey calls this *empathic listening*. It means putting yourself in the position of other people, looking at the world like they do and genuinely trying to understand their feelings. All this should be done without pushing your own personality to the side, because you need it to develop a good relationship.

For project managers, Covey's fifth habit is essential for effective communication. Understanding how the other person views the world helps you understand how to present your own story or actions. Furthermore, understanding the other person is an essential condition when managing your team through situational leadership. We will discuss this leadership style in more detail in the next section.

6. Synergize

Once you have mastered the first five habits, you are ready to move on to the sixth. This is where you start combining everything you have learned so far about individual effectiveness and collaboration. Synergy is achieved when the whole is greater than the sum of the parts. It is about respecting differences and using them to gain new insights. Instead of a decision being yours or theirs, it becomes something else – something more. Covey calls this *the third alternative*. Synergy leads to creative outcomes by utilizing the strengths of both the individuals and the group.

As a project manager, it is important to direct this process and decide what degree of synergy you wish to achieve. You will likely have different wishes at the start of the V-model than at the end. Early on, you need creative ideas and breakthroughs, which requires interaction between people with different insights. During the project execution, however, close collaboration is needed to effectively carry out the plan. This is easier when everyone wants the same things.

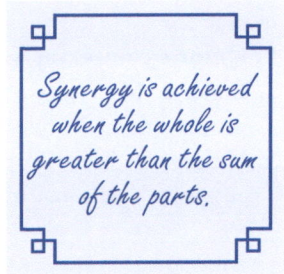

Synergy is achieved when the whole is greater than the sum of the parts.

7. Sharpen the saw

The final habit is about maintaining and improving your most valuable asset: you. Finding the time to work on yourself is often difficult when you live a busy life. Covey uses the example of a lumberjack with a dull saw. He neglects to sharpen his saw because he has so much sawing left to do. The message is clear: occasionally taking the time to sharpen ourselves enables us to then carry on far more effectively. Covey describes four dimensions in which we can sharpen ourselves:

1. **The physical dimension:** nutrition, exercise, rest and relaxation (note the ties to the second quadrant in figure 4.3).
2. **The spiritual dimension:** strive towards clear values, spiritual development and self-image (important for the second habit).
3. **The mental dimension:** the ability to read, analyze, write and plan.
4. **The social-emotional dimension:** empathic ability, helpfulness and achieving synergy (important for the fourth, fifth and sixth habit).

4.4   Situational leadership

Situational leadership together with the critical parameter offers control without micromanagement.

Motivating people is one of the most important qualities of a project manager. Your success largely depends on how good you are at this. Covey already demonstrated that effective leadership requires insight into who you are, the ability to understand how your employees and stakeholders think and knowing how to use this knowledge correctly. Managing your project employees correctly is called *situational leadership*. Like Covey's seven habits, this topic has also been covered by countless management books and publications. Nevertheless, I believe it is important to cover the meaning and application of situational leadership separately. If you miss the essence of this topic, it will be difficult to integrate its principles into your own leadership style. That would be a problem, because together with focusing on the critical parameter, situational leadership forms the ideal framework with which to closely monitor the details of your project without resorting to micromanagement.

I will explain the principles of situational leadership in three steps; for didactic reasons, but mostly because each step offers a great take away moment that you can use to your advantage in practice:

1. **Quinn's competing values framework:** being able to adopt various roles.
2. **Blake & Mouton's Managerial Grid model:** distinguishing between task-oriented and people-oriented leadership.
3. **Hersey & Blanchard's situational leadership:** basing your leadership style on the employee's task maturity.

Step 1: Quinn: being able to adopt various roles

It is like a handyman's toolkit in that you choose your tool depending on the job at hand, not the other way around. The same goes for leadership. It is important to master different leadership styles and apply each of them at the right time. That will make you more effective as a leader and keeps your behavior from becoming predictable and boring.

When I talk about this topic, I am sometimes asked: "Wasn't I told to stay close to myself?" That is indeed an important point to raise. Adopting different leadership styles does not mean that you have to fake it. Leading others still begins with knowing who you are and this will naturally affect your leadership style. The challenge lies in learning to adopt different roles within your personal style and consciously choosing which role to play in a given situation. It is fine to have personal preferences, that is what makes you who you are.

If you want to learn more about using the different leadership roles, it is a good idea to explore Robert Quinn's competing values framework (Quinn, 1994, 2015). In this framework, Quinn distinguishes between four classic complementary management models. No one model is better than any of the others; some are simply more effective in certain situations. Quinn challenges us to master as many roles as possible. He put the models and roles into a single figure and compared them using two dimensions:
1. The dimension with the extremes of *flexibility* and *control.*
2. The dimension with the extremes of an *internal* focus and an *external* focus.

Figure 4.4 shows that this results in eight roles. If side-by-side, they are somewhat similar. If opposite each other, they have contradictory properties (competing values).

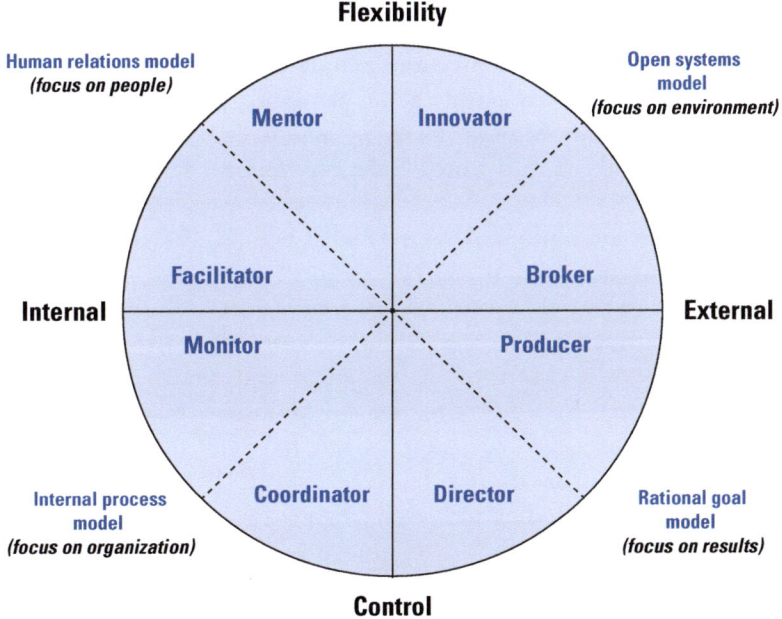

Figure 4.4   Quinn's competing values framework

Try to imagine how you can change roles – even within one series of activities – in order to become more effective, e.g. when presenting a proposal to the project board:

1. Director: you formulate the goal and develop a vision to reach the right decision.
2. Coordinator: you schedule the meeting and make sure the right people can attend.
3. Broker: prior to the meeting, you visit several attendees in person for a preliminary discussion of some important matters and to get a sense of their position.
4. Producer: you work hard on a properly substantiated and convincing presentation.
5. Innovator: you make sure there is a pleasant atmosphere during the presentation and you deal with questions and remarks in a flexible manner.
6. Facilitator: after your presentation, you put the ball in the group's court to get people to actively consider the issues and avoid giving them the feeling they are being pressured into making a certain choice.
7. Coordinator: once the decision has been made, you summarize everything succinctly and communicate the agreements and actions.
8. Monitor: afterwards, you check up on the status of all action points.

Consciously mix up your game.

Even within one series of activities, switching between different leadership styles will make you more effective. If you were, for example, to act solely as a producer, you will end up with a wonderful presentation but miss out on the benefits of prior informal coordination on certain matters. Furthermore, you might start to believe that "I am right, so I will be right." If you then encounter any opposition during the meeting, you might focus too much on convincing others. Like a good tennis player, make sure to mix up your game frequently…

Step 2: Blake & Mouton: task-oriented and people-oriented leadership

Whereas Quinn's framework was mostly about the synergy between different leadership roles, Robert Blake and Jane Mouton focus on how to lead employees and distinguish between task-oriented and people-oriented leadership (figure 4.5).

People-oriented leaders focus primarily on relational aspects. They explain *why* things are necessary, they appear interested and they take personal wishes into account. Task-oriented leaders focus on the substantive aspects of the work, on *how* tasks should be executed and on the quality of the results. Blake and Mouton summarize this with their Managerial Grid model (Blake & Mouton, 1964). Although several names for the corresponding leadership styles have been coined over the years, I find these to be the most appropriate: the *commander*, the *country club chairman*, the *easy rider* and the *team leader*. The latter focuses on involvement and motivation (people-oriented), but can also offer substantive (task-oriented) direction. According to Blake and Mouton, this is the most effective style. However, as with Quinn's framework, it is primarily about *consciously switching* between people- and task-oriented leadership.

Consider your own leadership style. Do you consciously distinguish between task- and people-oriented leadership?

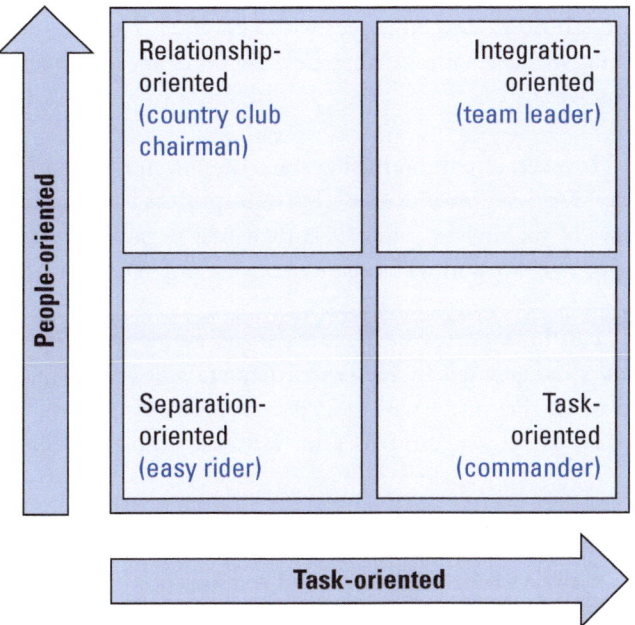

Figure 4.5   Blake and Mouton's Managerial Grid model

Step 3: Hersey and Blanchard: an employee's task maturity determines which leadership style to use

Understanding the various leadership styles is only part of what it takes to bring out the best in your people. When should you use which leadership style? Paul Hersey and Ken Blanchard answered this question with their theory of *situational leadership* (Hersey and Blanchard, 1977) by expanding upon the Managerial Grid model with the employee's maturity level. They later continued independently from their own company and gave the theory a new impulse with different names[5]. In this book, we opt for completeness and therefore show the names of both whenever that adds something. This is possible because the principles have remained the same.

In order to use the most appropriate leadership style, you must first assess your employees' maturity level, which consists of two aspects:

1. Ability: *competence*, tied to knowledge, skills and experience.

2. Willingness: *commitment*, tied to involvement, self-confidence, daring and motivation.

---

5   Hersey renamed maturity (M1-M4) to readiness (R1-R4) in his Situational Leadership Model. Blanchard coined the term development levels (D1-D4) in his Situational Leadership II model. Blanchard also introduced the words competence and commitment, where originally ability and willingness were chosen.

In their maturity (development level): employees will go through a process of growth. Hersey and Blanchard identify four stages during this process, which ultimately results in a higher degree of task maturity (development level):

D1 Enthusiastic beginner: a new employee with new tasks. These employees are motivated to take on everything in their path, yet they lack the necessary ability and tend to under- or overestimate themselves.

D2 Disillusioned learner: after a promising start, doubts and frustration begin to arise. In Blanchard's words: "*The honeymoon is over.*" These employees have acquired some ability, yet they are still unsure of themselves. They have their first negative experiences, they take on too much at once or they are annoyed because they are not yet given free rein.

D3 Capable but cautious performer: at this stage, employees have sufficient ability to carry out their tasks independently. However, they are still on thin ice. Their confidence is contextual and when they meet with unexpected problems, these employees may begin to hesitate or doubt. They need support and feedback from their manager to keep from reverting to D2.

D4 High achiever: these employees are able and willing to carry out their tasks on their own. They do what it takes to realize the desired results.

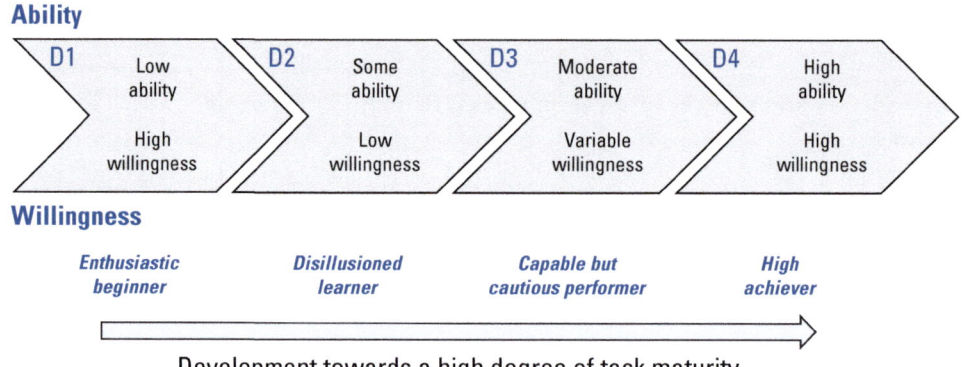

Figure 4.6   Development levels according to Hersey and Blanchard

As you can imagine, employees need more or less (task-oriented) directive behavior depending on their ability and more or less (people-oriented) supportive behavior depending on their willingness. Figure 4.7 once again represents the various maturity levels in four quadrants. The axes of ability and willingness have been reversed, so they begin with high and end with low. That makes it possible to add the axes of directive and supportive behavior along with the four situational leadership styles: directing, coaching, supporting and delegating (Blanchard) or telling, selling, participating, delegating (Hersey).

S1 Directing (telling): behavior that is mostly directive, rather than supportive. The project manager prescribes the *how* and gives the employee clear instructions to follow. He or she also inspects the execution and the delivered results. Supportive behavior should be applied sparingly, since this can be interpreted as weakness or the rewarding of inadequate performance. The responsibility for the final results is in the hands of the project manager. Note that if project managers cannot offer substantive direction themselves, they will assign this task to others.

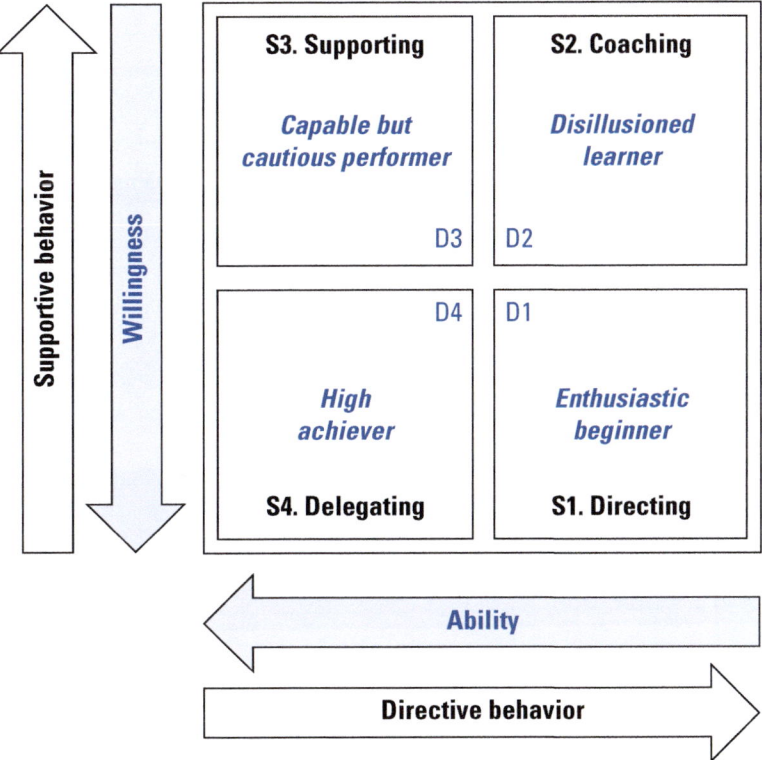

Figure 4.7   Maturity levels and associated leadership styles

S2 Coaching (selling): the project manager explains more about the *what* and the *why* in order to involve the employee in the activities. The task execution (the *how*) is still prescribed and the execution is inspected. However, the focus of the communication shifts to actively asking questions, explaining, stimulating and motivating.

S3 Supporting (participating): employees now have sufficient ability to translate *what* into *how* on their own. The project manager adopts a more hands-off approach, mainly acts as a sounding board and supports the employee when the latter needs help. S3 leadership is mostly about actively giving the employee attention and support.

S4 Delegating: with this leadership style, the employee is fully responsible for the final results. The project manager delegates the necessary authorities to the employee, who is free to choose how to carry out the tasks and safeguard the progress. The project manager mainly creates conditions, instead of acting in a directive or supportive manner.

With situational leadership, the project manager's success is not determined by his or her own preferred style, but by the ability to evaluate the employees' qualities and act accordingly. This brings us right back to Covey's concept of interdependence and "seek first to understand, then to be understood." Also remember that evaluating someone's maturity level is a dynamic process. It depends on the task at hand, yet the same task can result in different maturity levels for an employee depending on the situation (degree of complexity, insecurity, support from the environment etc.). The employee may, therefore, require a different style of situational leadership when performing the same task in a different context.

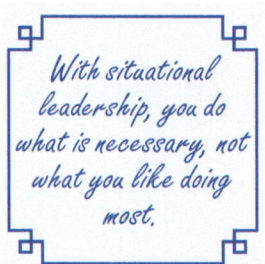

With situational leadership, you do what is necessary, not what you like doing most.

When using situational leadership, project managers have to rely to a large extent on their gut feeling and their ability to direct and let go at the right times. You cannot do the latter until your self-leadership is in order, as outlined in Covey's first three habits. Once you pull it off, though, situational leadership is an undisputed factor 10 skill. Managers who have mastered it are more effective and efficient, their employees are more motivated and they manage to bring out all the creativity their team has to offer.

Place the individual members of your team in the correct quadrant, based on their maturity level (D1 through D4). Ask yourself if you use the right situational leadership style (S1 through S4) for everyone.

Coaching leadership

You will probably know by now that mastering the application of situational leadership is an important part of "monitoring things closely without micromanaging." When used correctly, you do exactly what is necessary in the most effective way. This lets you monitor things quite closely, without appearing annoying or condescending to the employee. After all, focusing on details is done differently in each quadrant, e.g. through intensive soundboarding in S3 and by offering careful instructions in S1.

Figure 4.8 summarizes the entire situational leadership model and offers a preview of its application during the project execution. The figure also contains the term *coaching leadership*, which means you use the right kind of situational leadership to help the employee develop and grow. Some refer to the S2 and S3 quadrants as the coaching quadrants, although I personally believe that you can use coaching leadership in all quadrants. With coaching leadership, you empower your employees, use the right type of situational leadership, and develop their qualities to allow them to grow in their task maturity.

People sometimes say that it is difficult to delegate. That is understandable, because it requires both S4 leadership from the supervisor *and* D4 task maturity from the employee.

In my experience, however, the *transition from S2 to S3* may be even trickier for a supervisor. It means moving from "deciding how the employee carries out the tasks" to "surrendering to the employee's preferences while still maintaining control over the results." In practice, you will frequently move back and forth between S2 and S3 with the employee and learn for yourself that it forms a grey area between two fundamentally different leadership styles.

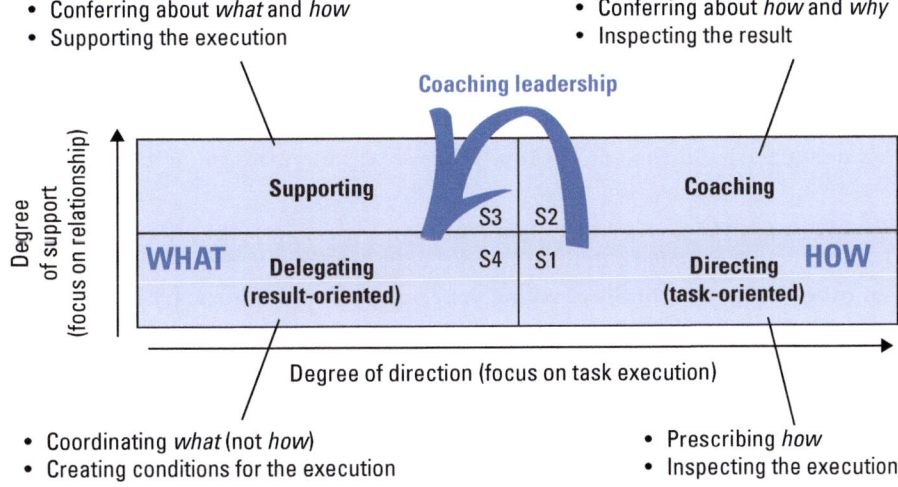

Figure 4.8   Situational and coaching leadership

I would like to conclude this chapter with some examples of the *incorrect* use of situational leadership:

- *Using directive behavior (S1) on high achievers (D4)*: the professional will see you as a micromanager and become demotivated. When we discuss the project motivator in chapter 7, we will see that the employee may even adapt to the (wrong) leadership style and revert to D2.
- *Overestimating D1 employees and treating them as high achievers (S4):* the employee will exhibit indecisive behavior or head down the wrong path. Furthermore, the chances are that you will discover your mistake too late because you (wrongly) assumed that "no news is good news."
- *Employees who view themselves as high achievers, even though they are not:* if only support is needed (meaning the employee is actually D3), the damage will not be too bad – although not everyone with a faulty self-image will be open to support or guidance. Should directive measures also be required, this can create problems if the task at hand requires a large degree of autonomy from the employee.

4.5   The project manager's factor 10

As we have seen, a project manager has many ways of becoming more effective; acting smart, flip-thinking, finding correlations, applying the right kind of situational leadership, being alert and the seven habits described by Stephen Covey all give you a veritable arsenal

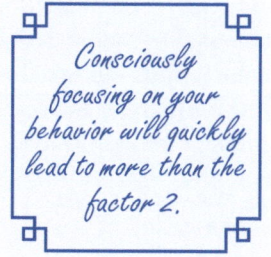

Consciously focusing on your behavior will quickly lead to more than the factor 2.

of means with which you can achieve more than with hard work, the factor 2, alone. If the aforementioned tips are hard to implement, remember that *consciously* applying them is more important than doing so *perfectly*. By consistently acting in a deliberate manner and thinking about the effectiveness of your actions, your common sense will create many factor 10 moments for you. Examples include deliberately choosing your seat during a meeting or taking a few minutes before a negotiation to consider what you want to get out of it and what you can concede to the opposing party. When you act consciously, you are well on your way towards achieving the factor 10. Your progress will stimulate you to keep at it.

Working on organizing or on the organization

The factor 10 can not only be applied to your own behavior, but also to the solutions you choose. Instead of automatically devoting your energy to procedures, try investing more in logic and human behavior.

Dare to invest in behavior instead of regulations.

Back in chapter 1, we concluded that additional regulations are often introduced in an organization in order to implement changes. There is another way, though, as you can see in figure 4.9. There are three types of rules: *written rules*, *logical rules* and *implicit rules*. New regulations fall into the category of written rules. Logical rules are not written down, but are derived from the structure of the organization or the system. Lastly, implicit rules are anchored in the behavior of employees and the organizational culture.

You might compare it to the rules and the game of football. The number of players, the size of the pitch, what offside is and how to decide who wins are examples of written rules. However, a team's playing together is a strategy that follows from the logic that you can utilize the strength of all team members by passing the ball around. A good team will do so automatically; it does not have to be officially recorded as a written rule. The same goes for the individual players' behavior during a game. Instead of prescribing this, you rely on the players' creativity and insight.

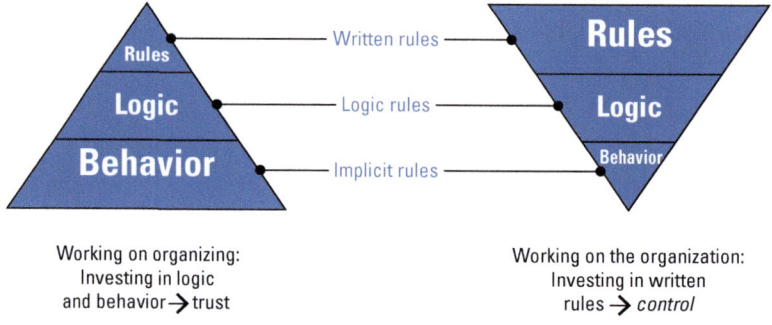

Figure 4.9   Implicit rules and written rules

Try applying this mechanism to your project. Do you want to invest in trust (behavioral culture, on the left in figure 4.9) or control (procedures, on the right side of the figure)? Instead of investing in more rules, try devoting your energy to changing the team's behavior or focus on logic. We all know the following example: a meeting that starts at 9:00 AM will often take all morning, while starting at 11:00 AM ensures everyone wants to be optimally effective so the meeting can conclude before lunchtime. You can also use this principle when you need input from people in your organization. Instead of devising rules by communicating deadlines and sending constant reminders, try setting up a short meeting during which everyone gets five minutes to present their input and a brief personal summary. Just watch, you will not have to push anyone to meet the deadline. Faced with the prospect of having to present their ideas to an audience, people will make sure their affairs are in order. That is how easy the factor 10 can be.

The factor 10 can be used by anyone, regardless of personal style!

Summary

- Working hard is factor 2, smart leadership and behavior form the factor 10.
- Leadership is about doing the right things; management is about doing things right. You need both!
- Use flip-thinking to take control by exhibiting seemingly counterproductive behavior. Do not fight reality, but create something new instead. This is another example of acting instead of reacting.
- Use Covey's seven habits of effective leadership, particularly:
  - The circles of influence and concern;
  - Covey's time management matrix (importance ⇔ urgent);
  - The emotional bank account.
- Covey's second habit is "begin with the end in mind." Make sure the landing strip is clearly visible from the very first moment of a project. This ensures everyone focuses on the path that leads to the goal. When reporting on the project, this results in communication in terms of time-to-go, costs-to-go, etc.
- You need situational leadership to achieve the factor 10:
  - There is no "best" leadership style. Effective leadership is situational. Do not be afraid to mix things up!
  - Distinguish between task- and people-oriented leadership;
  - Tailor your style to the employee's task maturity:
    - S1 Directing (task-oriented);
    - S2 Coaching;
    - S3 Supporting;
    - S4 Delegating (results-oriented).
- Anyone can use the factor 10. Applying it consciously is more important than doing so perfectly.

5 The plan part I: project breakdown

- ▼ How the 10% confrontation rule helps to prevent submarine behavior.
- ▼ Create your first influencing moment with the project charter.
- ▼ Why you should make a clear distinction between "understanding the project size" and "directing the execution."
- ▼ Easily create a complete overview of testable and delegable interim results with the product breakdown structure.
- ▼ How you can use the V-model and DfX to improve your project's foundation and make it proactive.

Do you have a go-to approach for developing a reliable plan that is supported by both the team and the client, or is the planning process something intuitive that you handle differently every time? During my initial years as a project leader, I sometimes spent a long time staring at the empty template for the project management plan. Where should I start? I quickly found my way once I began, but I occasionally forgot to coordinate with the stakeholders in the meantime. *I need to do that differently next time*, I thought while I patched things up. It usually worked out in the end, but I wanted a more structured approach for the planning process – one that would involve the team and help me to consistently inform and influence the stakeholders.[6]

I did not have a plan for making plans.

5.1 The ten steps of making a plan

Perhaps you also struggle with developing a project management plan. Rest assured that you are not alone. Many organizations – not just those new to project-based working – are unsure about the best way to develop a plan and project schedule. There is often no widely supported method that (novice) project managers can rely on. When making a plan, project managers generally have to figure things out on their own. This results in varying levels of quality, limited feedback and an amalgam of styles and approaches being used within the organization. There may be a template, but there are no guidelines regarding its use. We're not even talking about the fact that a planning process involves much more than just the writing of the project management plan. That document is an end result that was preceded by many steps of gathering information, conducting analyses, making decisions and drawing up proposals. Can project management methods, such as PRINCE2 and *PMBOK Guide* or IPMA's ICB competence framework, be of any help? To some extent, they can, although

---

6 This chapter ties into the following competences from IPMA's ICB4: Strategy, Results orientation, Project design, Requirements and objectives, Scope, Quality, Resources, Procurement, Select and balance.

these methods mostly describe *what* a plan needs to contain. They are less concerned with *how* to make the said plan and tend to leave that for the project managers and their organization to figure out.

Insufficient direction or guidance during the planning process creates the following risks:
- The project manager forgets steps or gets stuck during the process.
- The project management plan lacks structure or support from the work floor, making it hard to maintain or risking it will not be used at all.
- Because there is no clear approach, it is hard for the project manager to involve team members in the plan's development process.
- You need interim results in order to coordinate with stakeholders during the planning process. If there is no structured approach, these interim results or their substantiation are often missing.
- It becomes more difficult to exchange knowledge. Just as importantly, the interfaces and links between the (sub) plans become less explicit, which affects the synchronization of the subprojects during the execution phase of the project.

In this and the following chapter, I will explain how to develop a project management plan and how to optimally involve your team and stakeholders in this process. First, however, I want to introduce the 10% confrontation rule, which is an important tool for all activities during the definition phase.

The 10% confrontation rule
I had better come clean right away. Although I call it the 10% confrontation rule, I might as well call it the 8%, 15% or 20% confrontation rule. It has no scientific foundation; it is a tool that I use to avoid *submarine behavior*. You exhibit submarine behavior when you "dive under" at the start of an activity, work hard and only "surface" at the end when you are done. In other words, submarine behavior means there is no visibility or coordination with stakeholders during the activity. Focus, perfectionism and perseverance are good things, but they should be used in moderation.

 Do you ever exhibit submarine behavior?

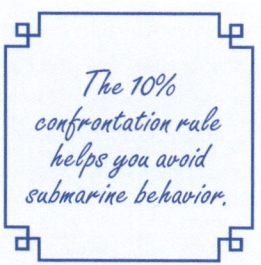

The 10% confrontation rule helps you avoid submarine behavior.

The 10% confrontation rule helps me avoid submarine behavior by making a commitment at the start of the activity to "surface" after about 10% of the lead time and present an interim result to the stakeholders. Figure 5.1 shows three activities along with examples for the 10% confrontation moment. It is important to understand that this moment is not voluntary; *instead of waiting to see if you have something to report, you make an agreement beforehand that you will report something*. That is exciting, because you will frequently not even know what you might present at the outset. Don't worry, you will in time. Making this commitment forces you to get on top of things quickly and identify the most important (proactive) aspects. This will usually take you less than an hour. You will be amazed at what you can achieve in such a short period of time by making a commitment and engaging with your environment. Talk about factor 10 behavior!

In addition to benefitting your communication with stakeholders, the 10% confrontation moment also helps you make choices on time. For example, it keeps you from spending too long preparing for something or working on the wrong things. No matter how important a good preparation is, it should never lead to tunnel vision. The final goal always comes first, so use the 10% confrontation rule to your advantage!

You have probably noticed that the 10% confrontation rule is a practical implementation of the "small V" covered in section 3.5. By forcing yourself to announce the first feedback moment when you set the activity's end date, you create a foundation for early coordination. That is both exciting and demanding, but it also gives you an automatic incentive that keeps you from hiding. *With the 10% confrontation rule, you basically force yourself to make the step from reactive to proactive to influencing.*

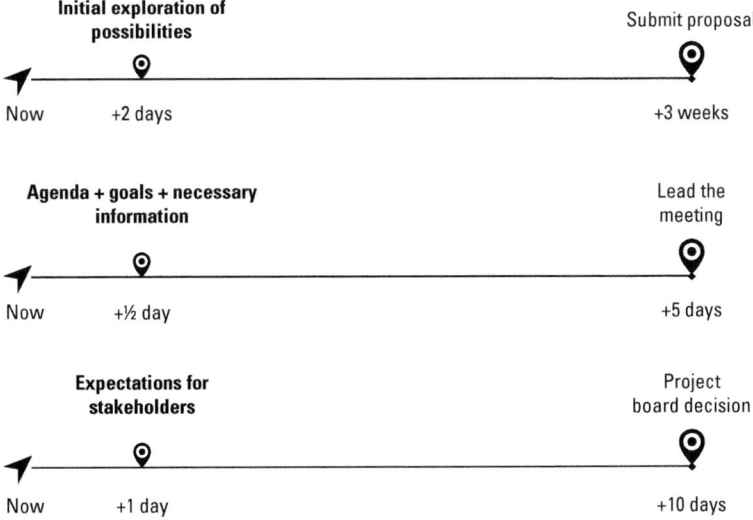

Figure 5.1   The 10% confrontation moment with interim results for three activities

The plan to develop a plan

When developing a project management plan, you can follow the ten steps outlined in figure 5.2. These will enable you to gather essential project information and create the right structure for a reliable path to the final goal. Furthermore, each step lets you involve (part of) the team in its execution. The steps work with both a traditional phased approach and in Agile development, as well as with a combination of both when your project consists of subprojects with waterfall and Agile/Scrum processes.

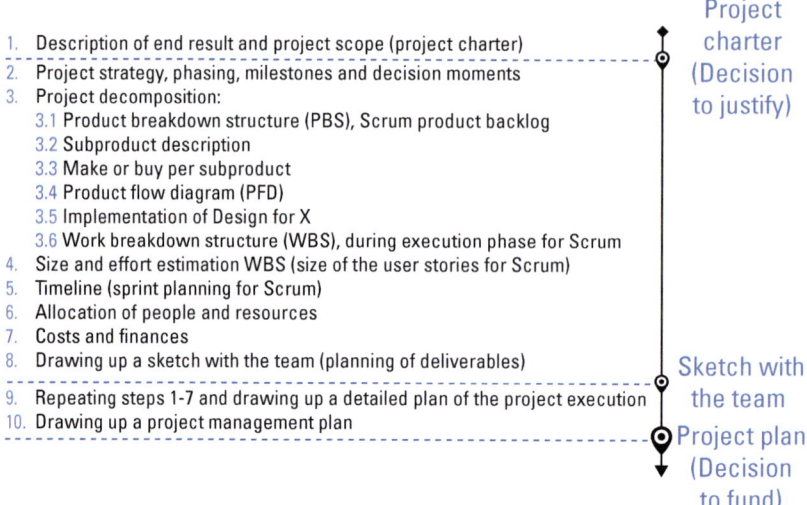

Figure 5.2   The ten steps of the planning process

The steps even incorporate the 10% confrontation rule *twice*; in step 1 and step 8. The time it takes to develop a finished project management plan is simply too long to go without close contact with the stakeholders. Submarine behavior is a real risk, which may cause your client to become uneasy and wonder about what you are doing. Clients may even lose their faith in you, especially if they have a go-getter mentality. Of course, you want to achieve the exact opposite and proactively influence the client instead. That leads to two important early feedback moments:

1. **Project charter**: a single page outlining the project's scope and goal and the key results to be delivered. Additionally, it lists the stakeholders, team members, project risks and the method of communication. *The project charter is the perfect opportunity to interact with your environment at an early stage.*
2. **Sketch with the team:** a general plan that contains sufficient detail to substantiate the project's timing and costs, the subresults (deliverables) to be delivered and the use of people and assets. It helps to *understand the size of the project* and differs from the detailed plan that will be drawn up later because it does not yet contain guidelines for the execution of the activities. The sketch with the team is a deliverable-based plan, not a plan of activities.

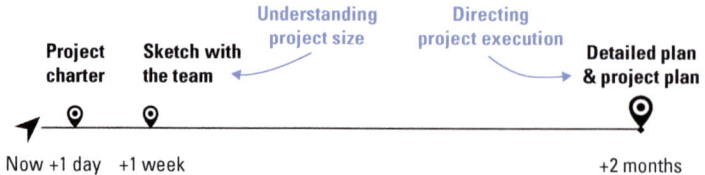

Figure 5.3   The planning process includes two 10% confrontation moments

As with a painter's charcoal sketch, you use the sketch with the team to determine the project's outline. This helps you manage your stakeholders' expectations early on. You go through quite a few steps in a relatively short amount of time. These steps are repeated when you draw up the *detailed plan* and refined with the help of additional information, feasibility studies and the completed (often substantive/technical) deliverables from the initiation phase. Furthermore, detail at the activity level is added to make the plan usable as *a guideline for the execution phase*. By only recording this information once the execution actually begins, you avoid unnecessary change management. The detailed plan is often created with the help of a planning tool such as Microsoft Project. For a project with a lead time of eighteen months, the process of developing a sketch takes roughly a week, while the rest of the definition phase takes two months or so. For a two-month project, a project plan (with a quotation) is often expected within a week, which means the sketch with the team has to be drawn up in about half a day.

5.2   Step 1: Project charter

The steps of the planning process cover the entire preparation and initiation phase. The key result of the project preparation phase is the *project charter*. It is perhaps a bit confusing that the project model we discussed in chapter 1 talked about the *project assignment*. I believe the term project charter, which is also used in the *PMBOK Guide*, is more accurate. Other methods, e.g. Six Sigma, also use this term, while PRINCE2 talks about a *project brief*.

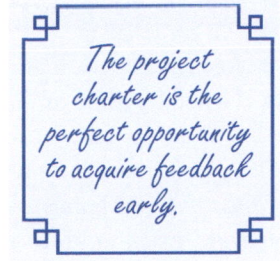

The project charter is the perfect opportunity to acquire feedback early.

The other deliverables from the preparation phase are the *business case* and the *project initiation plan*. Although the business case is important, it is really the client's responsibility. As a project manager, you will carefully examine the business case and help improve it by asking pertinent questions and suggesting possible modifications. You can view the project charter as your answer to the business case. The project initiation plan is your plan for the project initiation phase. It will contain, among other things, the ten steps of the planning process. This plan is important because it is used to coordinate expectations regarding the duration and costs of the initiation phase, as well to acquire the necessary assets to carry out the project initiation. It is important to stay pragmatic, though: the project initiation plan should not comprise more than one or two pages.

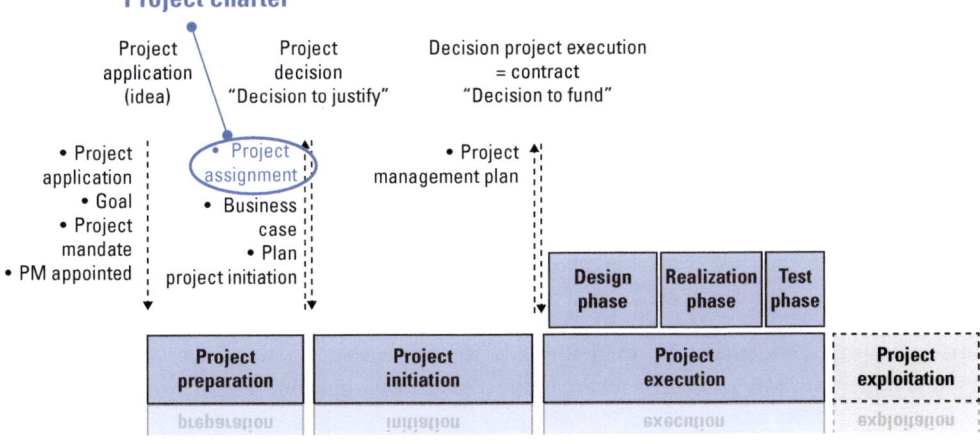

Figure 5.4   The project charter is the key result of the preparation phase

Contents of the project charter

The project charter contains the information and agreements needed in order to start the project. Think of, for example, the following elements:

- Background (context and motivation);
- Project definition:
  - Goal of the project;
  - Key project results;
  - Scope and delineation (what falls outside the project scope);
  - Interfaces;
  - Restrictions.
- Business justification (business case);
- General outline of client requirements;
- General outline of the project organization;
- Project strategy;
- Key risks;
- General outline of the project plan.

Of course, there are myriad ways to write down this information. Personally, I prefer *a format that can fit onto a single A4 page*, as seen in figure 5.5. Why? Firstly, because this gives you no reason at all to put off writing the project charter "because it is so much work." Secondly, limiting yourself to one page forces you to distil things to their essence. Finally, a folded A4 page will fit into your pocket, so you can always carry the project charter with you and further refine it during conversations with others. However, if you can achieve the same results with a different template, that is fine too. You can find many examples online.

The project charter gives you a head start.

Deliver the first version as early as possible

The project charter is one of the three deliverables that I believe should always be drawn up by the project manager. The other two are the *product breakdown structure* and the *heartbeat*, which we will cover later. A project charter is developed primarily for your own benefit; it creates a formal interim result that offers a wealth of valuable insight at an early stage. You can then use this insight during your (influencing) conversations with stakeholders. It is advisable to also conduct the *stakeholder analysis* during this phase (see section 2.3), because this tells you how to communicate with the various stakeholders involved in your project.

Do you want to surprise your client? Take the initiative and draw up a project charter soon after your initial meeting. You will likely be complimented on your professional approach.

Don't be fooled by the project charter's simple structure; it is not easy to translate your initial impressions into the essence of the project. The project charter has all the characteristics of a 10% confrontation moment: feeling like you are missing key information, recognizing shortcomings and wanting to fix them, which may lead to procrastination and a lack of communication. I therefore advise project managers to spend no more than two hours on the initial draft of their project charter, provided that they fill it out *in its entirety* (instead of getting stuck trying to perfect the project description). This means they can only use the information from the initial meeting, along with their own experience and some questions they may pose to other knowledge carriers. However, that is more than enough to get started and begin the follow-up meetings, using it as a head start. This follow-up process will be more effective than if you had not drawn up the project charter. The absence of such a charter would most likely still result in a period of plenty of thinking and analysis, but also one with a distinct lack of action because of submarine behavior…

Project name:	Project manager: Client:	
Project description (context and cause)	Project goal and financial impact (business case)	
Project scope (and delineation)	Stakeholders	
Project results (key deliverables, KPIs)	Key activities, timing	
Team members	Main risks	
Review and communication plan	Approval Name: Position: Signature: Date:	
	....	

Figure 5.5   The project charter

5.3   Step 2: Project strategy and phasing

Once the project charter has been drawn up, it is time to begin the project in earnest. However, first you should try to explicitly pass the "decision to justify" decision point with the project board or the client – even if they do not understand the need to do so. Try to come up with an approach that suits the organizational culture: schedule an official meeting, visit the stakeholders and get them to sign off, or send an email to your client and outline the agreements that were made.

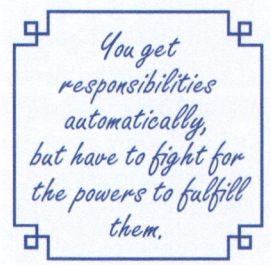

You get responsibilities automatically, but have to fight for the powers to fulfill them.

Why is this so important? Because this is the perfect moment to make your mandate explicit. You get nothing for nothing. As a project manager, responsibilities are given to you automatically, but you will have to fight for the power to fulfill them. Remember our discussion of flip-thinking in section 4.2: adopt a critical attitude at the start of the project and view the "decision to justify" moment as a transfer of the project from the client's hands into yours. Until that moment, it is still possible to negotiate; afterwards, *you* are officially responsible for the project realization.

Strategic approach
What is the best way to realize the project goals? Consider questions like:
■ What phasing structure and key interim results should you choose?
■ When should you use the Agile approach and when the traditional waterfall method?
■ How can you get to know the end user?
■ How should you deal with the stakeholders?
■ What will you undertake yourself, what will you outsource to partners?
■ How should you manage the risks?
■ Where can you expect changes to be made down the line?
■ How can you evaluate the specifications as soon as possible?
■ How can you motivate your team?

Developing your strategy requires insight, which you acquired during the preparation phase. You translate the strategy into a project phasing structure with themes for each phase. To begin with you can use the project model or the standard phasing structure that your organization uses. With the help of your strategy you can refine this phasing structure, e.g. by adding an additional phase because you want to evaluate an interim result with the end user. You can also decide what parts of the project to execute using the Agile approach and when to use the waterfall method instead. Above all, remember to keep it simple: *the project strategy should be clear, logical and translatable into a project phasing structure.*

Phasing and milestones
The project model already includes the basic phases. Phasing means dividing a project into distinct parts, each with its own predefined result. You can use phasing to achieve the following:
■ Structure a project;
■ Manage a project (dividing it into smaller chunks);
■ Deal with uncertainties (e.g. definition phase versus execution phase);
■ Stimulate decision-making.

People tend to overlook the power of stimulating decision-making. Particularly during the initiation phase, it can be valuable to split this phase and force decisions to be made on time, e.g. making the stakeholders choose between concepts, or to conduct a feasibility study, or a supplier selection process. The extra phase keeps such important decisions from taking up the entire initiation phase and complicating the planning process (figure 5.6).

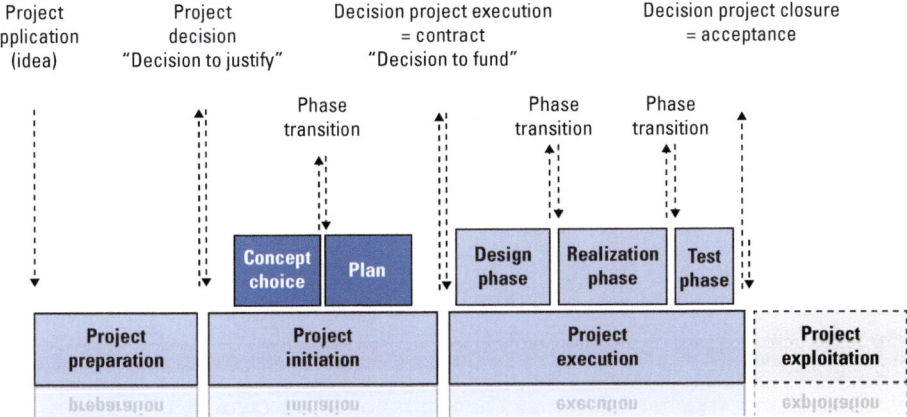

Figure 5.6   Dividing the project initiation phase into two phases to stimulate decision-making

At every *phase transition*, a phase evaluation is conducted. During such an evaluation, you should determine whether all interim results (deliverables) of the phase have been completed correctly. Such a moment is also known as a *milestone*. At a milestone, you also evaluate the status of management aspects, e.g. time, money, resources, quality and the critical parameters, in relation to the plan. Theoretically speaking, a milestone does not have to be a phase transition, although it is advisable to use this structure. A phase transition during which an important decision has to be made is called a *decision point*.

5.4   Steps 3.1 and 3.2: Product breakdown structure

How can you be sure that your plan includes everything you need to reach your final goal? With your plan you determine the project's lead time, the necessary budget and the desired resources. However, what don't you know yet? Whenever you make a plan it is important to have some insight into its completeness. Otherwise you cannot rely on it, since it only covers part of the project. Trying to identify "everything" will soon result in a near-endless list of items. To avoid getting lost, it is advisable to divide and structure the project: the *project decomposition*. This leads to both overview and detail.

Not a shopping list
You probably recognize this situation. You and your team are having a meeting to develop a plan for a new project. After some discussion you begin to feel uneasy. You do not want discussion, you want conclusions. Who will have the responsibility to draw up a final conclusion and make a commitment towards the client after the meeting? That's right: you! So, you get up, walk over to the whiteboard and speak the immortal words: "What do we have to do?"

A "things to do" shopping list lacks structure and coherence.

It is good that you have taken action. You also get what you ask for: within no time, the whiteboard is filled with actions. You managed to turn the meeting around and ended up with myriad ideas. The formerly passive group is calling out "things to do," while you struggle to keep up and write everything down fast enough. However, there is a downside to this approach. The list of actions on the whiteboard lacks coherence. That will come back to haunt you later, because all you are doing is writing a "shopping list."

Of course, there is nothing wrong with a shopping list – when you are going shopping. It is also quite useful as a *final overview* to manage the project execution at the activity level. However, it does not tell you anything about the connections between individual activities or the relationship between the activities and the final result you want to realize. You, therefore, cannot be sure that your list is complete. Furthermore, in the event of any changes, you will have to re-evaluate every single activity. Instead, it is advisable to start with an inventory of the required interim results and their correlations: the *product breakdown structure*.

The product breakdown structure
If, at the start of a project, you are not quite sure which interim results you have to deliver, drawing up a product breakdown structure (PBS) is an excellent way to gain more insight into the project. You create the PBS by dividing the desired end result into subproducts (sub-deliverables, interim results) step by step and repeating and refining this process until you have identified all required subproducts. This is known as product- or result-based planning. It ensures that all of the necessary interim results needed to realize the project goal are identified and described.

In addition to giving you a complete overview of the project, product-based planning with the PBS also offers the following advantages:
- It makes the project result-oriented;
- It offers a clear and visual overview of the project scope;
- It is a method that ties in well with the client's experience and the way your architect(s) and specialists think;
- The visual structure makes it easier for others to evaluate its completeness and add to it where necessary;
- The structure serves as the starting point to draw up the project schedule and determine the required assets and costs;
- By adding the specifications and testing requirements to the subproducts, they can be individually executed and completed - they become delegable;
- The decomposition also makes it possible to allocate many other properties of the final product, e.g. mass, energy consumption and cost price, to the subproducts;
- It makes it possible to divide the project into subprojects with clear interfaces between each other and the project environment;

■ The structure can also serve as a starting point for the project information and documentation systems, and for the operational systems of, for example, the logistics, purchasing and service departments.

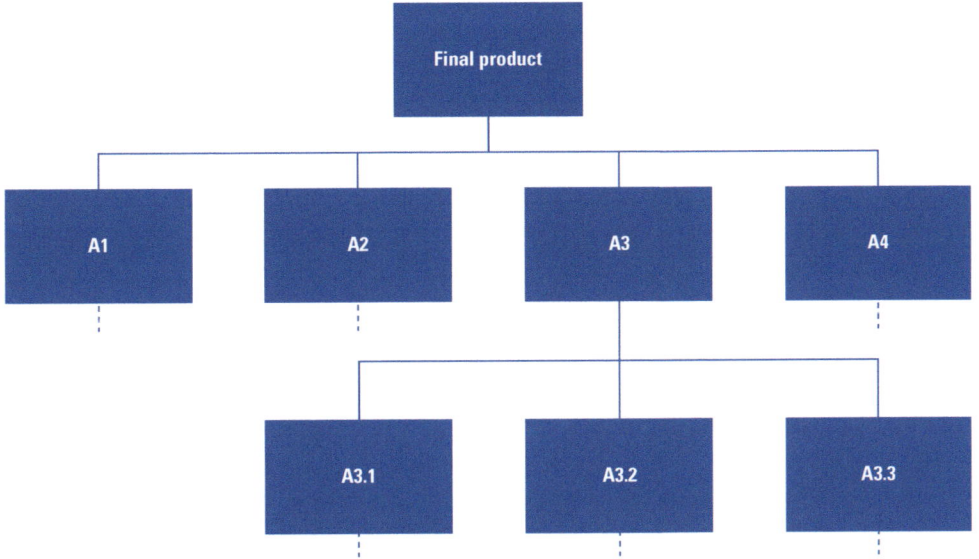

Figure 5.7   An example of the product breakdown structure (PBS)

The PBS is structured like a hierarchical tree, as can be seen in figure 5.7. This tree must be as complete as possible, because it will later form the foundation for the project management plan. The number of levels into which you divide the final result depends on two themes:

1. **Audience**: the desired detail per subproduct will depend on the responsible party or the executor. The client will mainly be interested in the top row of subproducts, because this usually provides insight into the project scope. For components that are outsourced to third parties based on a result commitment, you will usually not include any more detail yourself. However, subproducts that will be handled by your own team are divided up to the individual work level. The individual's maturity level is a factor here; S1 leadership calls for more detail than S4 leadership.

2. **Specifiability and testability**: divide the product into pieces that can be individually specified and tested. A division into details that cannot be specified or tested is not interesting and can even be a bit misleading.

More than an overview of components

It is important to understand that the PBS includes more than just subproducts that will be part of the final product. It is much more than an *exploded view* of the final result. A PBS should also include the interim products and interim results that are needed for the project execution. Think of, for instance, management documents, specifications, feasibility studies, prototypes, test documents, quality documents, etc.

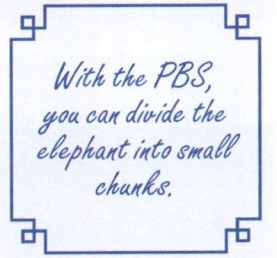

With the PBS, you can divide the elephant into small chunks.

Also remember to include *intakes* from outside the project (known as *external products* in PRINCE2), even though they do not come from your team. As a general rule, every interim result must be included somewhere in the PBS, otherwise it is not part of the project. It helps to consider the PBS as a *result* or *deliverable breakdown structure*. Many people fail to do this correctly. Consequently, their PBS only includes physical subproducts. To illustrate my point I like to use the recognizable example from figure 5.8 of moving furniture from one office space to another.

In this example, if you were to make the mistake of limiting the PBS to the physical aspects of the final result, the top row would only consist of the block marked "furniture moved to new space." The result would be that the project only includes part of the scope and when people are ready to begin moving the furniture, they discover that the new space has not been cleared out or fixed up yet. On top of that, the furniture has not been packed up yet either. That leads to stress for the project manager and a lot of improvisation during the project execution. This is why it is important to include *all* sub-deliverables, including clearing out and preparing the new space, packing up the furniture, and installing and getting the furniture ready for use again after its relocation. *The PBS is the foundation for all action!*

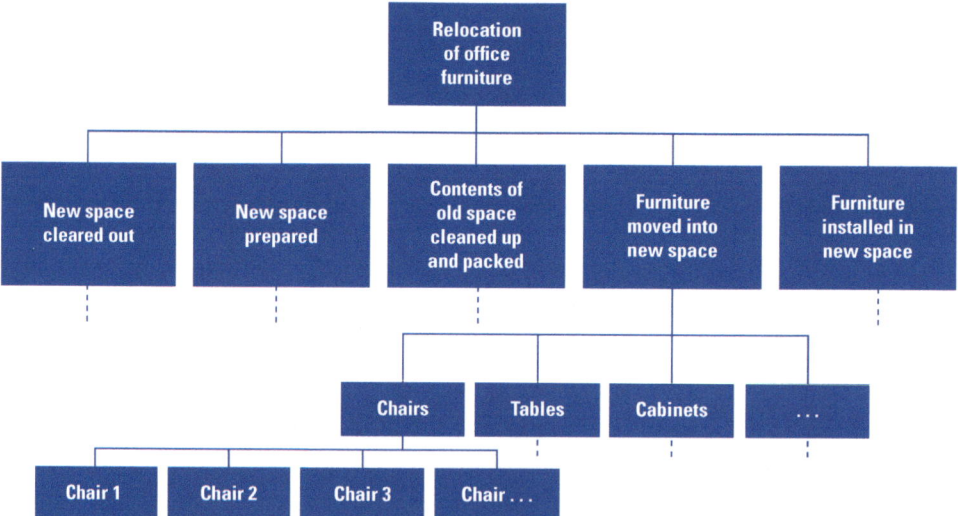

Figure 5.8   PBS for moving furniture from one space to another

Figure 5.8 clearly shows that the top row of the PBS illustrates the *scope* of the project. For example, this row shows that fixing up the old space after the furniture has been moved out is not part of the project. You should also note that the project plan based on this PBS will automatically show *interim success moments*. If nothing has been moved yet, but the new space has been fixed up and repainted, you can already show a tangible result to the client.

The PBS can also be used for projects that have nothing to do with product or service development. Let's say you are responsible for an organization's HRM activities. In the breakdown, the annual HRM plan could list the following results in the top row: increase employee satisfaction, recruit new employees, increase employee maturity level. You can then divide these items into subresults with the help of your team. You will be surprised about the items and ideas that come up during this group process.

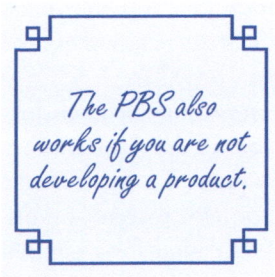

The PBS also works if you are not developing a product.

Do you still doubt the usefulness of the PBS? Next time you are developing a plan, force yourself to start with the PBS. After just an hour, you will begin to realize the advantages of having a structure of subresults.

Product descriptions and requirements management

The PBS consists of subresults instead of activities. You can easily test this by checking if your PBS consists of nouns. Activities (verbs) are only added later with the *work breakdown structure*. In other words, you use the PBS to describe *what* will be delivered, not *how* this will be done.

The product breakdown structure will only become truly usable when you have also translated the final product's specifications to the subproducts. This is the final step of the decomposition and it serves to make the subproducts SMART and delegable. For each subproduct, describe the following:

- Product name, code, etc.;
- Specifications that the subproduct has to meet;
- Specifications regarding the realization of the subproduct;
- Composition (list of parts of the subproduct);
- Delivery conditions (e.g. packaging);
- Measurable quality criteria, test protocol, test requirements, etc.

Translating the final product's specifications to the underlying subproducts is part of *requirements management*. With this, you create an opportunity for *bidirectional traceability of the specifications* throughout the system. What this means is that you can guarantee during the project execution that the delivered interim results will meet the necessary requirements in order to lead to the desired end result together. Dividing the project into subparts with subspecifications (*requirements breakdown*) makes the status transparent and traceable as

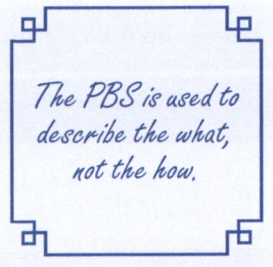

The PBS is used to describe the what, not the how.

you go through the V-model. This ties in perfectly with the TomTom behavior of making clear at all times what has already been completed and what still needs doing. Bidirectional traceability requires a clear PBS structure and it helps to make complicated matters more insightful and controllable. It is common to use a *traceability matrix* for this: a table that links the requirements of the sub-deliverables to those of the end result.

The way of documenting the product descriptions depends on the application. If, for example, you are developing components for the aviation or medical sector, such a description often comprises a small book and the traceability matrix is a complex database. However, do not let this scare you off. It is important to stay practical. A PBS in table form is a perfect foundation for a traceability matrix, as you can see in figure 5.9. Using your imagination, you probably picture additional columns for the critical parameters such as costs, mass and energy consumption, specified for each PBS element.

PBS level 1	PBS level 2	Final product specifications									
		R1	R2	R3	R4	R5	R6	R7	R8	R9	R10
Result A1		X		X		X				X	
	Result A1.1	X									
	Result A1.2					X					
	Result A1.3	X		X						X	
	Result A1.4			X						X	
Result A2			X		X			X			X
	Result A2.1		X					X			X
	Result A2.2					X					X
Result A3		X		X			X				
	Result A3.1			X							
	Result A3.2	X		X							
	Result A3.3						X				

Figure 5.9   Traceability matrix based on the PBS and the final product's specifications

Scrum and the PBS

How can you combine the PBS with the Scrum framework? We have already seen that the *product backlog* contains a list of items that the team will have to deliver. You could, therefore, view the items on the product backlog as the smallest (bottom-most) elements in the PBS. In Scrum, these items are known as *user stories*. A user story is functionality of the product that has a value for the user. Its implementation time must fit within the lead time of a sprint. The description has a standard structure, which ensures that the user story is drawn up from the user's point of view:

As a <type of user>, I want <some goal> so that <some reason>.

User stories are also the lowest level of the requirements breakdown (the specification structure) of the product. At a higher level, they combine into *epics*. Epics are functionalities that are interesting to the stakeholders and which are usually delivered during a sequence of multiple sprints. In Scrum, there is another level above the epics, known as *versions*. These are the official releases delivered to the client. Figure 5.10 shows an example of the specification structure used in Scrum. The associated PBS is seen in figure 5.11.

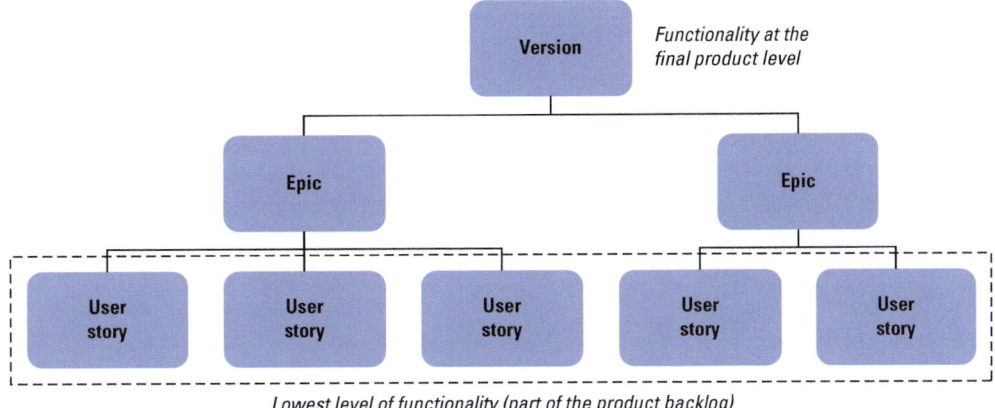

Figure 5.10   Scrum requirements breakdown (specifications)

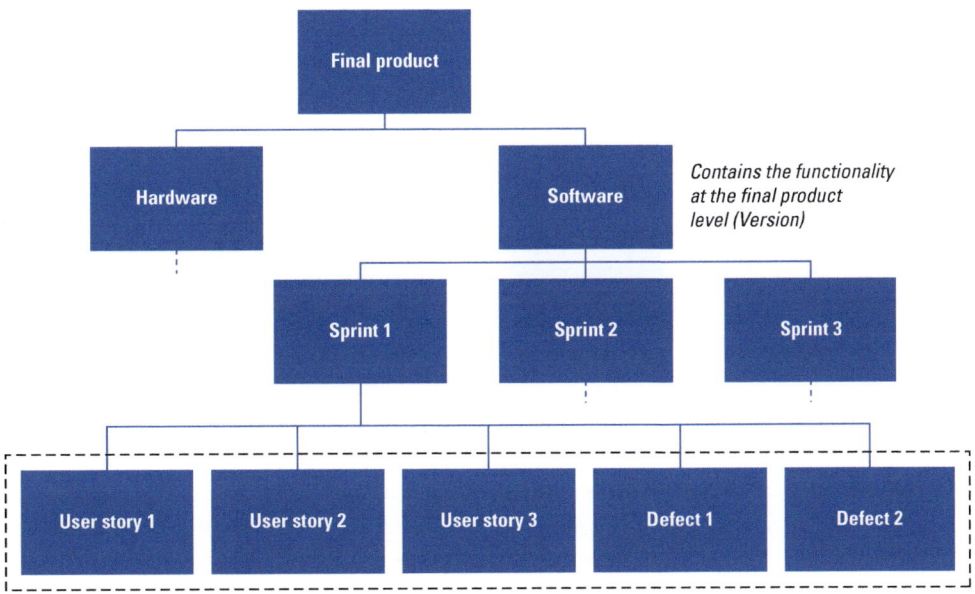

Figure 5.11   Scrum product breakdown structure (deliverables)

As it should, the PBS from figure 5.11 contains subresults and therefore the sprints to be delivered along with their allocated user stories. Furthermore, the product backlog includes *defects* (or bugs) in addition to the user stories. These are problems that were found during testing and which need to be resolved. They are, therefore, added to the development team's to-do list. Because defects do not add value for the client, they are not listed in the requirements breakdown.

5.5   Building a roller coaster

Who among us has not ridden a roller coaster at some point in their life? To make the development of the PBS more explicit, I will use the example of building a roller coaster. The development of a roller coaster is a project that offers a great mix of disciplines and project phases. Furthermore, a roller coaster is highly visual and therefore easy to understand for outsiders.

Project Roller Coaster
Your assignment to build a roller coaster is outlined in figure 5.12. Note that you do not have to understand all of the technical aspects; I only mention them to liven the scenario up a bit. It is not particularly relevant for the context of this book whether the track has a maximum acceleration of 3 or 4 G.

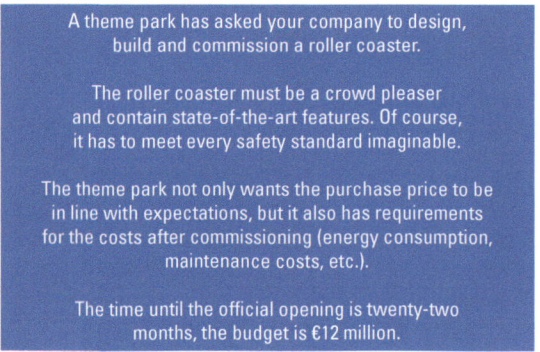

A theme park has asked your company to design, build and commission a roller coaster.

The roller coaster must be a crowd pleaser and contain state-of-the-art features. Of course, it has to meet every safety standard imaginable.

The theme park not only wants the purchase price to be in line with expectations, but it also has requirements for the costs after commissioning (energy consumption, maintenance costs, etc.).

The time until the official opening is twenty-two months, the budget is €12 million.

Figure 5.12   The assignment for project Roller Coaster

As you can see, the project has a broad scope that includes everything from design through to commissioning. Furthermore, the client – who has learned from previous projects – not only has requirements regarding the roller coaster's delivery time and cost price, but also concerning its operating costs. Of course, this will affect the project. The client has provided more information about these wishes, as seen in figure 5.13.

- Length of roller coaster track: 1,200 m
- Maximum height: 45 m
- Number of cars: 10
- Number of passengers per car: 4 (2x2)
- Top speed: 110 km/h
- Max acceleration: 3.8 G
- Number of inversions: 4 (2 loops, 1 corkscrew, 1 free fall)
- Duration: 2 min
- Service life: 30 years (3 million runs)
- 4D audio with music and FX (in the cars and along the track)
- Link to Facebook login via Wi-Fi and 3 points along the track at which pictures are taken (plus 1 picture taken from the car)

Figure 5.13   The specifications of project Roller Coaster

As I mentioned, it does not really matter whether the roller coaster contains one or two loops. What does matter is understanding that the client wants to implement a number of innovations, both to enhance the passengers' experience and boost the theme park's marketing and publicity. For example, the specification sheet lists 4D audio, which means sound coming from the car (from speakers positioned to the front and rear of the passengers) and the track itself. However, the most innovative feature is the link to social media. The client wants to do more than simply offer the standard option of buying a picture when you leave the ride. The idea is to get passengers to log into their own Facebook account before the ride starts and allow four pictures to be posted on their timelines. These pictures are taken at various points along the track and from the car itself. By the time the passengers get off the ride, their friends will already know what they just did. The client believes this is a perfect way to promote the new attraction.

To help you understand what the development of a roller coaster entails, the key components and project phases are outlined in figure 5.14.

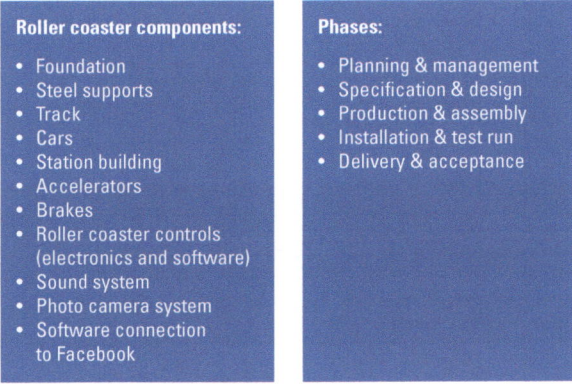

Figure 5.14   Components and phases of project Roller Coaster

Project charter project Roller Coaster
Figure 5.15 shows the initial version of the project charter for project Roller Coaster. It contains information that project managers can gather based on some interviews with the client and people in their own organization. Beware: *this information is fictitious*. I never worked on this project in practice. Nevertheless, I would feel comfortable taking on the project armed with this project charter.

The strength of the project charter lies in the fact that you gather information *early on in the project* and in the *description of the entire cycle* from context to agreements regarding communication. This means you will not get hung up on the details of only part of the project. Those details will be added later, during the planning process. You should not spend more than two hours on the initial version of the project charter. This boils down to around ten minutes per subject. Considering it will only take you two hours and comprise one page, there is no excuse to view the task as a giant hurdle and put it off.

You can use the initial version of the project charter to structure your meetings with the client. Because of the 10% confrontation rule, you will have gained a head start! You could, for instance, discuss the risks, such as the third item: "Facebook link not accepted by visitors." By discussing this issue now, you develop a positive relationship with the client, because the client considers this link an important aspect of the project goal. You could, for example, suggest that people who give access to their Facebook page get to use a VIP entrance with a shorter line. Armed with the project charter, you will be making deposits into your client's emotional bank account from day one, while developing a solid foundation for your project at the same time.

Project name: Roller Coaster	Project manager: Client:		
Project description (context and cause)	**Project goal and financial impact (business case)**		
Design, production and installation of a roller coaster. Roller coaster must be a crowd pleaser, both with its design and its integration with social media. In addition to cost price and delivery time, the cost of ownership is an important item.	Introduction of a new roller coaster that must be a crowd pleaser because of its design and the link to social media. The goal is a 10% increase in the number of visitors aged 16-30. Opening in 20 months, cost price €12 million + CoO target.		
Project scope (and delineation)	**Stakeholders**		
In scope: design, production, installation, delivery and maintenance. Clear plot including development of infrastructure. Out of scope: PR and marketing, exploitation and operation of the roller coaster after delivery. Making the plot available.	• Client: commercial director theme park • Other two theme park board members • Theme park staff involved in the ride • Target audience attraction visitors • Suppliers and partners development and production		
Project results (key deliverables, KPIs)	**Key activities, timing**		
• Design and artist impression for theme park PR • Plot developed including infrastructure • Prototype car available and tested • Music and sound FX available • Delivery of roller coaster after completion of all tests	• Develop system architecture • Draw up contracts with suppliers • Design roller coaster including check of component specifications • Production and assembly of subsystems • On-site system installation, test and delivery		
Team members	**Main risks**		
Core team (team leaders): system architect, subcontract manager, hardware project leader, software project leader, test project leader, installation & support project leader	• Development starts too late because of design decisions • System performance not possible with standard components (already released and available) • Facebook link not accepted by visitors		
Review and communication plan	**Approval** Name:	Position:	Signature:	Date:
• Internal: weekly meetings • External: biweekly meetings with client	············ ············ ············	············ ············ ············	············ ············ ············	············ ············ ············

Figure 5.15   Initial project charter for project Roller Coaster

Strategy and phasing project Roller Coaster

With the project charter in hand, step 2, the strategy and phasing, is easy to make. The phasing structure for this development project is a fairly standard one. It has already been partially detailed in the project charter under *key activities*. When it comes to the strategy, there are some choices left to make, such as whether to use a traditional or Agile development approach. Developing a roller coaster is not that difficult on a technical level for a specialized organization, since many elements can be reused from earlier projects. If we use the Cynefin method, we see that this is mostly a *complicated* project with relatively few uncertainties (see section 1.3). However, some elements are *complex*, e.g. the implementation of the link to social media and the feasibility of the objectives regarding energy consumption and cost of ownership during the roller coaster's operational life cycle.

It is decided to use the Agile approach for the software development – not because of the large number of uncertainties in terms of software functionality, but because it is important to get a clear idea of the feasibility of the Facebook photo upload feature at an early stage of the project. Furthermore, you want to use the interim sprint releases for tests of the hardware subsystems, which are mainly developed using the waterfall method. To maintain a focus on safeguarding the system's energy and maintenance costs, DfX is used for several critical parameters. It is inadvisable to only test these aspects during the system tests at the end of the project. Figure 5.16 details the project strategy. As with the project charter, this representation will fit onto a single sheet of paper.

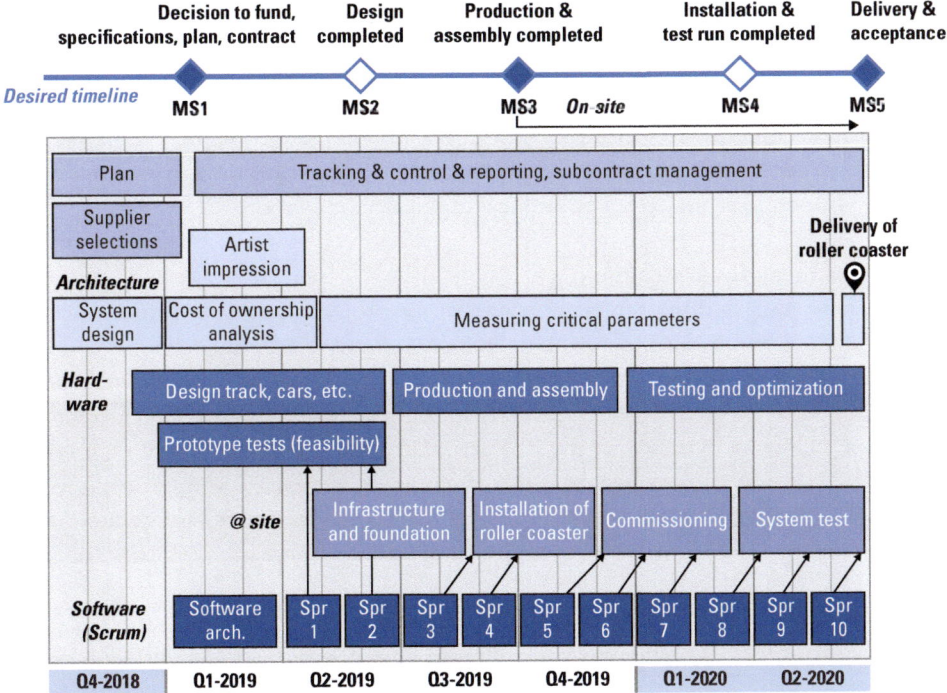

Figure 5.16   The project strategy of project Roller Coaster

You are probably wondering: *will you know all this at the start of the project?* The answer is: yes and no. A lot will still be unclear and you will not have a PBS and certainly no detailed plan as yet. However, Covey's second habit of "beginning with the end in mind" will help a lot – or rather, it will show you that you do not have much to choose. The figure primarily details how the project should proceed in order to realize the goals, which is something you can probably come up with yourself at the start of the project. It is, therefore, not a substantiation of the project's feasibility; that comes later when you develop the plan. It complements the project charter and serves as a way to discuss the project approach with your team and the stakeholders. You can use this graphical representation throughout the entire project to provide visual insight into its status.

You will find that clients love to get this kind of information early in the project. On top of that, you force yourself and your environment to reflect on the entire project, rather than getting stuck on just a few details. Remember what the TomTom has taught us: regardless of any uncertainties, always show the path to the final goal and the consequences! To make sure your strategy is not mistaken for a committed plan, the time axis with the milestones is marked "desired timeline." I sometimes refer to this timeline as the *laws of nature of the project.* These are milestones that are pretty much a given if you think back from the project's end point. That means the project manager did not come up with them; they are the result of the client's demand. Presenting this overview at an early stage will help you get to the point quickly and separate the wheat from the chaff. Because stakeholders quickly gain an insight into the consequences of their wishes, you create an atmosphere in which decisions are made together. Combined with the project charter, this makes for a perfect opportunity to present yourself as a proactive and influencing project manager.

The product breakdown structure

Once you have discussed the project charter and the project strategy with the stakeholders, you can get to work on the PBS.[7] It may look something like figure 5.17. Of course, it is not possible to depict the entire PBS here. Instead, a complete row is shown and only one subproduct is then explored in more detail. Also, this example only contains three rows. You can make several choices regarding the PBS structure. This figure begins with a *functionally oriented* division into project phases, after which all roller coaster components per phase are listed. That approach makes sense for this project, because you will integrate the entire system yourself and are responsible for all project phases.

A good PBS suits both the content and the organization.

You could also use the approach seen in figure 5.18. In this figure, the roller coaster components are listed in the top row and the phasing is repeated at a lower level for each component. This *product-oriented* division is more useful in a situation in which you outsource all components to partners at a high level. You assign an entire tree and a full development life cycle, e.g. for "Cars" or "Controls & software," to each of these partners.

The functionally and product-oriented structures may be different, but they still use the same building blocks. These are just placed in different positions in the PBS because the projects are organized differently. *A good PBS therefore not only suits the project content, but also the project organization.* After all, it is easier to delegate the responsibility for project components if said components are included in the PBS as clearly delineated structures.

---

7 If you want to examine the full PBS of project Roller Coaster, you can download it at www.roelwessels.com

That means they can be developed and tested as independent subsystems and there will be no confusion about the product and project interfaces.

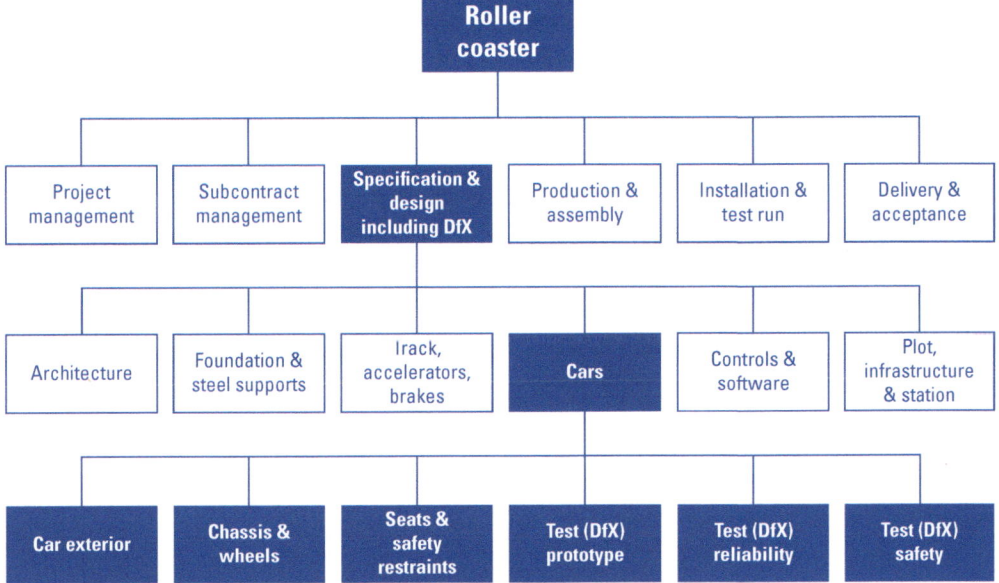

Figure 5.17 Product breakdown structure project Roller Coaster (functionally oriented)

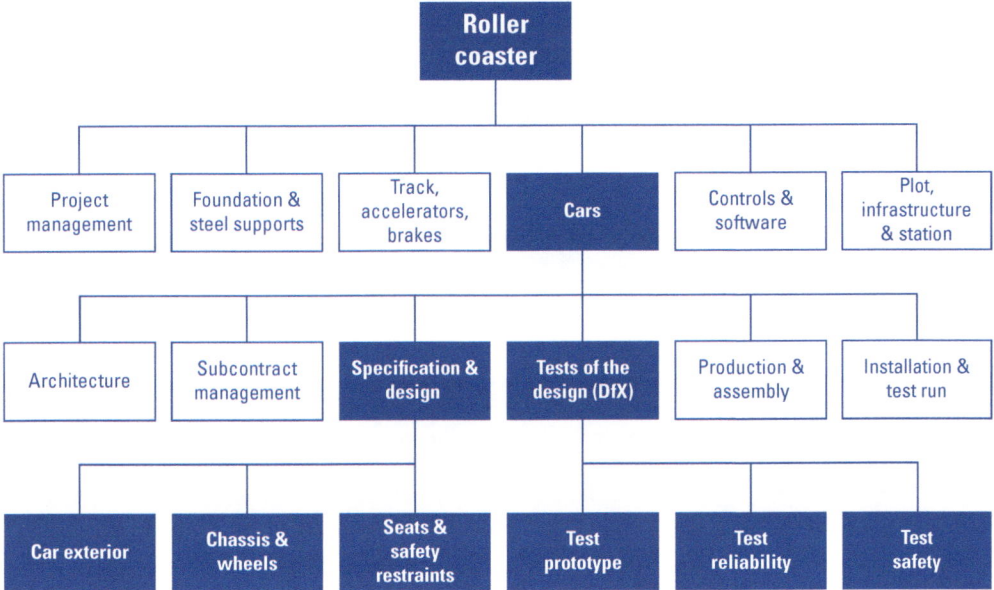

Figure 5.18 A different structure for the PBS of project Roller Coaster (product-oriented)

Wax on… wax off…

You probably know this famous line from the 1984 movie *The Karate Kid*: "Wax on… wax off." In this film, teenager Daniel wants to become a karate champion. He receives help from former karate instructor Mr. Miyagi, who slowly develops into a father figure for Daniel. Miyagi's training is highly unusual and has him doing things like waxing cars, sanding a floor and painting a fence. *Wax on… wax off*, again and again and again. Each exercise is linked to a specific move that builds strength and embeds the move in Daniel's muscle memory, so he can later apply them during his karate matches. However, the student cannot see this link and becomes frustrated because he thinks he is not learning anything about karate. He goes through every stage of development towards task maturity, including that of disillusioned learner. Later, he discovers that these seemingly meaningless exercises, combined with a daily exercise regime, form the path to expertise. He ends up winning the championship.

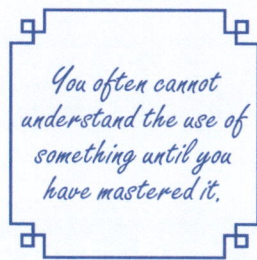
You often cannot understand the use of something until you have mastered it.

The same principle applies to the planning process. The eventual detailed plan with activities, resources and deadlines must be preceded by plenty of exercise and sometimes seemingly irrelevant "wax on, wax off" activities. Drawing up the project charter and the PBS are activities that might seem futile at first. You will not be able to fully understand the benefits they offer until you have mastered the business of project management. More often than not, you will not have a Miyagi in your environment to rely on and motivate you to keep going. Your client will not ask for it, your supervisor probably won't either and your team would be only too happy to move straight to the activity level.

Figure 5.19   The Karate Kid, Wax on… wax off…

Instead of wasting your time doubting the usefulness of the project charter and the PBS, just do it! When you have something tangible to show them, your team members will begin to realize the benefits; for example, because they discover subresults that would otherwise have been overlooked, or because people realize that thinking about testability at an early stage affects the definition of a subproduct. A project manager must, therefore, not only master the planning process, but also have the ability to motivate the environment and offer task-oriented support during this process.

5.6 Steps 3.3 to 3.5: Product Flow Diagram and DfX

Once the PBS has been drawn up, it is time for the next step: determining the correlation between subproducts (sub-deliverables) in time, because the PBS does not include that information. This also gives you the opportunity to further improve the PBS using the V-model and Design for X, so that risks can be reduced earlier on in the project.

Make or buy per subproduct (step 3.3)

First, however, it is a good idea to indicate in the PBS which sub-deliverables you will realize with your project team and which will be delivered by partners or suppliers. This once again illustrates the importance of making the PBS as complete as possible: *it must also include the sub-deliverables that you will not develop yourself, but which are needed for the end result.* You will have to monitor the progress and quality of these sub-deliverables as well. You often conduct the make or buy decision integrally while drawing up the PBS, because it

Make sure to only outsource clearly delineated subproducts.

is advisable to outsource *entire trees* of the PBS, for which the specifications and interfaces with the rest of the project are clear. Make or buy therefore affects the structure of the PBS. Furthermore, you will not draw up the details of the sub-deliverables that you outsource yourself. That responsibility (and freedom) is left to the executor. You describe the *what*, the supplier decides on the *how*. Figure 5.20 clearly illustrates the consequences of make or buy for the PBS.

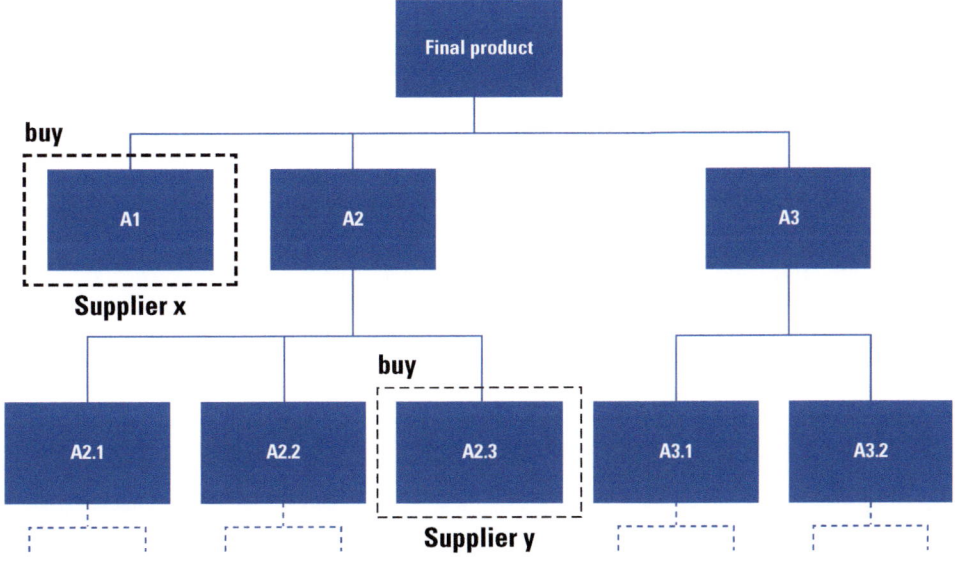

Figure 5.20   Make or buy decisions in the PBS

The Product Flow Diagram (step 3.4)

The PBS gives you a lot of information, but it does not tell you the order in which the sub-deliverables are realized. That is why you should also draw up a *Product Flow Diagram (PFD)*. This flow diagram, which is described in great detail in PRINCE2, presents the sub-deliverables from the PBS along with their correlations, leading up to the project result. The order of their realization is represented with arrows. Generally speaking, all PBS sub-deliverables are included, with the exception of periodical management products such as progress reports. However, do not go overboard with the amount of detail; acquiring insight into correlations is the primary goal at this stage of the planning process. When drawing up the PFD, you will likely discover sub-deliverables that are not included in your PBS as yet. Be sure to add these to your PBS, because its structure should remain the foundation for your plan. In other words, the PFD is a great way to verify the completeness of your PBS.

Improve your PBS by creating early integration opportunities.

An interesting form of the Product Flow Diagram is the *system integration diagram*, which describes the phase of the project during which the subproducts are integrated into a single end product on the right side of the V-model. The integration phase is often a poorly substantiated part of the plan, which may lead to surprises and setbacks along the way. The system integration diagram creates overview in advance and presents you with opportunities to improve your PBS, as shown in figure 5.21. As you can see, the initial integration diagram usually only leads to the simultaneous integration of all subproducts at the end of the project. This is also known as *big-bang* integration (note the continuous arrows). For a proactive project manager, this is not good enough. The trick is to create moments earlier on at which subproducts can be tested together (the dotted arrows in the figure). This may require modifications of the specifications of subproducts or even additional PBS elements. However, this extra effort is worth it because the risks involved in the integration are reduced. The figure also shows that the Agile sprint results can be used to test other system components at an early stage. The challenge lies in defining and allocating the right product backlog features to the right sprint in order to facilitate the desired tests.

Implementing Design for X

After improving the PBS with the PFD, we can also begin putting Design for X into practice. Place the V-model on top of the PFD and determine when your project's critical parameters are tested. For project Roller Coaster, these critical parameters include:

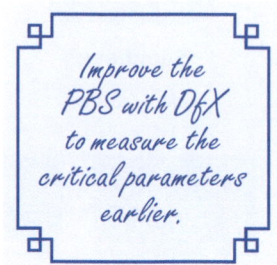

Improve the PBS with DfX to measure the critical parameters earlier.

- Cost price;
- Maximum acceleration (G-force);
- Cost of ownership – energy consumption;
- Cost of ownership – maintenance;
- System reliability.

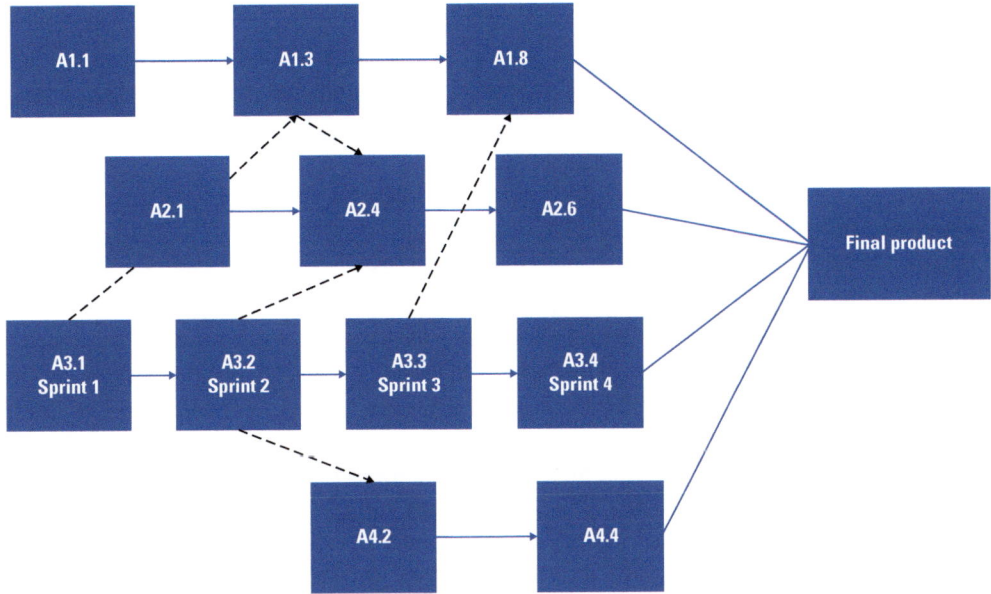

Figure 5.21   System integration diagram where the dotted arrows represent earlier opportunities for integration and testing

It is likely that most test moments only occur on the right side of the V-model in your initial version. *You and your team should therefore come up with ways to verify the critical parameters earlier in the V.* This will also result in additional (sub-)deliverables for the PBS. Figure 5.22 shows several additional defined deliverables for the critical parameter "Energy consumption" of project Roller Coaster. Your project will gradually develop into a complete PBS with elements that enforce proactive behavior and early risk reduction.

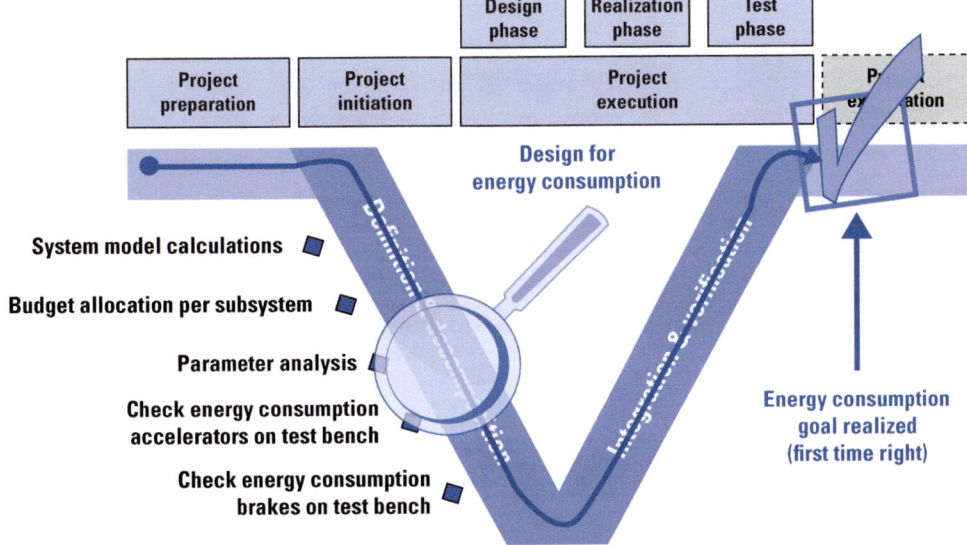

Figure 5.22   Expanding the PBS with Design for X (energy consumption)

5.7   Step 3.6: Work breakdown structure

I want to conclude this chapter by discussing the work breakdown structure and a somewhat unique philosophy. I am talking about the difference between the *product breakdown structure (PBS)* and the *work breakdown structure (WBS)*.

WBS versus PBS

Is there even a difference between the WBS and the PBS? I sometimes say: "*Only when you understand the differences can you say they concern the same thing.*" Like the PBS, the WBS is a hierarchical decomposition of a project. Instead of subproducts, however, the project is divided into executable work packages. Theoretically speaking, there is a difference. The PBS tells you which *subresults* must be delivered to realize the end result, while the WBS shows you how the work must be divided into *work packages* to achieve the same end result.

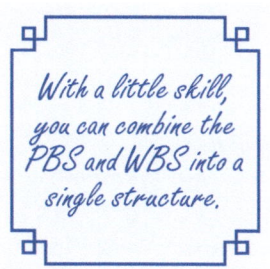

With a little skill, you can combine the PBS and WBS into a single structure.

Those purists claiming that you must first develop a PBS before drawing up a WBS certainly have a point.

Personally, I believe this approach to be impractical. It goes against my goal of developing a single basic structure for the project. That is why I am in favor of combining both by expanding the PBS with activities on the bottom row and choosing a structure that also neatly represents the organizational context. This allows you to combine both the delivery of subresults and the organization of the work into a single complete PBS/WBS overview. Alternatively, you could turn this approach around by developing a WBS with a result-oriented structure.

This means that, although the PBS and the WBS are different decompositions of the same project, I combine the two into a single PBS/WBS decomposition[8]. I do that *by viewing the WBS as an extension of the bottom of the PBS*, as seen in figure 5.23. The PBS represents the (interim) results and therefore *what* you deliver. The WBS adds to the PBS's bottom level the activities needed to realize these results and illustrates *how* to deliver. Together, they form a single complete overview that is both result-oriented and work-oriented. If you were to rotate it ninety degrees anti-clockwise, it would actually be quite similar to a Gantt chart (detailed plan). This Gantt chart with WBS activities has a solid structure because it is based on the PBS. Furthermore, clearly distinguishing between PBS deliverables (*what*) and WBS activities (*how*) will help you use situational leadership during the project execution.

The WBS in a traditional and an Agile environment

Before delving much deeper into the WBS in chapter 6, it is a good idea to ask yourself why you should even develop a WBS. Here are two major reasons:

1. To determine the *size* of the sub-deliverables in the PBS (or the Scrum product backlog), e.g. in terms of costs and lead time. The WBS can be a useful tool here.

---

8   The MIL-STD-881D standard, used by all Departments and Agencies of the Department of Defense of the USA, adopted a similar hybrid PBS/WBS (typically called a WBS in this standard).

2. To define the *tasks* (activities) that must be carried out during the execution phase. The WBS itself is the desired result.

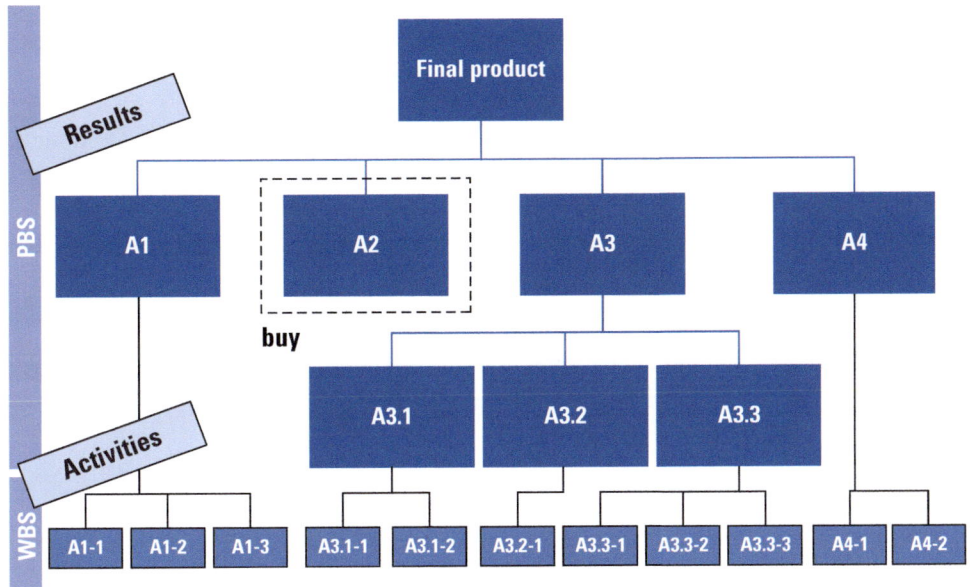

Figure 5.23   Expanding the PBS with the WBS activities derived from the PBS subresults

In general, you want to tackle the first point before the second. Knowing the size of the sub-deliverables will help you manage expectations, make decisions and draw up the project budget. The sooner you have this information, the better. The second point is also important, but you only need to know this once the project execution actually begins. *The first point must, therefore, be addressed in the sketch with the team, while defining the tasks can be put off until you start developing the detailed plan.* We will cover both the sketch with the team and the detailed plan in the following chapter.

The situation is slightly more nuanced when using Scrum. The activities in the WBS are only defined prior to the sprint in which they will be carried out. This definition occurs during the sprint planning meeting (see Pl in figure 1.12) and the activities are covered in more detail during the daily stand-up meetings. All this is done by the development team itself – under the scrum master's supervision – during the execution phase. That is why you will not see the WBS of the Scrum subprojects in the project manager's detailed plan. Of course, a good estimate of the size of the product backlog is needed to plan the sprints. The first point listed above is, therefore, also an important step in Scrum in order to develop the sketch with the team, although you will usually not need a WBS for that because the product backlog items are usually small enough to be estimated directly in terms of size. We will come back to this point in chapter 6.

Determining the size of an activity in the WBS

When you have defined all WBS activities, your project decomposition is complete. All you have to do now is turn it into a schedule. We will discuss this in chapter 6, in which I cover the second part of the planning process. I want to end this chapter by telling you which parameter is used to define the size of a WBS activity: the *number of hours* it takes to carry out an activity (often called *Work* or *Effort* in planning tools). It is not the lead time, because you can only determine that when you know how much capacity/manpower you can allocate to the activity. Like the PBS, the WBS follows the 100% rule: all (internal) activities together must add up to the total project budget in hours. Estimating the amount of work in hours is an important process with a rational and a psychological side, because it affects people in a major way.

With this, we shift our focus in the planning process from analytical structuring in part I of the book to the psychological aspects of leadership and motivation in part II.

Summary

◉ Avoid submarine behavior by using the 10% confrontation rule for important activities.

◉ Planning is mostly about structuring and it should lead to support and coordination with your team and stakeholders.

◉ Take inspiration from the ten steps of the planning process and experience for yourself that they – after some practice – will lead to:

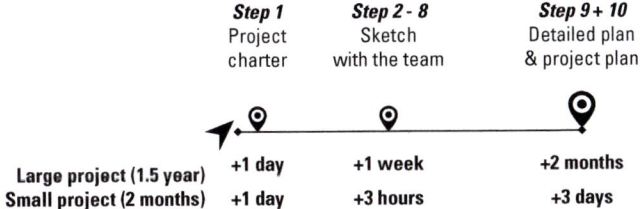

	Step 1 Project charter	**Step 2 - 8** Sketch with the team	**Step 9 + 10** Detailed plan & project plan
Large project (1.5 year)	+1 day	+1 week	+2 months
Small project (2 months)	+1 day	+3 hours	+3 days

◉ The project charter is a single-page overview of your project. It is the perfect opportunity to interact with your environment at an early stage.

◉ You combine early confrontation, overview, detail and agility by making a clear distinction in the planning process between:

1. **Understanding project size**: in order to manage expectations, you need to know the size of the complete project as early as possible. This results in the sketch with the team based on the sub-deliverables of the PBS and/or Scrum product backlog. The WBS can be a useful tool to determine the size of these sub-deliverables, but its use is optional.

2. **Directing project execution**: task-related information is only needed once the execution starts and can be determined separately per phase or sprint to prevent unnecessary change management. This results in the detailed plan which includes the WBS activities. In Scrum, the team members usually manage their activity plan on the scrum board, so there is no official detailed plan.

◉ The sketch with the team is a general outline of the plan, although it includes sufficient detail to properly substantiate timing, costs, the results to be delivered and the use of people and assets. The sketch with the team is a plan based on deliverables rather than activities, so it cannot be used as a guideline for the project execution.

◉ Use the product breakdown structure (PBS) to easily divide the project into a complete overview of subresults (sub-deliverables): the *what* of your project.

◉ The Scrum product backlog contains user stories (and defects). These user stories can also be found at the bottom of the PBS as the smallest specified sub-deliverables.

◉ The PBS is a living project database. Improve the PBS – before drawing up the detailed plan – with DfX and early integration moments and by coordinating with your stakeholders.

◉ A good PBS suits both the content and the organization.

- You can expand the PBS with the WBS activities needed to deliver the PBS sub-deliverables. In Scrum, this is only done during the execution phase at the start of each sprint.
- The WBS helps you determine the size of the sub-deliverables in the PBS (for the sketch with the team) and outlines which activities need to be carried out during the execution phase (for the detailed plan).

6 The plan part II: sketch with the team and detailed plan

- ↱ How to use the knowledge of your team to determine the PBS/WBS size.
- ↱ Why safety margins only lead to overrun.
- ↱ From estimate to successful execution in four steps.
- ↱ Why having the sketch with the team available early on is so important for both Agile and traditional project management.
- ↱ How to make planning tools work for you.

By drawing up the PBS and the WBS, you have created an important foundation for a successful project execution. You now have a complete overview of subresults and activities that is logically structured by content and organization. You may have noticed that the step-by-step development of a plan creates ample coordination opportunities: contact moments with your team members and stakeholders to acquire information and coordinate. These are all opportunities to avoid submarine behavior and influence the project course instead.[9]

If you want explicit details concerning what those contact moments might look like, they are shown in figure 6.1. It is based on a larger project with subprojects which are managed by team leaders (also known as subproject leaders). After defining the top row of subproducts in the PBS, you can give these team leaders the responsibility to develop their part of the PBS with their team. This method of *organizing for delegation* is efficient for you and allows you to make optimal use of the knowledge of your team. A similar step will occur later on when you develop the WBS and assign responsibility to the team member (or Scrum team) that will actually carry out the activities in question. In this manner, *the planning process becomes a team effort* and you create more support for the project execution. This method will also work for a smaller project without subprojects, with the exception that team members are directly involved in creating the PBS because there are no team leaders.

After completing the PBS/WBS combination, it is time to determine the size of the work so the activities can be translated into a schedule. This schedule is initially part of the deliverable-based sketch with the team. Later, it is converted into the final activity-based detailed plan that can be used to manage the project execution.

---

9 This chapter ties into the following competences from IPMA's ICB4: Negotiation, Time, Organisation and information, Finance, Resources, Plan and control, Select and balance.

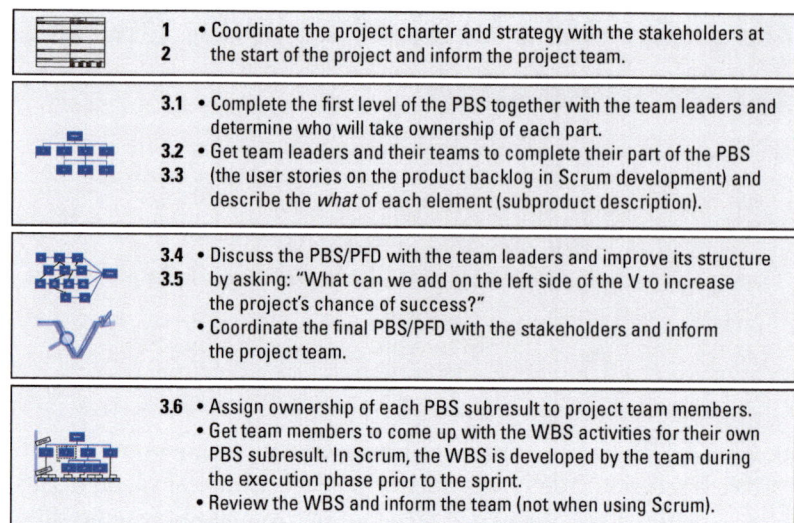

	1 2	• Coordinate the project charter and strategy with the stakeholders at the start of the project and inform the project team.
	3.1 3.2 3.3	• Complete the first level of the PBS together with the team leaders and determine who will take ownership of each part. • Get team leaders and their teams to complete their part of the PBS (the user stories on the product backlog in Scrum development) and describe the *what* of each element (subproduct description).
	3.4 3.5	• Discuss the PBS/PFD with the team leaders and improve its structure by asking: "What can we add on the left side of the V to increase the project's chance of success?" • Coordinate the final PBS/PFD with the stakeholders and inform the project team.
	3.6	• Assign ownership of each PBS subresult to project team members. • Get team members to come up with the WBS activities for their own PBS subresult. In Scrum, the WBS is developed by the team during the execution phase prior to the sprint. • Review the WBS and inform the team (not when using Scrum).

Figure 6.1   Turn the planning process into a team effort with delegation and feedback moments

6.1   Step 4: Size & effort estimation

A good hour's estimate is essential for a project manager in order to get the timeframe and project budget under control. By expanding the PBS with the WBS and then assigning hours to that, you end up with a complete database of the project size and also create the foundation for a good plan. In addition, the hours estimate is a way to get support and commitment from the team – or to lose it…

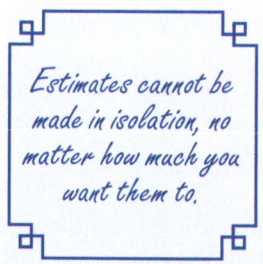

Estimates cannot be made in isolation, no matter how much you want them to.

Determining the size of the work can be a confusing task. Project managers may have an insufficient understanding of the methods and lose their way as a result. You can recognize those situations from remarks like "my team members all have trouble sticking to the plan" or "I have to double all my estimates for that team member." I sometimes wonder where the problem really lies…

 Do you use your team's input for the estimate of hours or have you given up on that?

Is it hard to estimate the amount of work? I believe that question has two possible answers. *No*, because all you are doing is dividing the work into understandable tasks and adding up the hours. *Yes*, because you face questions like:
- How do you determine the size of the work with traditional and Agile methods?
- How do you account for your team members' different approaches to the work?
- How can you make your estimates less dependent on the person doing the work?
- How can you incorporate risk management in your estimates?

- How can you use the knowledge of your team when making your estimates?
- Why do windfalls and setbacks regarding the lead time not cancel each other out?
- How can you keep employees from including extra time in their estimates and then lacking a sense of urgency because of these buffers?
- How can you maintain your team's support when "bottom-up" estimates are affected by "top-down" limitations?
- How can you keep your employees committed, despite their dependence on external influences (tardy input from others, changes in scope, etc.)?

Estimates cannot be made in isolation. They depend on the context. Furthermore, you need to find a balance between elements that seemingly clash with each other: your estimates must be both *realistic* and *challenging*, because the project budget will run too high otherwise. All this illustrates that you will always have to deal with the people on your team and the practical reality of project execution when estimating the work size. It is important to understand this in order to truly build upon your team's input and take advantage of your team's motivation to achieve the plan.

When it comes to estimating the work size of a project, there are differences in the approaches used by traditional and Agile methods. Still, these differences are not as significant as some people think. Estimates are made by cutting the desired subresult into smaller and smaller pieces until you understand the size of each piece. With traditional methods, these smallest pieces are usually the WBS elements. With Scrum, they are the user stories on the product backlog at the bottom of the PBS. Because these user stories are relatively small (it must be

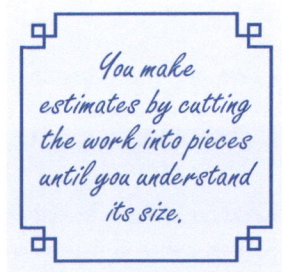

You make estimates by cutting the work into pieces until you understand its size.

possible to realize them in a single sprint), it is fairly easy to estimate their size directly, e.g. with Planning Poker. A project manager, therefore, does not need the WBS to draw up the plan and the Scrum team develops the WBS for itself to understand the tasks it must execute during a sprint. Because you are able to estimate the size of the user stories directly, you therefore do not need a WBS in Scrum until the execution actually starts. Of course, this is also possible with traditional methods, as long as you cut the PBS into sufficiently small chunks.

Some terminology
Before we continue, I want to explain some terminology. These concepts form the foundation for the planning process and they are used by most planning tools as well. Figure 6.2 illustrates the relationship between these terms.

Size refers to the size of the task, e.g. the surface area in square meters of a wall that needs painting. Size therefore says something about the scope of the work, independent of resources. Size is linked to a WBS element together with *effort*.

Effort/work describes the number of labor units required to carry out a task, e.g. the number of hours it takes to paint a wall. Effort is the most important WBS characteristic that has to be estimated if the activity is *effort-driven*.

Duration is the lead time required to complete a task, e.g. three days to paint the top floor of a house. For effort-driven activities, the lead time is related to the *effort* and the amount of *capacity* deployed. For *duration-driven* activities, the lead time is determined directly.

Effort-driven applies to most activities. This means that their size is primarily determined by the amount of work in hours. Painting a house is an example of an effort-driven task: if it takes one person twenty-four hours to finish the work, that amounts to three working days. If you assign three people, the work still takes twenty-four hours, but the lead time is reduced to a single working day. The *effort* does not change, yet the *duration* depends on the capacity deployed.

Duration-driven activities have a set lead time. Examples include transporting paint supplies in a van or the drying of the paint: their lead time cannot be reduced by assigning more people.

Costs are the costs involved in the project execution. These costs consist of multiple components: personnel costs, materials, outsourcing, etc. The personnel costs are derived from the effort multiplied by the hourly rate.

Capacity/units describes the number of resources, often in the form of a percentage. Two painters with full-time availability result in a capacity of 200%. Make sure to account for employees' maximum availability during each week of the project (forty hours or perhaps a lesser figure of thirty-six hours due to training or a departmental meeting outside the project).

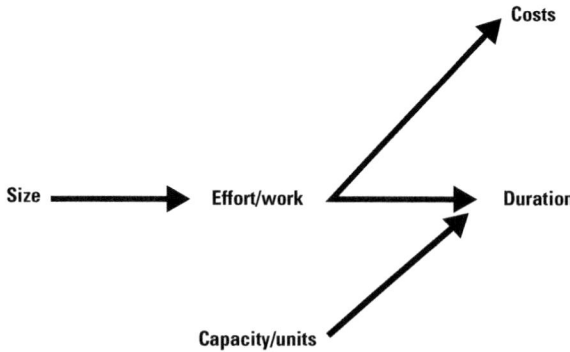

Figure 6.2   The relationship between size, effort, duration (if effort-driven), capacity and costs

First determine the size

No matter how tempting it is to immediately write down the number of hours a task will take, it is advisable to first determine the size of the work. Why? Because by doing so, you also record the activity's scope. This was probably already done implicitly when you created the PBS, but you can make it explicit by simply adding one column to your activity overview. I will use the example of the painter again to illustrate the advantage this presents.

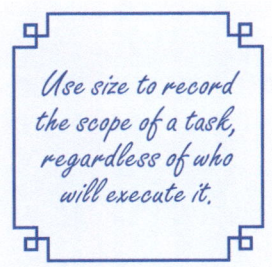

Use size to record the scope of a task, regardless of who will execute it.

Let's say you are a painter who is still a bit inexperienced when it comes to drawing up quotations. You walk through the building with your client and discuss which walls need painting. In your quote you mention that the work will take forty hours and you calculate a total price based on your hourly rate. Later, when you are about to start the work, the client says that he wants a different room painted instead. This room is bigger than the last. If your quote clearly states the number of square meters that the job consists of, you can quickly reach a new agreement for the bigger room. However, the discussion might turn personal if you failed to do so. The client may claim that the two rooms are hardly different at all and say that you will just have to work a bit faster. *Effort depends on the person; size does not.*

By first determining the *size* of a task, you get:
- A way to evaluate the mutual understanding of the job at hand before employees make their time estimate;
- A way to record the scope of a task for the client;
- A way to make the estimation of the scope of the task independent from the executor;
- A tool to objectively determine the impact of a change;
- A reference to determine the effort based on data from previous projects, e.g. the number of hours (effort) it takes to paint a square meter of wall (size).

By recording the *size*, you increase the quality of your estimation of the work. Figure 6.3 shows some examples of size. This figure also shows the unit used to describe the size of a Scrum user story: the *story point*. You can read more about how that works in the following section.

Delphi method (general)

During knowledge-intensive projects, it is important to utilize the knowledge of as many people as possible. How can you do that? When multiple people possess knowledge of the size of the work, you can apply the *Delphi method* (Helmer, 1963). This method is used when no scientifically substantiated answer is available, but you can make use of the knowledge, experience and intuition of experts. With the Delphi method, a carefully selected number of experts are (often anonymously) asked for their opinion during several rounds of questioning. Each round concludes with the experts receiving feedback on the results, which allows them to learn about the opinions of their fellow experts. This affects their views and may cause them to change their opinion. After several rounds of this, the experts' different insights should have converged into a unified and widely supported answer.

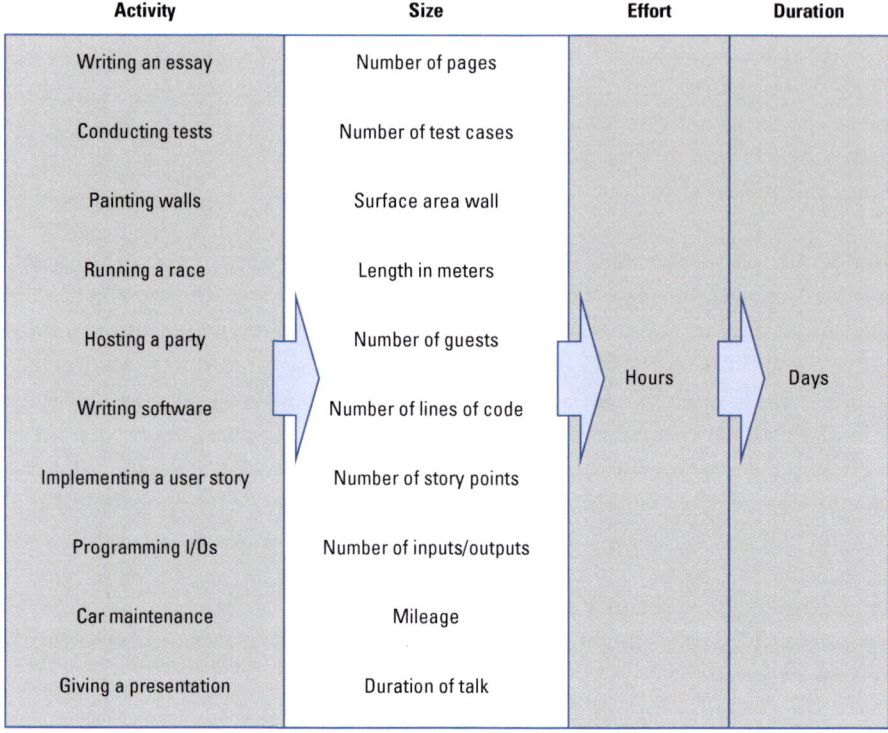

Activity	Size	Effort	Duration
Writing an essay	Number of pages		
Conducting tests	Number of test cases		
Painting walls	Surface area wall		
Running a race	Length in meters		
Hosting a party	Number of guests	Hours	Days
Writing software	Number of lines of code		
Implementing a user story	Number of story points		
Programming I/Os	Number of inputs/outputs		
Car maintenance	Mileage		
Giving a presentation	Duration of talk		

Figure 6.3   Examples of the size of activities

The Delphi method was first described in the 1950s and used in the American defense industry. These days, it is used in a wide variety of fields. The name refers to the famous Oracle of Delphi, which is odd because there is nothing mystical about this method; it merely utilizes pre-existing knowledge.

How can you apply this method when making size and effort estimates during projects? Above all, it is important to stay practical. The anonymity principle intended to eliminate the social pressure felt by the experts usually does not apply. As a result, two rounds are often sufficient: an individual round and a round with all experts together.

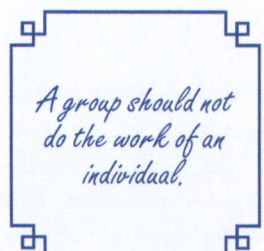

A group should not do the work of an individual.

Round 1 (individual): distribute the Excel file with the PBS/WBS and have every expert make an individual estimate of the effort required per WBS activity[10]. Make sure to only select activities that fall within the experts' areas of expertise.

10 Of course, you can also apply the Delphi method directly to higher levels of the PBS/WBS.

Round 2 (group): compile the input into a single overview as seen in figure 6.4. It is immediately clear where the differences in insight lie. They have been marked in the figure. These are the only elements that you need to discuss further. Having the expert who came up with a markedly different estimate from the rest of the group explain his or her choice will often lead to new insights for the other experts. The group then determines what estimate to include in the plan. In addition to combining the knowledge of multiple people, this approach is a great example of handling the group's time efficiently. Only those aspects that benefit from everyone's input are discussed by the whole group, while the rest can be automatically derived from the individually prepared input.

PBS level 1 (deliverable)	PBS level 2 (deliverable)	WBS (activity)	Effort estimation (hours)						
			Round 1 (individual)						Round 2 (group)
			Expert 1	Expert 2	Expert 3	Average	Standard deviation	Choice	Clarification
Result A1									
	Result A1.1								
		Activity A1.1-1	16	12	15	14	2	14	
		Activity A1.1-2	12	10	10	11	1	12	
		Activity A1.1-3	4	4	6	5	1	5	
		Activity A1.1-4	4	5	6	5	1	5	
	Result A1.2								
		Activity A1.2-1	12	40	32	28	14	30	Better understanding of content
		Activity A1.2-2	4	2	4	3	1	4	
Result A2									
	Result A2.1								
		Activity A2.1-1	4	24	6	11	11	24	Risks recognized
		Activity A2.1-2	6	4	6	5	1	5	
	Result A2.2								
		Activity A2.2-1	10	12	12	11	1	12	
		Activity A2.2-2	20	16	36	24	11	20	Risk outlier 36 low
		Activity A2.2-3	20	16	16	17	2	16	
Result A3									
		Activity A3-1	32	8	8	16	14	8	Unclear scope
		Activity A3-2	12	10	8	10	2	12	
		Activity A3-3	8	8	8	8	0	8	
		Activity A3-4	6	8	8	7	1	8	

Figure 6.4   Effort estimate of WBS elements using the Delphi method

Planning Poker

Scrum uses a technique derived from the Delphi method to make estimates in a team context: *Planning Poker*.

Before I explain what Planning Poker is, I first want to say the following about estimates in Scrum. Because the duration of a Scrum sprint is set, the lead time per sprint is known in advance, as is the available effort from the team (depending on the number of team members, of course). For that reason, there is no need to determine how much effort the implementation of a user story will take when developing your plan; it is enough to know how many user stories you can fit into a sprint. You can find this out by determining the size of the user stories (and the capacity of a sprint). Determining the effort of the WBS activities (tasks) in Scrum is only done during the execution phase prior to the sprint when drawing up the sprint backlog (see figure 6.5). That makes sense, because you want to draw up the activity plan as late as possible to account for possible changes per sprint.

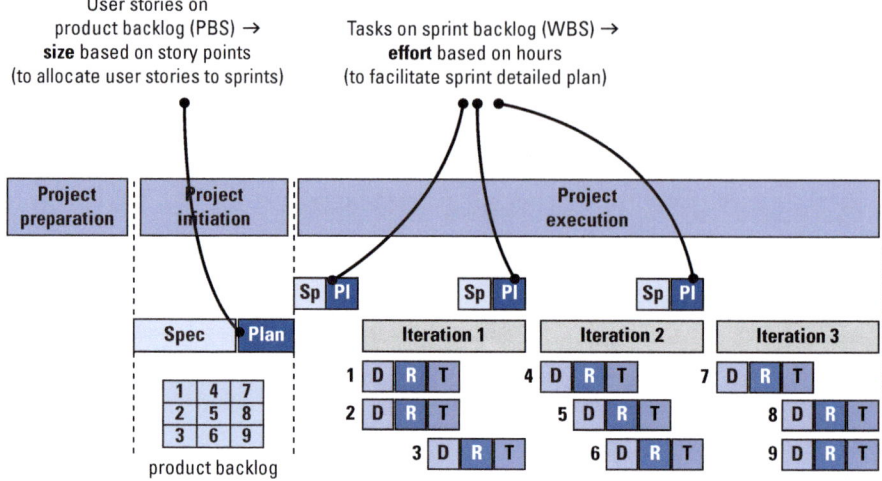

Figure 6.5   The moments of size and effort estimation in Scrum

The size of the user stories is usually expressed in *story points*. A story point is an abstract and *relative* unit with which to relate the size of the user story to a known piece of work. This means story points are not directly related to hours and are dependent on the team. The main goal is to "fill" the sprints. With Planning Poker, the team estimates the size of the user stories during the project initiation phase in a game-like manner by using a set of cards, a piece of software or an app. The cards have the following numbers on them: 0, 0.5, 1, 2, 3, 5, 8, 13, 20, 40 and 100. These numbers are based on the Fibonacci sequence, which represents the fact that uncertainty grows in proportion to the size of the user story.

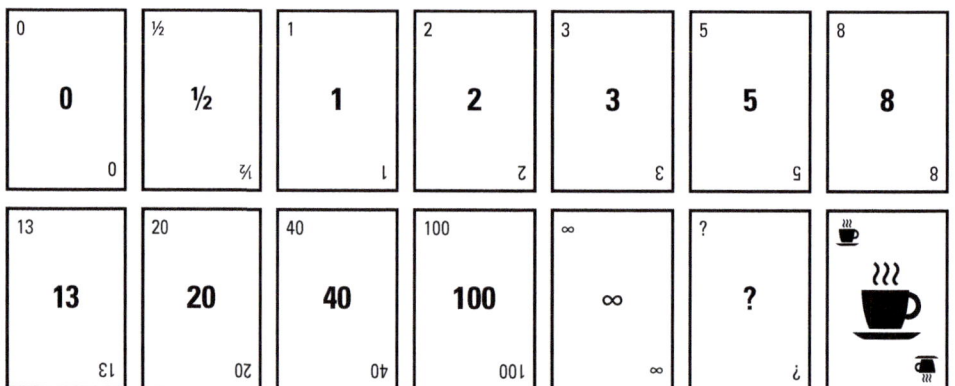

Figure 6.6   Planning Poker

This method has many similarities to the Delphi method:
1. The product owner explains the user story.
2. The team members ask questions, discuss assumptions and risks, and determine the necessary tasks (so they are thinking about the WBS…).

3. The scrum master asks all team members to make an individual estimate of the work and pick a card from their own set.
4. The team members reveal their cards at the same time and the persons with the highest and lowest estimates explain their choice.
5. Steps 3 and 4 are repeated until a consensus is reached.

Planning Poker results in adequate estimates and an efficient process and it stimulates an active attitude from all team members. Remember that the goal is to determine the size of the user stories (the subresults) on the product backlog in relative story points, not the effort of the associated Scrum tasks. The latter is done during the sprint planning meeting prior to the sprints and during the daily stand-up meetings. At that point, it will be about defining the WBS activities and it is advisable to estimate the work in hours, just as with traditional project management methods.

Three-point estimation technique
How do you deal with the fact that your team members all have different areas of expertise, which keeps them from conducting a Delphi analysis as a group? There are several ways to do that. I prefer the *three-point estimation technique* from the PERT network planning method. This technique requires team members to make three time estimates per activity: the *best-case* estimate, the *worst-case* estimate and the *most likely* estimate (the completion time with the highest probability). By asking for three estimates, you get more information than if the executor only offers one estimate. After all, you do not know which context the employee has in mind. People tend to have different preferences when it comes to including a risk buffer in their estimates. Furthermore, the three-point estimation technique forces employees to think about what might go wrong and what needs to be done to complete the activity in the shortest time possible. This will all benefit the quality of the final plan.

Which of the three estimates should you use for your plan? To understand that, it is important to delve deeper into the probability distribution of an activity's time to completion. It turns out this is not symmetrical! The physicist and business management guru Eliyahu Goldratt explains this phenomenon in *Critical Chain* (Goldratt, 1997). First of all, he discusses shooting a well-calibrated rifle at a target and the marksman's chance of hitting the bull's eye. It is not 100%, but it is still larger than the chance of hitting any other random point of the target. The probability distribution is a normal distribution and has the classic bell shape. The better the marksman is, the narrower and higher the normal distribution around the bull's eye will be. Next, he applies this philosophy to one of his students driving home from the university. He asks the student how long it takes to drive home. Reflexively, the student replies: "Thirty-five minutes." When asked what that answer is based on, the student says that it depends on the conditions. If there is little traffic in the evening and the lights are all green, the trip can be completed in ten minutes. However, it takes longer during rush hour. It would take even longer if the student was to get a flat tire along the way or stop for a drink in a bar. In that case, the trip may take as long as three hours. In the end, the probability distribution is not a normal distribution, but an asymmetrical one as seen in figure 6.7.

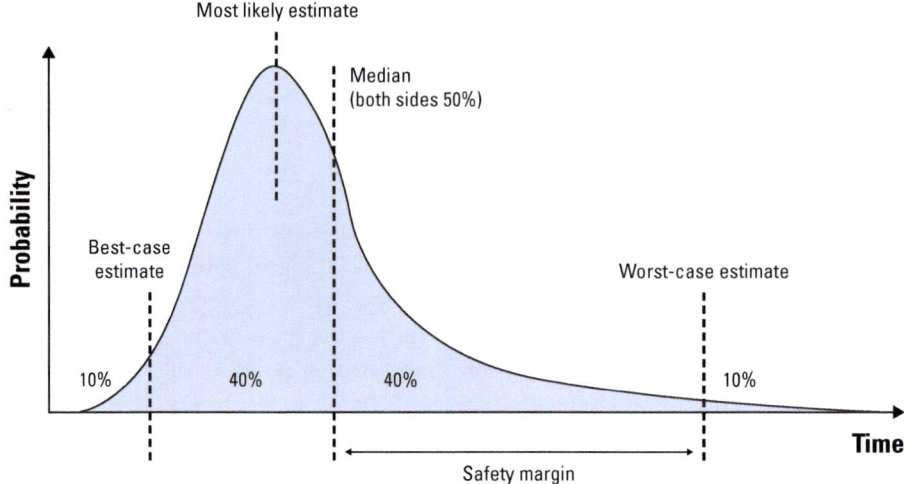

Figure 6.7   The asymmetrical probability distribution of an activity's time to completion

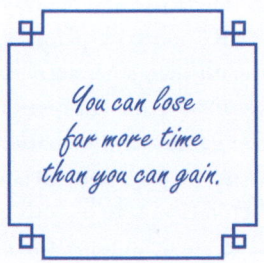

You can lose far more time than you can gain.

This has serious implications! People tend to build in a significant safety margin when making an estimate to safeguard against unforeseen circumstances, unless they are inexperienced or naive and enthusiastically believe that they can realize their best-case estimate no matter what. *However, you can lose far more time in a worst-case scenario than you can gain in a best-case scenario.* This is a phenomenon that most project managers are aware of, either intuitively or because of past experience, but it is hard to account for during the estimation process. The three-point estimation technique provides insight into the employee's stance on the *safety margin*. Furthermore, you can calculate the median and use that as the estimate to include in your plan:

Median = (best case + (4 x most likely) + worst case) / 6

Perhaps you also want to know how accurate this calculation is. To find that out, you can calculate the standard deviation. If the best- and worst-case estimates are far apart, this will result in a high standard deviation. This should tell you that the activity is risky or plagued by uncertainty and therefore calls for extra attention by taking risk-reducing measures or including a buffer. The formula used to calculate the standard deviation is as follows:

Standard deviation = (worst case − best case) / 6

Figure 6.8 shows how you can integrate the three-point estimation technique into your WBS activity overview.

PBS level 1 (deliverable)	PBS level 2 (deliverable)	WBS (activity)	Effort estimation (hours) Estimates by individuals				
			Best case	Worst case	Most likely	Median (choice)	Standard deviation
Result A1							
	Result A1.1						
		Activity A1.1-1	8	16	10	11	1.33
		Activity A1.1-2	6	20	10	11	2.33
		Activity A1.1-3	3	6	4	4	0.50
		Activity A1.1-4	4	6	6	6	0.33
	Result A1.2						
		Activity A1.2-1	16	40	24	25	4.00
		Activity A1.2-2	4	10	6	6	1.00
Result A2							
	Result A2.1						
		Activity A2.1-1	16	40	32	31	4.00
		Activity A2.1-2	4	6	4	4	0.33
	Result A2.2						
		Activity A2.2-1	8	20	14	14	2.00
		Activity A2.2-2	16	40	20	23	4.00
		Activity A2.2-3	12	20	16	16	1.33
Result A3							
		Activity A3-1	6	20	10	11	2.33
		Activity A3-2	8	12	10	10	0.67
		Activity A3-3	6	12	8	8	1.00
		Activity A3-4	6	8	6	6	0.33

Figure 6.8   Effort estimate of WBS elements using the three-point estimation technique

6.2   The rational and psychological sides of hour estimates

At the end of the previous chapter I already mentioned that we would be dealing with an interesting yet highly complicated player: humans. Human behavior affects the estimates we make. *The more pressure comes with a commitment, the larger we want our safety margin to be.* Murphy's law is a constant risk. We will also have to deal with the people behind the numbers during the project execution. Because if we do not correctly take safety margins into account in our approach, we will develop a plan that is theoretically feasible, yet we will still lose our grip on the project due to a lack of urgency. Then we'll be in trouble!

You'll be in trouble then!
Let's say you are a project manager who assumes that employees are perfectly capable of managing their own time and that their estimates should be taken seriously. You trust your people and generously give them all the time they asked for to get the job done. If you give them the time specified in their worst-case estimates, the task will surely be realized by the agreed-upon deadline, right?

On Monday morning, you ask one of your employees about the best- and worst-case estimates for completing a task. The employee says that it should be possible to get the task done in four hours if all goes well. However, it may also take several days, because there are quite a few uncertain external factors involved. You then say that you expect the job to be done by Friday. Feeling good about yourself and without a doubt on your mind, you move on to other tasks. You reap what you sow...

Will employees in this situation get started on the task immediately, bolstered by their supervisor's faith in them? Probably not. There are plenty of other urgent things to work on

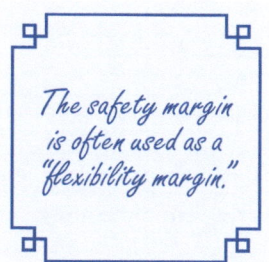

The safety margin is often used as a "flexibility margin."

first. When a different project manager asks them on Tuesday if they have some time for an urgent job, they can hardly refuse. After all, there is plenty of time left before Friday to complete a task that should really only take four hours. Before they know it, it is Thursday afternoon and high time to get started on the agreed-upon task. Then they discover that they need an important piece of information, but the colleague who has that information is off work that day. This feels like force majeure. On top of that, they should have ordered a part on Tuesday to be able to move ahead. That would have taken them twenty minutes, but they neglected to do so. On Friday, there are a few other setbacks outside their control, which take up another three hours. The feeling of force majeure grows. Friday afternoon comes around and your employee remembers the promise to the family to get home as soon as possible because they are all going to a party that evening. It might be better to wait until Monday to tell you that the job is not yet done due to external circumstances…

Force majeure? An outsider would probably disagree, but your team member is convinced that it was an unfortunate series of events and he or she is not to blame for the delay. What does this mean for you as a project manager? You are in trouble!

In practical terms, because you invested in the worst-case scenario and are still left without any tangible results. Emotionally, because you were too naïve and trusting. Your employee took advantage of the safety and space that you provided. That is how it often goes with the safety margins of project activities. Subconsciously, these are used as *flexibility margins*, because the buffer eliminates people's sense of urgency. They still believe in their best-case estimate and will only start to feel the pressure when the safety margin is used up. By then, there is no more room to allow for unexpected setbacks (see figure 6.9). The student syndrome affects us all…

 Do you ever unconsciously take away your employees' sense of urgency as a project manager?

The execution is even more important than the estimate

As you can see, making estimates is important, but the execution determines the actual success. As a project manager you are doubly at risk if there are unforeseen problems with the execution of a task. You gave your employee an extra margin that cost both time and money, yet the task was still not completed on time.

So, is there any point at all in making estimates? Fortunately, there is. You just have to do more to reap the rewards. This does not have to negatively affect the employee in any way and you can even increase the support you receive from your team members. I have detailed this approach in figure 6.10. First of all, it is advisable to replace your observing attitude with an active one. Although there is nothing wrong with creating numerical insight

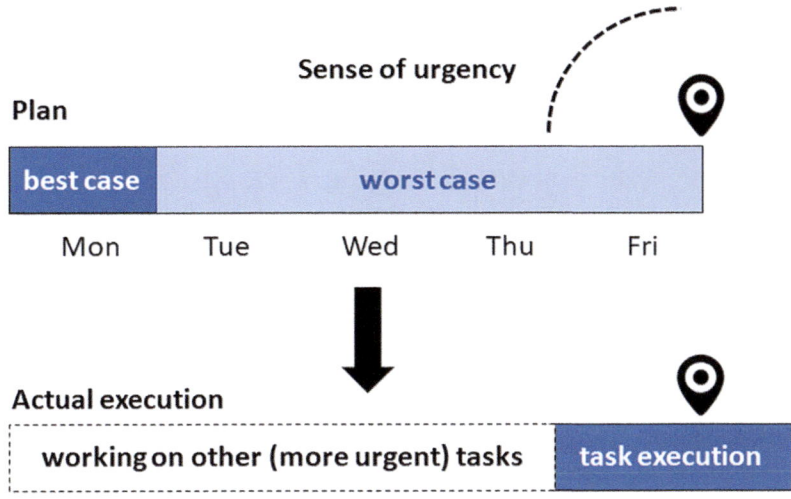

Figure 6.9   Working with safety margins can actually increase the chance of a delay

into the differences between the best- and worst-case scenarios, why stop there? Ask your team member about the reasons for any major differences and work together to define *risk-reducing actions* to lower the worst-case estimate. Add these actions to the PBS/WBS. Think of, for example, a verification moment to safeguard input beforehand or providing support during the execution of the risky part of a task.

It is also advisable to not afford the executor the remaining safety margin in advance. Instead, you should only do so in the event of an actual setback. *Turn individual buffers into a project buffer that you are the owner of* and place this buffer at the end of the project phase (or the project), rather than after the activity. This is an important conclusion arising out of Goldratt's theory and we will come back to it later. Finally, you can do what we have already discussed in section 3.5: *develop earlier interim results for your activity*. This helps you to prevent the student syndrome while also stimulating confrontation and communication in the interim.

Why every minus counts

I remember it all too well: I walked into the office of the (then) head of product development at a time when project after project missed its deadline. Turbulence in the market resulted in many changes to the scope of projects. The chief of product development was desperate and asked me why we never managed to finish a project on time. He was one of those people who prefer to rationally focus on the facts. I sometimes got the feeling he even tried to understand human behavior through mathematics. I told him: "Unfortunately, minuses

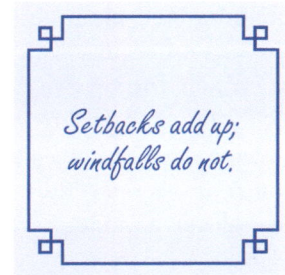

Setbacks add up; windfalls do not.

add up in project management, while pluses don't. We will have to be much more careful throughout the entire project that our progress is not unknowingly lost to all kinds of small setbacks or scope changes."

1 Three-point estimation			

WBS (activity)	Best case	Worst case	Most likely
Activity A1.1-1	8	16	10
Activity A1.1-2	6	20	10
Activity A1.1-3	3	6	4
Activity A1.1-4	4	6	6

2 Define risk-reducing measures with the employee

3 Turn individual buffers into a project buffer

4 Develop earlier interim results per activity

Figure 6.10   From estimate to successful realization in four steps

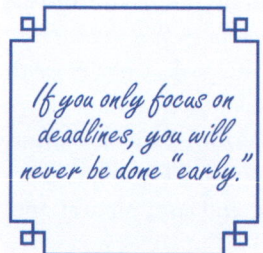

If you only focus on deadlines, you will never be done "early."

What I meant was that all activities in a project are basically interconnected. When an activity misses its deadline, it affects all subsequent activities. If one activity after another runs too long, you can add up the delays. However, what happens when activities are finished before their deadline? Will the next activity start sooner? Probably not, because the person responsible will follow his or her own original plan. Furthermore, it is not uncommon for people who finish their work early to not say anything. Why is that? Because they will not be rewarded for their efforts and may actually be punished. "You are done already? Why don't you help clean up someone else's mess then?" Finishing early might also give others the impression that your estimates are inaccurate, which means you are given less time in the future. Instead, we choose to hand in our results right on time. As a project manager, I therefore preferred to keep a very close eye on the project's progress from the very start, because every "minus" added up to the delay of the end date. I quickly discovered just how much time was lost during the early phases of a project if I was not careful. Without any of us realizing it, minuses were adding up quickly!

This insight was based on my own common sense. Later, I read about it in a more complete context in Goldratt's *Critical Chain*. It became clear to me that *estimates always contain a safety margin* and that this does not necessarily benefit the success of the project – no matter how counterintuitive that sounds. Even worse, I found that setting a deadline made people focus only on that deadline. They stopped trying to deliver their results any earlier. Note that this does not necessarily indicate any malicious intent on the part of the employees, they probably let more urgent tasks come first. For that reason alone, it is dangerous to direct a project by focusing solely on milestones with interim periods of, for example, eight weeks. As with the previous "Friday deadline" example at the beginning of this section, all team members will use up their eight weeks and the project will end up "just" missing its deadline…

How should you deal with this? When we talk about *heartbeat* in chapter 8, we will see that it is important to focus on aspects other than the deadline during the execution phase. However, you can already take a valuable step while developing your plan by replacing the individual buffers with a shared project buffer. It helps to prevent any reserves from being used up during each separate activity. The project buffer is managed by the project manager and it will only be used in the event of a setback. *Note that employees should not be punished for failing in that case, because they did their best to stick to a challenging plan without a buffer.*

Figure 6.10 shows project members completing their activities as a kind of relay race. The activities are scheduled so close to one another (based on the best-case or most likely scenario) that the set deadlines become less relevant than proper coordination between team members. As with a real relay race, communicating with your team members is more important than recording start and end times with safety margins. The project manager ends up with a team that plans to be done earlier than the set deadline and tailors the communication accordingly. Instead of "when will the project be done?" the important question becomes "how large is the project buffer now?" If the remaining buffer is twenty days and there are no unforeseen setbacks along the way, the project will be finished twenty days before the deadline.

Remember that it is not easy for a project manager to properly manage this process. You must be able to explain that giving up their personal buffers will ultimately benefit the project members. It can help to "give back" part of the remaining project buffer to the team at the end of the project as time in which to do some fun and interesting work. Win-win! It is also important not to be overly naïve towards the project board and your stakeholders. There is no guarantee that they are ready to accept this method. It is not uncommon for a project board to

Do not be more transparent than the other party can handle.

take the project buffer away from the project manager and use it for different purposes (i.e. by shortening the project deadline). *Whether you have to be transparent about the available buffer to the project board depends on the board's maturity level and the degree of trust between you.* I recommend only being as transparent as the other party can handle!

The Agile Scrum process

What about the buffers in Scrum? Everything I mentioned above is basically inherent in the Scrum process itself. Among other things, the power of Agile lies in the fact that not all functions on the product backlog are "must haves." There is room to accommodate setbacks, which creates a project buffer during the final few sprints. Additionally, the daily stand-up meetings ensure that the relay-race effect occurs automatically. Every day, the team members decide what they will work on based upon the best-case scenario. *There is no need to set deadlines during the sprint, so there are no safety margins or individual buffers that eliminate the sense of urgency people feel.* Consequently, if there are any setbacks along the way, this simply means that fewer backlog items will be completed during the sprint. That is fine, as long as the setbacks do not outweigh the size of the optional backlog items in the final few sprints (the buffer).

Scrum results in project buffers and relay-race behavior automatically.

In traditional organizations that are using the Scrum approach for the first time, I sometimes hear people say that it goes against their idea of commitment if functionality can be put off until the next sprint just like that. I try to alleviate this concern by explaining that Scrum is able to create room for (extra) optional items as a project buffer because the sprints do not include individual buffers. The team members will strive for the maximum result without any reserves and the more successful they are, the more extra functionality they will be able to implement during the final sprints. Management's acceptance of this fact can be a slow process that is quite similar to the discussion from the previous section on transparent communication about the project buffer. Once again, do not be naïve and remember that a change process like this proceeds quickest when you emphasize the good results of the Scrum process. Focus on the positives!

6.3   Steps 5 to 8: Drawing up the sketch with the team

How can you turn all this into a concrete plan? Simply by adding two columns to the existing PBS/WBS table under effort: *plan* and *buffer*. *Plan* is the estimate that you will ultimately use in your planning documents. If you used the tips from figure 6.10, this is not the worst-case estimate and you have added additional risk-reducing actions to the PBS/WBS. You reserve all or part of the difference between the numbers in the *worst-case (WC)* and *plan* columns for the (project) *buffer*. Of course, you are free to make choices here. This will depend on the type of activity, the executor's preference, the pressure on the project budget and your own preference. Figure 6.11 shows the three-point estimation for several tasks from project Roller Coaster, as well as the values that are ultimately selected for plan and buffer. Note that no hours are allocated to review activities, because these hours are bundled together and budgeted as a separate group task in the final plan.

PBS level 1-3 (deliverables)	WBS (activity)	Other costs	Size activity	Effort (hours)				
				BC	WC	ML	Plan	Buffer
Specification and design								
System architecture								
- **System concept**								
	Create concept study with different roller coaster concepts		3 concepts	16	32	20	20	12
	Analyze roller coaster concepts		6 key parameters	16	24	20	20	4
	Review concept study						0	
	Present concept study to customer and select concept			4	6	3	4	0
	Update concept study based on concept choice			4	6	4	4	0
- **System architecture**								
	Define system architecture		32 pages	32	50	40	40	10
	Review system architecture						0	
	Update & release system architecture			8	12	8	8	0
- **Critical parameters per subsystem**								
	Define critical parameters		4-8 crit. param.	4	6	4	4	0
	Define budget allocation per subsystem		4-8 par/11 subsys.	8	8	8	8	0
	Review and communicate budget allocation						0	
Track								
- **Track modeling (incl. validation)**								
	Create track model to simulate system performance		60% reuse	12	20	16	16	4
	Validate track model (based on existing roller coasters)		2 roller coasters	8	12	8	8	4
	Perform parameter study to understand system behavior		6-10 parameters	12	16	12	12	0
- **Track design**								
	Create track design (CAD model)		Historical data	32	48	40	40	8
	Check system performance with track model simulations		Historical data	16	32	24	20	8
	Perform mechanical stress analysis		Historical data	16	24	20	20	4
	Perform FMEA on track design			16	24	16	16	0
	Create track test protocols and quality check plan			8	12	8	8	0
	Create track maintenance and spare parts documentation			8	10	8	8	0
	Review track design						0	
	Update & release track design			8	8	8	8	0
Sound system (buy)								
- **Sound system design (by supplier)**								
	Receive sound system design (from supplier)	€ 115,000					0	
	Review sound system design			8	8	8	8	0
	Approve sound system design			4	4	4	4	0

Figure 6.11 PBS/WBS table with estimates and chosen results for plan and buffer

This results in an hour budget that is challenging, supported by the team members, avoids the student syndrome and allows room for setbacks because of the project buffers. Attentive readers may have noticed the *other costs* column. This column was added to meet the 100% rule of the PBS/WBS. Ultimately, we want to be able to derive the entire cost of the project from the table. When all deliverables and activities are included, the personnel costs can easily be derived from the hour budget. However, outsourced deliverables are not paid for based on internal hours. By including the costs of outsourcing in a separate column, these costs can also be represented in the table.

Timeline, allocation of people and resources, and costs

From here, it is an easy step to the deliverable-based sketch with the team. By adding columns with week numbers and months, you can add a time grid to the existing information. This is done for part of project Roller Coaster in figure 6.12. The table also includes three columns that are concerned with translating effort into duration:

- The executor (who);
- The allocated capacity;
- The duration (with Scrum, the duration per sprint is, of course, a given and it is instead about which backlog items have been allocated to which sprint).

You can calculate the duration after writing down who will work on the deliverable and with what capacity. By rounding up to weeks, you can draw a bar in the time grid for each deliverable. If you copy the allocated capacity in the time-grid, you can add it up at the bottom of the plan (separately for each discipline, if you wish). *By doing so, you create an overview of all deliverables, their respective order, the delivery moments, the resource allocation, the budgeted number of hours and the costs.* Note that figure 6.12 only shows the relevant columns in order to improve the table's legibility. This means that the columns used to estimate size and effort, as mentioned in previous sections, are also included in the Excel file, but they are hidden in this figure. *The goal is to record all data in a single comprehensive overview.* You can find the complete sketch with the team of project Roller Coaster at www. roelwessels.com.

The sketch with the team combines speed, detail and comprehensiveness.

As you can see, the sketch with the team is based on detailed information, yet it does not show any more information than necessary. *That is why only deliverables are shown and activities are left out.* This keeps things practical, modifiable and suitable for both traditional and Agile planning methods. The information pertaining to the activities is included as summed effort for the deliverable in question (not for Scrum, of course, where the size is determined based on story points). You will only need the activity level once the execution phase begins. It will be included in the detailed plan that is to come, *but not until the sketch with the team has resolved the key points of discussion concerning the project.*

The figure shows that *the 100% principle is essential.* Consider the production of the prototype of the roller coaster car, which is handled by external suppliers. If you neglect to include these deliverables in your own plan, you would lose sight of their costs, timing, and dependencies. By including the costs as part of *other costs* and listing the deliverables with a capacity of 0 FTE, outsourced work can be fully included in your plan without issue. You are also free to expand the table as you see fit with columns for deliverable properties, e.g. the target values of the critical parameters. This will turn the sketch with the team into a valuable project database.

PBS level 1-3 (deliverables)	Other Costs	Effort [hours] plan	Who?	Cap [FTE]	Dura-tion [days]
Specification and design					
Track					
- Track performance specification		16	ME2	1	2
- Track modeling (incl. validation)		36	ME2	1	5
- Track design		120	ME2	1	15
Cars					
- Car performance specification		16	ME4	1	2
- Car exterior design		52	ME5	1	7
- Car rolling chassis design		92	ME4	1	12
- Car seats and safety restraints design		72	ME6	1	9
- Car prototype test		100	TE1	1	13
- Car reliability lifetime test bench design		40	ME6	1	5
- Car safety test		60	TE2	1	8
- Car accelerated lifetime / reliability test		60	TE3	0.25	30
- Car specification and design update		16	ME4	1	2
Software					
- Software performance specification		28	Swarch	0.5	7
- Software architecture		108	Swarch	1	14
- Software sprint plan		16	Swarch	1	2
- Prepare next sprints		850	Swarch	0.5	213
- Sprint 1 (feasibility + FB functionality)		960	Swteam	5	24
- Sprint 2 (basic functions controls + photo upload)		960	Swteam	5	24
- Sprint 3 (all functions controls)		960	Swteam	5	24
- Sprint 4 (start installation @site)		576	Swteam	3	24
- Sprint 5 (installation issues solved)		576	Swteam	3	24
- Sprint 6 (full functionality release)		576	Swteam	3	24
- Sprint 7 (test issues solved)		576	Swteam	3	24
- Sprint 8 (start system optimization)		384	Swteam	2	24
- Sprint 9 (optimization test issues solved)		384	Swteam	2	24
- Sprint 10 (final release for acceptance)		384	Swteam	2	24
Facebook connection					
- Facebook connection performance specification		20	Swarch	0.5	5
- Design and feasibility Wi-Fi check-in		20	Swarch	0.5	5
- Design and feasibility photo synchro		36	Swarch	0.5	9
- Design and feasibility photo upload		20	Swarch	0.5	5
Production & assembly					
Car prototype production	€1,150,000	80			
Track production by supplier					
- Car exterior production (buy)	€18,000	37	supplier	0	5
- Car chassis production (buy)	€35,000	39	supplier	0	5
- Car seats and safety restraints production (buy)	€22,000	41	supplier	0	5
- Integration and assembly car prototype		72	workshop	5	2
Car final series production (10 + 2 spare)					
- Car exterior production (buy)	€84,000	78	supplier	0	5
- Car chassis production (buy)	€150,000	78	supplier	0	5
- Car seats and safety restraints production (buy)	€60,000	78	supplier	0	5
- Integration and assembly 12 cars		272	workshop	5	7
Installation & test run					
Track basic installation					
- Steel supports installation (buy)	€170,000		supplier	0	
- Track installation (buy)	€240,000		supplier	0	
Totaal	**€1,929,000**	4236	13125		

Figure 6.12   Sketch with the team for part of project Roller Coaster

The sketch with the team also shows that Agile software activities can easily be combined with waterfall mechanical activities. All you have to do is choose whether to place the sprints

With just a few clever choices, you can combine the Agile and waterfall methods.

– which combine design, realization and testing – under "specification & design" or "production & assembly." Given that the key part of software development falls under design, I usually opt for the former. Note that you can still include the results of the sprints under production & assembly as well, as long as you clarify that these do not represent extra activities. You can do so by assigning an owner, but not a capacity in hours. Furthermore, I usually give each sprint a name that clearly indicates what functionality it will produce. This also serves to clarify the relationship with the hardware interim results they are to be tested with. Sprint 1 and sprint 2, for example, result in the software functionality that can be used to test concept choices and the Facebook link "on the left side of the V." If you do not want to fully adhere to the Scrum process, you can still plan the iterations in a similar manner. However, instead of using the name "sprint," it may be advisable to choose a name like *delivery pack*. That means you are not restricted by the fixed sprint duration, while still clarifying that you plan to iteratively deliver completed packs of subfunctionality.

Determining the critical path

When we developed the sketch with the team, we used our common sense to translate the PBS/WBS structure into a time schedule. Later, when you are drawing up the detailed plan, you will utilize a planning tool to help you with this. Does that mean you do not need to know anything at all about flow diagram techniques? Actually, you do. Even if you do not use it actively, it is advisable to practice the use of a methodology such as a *precedence diagram* at least once. This teaches you to understand how your planning tool "thinks" and how, for instance, the critical path is determined.

The precedence diagram is an *activity on node* network planning technique. This means that activities are represented as nodes and the dependencies between them are visualized as arrows running between the nodes. For each node, the following is determined based on the duration (D): the earliest start (ES), the earliest finish (EF), the latest start (LS), the latest finish (LF) and the total slack or float (S). You fill out the precedence diagram by first calculating the ES and EF (top) of all activities, starting with the first activity on the left and gradually moving to the right from one activity to the next. You fill out the bottom of the diagram (LS and LF) in a similar manner, except that you start with the last activity and end at the beginning. You can determine the total slack per activity by calculating LS-ES or LF-EF. Figure 6.13 contains an example of a precedence diagram.

You determine the *critical path* by marking all activities whose total slack equals 0. The total slack is the amount of extra time an activity may take without this affecting the lead time of the project as a whole. It is essential that a project manager knows the project's critical path. This is the project's bottleneck and it should not be overlooked. Planning tools (see section 6.4) automatically calculate and show the critical path.

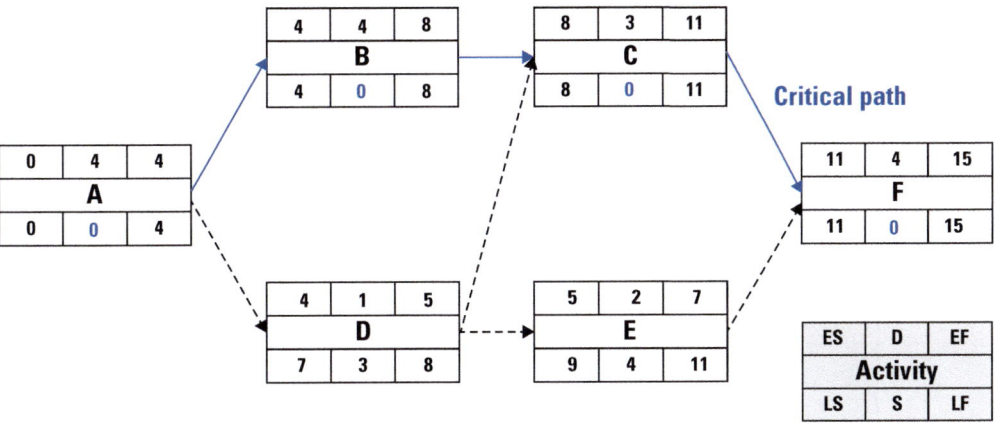

Figure 6.13   An example of a precedence diagram

Visualizing challenges with the sketch with the team
Making the final sketch with the team (figure 6.12) is something project managers do on their own or together with their team. In any case, compiling everything for the first time will certainly bring challenges to light. It is common for the team's bottom-up estimates to exceed the top-down project budget or the desired lead time. You may also hear suppliers say that they cannot deliver at the right time or for the right price. When you finish the first version of the sketch with the team, it is therefore advisable to meet with the key members of your team and work together to come up with actions to shorten lead times and reduce costs. Think of, for example, implementing parallel processes, developing smarter solutions, identifying alternate design choices, listing additional wishes to present to suppliers, submitting proposed scope changes to the client, etc.

The sketch with the team is a tremendously useful tool that you can use to identify a project's key challenges at an early stage and tackle them together with your team. This allows you to proactively manage your stakeholders' expectations long before an official detailed plan has been drawn up. The overview of delegation and coordination opportunities in the time leading up to the sketch with the team is summarized in figure 6.14. You might have missed these opportunities if you had jumped straight into developing a complex detailed plan. In that case, you would have wasted a few precious weeks on submarine behavior.

6.4   Step 9: Tips & tricks for the detailed plan

By finishing the sketch with the team, you have created an important foundation for your project's success. You have given everyone involved in the project peace of mind and gathered enough information to optimally manage your stakeholders. *This is another step on the way from reactive to proactive to influencing.*

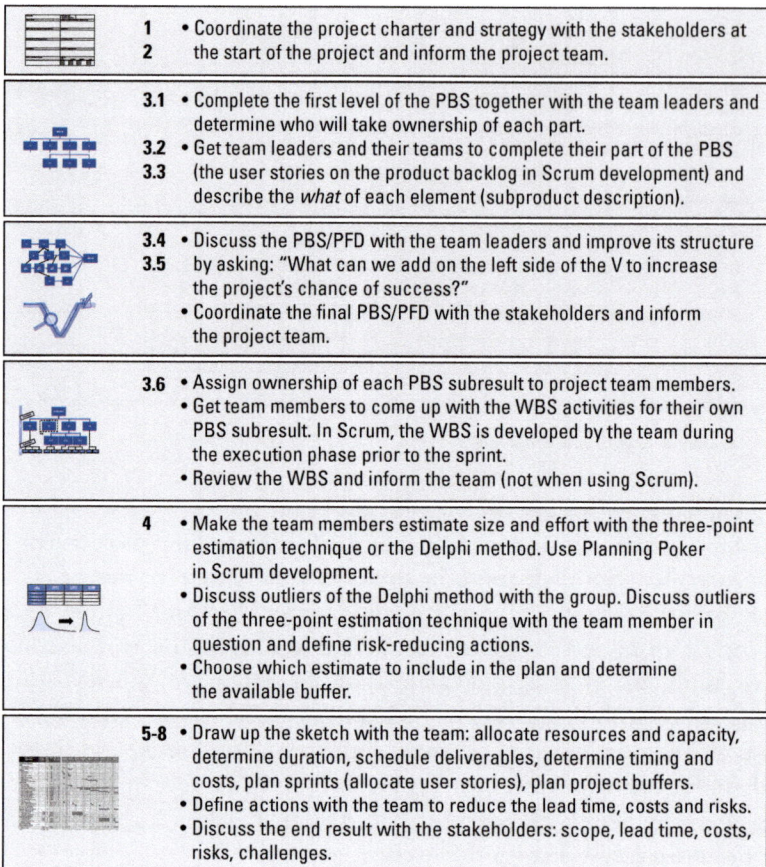

	1 **2**	• Coordinate the project charter and strategy with the stakeholders at the start of the project and inform the project team.
	3.1 **3.2** **3.3**	• Complete the first level of the PBS together with the team leaders and determine who will take ownership of each part. • Get team leaders and their teams to complete their part of the PBS (the user stories on the product backlog in Scrum development) and describe the *what* of each element (subproduct description).
	3.4 **3.5**	• Discuss the PBS/PFD with the team leaders and improve its structure by asking: "What can we add on the left side of the V to increase the project's chance of success?" • Coordinate the final PBS/PFD with the stakeholders and inform the project team.
	3.6	• Assign ownership of each PBS subresult to project team members. • Get team members to come up with the WBS activities for their own PBS subresult. In Scrum, the WBS is developed by the team during the execution phase prior to the sprint. • Review the WBS and inform the team (not when using Scrum).
	4	• Make the team members estimate size and effort with the three-point estimation technique or the Delphi method. Use Planning Poker in Scrum development. • Discuss outliers of the Delphi method with the group. Discuss outliers of the three-point estimation technique with the team member in question and define risk-reducing actions. • Choose which estimate to include in the plan and determine the available buffer.
	5-8	• Draw up the sketch with the team: allocate resources and capacity, determine duration, schedule deliverables, determine timing and costs, plan sprints (allocate user stories), plan project buffers. • Define actions with the team to reduce the lead time, costs and risks. • Discuss the end result with the stakeholders: scope, lead time, costs, risks, challenges.

Figure 6.14   Delegation and coordination opportunities in the time leading up to the sketch with the team

Now it is time for the other 90% of the project initiation phase: drawing up the architecture, detailing the technical specifications, conducting feasibility studies, selecting suppliers, engaging in contract negotiations, setting up the project organization and developing the *detailed plan* and the *project management plan*.

In the detailed plan, you will continue your work on the WBS activity level, which you need in order to properly manage the execution phase (except for Scrum subprojects). The existing PBS/WBS structure can be reused here. Instead of starting over, you copy it directly to your planning tool. After all, the PBS/WBS structure represents the technical and organizational context of your project. It is complete and – because of the discussions based on the sketch with the team – mature and stable. *The contours of the project are clear, so you can now start filling in the blanks.*

Special software, e.g. Microsoft Project, is commonly used to develop and manage a detailed plan. Such a tool can present the plan as a network diagram (PERT), but it is most commonly used in the *Gantt chart view*, in which each task is shown on a separate row as a time bar. Although many users take an introductory course, they are still unsure about how

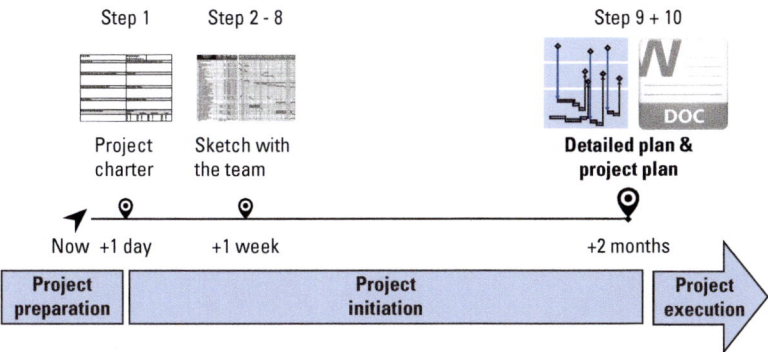

Figure 6.15 Project preparation and initiation for the project manager

to make optimal use of the tool in their own work processes. Just as mastering Word does not automatically make someone a good writer, knowing how to use a planning tool will not instantly make you a great planner.

Many users of planning tools claim to struggle with the following challenges:

- They get caught up in the details and work for the tool instead of the other way around;
- There are too many uncertainties, so it is not yet possible to develop a plan;
- There is no time to develop a detailed plan;
- Although a planning template exists, the organization lacks a clear vision on how to use it during projects;
- The detailed plan is never finished because changes are constantly being made;
- The detailed plan is developed but not used;
- The detailed plan does not help to gain the team's commitment;
- The detailed plan does not help with the communication with stakeholders.

> *Don't start working on the detailed plan until the key issues have been resolved.*

Added to this is the fact that all the interconnections often make a Gantt chart so complex that it is hard to keep an overview. You can only see a small part of the project schedule onscreen at any one time and it sometimes feels like trying to read a book through a keyhole. This lack of overview only leads to more frustration. Who hasn't been in a situation where you, for instance, move an activity up three days, only to find out later that the project's end date has moved up two whole weeks…

 Do you work for your planning tool or does it work for you?

I have come up with three tips to make more effective use of your planning tool in your own work process. These tips result in the following benefits:

A. Detail and flexibility: *the level of detail should not become a hindrance and lead to a fear of updating.*

B. Simulation opportunities: *the detailed plan should be a model of the project and give you the opportunity to gain insight into the effects of alternatives.*

C. Communication tool for the team and the client: *the planning tool should be a communication tool for multiple audiences and form the foundation for tracking and control.*

D. Showing problem areas, not just consequences: *a schedule with interdependent tasks will automatically pass on a delay to the subsequent activity, but is that really what you want as a project manager?*

E. The project manager makes the decisions, not the tool: *the tool must provide the correct insights and enable the project manager to take optimal, effective action when necessary.*

Although the detailed plan for project Roller Coaster was created using MS Project, the method used in the following three tips works with any kind of planning software.

Tip 1: stop connecting!

Stop connecting? That is an odd thing to say. Creating connections is one of the core principles of any planning tool. There exists a certain order between activities and by recording the first activity in time, all subsequent activities are automatically recorded as well. Whenever one activity moves, the rest moves along with it. That is both logical and desirable.

However, as your detailed plan expands, the chances are that these connections turn into an indecipherable jumble which can impact your project in unpredictable ways. Moving tasks on your screen may have unwanted consequences for tasks that you are not currently looking at. I therefore recommend only connecting activities *directly* if they cannot be carried out

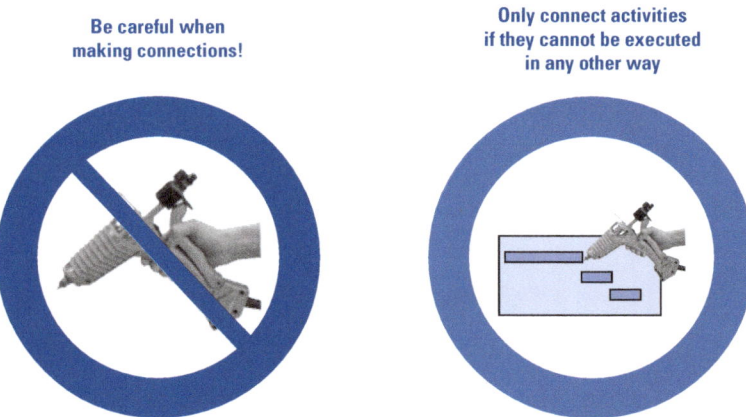

Figure 6.16   Only connect activities in the detailed plan that cannot be executed in any other way

together in any other way. Think of, for example, preparing, drawing up, reviewing and updating a document or activities that can only be conducted by one person, and, therefore, will always take place in the same order.

Make your detailed plan flexible by linking it to a project interface.

"Won't this create floating blocks of activities," you might ask? The answer is yes, and that is something we don't want – and yet we do. We will connect these floating blocks to each other at the "top of the detailed plan" as seen in figure 6.17. By not using the rows at the top of the planning tool as tasks, but rather as *input* or *output*, you can create a *control panel* of sorts. You can use this to manually control the starting points of the blocks and visualize the ends of the blocks as results at the top of the detailed plan. Of course, you can also connect these inputs and outputs directly in this control panel. This has the same effect as doing so at the bottom of the detailed plan, except the former solution is much clearer. On top of that, you can easily sever or replace the connections between the blocks of activities.

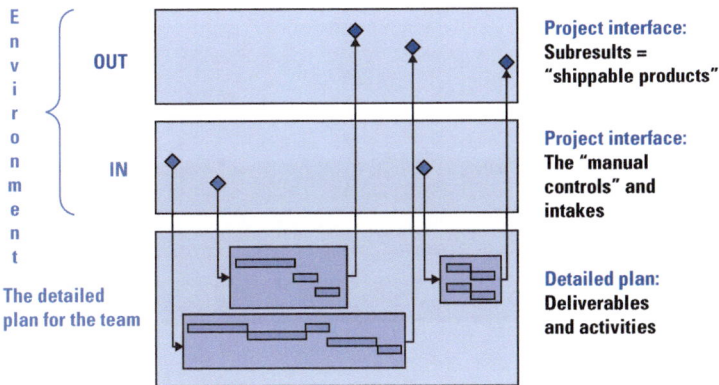

Figure 6.17   Create controls and readout instruments at the top of the detailed plan

This allows you to turn an entirely interconnected plan into something much clearer that is also easier to modify and update. The inputs and outputs also reflect the relationship to the outside world via the *project interface*. For example, you could add suppliers' delivery times or the *intakes* from other projects to the inputs. For the outputs, the trick is particularly to connect those moments from the detailed plan that can be seen as deliveries to the outside world, i.e. subresults that, for example, generate feedback. I therefore tend to refer to these as *shippable products*, in line with the name of the results of the sprints in Scrum.

The project interface helps with simulation and communication.

The individual controls allow you to easily analyze alternative scenarios. You can, for instance, study the effects on the project's lead time by placing two consecutive processes in parallel. Of course, this also impacts the deployed capacity, which the resource overview will immediately reflect. You can also take a stronger position when a supplier reports that the completion of a deliverable is delayed by a week. Being able to tell the supplier exactly how this delay affects a major milestone or the project's end date is far more effective than only stating that such delays are undesirable.

The principle of connecting points from the detailed plan to the project interface can also be used to compare the project's status to the goals. Create two rows per milestone, connect one row to the milestone moment in the detailed plan and fill in the agreed-upon delivery time in the other row. Similarly, you can provide insight into the verification moments of the critical parameters. This leads to the situation shown in figure 6.18: the detailed plan is hidden under the hood, while the top of the plan acts as the dashboard and steering wheel. In the project interface, you can then specify your communication with the outside world for each target audience by including different subresults in the list for each stakeholder. You can also choose how to present the results, e.g. a milestone with or without a project buffer. Finally, you can sort intakes per supplier, which makes it easy to monitor them on a weekly basis via telephone. Go to www.roelwessels.com to see exactly how this method has been applied to the detailed plan of project Roller Coaster.

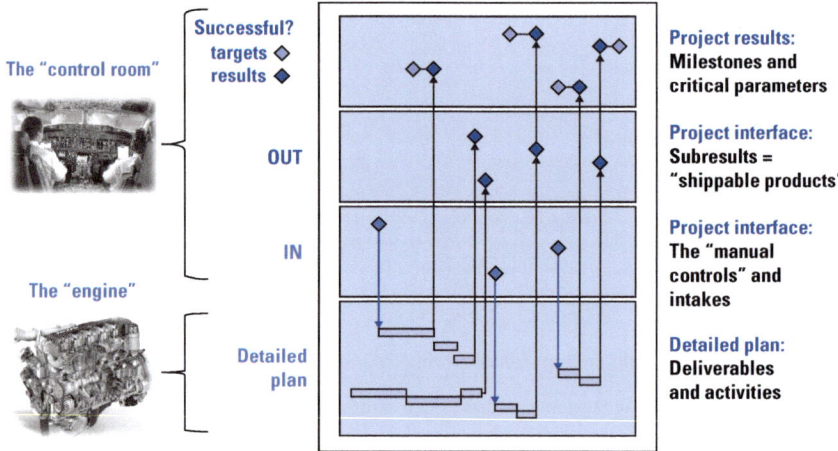

Figure 6.18   Control and report from the "control room" of your detailed plan

The project interface is also a way to allow subproject leaders to manage their own detailed plan, without this affecting the connections between subprojects. All they have to do is coordinate their respective interfaces (as each other's client or supplier). The dotted lines in figure 6.19 show the dependencies between each subproject leader's plan that have to be coordinated. This keeps you from having to record everything in one giant unmanageable detailed plan. It also ensures that the ownership of a subproject lies in the hands of the responsible subproject leader, not in yours.

Tip 2: identify the problem areas, not the consequences
There are many other advantages to connecting tactical points via the project interface instead of keeping them hidden in the detailed plan. Let's say you are working on a project with a lead time of one year. During the first week of the project there is a three-day delay

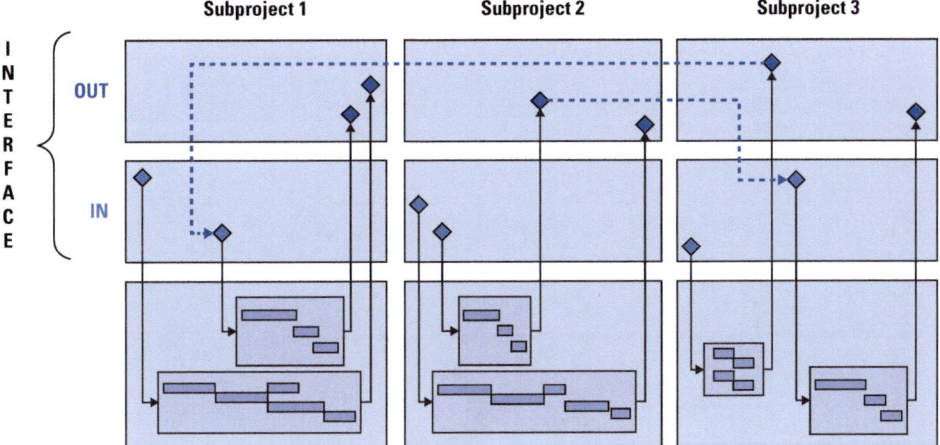

Figure 6.19   Synchronizing separate planning schedules via the project interface

on the critical path. What does your planning tool tell you? That's right: the project's end date will also be delayed by three days. We cannot blame the tool for this, because that would be an accurate prediction if no measures are taken. Therein lies the rub, however; of course, you are going to take action! You have more than three hundred days to make up for the three days that you lost! Even though you as a project manager may understand what the planning tool is telling you, most clients will not. They will not be happy if project control reports that the project has already fallen behind schedule after just one week. Surely, that is not what you want?

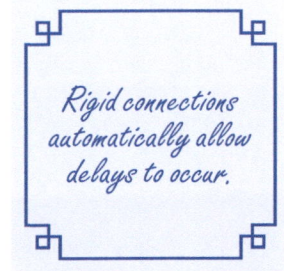

Rigid connections automatically allow delays to occur.

By working via the project interface, you can kill two birds with one stone. Figure 6.20 shows what happens if there is a delay at the start of a project that consists of a development process and a testing process. When everything is connected, the planning tool will report that the project's end date will be moved back because of the delay (situation A). Organizations often (subconsciously) accept delays at the start of a project, e.g. by focusing mainly on deadlines and wasting the available safety margin. We have already covered this in section 6.2. People believe there is plenty of time left to resolve the problem (later). The result is that the test department has to make up for the delay at the end of the project. The organization's leadership is not very helpful, but neither is the planning tool itself. It reports that all connected activities after the delay will also start and end later. Before you know it, the people involved in the later stages of the project have accepted and incorporated the delay!

By removing the automatic connection from a number of essential milestones in the project interface, you keep the tool from automatically accepting the delay. Even better, you can get the tool to show you where the problem lies, with the development activities (variant B). As a project manager, you can report that there was a setback at the start of the project, but

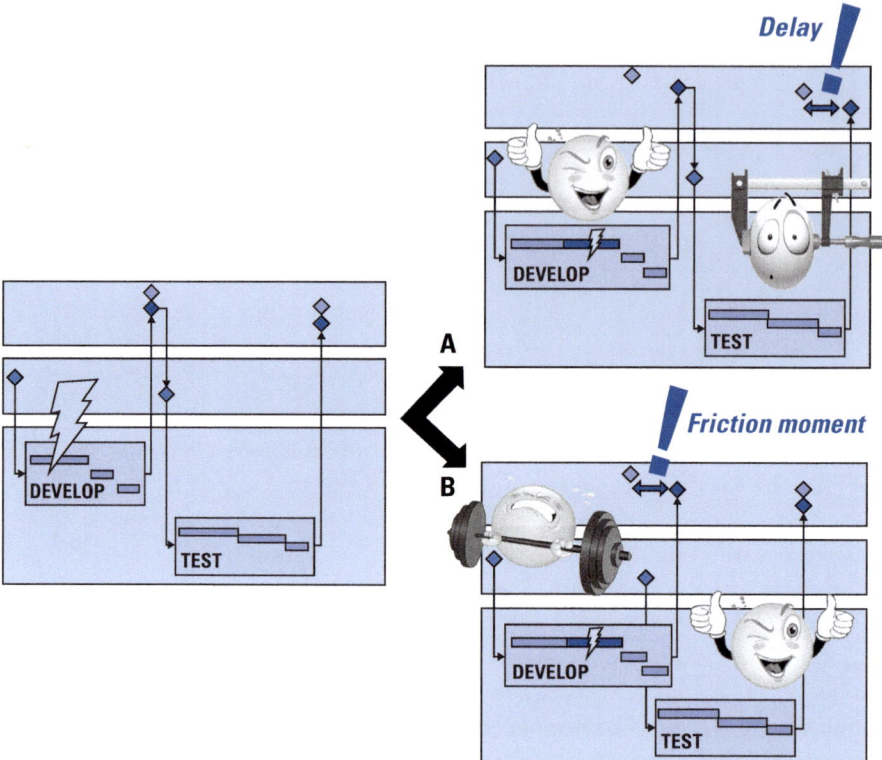

Figure 6.20   Identify problem areas when there is still time to act

Replace a delay at the end by a friction moment during the project.

that you have not yet accepted this delay. It, therefore, does not represent a delay to the project end date, but rather a *friction moment between the development and test phases.* Instead of accepting the delay, you collaborate with the team in question to come up with actions that will allow you to resolve the issue where you should - during the development phase itself. As you can see, the way in which you utilize the planning tool can keep "minuses" from stacking up (unnoticed) during the start of the project. We will come back to this topic in chapter 8.

Tip 3: avoid the "group photo" effect

What happens when a group photo is first shown to the group in question? Do people think: "Oh, what a nice picture. The group looks great." I do not believe so. Most people's first instinct is to look for themselves in the picture.

The same effect occurs when you show people an extensive *Gantt chart.* It contains so many time bars with the names of executors written in them that you cannot expect to get a proper answer to the question of whether people believe in the plan. All they are doing is trying to find their own tasks, which can be quite difficult in such an overview. How can you improve communication of the detailed plan to your team members? The answer may surprise you: in the form of a to-do shopping list! It is okay – and even extremely useful – to do so at this stage.

Personally, I export the (updated) detailed plan in MS Project to Excel every week. I then filter the tasks to be carried out using a standard layout. Next, I sort the tasks by their delivery moments, preferably in the form of a week number. Figure 6.21 shows an example of such a shopping list. It has been filtered for a single team member, the architect. Furthermore, most planning tools allow you to add additional "customized" columns, which you can use to assign other properties to the tasks, e.g. their respective subproject, sprint, client, etc. This lets you create shopping lists that you filter using these properties.

The shopping list finally comes in handy.

Planned finish	WBS	Deliverable	Activity	Allocation	Planned start	Realized finish	Status
2019.24	1.1	Summary 1\	Task 1	Architect	2019.23	2019.25	FINAL
2019.24	1.6	Summary 1\	Task 6	Architect	2019.24	2019.30	FINAL
2019.25	1.2	Summary 1\	Task 2	Architect	2019.25	2019.25	FINAL
2019.25	1.4	Summary 1\	Task 4	Architect	2019.25	2019.25	FINAL
2019.26	1.3	Summary 1\	Task 3	Architect	2019.25	2019.26	FINAL
2019.26	1.7	Summary 1\	Task 7	Architect	2019.25	2019.26	FINAL
2019.27	1.5	Summary 1\	Task 5	Architect	2019.25	2019.30	FINAL
2019.32	2.1	Summary 1\	Task 1	Architect	2019.27		
2019.33	2.5	Summary 1\	Task 4	Architect	2019.33		
2019.34	2.6	Summary 1\	Task 5	Architect	2019.33		
2019.35	2.2	Summary 1\	Task 2	Architect	2019.33		
2019.36	2.8	Summary 1\	Task 7	Architect	2019.34		
2019.37	2.4	Summary 1\	Task 3	Architect	2019.36		
2019.37	2.7	Summary 1\	Task 6	Architect	2019.35		

Figure 6.21   Extraction of tasks for a selected audience

An extraction like this contains everything you need to work towards the project's end goal in much the same way as a TomTom: a sorted countdown list that shows the remaining activities and deliverables at all times. Under "Status," you see the word "*FINAL.*" It is used when a task is 100% complete. In chapter 9, *The blind check*, I will explain why I prefer to show tasks as being either 0% or 100% completed. I ignore everything in between because this is generally little more than wishful thinking. The only way to strike a task off the list is, therefore, by completing it entirely…

6.5   Step 10: Project management plan and go

After all that has come before, the final step – writing the project management plan – is simply a matter of doing it. All essential discussion points have already been taken care of during the development of the project charter, the sketch with the team and the detailed plan. Drawing up the project management plan is, therefore, primarily about writing and structuring everything into a single document.

Project management plan (PMP)

How comprehensive your project management plan will be depends upon the scope of your project, your own preferences, the wishes of your stakeholders and the organizational culture. For smaller projects, you may not even have to draw up a document at all, you might simply include all relevant information in the quotation. You will have to weigh the time it takes to develop the PMP against the benefits of having a single clear document that helps with communication and execution during the project.

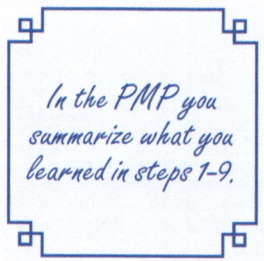

In the PMP you summarize what you learned in steps 1-9.

Figure 6.22 contains an overview of the elements of a project management plan. You can look at this in one of two ways: "Gee, I have to write down a lot of information" or "Wow, I have gathered a lot of information already!" The latter is absolutely true: all the information you need will already be available to you if you have followed the entire ten-step plan so far. This makes a huge difference. I remember how I struggled with the template of the project management plan during my first project. I spent two hours staring at the paragraph marked "intakes" without having a clue as to what I should write down there. I only learned later that you cannot write a project management plan by starting with an empty template. It is not about filling in the blanks. Rather, it is the final summary of your search for overview, structure and the appropriate actions to execute the project in such a manner that its goals can be realized.

Making the decision to fund

After finishing the project management plan, you will be ready to move on to the project execution phase. The project management plan is an important document for the project board when approving the *decision to fund* phase transition. Of course, all other deliverables from the initiation phase should also be completed, if only because they served as input for parts of the project management plan. When the decision to fund is made, the client and the contractor both accept certain responsibilities and the project execution can begin with confidence.

General
- Change history and authorization table

Introduction
- Project goals
- Project history
- Request from the client/stakeholders
- Scope and delineation of the project
- Reference documents

The assignment
- Project results to be delivered (possibly in the form of a Scrum product backlog)
- Priorities

Project approach and strategy
- Clients (internal and external) who receive deliverables
- Phasing and project approach (e.g. Scrum, V-model)
- List of all deliverables (PBS): client, project phase, delivery moment (must tie into the project interface of the detailed plan and the Scrum product backlog)
- Project intakes: supplier, project phase, delivery moment (must tie into the project interface of the detailed plan)
- Timing and costs per phase, total budget
- Assumptions

Organization
- Team composition
- Resource allocation on a monthly/weekly basis
- Project board composition
- Non-human resources (test systems, equipment, etc.)

Risk management
- Risk table: risk, probability, consequences, preventative measure, corrective measure if the risk should occur (including linking these activities to the detailed plan)

Detailed plan
- Reference to the detailed plan in the planning tool

Quality plan (sometimes as a separate document)
- Quality assurance method
- Review and evaluation method for results (including linking these quality activities to the detailed plan)

Configuration management plan (sometimes as a separate document)
- Releases (sprints) with scheduled deliverables
- Configuration items, identification, life cycle, control and auditing/reporting (including linking these CM activities to the detailed plan)

Communication plan (sometimes as a separate document)
- Internal meetings and communication method (when, to whom, via which medium)
- External meeting and communication method (when, to whom, via which medium)

Figure 6.22   The contents of a project management plan

Summary

- Determine the size of your project by conducting size and effort estimations on the WBS using the:
  - Delphi method (group of specialists);
  - Three-point estimation technique (individual team members).
- Your ultimate goal is to determine the *effort* (in hours), but you first need to understand the *size* of a task.
- Estimates depend on the context and partly consist of a safety margin to account for setbacks. Prevent your project from missing its deadline despite these safety margins with the following four steps:
  - Use the three-point estimation technique;
  - Add risk-reducing actions;
  - Replace individual buffers with a single project buffer;
  - Add interim results at an earlier stage.
- An Agile project can also be planned using the ten-step plan. The product backlog can be related to the PBS because they both contain subresults. You can determine the size of the user stories on the product backlog with Planning Poker (derived from the Delphi method), utilizing the relative story point unit. The WBS activity level is not recorded in the detailed plan in Scrum; instead, it is only determined by the team while defining the sprint backlog during the execution phase prior to each sprint.
- The sketch with the team provides a time schedule of all deliverables with resource allocation and costs. Use it to proactively manage your stakeholders' expectations and do not start working on the activity-based detailed plan until the key issues have been resolved.
- Use the following tips to make a detailed plan that will truly help you with the project execution:
  - Connect strategic points at the top of the plan via the project interface;
  - Identify problem areas, not just consequences, creating friction moments in your plan instead of blindly accepting delays;
  - Communicate the plan during the project execution phase by creating to-do shopping lists that you filter for each target audience.

7 The project motivator

- ◄ Why the difference between autonomous and controlled motivation is so important.
- ◄ You reap what you sow but how can you make the most of this?
- ◄ What are the the temporary project organization and the project board?
- ◄ Why a project manager is also a change manager.
- ◄ How creativity works and the ways in which you can utilize creativity-focused leadership.

Now that the plan has been developed and approved, "all" you have to do is execute it. When the execution is in the hands of a highly motivated team, a project manager possesses an important factor 10 element. Being surrounded by motivated people energizes you and creates the ultimate feeling of "smooth sailing": delegating tasks is easier, people's adaptability increases, they do not respond to challenges by saying "yes, but," and setbacks do not weigh as heavily. As a project leader, you therefore depend largely on the motivation of your team. Fortunately, you can affect this process in significant ways, as we will see later in this chapter.[11]

7.1 Deci and Ryan's self-determination theory

A great deal of research has been conducted into the field of motivation and engagement. One of the most influential theories is Edward Deci and Richard Ryan's *self-determination theory* (Deci & Ryan, 2002). In principle, this theory focuses on the motivation of students and the effectiveness of their learning process, but it can also be applied seamlessly to the motivation process during projects because it explains how people become excited and engaged.

According to Deci and Ryan, every human being has three basic psychological needs: the need for *competence*, *autonomy* and *relatedness*. The need for competence is about trusting in your own ability to perform your tasks well. The need for autonomy is about making your own choices and being able to operate with a certain degree of independence. The need for relatedness is about feeling accepted, appreciated and connected to your fellow project members. It also concerns your connection to the project goal, what you are doing it all for, for whom and why. Knowing all this, you can probably conclude that project managers have several ways to affect their team members' three basic needs. This means you are not only dependent on your team members' motivation, their motivation is also largely affected by

---

11 This chapter ties into the following competences from IPMA's ICB4: Governance, structures and processes, Power and interest, Culture and values, Personal communication, Relations and engagement, Leadership, Teamwork, Conflict and crisis, Resourcefulness, Negotiation, Organisation and information, Stakeholders, Change and transformation.

your actions. Project leaders who see themselves as *project motivators* from the very start of a project will hold an important key to success.

Autonomous motivation versus controlled motivation

If we delve a bit deeper into the subject of autonomy, we can make some explicit connections to topics already covered in the previous chapters. Deci and Ryan conducted a study among two groups of students. Both groups were presented with the same puzzle that they had to develop solutions for. The first group was paid for each solution they turned in. The second group was not promised a reward at all. After the assignment was completed, the test subjects were given the chance to keep playing. It turned out that the people in the first group were far less motivated to keep going than those in the second group. The rewards they received made them play for a reason other than their own enjoyment. They were no longer driven by their intrinsic motivation.

Motivating based on control destroys intrinsic motivation.

Curiosity and intrinsic motivation are naturally present in people, but they are also vulnerable. Project managers who want to perform well with their team will have to deal with that. At the start of a project, people will not be motivated instantly. In response, many supervisors tend to start pushing their employees to perform. However, the self-determination theory shows that being pushed is actually counterproductive. This is known as the *paradox of achievement*. Giving out rewards is another way to exert control over other people, which also reduces their autonomy to act on their intrinsic motivation and take responsibility.

Figure 7.1 presents a detailed overview of this topic. *Intrinsic motivation* is the ultimate goal. It is born purely out of one's interest in, and enjoyment of, the activity itself. Intrinsically motivated people show more understanding, work harder and are more perseverant and creative. However, no project consists solely of fun tasks. That is why we will often have to rely on externally oriented motivation: *extrinsic motivation*.

The model shows that *extrinsic motivation* is not necessarily a bad thing. There exist "good" and "bad" external influences. Good external influence gives people a sense of autonomy, just like intrinsic motivation. Being able to make their own choices and act independently will energize your employees. On the other hand, being motivated through control, the obligations forced upon them or guilt will both drain their energy. *Deci and Ryan show that the difference between autonomous and controlled motivation is more important than the difference between intrinsic and extrinsic motivation.* That is good news for project motivators.

Both identified and integrated regulation fall under the banner of (external) autonomous motivation. In the case of identified regulation, team members will not carry out a task because they enjoy it, but because they will get something out of it – not a reward, mind you, but something that ties into their personal goals or development. People act because they choose to do so, not because they must. The other form, integrated regulation, is most similar to intrinsic motivation. Once again, the activity itself is not the primary driving force, but the reasons behind the activity tie in perfectly with someone's personal beliefs and values. In other words, people follow their heart and act because they want to act.

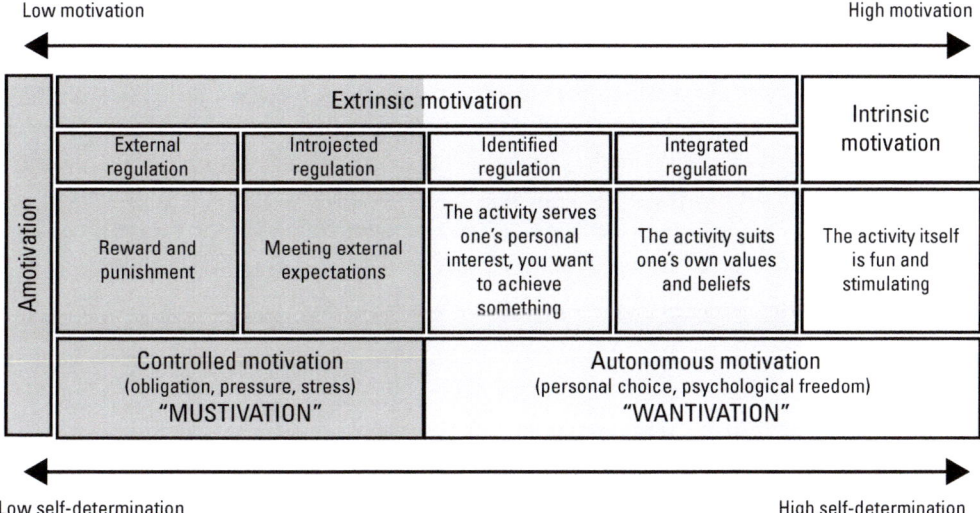

Figure 7.1   Deci and Ryan's motivation continuum

Monitoring things closely and giving plenty of space

The previous sections demonstrate that your behavior as a project manager is a major factor in your team's motivation and performance. Remember that *the devil is in the detail*. Your choice of words alone can make a huge difference. Managers who, at the end of a meeting, say something like "During our next meeting, we will see if you managed to do everything we discussed" are focusing on control and should expect a lesser performance. On the other hand, if they say something along the lines of "I am curious to see if this feedback can help you," they stimulate the employee's autonomy and his or her desire to realize some positive effect. As you have probably guessed, this ties in perfectly with situational leadership, as discussed in section 4.4. If people need S3 leadership, it would be a bad idea to tell them that you will come by tomorrow to see how well they have performed their task. By doing so, you are interfering with the *how*. I usually deal with this by telling my team members that I want to visit them out of interest and curiosity. Instead of smothering their autonomy, it nurtures their feeling of relatedness. The principle of multiplier and diminisher behavior, as discussed in section 1.2, also ties into Deci and Ryan's theory. A diminisher focuses on control, while a multiplier strives to invest in the other person's autonomy.

Good project motivators are conscious of the way they communicate. Using controlling language can have a counterproductive effect, as can focusing solely on deadlines and ignoring the process. You can bolster motivation by offering your team members freedom of choice, acceptance and appreciation. *Yet*

Performing well and giving someone space can even amplify each other.

you still want to maintain control over your project. You can! Firstly, by exercising the right kind of *situational leadership* and focusing solely on what the employee needs. Secondly, by not trying to control everything when measuring progress, but by zooming in on what is essential to the result: the *critical parameters.* Your team members are not likely to view this as controlling, but rather as recognition of their area of expertise. Thirdly, *by closely involving your team members in the development of the plan,* which creates room for their input and gives them insight into the process. Finally, you have to understand that you have little choice but to apply dominant crisis management if you discover that things are not going the way they should at the last moment. Letting things get that far is, therefore, not an option for a motivating project manager; you will have to spot any problems sooner. This is where the "warming up" of *confrontation moments* earlier in the V-model comes in handy. It is definitely possible to maintain control over your project while also giving your people plenty of room. In fact, the two can amplify each other. This is one way to resolve the &-&-&-paradox of "monitoring things closely while giving plenty of space."

7.2   You reap what you sow

From all this, we can draw a conclusion that should not really come as a surprise: you reap what you sow. The American social psychologist Douglas McGregor reached the same conclusion after conducting his research.

McGregor's Theory X and Theory Y

McGregor researched how managers view their employees. He concluded that they have one of two perceptions, which he refers to as *Theory X* and *Theory Y* (McGregor, 1960):

- **Theory X** managers have a *negative* perception of mankind. That is also how they talk about their employees: "They will do their work poorly if you let them, they do not want to accept any responsibility and they need to be coerced and controlled to perform well."
- **Theory Y** managers have a *positive* perception of mankind. They view their employees as people who naturally take initiative, want to accept responsibility and do their work well.

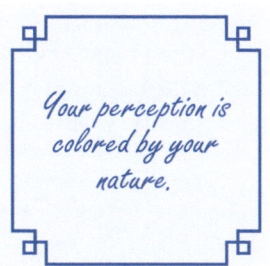

Your perception is colored by your nature.

Managers with a negative perception of people are more likely to adopt an authoritarian leadership style (S1 leadership). They believe in rewards and punishment and they hardly involve their employees in decision-making processes: more examples of diminisher behavior. Theory X managers squash any nuances related to the estimation of activities by putting their employees under as much pressure as possible. They do so by giving their employees more and more work until they speak up. These managers believe that the team does not have enough to do until it starts complaining about the workload. This is a rather blunt way of avoiding having to struggle with estimates and safety margins…

However, McGregor states that *managers reap what they sow.* Employees adapt their behavior to the way they are managed. They sense that their input is not rewarded in an authoritarian system and there is no point in trying harder. When asked to present their hour estimations, they are more likely to include a larger safety buffer. They rapidly lose their intrinsic motivation and Theory X therefore becomes a *self-fulfilling prophecy.* Consequently, authoritarian managers have their perception of the team confirmed and they are caught in a vicious circle. They can get away with this in an environment where S1 leadership is standard (e.g. for unschooled production activities). However, the use of this leadership style will be much harder to maintain when dealing with knowledge workers who possess knowledge that the manager lacks, or with project staff who work in different locations and are therefore harder to control.

 Do you know any examples of this self-fulfilling prophecy for Theory X managers?

Acting out of a positive perception of people and exhibiting the right kind of exemplary behavior is, therefore, the perfect formula to ensure you have motivated employees who want to take responsibility for their work. A good shepherd knows when to lead his flock, but also when to trail behind. After all, the sheep know far more about where to find the best grass and water. This behavior is not easy, especially when you feel the pressure to perform with your team during the heat of battle. In those situations, it can be tempting to push your agenda

Take control to let others be autonomous.

onto your team. Nevertheless, you will achieve better results in the long run if you act in a subservient manner and focus primarily on allowing the professionals to do their job. You generate output by focusing on the right input: creating the right conditions and fulfilling the preconditions. One of these conditions is about setting the right goals (the *what*) and offering structure and support through the right kind of situational leadership. This means you still play an essential role as a leader! If you ask for too much autonomy, or if you do not offer enough structure, your project will not be successful either. Moving between freedom and structure is a delicate *balancing act* that calls for a ton of expertise from a project manager who operates out of a belief in Theory Y. Allowing others to be autonomous does not mean that you don't need to take any control yourself – on the contrary!

A project equals change, equals resistance

I struggled quite a bit with this during my first few projects. I encountered resistance from my environment, so what was I doing wrong? Later, I realized that this has a lot to do with the fact that a project is usually a *temporary organization* within a permanent organization that is reluctant to give up its powers. As we mentioned in section 5.3: "Responsibilities are given to you, but the power to fulfill them has to be fought for." The following helped me to put the resistance I encountered in the right perspective and even view it as a compliment of sorts: *a project = change = resistance.*

Encountering resistance is all part of the game! The reverse may also be true: if you do not encounter any resistance at all, you may not be moving fast enough or your actions are not having the desired impact. Above all, you should not take resistance personally or start doubting yourself. The project environment knows what it has, but not what it will get. The logical first reaction will therefore be: "Yes, but…" Instead of being caught off guard by resistance, consider it a normal part of any project. You should, therefore, start working on motivation and engagement in your project immediately, even if there does not appear to be a need to do so yet. In the same vein as "start communicating while the project is still fun," we can also say: "*start motivating your environment before you encounter resistance.*"

Motivation summarized

Let's summarize what we have learned so far. You use motivation to inspire your team members to take action and accept the responsibility for completing their tasks independently. Deci and Ryan offer a neat framework to present all this in an easy-to-understand format, in which we can integrate the aforementioned topics from this book (see figure 7.2). That is what I love about it: leadership is not about different techniques for each situation, rather, it is a logical and coherent set of basic principles that you use again and again, for example when motivating your team members, conducting stakeholder management, developing a plan, managing people's expectations, controlling the project scope or managing the project execution.

Start motivating before you encounter resistance.

The basic principles of leadership are universally applicable. Clarifying and communicating the project's scope and goals at an early stage is always useful. Good situational leadership is always useful. Agile behavior is always useful, even if there are only few changes. Proactive behavior supported by the V-model is always useful. Focusing on output by monitoring the critical parameters is always useful. Proactively approaching your stakeholders is always useful. Properly and flexibly structuring your plan is always useful. Actively involving your team in the development of the plan is always useful. Closely monitoring the situation and making timely adjustments is always useful. Applying Covey's seven habits is always useful. I could keep going…

Moving from reactive to proactive to influencing is therefore mostly about applying these basic principles. If you are succeeding in one domain, the effects will frequently be felt elsewhere. However, applying them together does require a degree of expertise. Authentic motivators are all about win-win and entice their environment to take action. They also want results, though, so the challenge is to find the right balance between giving people freedom and creating evaluation moments. The more experience you have, the easier it will be to play this game well and deal with the discrepancies. Everything will become factor 10 behavior and you will start to trust more and more in the fact that all the energy you put in will be paid back in spades!

Flip-thinking and motivation

Figure 7.2 sums up everything involved in motivation-oriented leadership. Note that this does not mean all of the action has to come from the project manager. For example, when using situational leadership and moving from coaching (S2) to supporting (S3) to delegating (S4), it can be helpful to tell the employee that it is difficult for you to let go of the reins – not because you are bad at delegating, but because there is so much at stake. The employee will realize that operating autonomously is a rare privilege and will become intrinsically motivated not to damage your trust. *Acting vulnerably* can create a powerful impulse, but it requires strong leadership from you. As Covey said: "you can only achieve interdependence by first being independent."

Competence	Autonomy	Relatedness
Provide insight into the project context and what is expected of the employee	Explain goals and frameworks (what and why)	Create a shared view on the project goals and align them with personal goals (win-win)
Situational leadership: offer sufficient task-oriented leadership	Situational leadership: do not offer too much task-oriented leadership	Situational leadership: offer sufficient people-oriented support
Situational leadership: offer the right people-oriented support (trust and positive feedback)	Put results first (what), but give employees the opportunity to choose their own method (how)	Appreciate successes and offer support if errors are made, even in stressful situations
When appointing tasks, keep the employee's required and inherent competences in mind	Involve employees in the planning process and leave room for personal input	Create an open atmosphere in which everyone can speak their mind and listen to each other
Make sure the context of the tasks is clear and challenging	Involve employees in the decision-making process and encourage them to take the initiative	Stimulate personal development and participation in networks
Create the right learning process from one task to the next within the project	Remind employees of their personal responsibility	Stimulate collaboration and teambuilding
Be proactive and use the V-model to allow team members to grow in their role in a structured manner	Be proactive and use the V-model to give team members the opportunity to show personal involvement	Be proactive and use the V-model to avoid crises and to continue offering the right support

Figure 7.2   An overview of topics from this book and how they each meet Deci and Ryan's three basic needs

Less is often more. Let others feel that you are giving them more responsibility and *visibly* create some distance. Quinn's concept of switching leadership styles plays into this, you are changing from a director into a mentor. Gradually start putting more energy into the coordination beforehand and less into correction after the fact. This stimulates the employee's autonomous and intrinsic motivation, *from correcting to coordinating.* Try the following: tell team members, whom you always used to accompany on visits to a supplier, that they can also handle this task on their own. You do want something in return, though, a good *briefing*

From correcting to coordinating.

beforehand and a *debriefing* after they get back. Both do not have to take more than fifteen minutes. During the briefing, ask the employees in a coaching manner what the dos and don'ts are and under what circumstances or unexpected turns of events would they like to be allowed to disturb you. Chances are that they complete their task with flying colors because of this preparation and your explicit support. When they return excitedly to give you a debriefing, they will be bursting with energy. In this manner, growing and helping people grow is actually a lot of fun.

Compliments and rewards

We have already seen that rewards and punishment fall into the category of controlled motivation, which has a counterproductive effect compared to autonomous motivation. Does that mean you should never reward your team members at all? I personally believe that rewarding and complimenting people is very important, provided that you do so as a sign of appreciation, not in an attempt to control the other person. In such a case, it can reinforce their competence, autonomy and feeling of relatedness. This means it is important *how* you reward and compliment people. The following characteristics of a good compliment can help you figure that out:

- The compliment must be *genuine* (you must not have a hidden agenda);
- The compliment must be *specific* (to what behavior does it pertain);
- The compliment must be *appropriate* (it must suit the degree of appreciation);
- The compliment must be *deserved* (the performed task must be a real challenge);
- The compliment must be *timely* (if you give it six months later during a performance evaluation, the magic will be gone).

These requirements can sometimes cause problems. No matter how genuine your compliment is, it often also serves as a stimulus to get employees to repeat their good behavior. You do not have to downplay this fact; it is only logical that multiple interests are in play. As long as you are open about that, no one will bat an eye. Check your intention and look for the win-win. It is also possible that a manager might hold some strong beliefs, e.g. that someone will work less hard after receiving a compliment. I believe this idea stems from McGregor's Theory X and is, therefore, a projection of one's own negative experience. A properly given compliment can, in fact, result in additional motivation and inspire someone to work harder.

Giving compliments and rewards calls for an active attitude on the part of the project leader. How often do we overlook important moments because we are preoccupied? Dare to celebrate successes and dare to follow your gut feeling. For instance, I like to reward people for their *behavior* before the final goal has been realized. Consider this example of a barbeque at my home. Because a barbeque is not something you would do in the winter, I once rewarded a software development team in the summer – well before the software had proven its usefulness in the client's organization. It might seem counterproductive, but what easier way is there to show your appreciation for the progress being made and your trust in the team than by rewarding them before the final score is on the board? Should things become more difficult later on in the project, the team members will not hang you out to dry. Instead, they will be all the more motivated to earn the trust you put in them. Another case of flip-thinking…

When rewarding people with the goal of improving their motivation, it is also important to take Herzberg's theory into account. Fredrick Herzberg suggests that there are two groups of factors that play entirely different roles in long-term motivation and job satisfaction: *satisfiers* and *dissatisfiers* (Herzberg, 1959). Dissatisfiers or hygiene factors lead to dissatisfaction if they are not met. If they have been met, however, they do not result in any additional motivation. The reverse is true for satisfiers, which can directly contribute to one's motivation and job satisfaction. As you might expect, not meeting these conditions does not immediately result in dissatisfaction. Herzberg says that you motivate people by focusing on the satisfiers, but that giving (just) enough attention to the dissatisfiers is an important precondition for that.

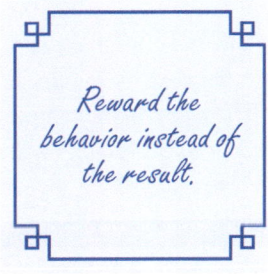

Reward the behavior instead of the result.

Herzberg's theory shows that a financial bonus (more salary), a hygiene factor, is not a stimulus to perform better in the long run – although it is important that you pay people enough, because money should not be a source of friction. If you want to motivate people, it is better to focus on satisfiers like recognition, appreciation or growth opportunities. These intrinsically motivating items do lead to a higher degree of job satisfaction, as seen in figure 7.3.

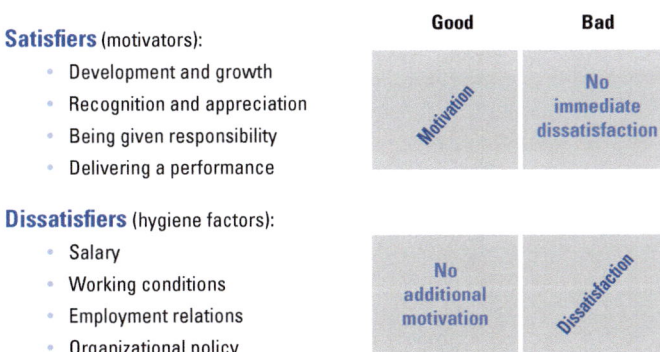

Satisfiers (motivators):
- Development and growth
- Recognition and appreciation
- Being given responsibility
- Delivering a performance

Dissatisfiers (hygiene factors):
- Salary
- Working conditions
- Employment relations
- Organizational policy

Figure 7.3   Herzberg's motivators and hygiene factors

I would like to conclude this discussion of rewards with an anecdote that presented me with some interesting eye openers. A team of circa forty five project members was working on the final stages of a project that was crucial to the company's survival. There was a lot of pressure to deliver the new product on time, which meant that the team was pushed hard to perform. Many employees worked late, while some people were so caught up in the project that they would not listen when told to go home and spend some time with their family. That is why the project management team had come up with the idea of picking three people every month who had performed exceptionally well and showing them some extra appreciation. The proposed reward was a gift card for a dinner for two, so the nominated employees could take their partner out to dinner. After all, their partners were also affected by the stress and long hours.

Receiving appreciation feels great – and so does giving it.

At first, the HRM department was not particularly cooperative. Their view was that the reward would have to be used for all projects. The project management team was disappointed, because then it would no longer be _deserved_ and _genuine_. Moreover, implementing the idea throughout the company would delay things, even though it was so important that the rewards were given in a _timely_ manner. After some serious stakeholder management, the team nevertheless got permission to implement the idea.

It was at this point that the HRM department surprised me. They wanted to increase the reward by adding a bouquet of flowers that would be delivered to the employee's house instead of to the workplace. What a brilliant idea! I saw several people put the phone down after an emotional chat with their partner, having been told that their work must be really important to receive this kind of appreciation. Conclusion: appreciation is not about the size of the reward, but about _how_ you show it. On top of that, the people in charge of the nomination and execution process loved their job. This goes to show that _receiving appreciation feels great – and so does giving it!_

7.3   The (temporary) project organization and the project board

We have not talked much about the project organization so far, except for when I mentioned in section 5.5 during the development of the product breakdown structure that there are many advantages to tailoring the PBS not only to the project content but also to the project organization. Now it is time to delve deeper into this aspect, because influencing the structure of the project organization has a ton of factor 10 potential. Of course, not all of the elements you want to influence are located inside your circle of influence, but you will discover that you can affect this process in more ways than you think.

It is important to recognize that the project organization is a temporary organization, which basically does not even exist at the start of the project. If you ignore this fact, you may encounter some nasty surprises: parts of the team have not yet been formed, the project board or even the client has not been appointed, nor have the mandate and powers been drawn up. However, interfering in this process at the start of a project can be essential to its success.

Model of the temporary project organization

I prefer to use the PRINCE2 organization model (figure 7.4) to create insight into the project organization. The model has the option to include subprojects that are supervised by subproject leaders or team leaders who report to the project manager. If the project scope is limited, this intermediate layer can be left out and the project manager manages the team members directly. The division into subprojects determines the interfaces and the coordination between these subprojects, as mentioned during our discussion of the planning process in figure 6.19. It is important to realize that employees from the permanent organization are given a *role* in the project organization, which comes with its own tasks, responsibilities and powers. People retain a position in the permanent organization and have a delegated role in the project organization.

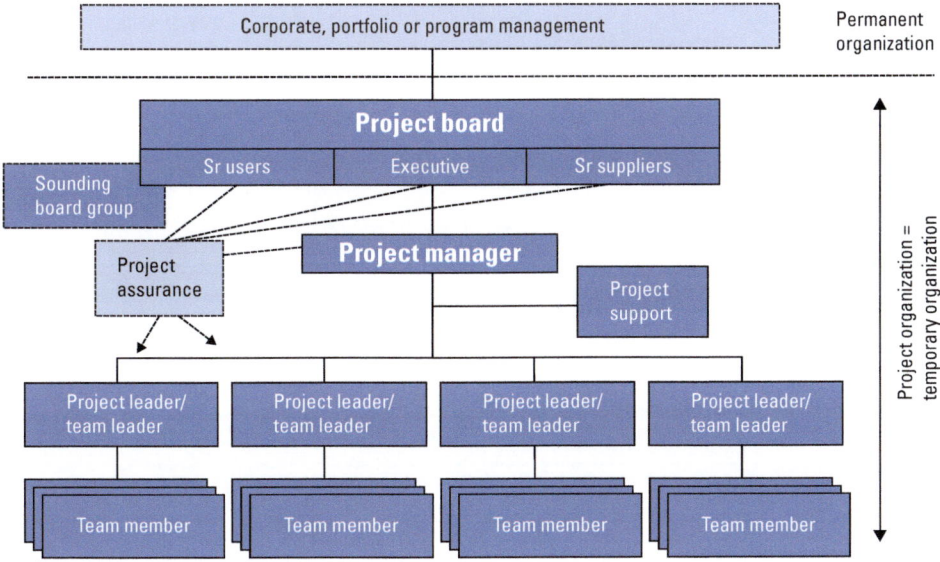

Figure 7.4   Model of a project organization

The project sometimes receives *project support* to manage the detailed plan, moderate reviews, etc. Furthermore, there is project assurance, whose members by definition do not report directly to the project manager, but to the permanent organization. Examples include a controller who reports to the financial director or quality coordinators who report to the respective department head. In the project organization model, the temporary project organization is located below the dotted line (with the exception of project assurance). This

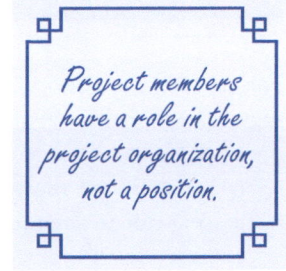

Project members have a role in the project organization, not a position.

presents a clear overview of the part of the organization that must be filled at the start of the project and be given a mandate from the permanent organization.

If there are multiple ongoing projects, each project will have to have its own project organization in place. If a company's primary operating method is project execution, you will often find a matrix project organization as seen in figure 7.5. The projects still follow the project organization model, but the organization is set up in such a way that two goals are met: being able to *flexibly* assign people to projects and providing *anchoring* of specialist knowledge in the departments (line organization). The projects "hire" project members from the departments, who in turn provide the appropriate staff, education and substantive support. Project members therefore report to two supervisors: the functional supervisor from the permanent organization (the department head) and the operational supervisor from the temporary project organization (the project manager). The project manager is responsible for the project's progress and decides *what* the team members must deliver and when, while the functional supervisor determines *how* they should do this. This combination of project progress and quality assurance can create friction when team members receive conflicting tasks from both sides. It is, therefore, essential that the project and line organizations coordinate properly.

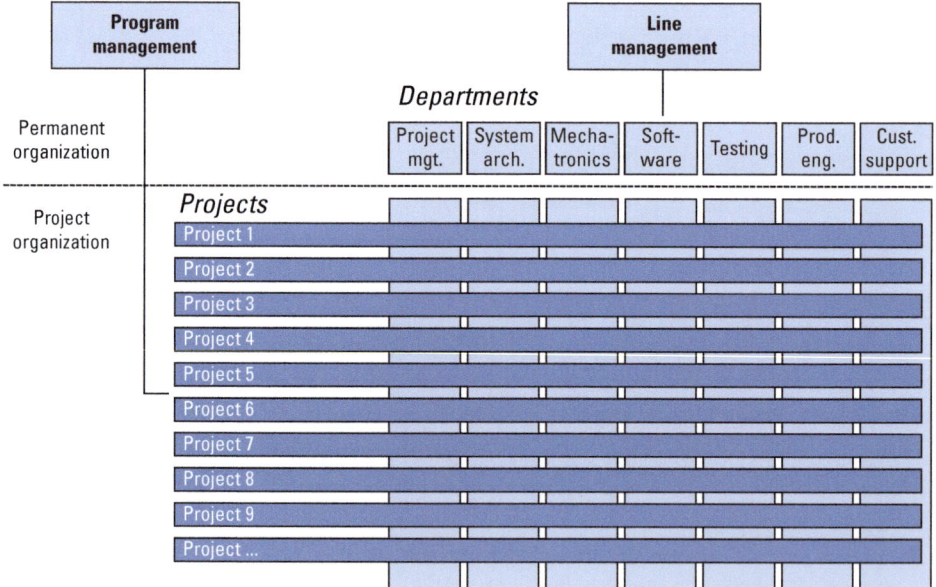

Figure 7.5   Matrix organization

For project motivators, it is important to understand the interests of the permanent organization and actively ensure that team members are given the right powers. Furthermore, they need to make sure that the departments support the project management plan, that team members are motivated to execute the plan and that the line organization plays a facilitating role in the project.

The project board

As you can see in the organizational model in figure 7.4, the project board (or project steering committee) is also part of the temporary project organization. At least, that is the case with PRINCE2, the project management method which I believe presents the project board in the clearest and best light. The project board is the highest decision-making body involved in the project. Its task is to ensure that the requirements and goals of the project are realized. PRINCE2 states that users and suppliers involved in the project must be represented at the management level on the project board. These project board members must also have the power to make decisions on behalf of the group they represent. In addition to the executive, the project board is, therefore, made up of:

■ *Senior users* who represent the interests (and priorities) of the users or clients of the project. For example, think of business, sales or product managers. Senior users can also have a sounding board group to involve their members or the interests of the end user.

■ *Senior suppliers* who represent the interests of the people who design, develop or implement the actual project results (both internally and externally), e.g. department managers or the heads of purchasing, logistics, IT or product development.

The project board must have an active role in the project, especially when it comes to decisiveness. In practice, however, the project board's decisiveness and accountability are sometimes under pressure. Furthermore, the board's composition is important: who takes on which role? This can lead to misunderstandings when organizations automatically appoint the management team or the board of directors (both parts of the permanent organization) as the project board. Although it is not necessarily wrong to do so, it may result in some management team members interfering in the project without having the "authority" to do so. More importantly, some project board positions may be left unfilled. As a project manager, you should therefore take the initiative to evaluate the situation and talk to the chairman/executive if, for instance, there is no one on the project board to represent the client's interests, or if it would be advisable to invite the head of purchasing because many project activities will be outsourced. Having a decisive project board is a major factor in your project's success!

 Does the composition of your project board meet these requirements?

If you cannot do it formally, take the informal route

As mentioned, proactive project managers try to influence the composition and the actions of the project board to which they ultimately have to report themselves. That might seem strange, but you should remember that your relationship with the project board largely determines your project's success. Manage yourself, manage your team, manage your environment! In addition to that, what should you do if no project board has been formed yet? Rejoice: *you have every opportunity to help form the project board based on your own stakeholder analysis!*

Manage yourself, manage your team, manage your environment!

However, you may also encounter the opposite situation: perhaps there is a project board, but it lacks the necessary effectiveness or members with the right mandate. If your recommended changes are ignored, choose your battles wisely, you can always form your own *informal* project board. Have coffee once every two weeks with the person whom you see as a decision maker in the organization or schedule regular meetings with the supervisors who must ultimately embrace your project result and implement it in their organization. *In the end, it all boils down to stakeholder management and the circle of influence.* If you cannot get what you need from the project board, take the informal route.

7.4   Why the start requires perseverance

In the first chapter of this book we concluded that the project preparation phase is enormously important to the project as a whole. This is where you lay down the foundation for success, where you start raising expectations and where you have myriad options to influence the stakeholders. However, this phase is not all smooth sailing.

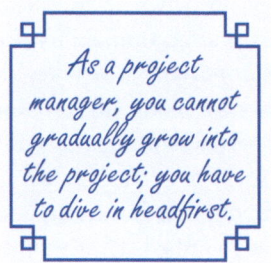

As a project manager, you cannot gradually grow into the project; you have to dive in headfirst.

The project S-curve
Because the start of the project is so important, a project manager hardly has any time to "grow into the project." You have to utilize your soft skills from the very first moment: *you have to dive in headfirst.* At the same time, the environment is not likely to make things any easier for you. Most elements that can support you are not in place yet. Motivating your team requires time and patience, your stakeholders' emotional bank account is initially empty, little is yet known about the project goals and no clear project approach has yet been defined. To top it all off, the start of the project is not a phase during which you can easily show results. *Initiating action and building trust are under pressure.*

I have tried to represent this tension in figure 7.6. It shows that your project is *always a change process as well.* Your environment develops along an S-curve and during the definition phase you will have to overcome the hurdles of team motivation, the emotional bank account, knowledge of the end goal, etc., – which is difficult enough in itself. It also shows why projects often fail, even with a project management plan in place that was theoretically sound.

As a project manager, you are also a change manager.

There is little you can do about this, you will have to accept this fact and adapt accordingly. You can, for example, devote extra energy to activities at the start of the project to compensate for less than ideal conditions. Furthermore, remember that the impact of your actions will initially be limited. We have already taken this effect into account in the previous chapters, e.g. by focusing on early communication with the stakeholders, actively showing interim results, starting with a project charter and dividing the planning process into separate communicable steps. In short, you can certainly influence this change process with the way in which you tackle the project. As a project manager, you are also a change manager!

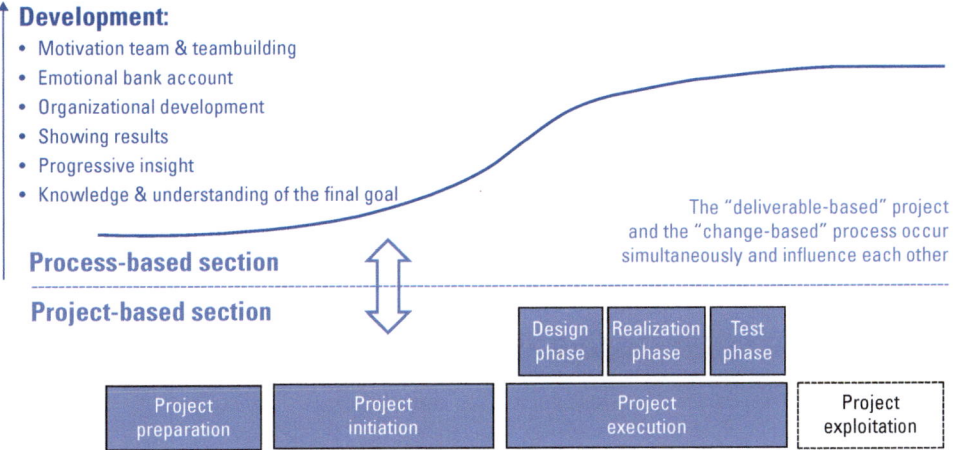

Figure 7.6   The project S-curve: a project is also a change process

Team maturity

Bruce Tuckman's stages of group development are a great example of this project S-curve. These are the stages that a team goes through in order to reach a state of effective collaboration: *Forming – Storming – Norming – Performing* (Tuckman, 1965).

Tuckman states that all teams go through four phases before their collaboration truly flourishes (see figure 7.7). However, many teams get stuck on a particular phase, so they never realize their full potential. During the *forming* phase, the team members get to know each other. People are hesitant, avoid conflicts and prefer to operate in a task-oriented manner (the team members will not show much initiative yet). Next is the *storming* phase, during which interpersonal relationships and role divisions become clearer and conflicts arise. Many teams do not make it through this phase. If they do, they move on to the *norming* phase: people know and accept each other's role and task division and begin to focus on the common goals. Finally, the team finds its flow and reaches the *performing* phase. This phase is all about collaboration and taking responsibility. The team requires little management at this point. Ultimately, every team reaches the fifth and final phase, the *adjourning* phase, during which it is modified or dissolved.

Figure 7.8 shows the S-curve of the team development process. At the start of the project you are clearly dealing with a different kind of team dynamic than during subsequent phases. If you understand and accept this fact, you can act accordingly. For example, the team will require a more directive leadership style (S1) at first, regardless of the level of task maturity of its individual members. Early on, team members want direction and clarity. Once you reach the storming phase, it is good to

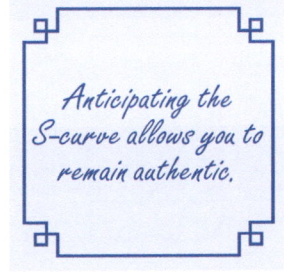

Anticipating the S-curve allows you to remain authentic.

Forming	Storming	Norming	Performing	Adjourning
• Hesitant • Insecure • Searching for a leader • Development of subgroups due to insecurity • Polite to each other • Searching for personal interests • Focus on task aspects	• Individual search process visible • Personal conflicts about role division • Competing about status • Close bonds and hostile relationships • Evil outside world is often blamed for tension	• Acceptance of differences of opinion and insight • Feeling of shared responsibility • Common goals • Collective decision-making • Good relationships between team members	• Team members have found their roles • Performances are seemingly effortless • People are self-learning and want to improve • Team can deal with setbacks and changes	• As a result of team changes, the team relapses to earlier phases • This is sometimes done deliberately to avoid group blindness (Not invented here syndrome)

Figure 7.7 The path towards team maturity according to Tuckman

remember that there is no need to doubt your own leadership skills. This is all part of the growth process. Before I knew about Tuckman's model, I sometimes blamed myself when

Do not take resistance personally.

I was unable to keep the team away from this phase. Later, I heard an experienced project manager deftly put things into perspective by saying to his team: "Finally, a storm is coming. This is starting to look like a real project!" Next, he opened the conflicts and differences of opinion up for discussion and clearly explained the frameworks and goals once more (S2 leadership style). Anticipating and understanding the project and group dynamic can lead to simple and disarming behavior. On the other hand, you could also deliberately stoke the fire to make sure the storming phase starts sooner and is over quicker. That is another example of factor 10 behavior!

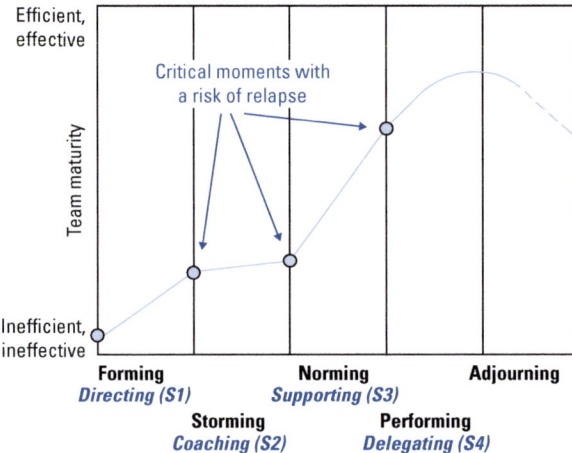

Figure 7.8 Project S-curve during team development and the associated leadership style at team level

The S-curve tells you that the project environment still has to get used to your project and that content-driven coordination alone will not be enough. You should, therefore, act as a change manager and project motivator from the start. Do not let resistance put you off. Another valuable tip is not to take the resistance personally. Of course, that is easier said than done. If you have spent a long time working on your plan and have resolved many bottlenecks along the way, it is hard to just shrug off comments such as "I don't like it" or "It's too expensive." You might start reacting instead of acting. Remember that the TomTom would never do that; you cannot let it get to you. Personally, I like to look at a situation that affects me on a personal level as a tennis match: both sides are trying their best to win, not to make the other party lose or annoy them. This philosophy helps me put things in perspective when the other party gets in my way. Instead, I devote my energy to coming up with a great *return*.

7.5   Directing creativity

I want to finish this chapter by discussing a topic that presents a major challenge to any project motivator: directing creativity! This is about giving your team members the freedom they need to be optimally creative, while simultaneously meeting strict deadlines. We will cover such questions as "Can you capture creativity?", "Can you control and stimulate creativity with certain processes?" and "Can creativity get in your way or even obstruct existing processes?" First, however, we must discuss another challenge for project managers, their schizophrenic role of motivator and realist.

The project leader as a motivator and a realist
You will probably be familiar with this situation: one moment, you are motivating your team members, creating the right conditions, communicating in a positive manner and actively removing obstacles along the way. You are a true *motivator*. An hour later, you have to report to the project board. You notice that the board members do not feel a sufficient degree of urgency as yet, that they are very positive about delivery dates and are primarily focused on further expanding the project scope. You must be extremely careful with the dates

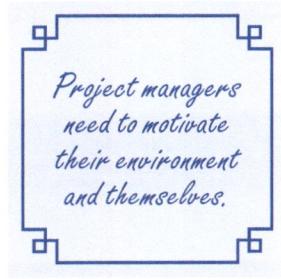

Project managers need to motivate their environment and themselves.

you mention and how you communicate, because you can set the wrong expectations before you know it. You have, therefore, properly substantiated your story and ensure that you plant the project board's feet firmly on the ground again. You are a *realist*. Earlier in this book, we talked about how the ability to switch between different leadership roles is an important success factor in project management. However, moving between the roles of motivator and realist takes a lot out of many project managers and can often leave them feeling lonely and schizophrenic.

?   *Do you recognize this occasionally lonely feeling of having to be both a motivator and a realist?*

Still, this is all part of the game. One moment, you will be explaining to the project board members that the change they are proposing is really not a good idea, while next you have to motivate the team to look into the board's request anyway. Without input or substantiation, you have nothing to go on during your next meeting with the project board. The schizophrenic combination of being both a motivator and a realist can take a lot out of you. *Project managers motivate the project environment, but they must also motivate themselves.* After all, when the chips are down and even you have momentarily given up, who is left to keep the project on track?

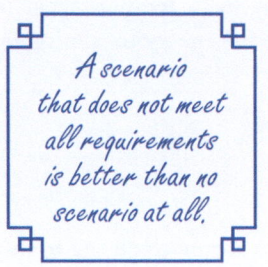

A scenario that does not meet all requirements is better than no scenario at all.

A successful project leader must know how to call on the team's strengths even during difficult situations and prevent everyone from simply giving up. Only by taking action and working even harder can the team achieve results and create arguments to convince the stakeholders. It is up to you to maintain control as both a motivator and a realist. You must stay goal- and solution-oriented. Remember what the TomTom has taught you: *always show a scenario that leads to the final goal.* Even if the scenario in question does not meet all requirements, it will still be better than no scenario at all. Clients often respond poorly to remarks such as "It cannot be done." On the other hand, they will likely start thinking more positively if you present them with options, even ones that do not (yet) meet every requirement.

Creativity: how we think

Over the years, countless scientists have attempted to describe the creative process using a wide variety of theories. These theories can coexist without difficulty. In fact, they complement each other in certain key areas.

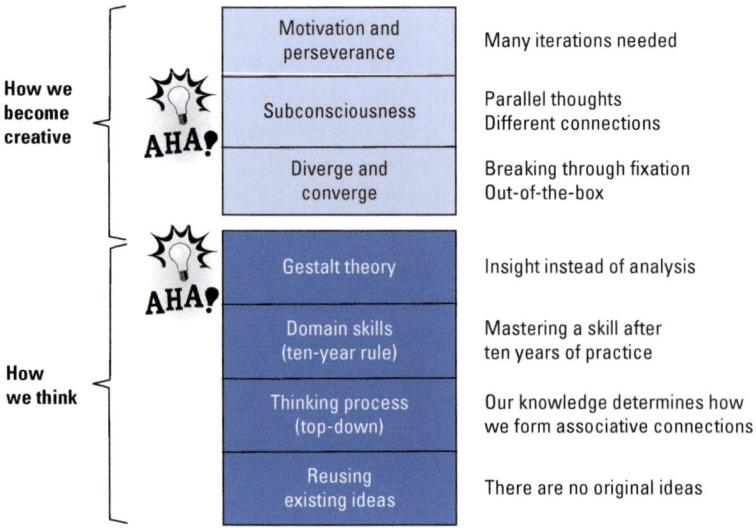

Figure 7.9   How we think and how we become creative

With figure 7.9, I have tried to help you understand the creative process by "stacking" the available theories. The bottom blocks describe how we think. The first one is a doozy already: new ideas are almost always derived from older, existing ideas. Allen Newell and Herbert Simon's theory states that creative thought processes are similar to standard thought processes (Newell & Simon, 1972). This is reflected in the succession of inventions, but also when we look at artists who never leave their homes without a notebook. Rather than coming up with something entirely new, it is about making new connections. When we have ideas and create new connections, our thought process is knowledge-driven, as described in the second block: your existing knowledge determines how your brain interprets the sensory input it receives. The more you already know of a topic, the easier it will be to store new information about it. This idea is supported by John Hayes' *ten-year rule* (Hayes, 1989), shown in the next block. Based on a study among many artists, Hayes discovered that it takes ten thousand hours or ten years of experience before true creative breakthroughs occur. Knowledge and experience, i.e. your domain skills, determine your solution space (the ideas you have) and the solution method (how you form connections). Finally, Max Wertheimer's *Gestalt theory* (Wertheimer, 1982) states that we perceive the world as whole units and patterns. You have probably seen images like those in figure 7.10 before. The Gestalt theory is also used when you read the following text:

Aoccdrnig to a rscheearch at Cmabrigde Uinervtisy, it deosn't mttaer in waht oredr the ltteers in a wrod are, the olny iprmoatnt tihng is taht the frist and lsat ltteer be at the rghit pclae.

The Gestalt theory demonstrates that our brain uses *insight rather than analysis* when it interprets sensory input. That explains why you recognize things all of a sudden, instead of gradually; an *Aha-erlebnis*.

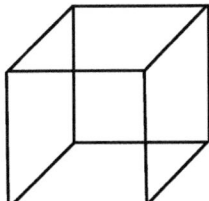  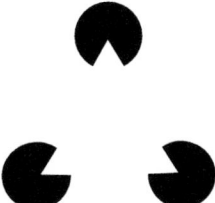

Figure 7.10   Examples of the Gestalt theory

Diverging and converging
Now we know how we think, but what does this teach us about creativity? *Creativity is about breaking through patterns and habits.* The fact that our brain relies on these patterns and our existing knowledge is precisely what makes creative thinking so difficult. Possessing knowledge and seeing patterns can be counterproductive, it leads to fixation. That is why *divergent* thinking, i.e. breaking away from set patterns and habits, is so important. The psychologist Joy Paul Guilford concluded that creativity is the result of out-of-the-box thinking, breaking through one's fixation, not immediately thinking in solutions and therefore coming up with different ideas and forming new connections (Guilford, 1950).

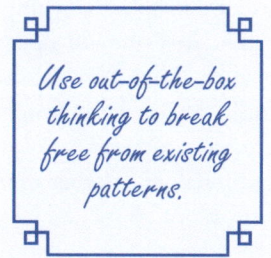

Use out-of-the-box thinking to break free from existing patterns.

To this, you can add the theory developed by the mathematician and philosopher Henri Poincaré, which states that our brain can have multiple *parallel thoughts* at once (Poincaré, 1913). Only one of these thoughts will be "visible" in our consciousness, yet the other thoughts are active at the same time in our *subconsciousness*. From there, they can suddenly produce ideas and solutions that could not have resulted from conscious thinking. This is another example of a sudden *Aha-erlebnis*. You can make clever use of this concept by moving on to a different task when your thought process is momentarily stuck. Whether you believe in this theory or not, the change of pace will do you good anyway. *Break through your fixation and utilize your subconscious thought processes!*

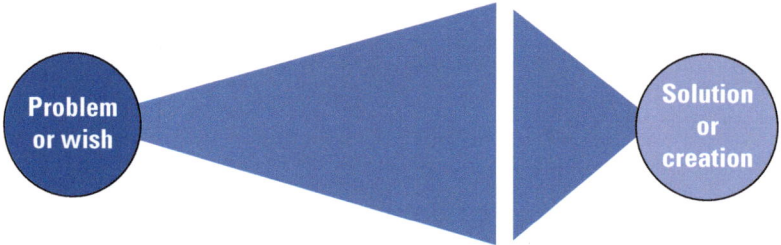

Figure 7.11   First diverge and break through your fixation, then converge again

No matter how important divergence is, you will eventually have to converge again. Otherwise, the process will not result in a solution, choice or other desired result. This means that the creative process of diverging and converging is mostly about perseverance. Genuine breakthroughs are the result of many iterations. As Thomas Edison once said: "Genius is 1% inspiration and 99% perspiration."

Creativity-focused leadership

This insight into how we think and how we become creative shows that it is not so much about whether people are creative, but more about how you can bring out their creativity – at the individual level, but also at the team level. It should also be clear that stimulating creativity involves more than just motivating people. It is important to tap into your team members' creativity in a tactical way. Since you are not just looking for divergence, you want to stay on top of the convergence process (making decisions and achieving results) as well. Brainstorming sessions that lead to a ton of ideas but few conclusions and results are of no real use to anyone. Focusing on creativity is, therefore, about striking the right balance between offering freedom and creating structure.

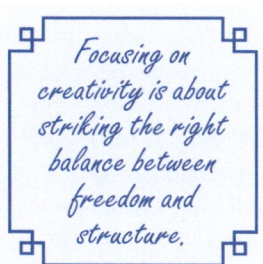

Focusing on creativity is about striking the right balance between freedom and structure.

Leadership plays an important role in this regard. Jeff Gaspersz covers this in *Compete with creativity* (Gaspersz, 2005). He defines the climate in which creativity can flourish as an environment with a high degree of diversity, plenty of knowledge sharing and cross-fertilization and enough calm to allow for divergence. Furthermore, challenging goals must result in creative tension, which inspires people to abandon the familiar paths and dare to experiment. This results in a different level of risk compared with other activities. Consequently, it is important that failures are tolerated and people understand they can learn from each other's mistakes. Finally, there must be room for internal entrepreneurship, which results in autonomous motivation, a desire to act and a high degree of perseverance.

Gaspersz suggests that creativity-focused leadership is essential in order to create such a climate. The leaders in question do not have to be creative themselves, as long as they manage to build an environment in which people feel challenged and have a desire to be creative and achieve results. This creativity-focused leader has the following tasks:
■ Setting clear and challenging goals;
■ Correctly utilizing situational leadership;
■ Stimulating out-of-the-box thinking and daring initiatives;

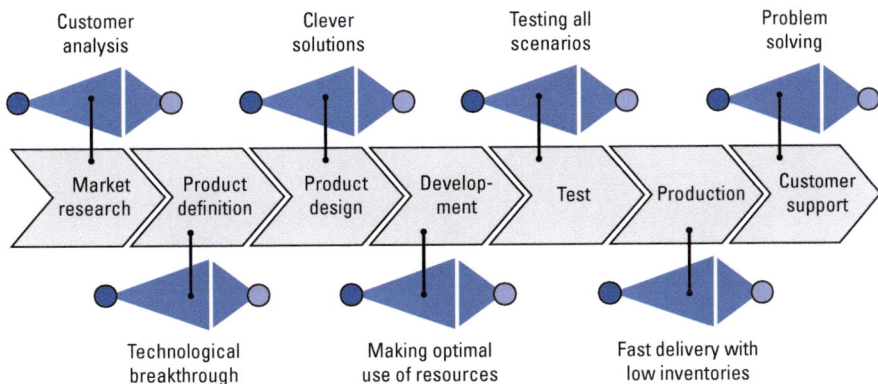

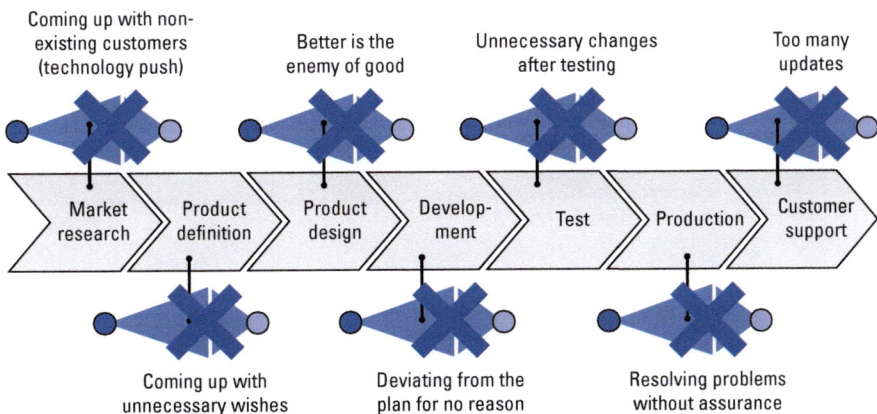

Figure 7.12   A creativity-focused leader must also be able to rein in a team's creativity

- Daring to diverge, yet also managing to converge;
- Creating teams with the right diversity;
- Making teams effective (despite any differences of opinion);
- Facilitating knowledge sharing and cross-fertilization;
- Motivating, fostering creative tension and offering a sense of security (tolerance for failure) at the same time;
- Activating creativity at the right moment and reining it in when necessary.

With this behavior, project motivators can allow their team to make optimal use of its creativity and come up with smarter solutions. Focusing on creativity is, therefore, the ultimate form of the &-&-&-paradox of "monitoring things closely and giving your team plenty of space." You give your team members the space they need, while also controlling when it is time to diverge or converge. You can achieve this by having a clear project management plan and deploying the right kind of operational leadership. Figure 7.12 shows that there are even moments when creativity is not required at all, and you have to rein it in…

Summary

- A project = change = resistance.
- Project motivators start motivating before they encounter resistance.
- There are several ways to motivate people. Above all, it is important to distinguish between autonomous and controlled motivation ('wantivation' versus 'mustivation').
- When motivating others, you must satisfy their basic psychological needs: competence, autonomy and relatedness.
- Employees adapt to how they are managed. Acting out of a positive perception of people will therefore create the strongest feeling of responsibility in your team.
- Dare to celebrate successes and understand the benefits of rewarding people's behavior even before the final results are in.
- The project board is the highest decision-making body within a project. It represents the interests of the users and suppliers of the project at the management level.
- The project S-curve shows that everything grows during a project, yet you must dive in headfirst. As a project manager, you are also a change manager.
- The pressure to be both a motivator and a realist can make you feel schizophrenic and numb. Remember the TomTom and how it never stops communicating or suggesting possible scenarios.
- Creativity is about breaking through patterns and forming new connections: divergence and convergence.
- Focusing on creativity is about striking the right balance between offering freedom and creating structure. It is the ultimate example of the &-&-&-paradox of "monitoring things closely and giving the team plenty of space."

8 Heartbeat

- ◂ How to translate goals and plans into execution.
- ◂ Why you need rhythm for control, communication and the establishment of learning ability.
- ◂ Why focusing solely on milestones and deadlines is not a good idea.
- ◂ How rhythm leads to progress without coercion for self-organizing teams and professionals.
- ◂ The role of the heartbeat in the EOS model and OKR.

With the knowledge gained from chapters 5 and 6, you have now reached the point at which your project management plan will be ready for use during the execution phase, but how can you tell during this phase whether you are still on schedule? In addition, Covey's second habit of "beginning with the end in mind" sounds like a good idea, but how does it relate to project management? And finally, we mentioned in chapter 7 that acknowledging the change process which is inherent in any project is an important factor in the project's success. So how should you direct this process? How can you accelerate the project S-curve of the team's motivation, the stakeholders' support, the understanding of the project goals and the insight into the trend of the critical parameters? In this chapter, I will discuss an essential element of the project execution: the heartbeat.[12]

8.1 Progress through rhythm, cadence and trance

It is every project manager's worst nightmare: finding out at the very last moment that you will not be able to meet the deadline after all. In hindsight, it always feels like an avoidable problem. Nevertheless, we have all been there at one time or another. One reason is that many projects are directed in a *milestone-driven* manner. It starts with the assignment itself: "This must be done in four weeks' time." Can you see how this approach can easily lead to the student syndrome? Four weeks feels like a very long time, so any sense of urgency is eliminated from the outset. Furthermore, the way in which the assignment is described does not encourage the development of a plan for those four weeks. The executor, therefore, cannot answer the question: *"What will you do tomorrow?"*

How can you check during the execution of this assignment whether it is still on schedule? Simply put, you can't. When working on a milestone-driven assignment, people often (subconsciously) make a faulty calculation in evaluating the status of the project:

Remaining time = deadline − time spent

Remaining costs = budget − costs incurred

---

12 This chapter ties into the following competences from IPMA's ICB4: Results orientation, Time, Quality, Plan and control, Risk and opportunity, Change and transformation.

This suggests that halfway through a four-week assignment, you will have two weeks left. The problem lies in the belief that the remaining time equals the *required time*. Depending on the overview and insight of the team member, project manager or project board, this belief may persist for a while. Eventually, however, someone will realize: *"We are not going to make it."* Only with the deadline in sight will people discover that the required time exceeds the available remaining time. As this realization only comes at the last minute, there is no time left to take any action. In terms of communication, this creates two problems: you inform others of a *fait accompli* and you do so *too late*.

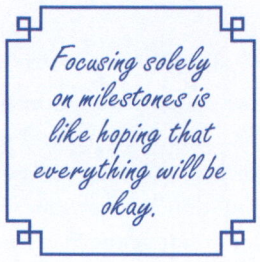

Focusing solely on milestones is like hoping that everything will be okay.

Focusing solely on milestones is no good. Frankly, it is little more than sitting around and hoping everything will be okay in the end. It is reactive behavior that goes entirely against the advice of our inspirator TomTom, who showed us that the required time must be based on the *actual path* that you still have to cover. However, to calculate the required time you have to know this path. Luckily, we have already seen how this can be achieved: by dividing the path to the final goal into smaller sections, i.e. *subresults and activities*, derived from the PBS and WBS. This allows you to evaluate the project's status during its execution and make any necessary adjustments on time. It also ensures you work with the end in mind. From the very start of the project, you will have the landing strip in sight, because you know at all times what still needs to be done: *deliverables-to-go, activities-to-go, hours-to-go, time-to-go, costs-to-go,* etc. These are things you *can* focus on! Now you just have to find the discipline to actually do all this, but we will overcome that hurdle with the rhythm of the heartbeat!

 Do you focus solely on the final deadline or on earlier activities and interim results?

A ten-kilometer long track speed skating race is actually 25 x 400 meters
I often explain the meaning of the heartbeat and its application in the field of project management by comparing a project to a ten-kilometer ice skating race. Like a project, it is a lengthy and unclear process with an inherent risk of procrastination and a chance to lose valuable time at the start.

Yet that is not what happens! The ten-kilometer race is divided into twenty five 400-meter laps. The skaters' times are measured after every lap, which results in two figures, their lap time and their total time. Both are compared to the plan, which may be the skaters' own reference schedules, their opponent's lap times or the charts for the track or world record. After each lap, it will be instantly clear how the skaters are doing, which gives them peace of mind. They do not have to worry about their times during the race. Instead, they can focus on the execution, their technique, body posture and strokes. Whenever they complete a 400-meter lap, they will receive the latest lap time and advice from their coach. The audience also knows what a good lap time looks like. We all get excited when skaters start to accelerate near the end of a race and their lap times drop to the low thirties. From the very start of the race, the skaters, their coach and the audience are counting down to the finish line. Ten thousand boring meters are turned into an infectious rhythm of twenty-five laps.

What the 400-meter lap is to a skater in the metaphor above, the PDCA (plan-do-check-act) cycle period is to a project manager. A constant heartbeat can create structure during a long and boring process and is essential to starting up the PDCA cycle. Without a heartbeat, humans cannot live and a project cannot progress. You should, therefore, divide your project into a strict rhythm of PDCA periods. These periods are usually a week long, although you are free to choose whatever frequency you prefer. A constant and high project heartbeat offers a range of advantages:

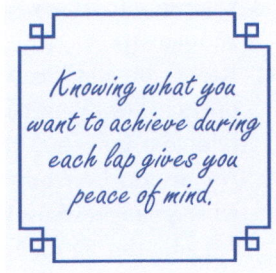

Knowing what you want to achieve during each lap gives you peace of mind.

- You keep yourself from only working hard when the end is in sight or, vice versa, from blindly powering ahead until the deadline and only then checking to see how far you have progressed. Projecting the plan onto the project heartbeat creates structure from the very beginning, just like the lap time schedule does for the skater.

- At the start of each lap (week), you will know exactly what you have to do that week to realize the project goal. At the end of a lap, you can easily assess how you did compared to the plan and what you may need to improve next time.

- During each lap, you know what you have to do to stay on schedule, even without consulting the overall project plan. You and your team can focus entirely on your current tasks.

- At the end of each lap, you receive an update that tells you how far along the project is in relation to the final goal. Additionally, you can make adjustments if necessary. A high project heartbeat increases your *agility*.

- You create focus on the activities of a process well before the deadline. The heartbeat divides the project into multiple cycles, each with its own activities and interim results to be delivered. Consequently, you move from reactively focusing on the final deadline to proactively focusing on activities and deliverables per heartbeat, as seen in figure 8.1:

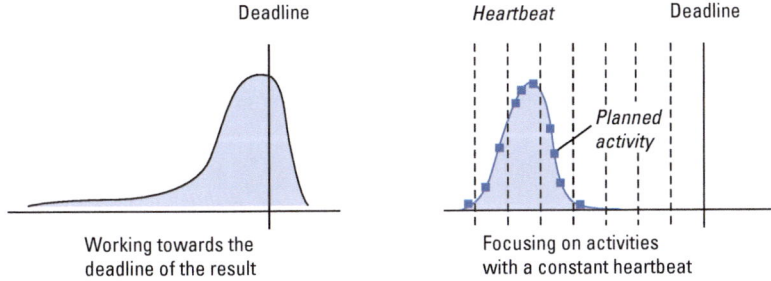

Figure 8.1   The effects of deadline- and activity-driven direction

- You ensure that you do enough work on the right things and do not naively accept changes at the start of the project. The project heartbeat helps avoid the "minuses" we talked about in section 6.2 and puts constant (yet not excessive) pressure on the entire project, instead of creating a peak in workload and stress near the end.

■ Your *stakeholders* will also grow accustomed to the rhythm of your reports. Your high rhythm will become the standard and you will no longer have different stakeholders come up to you day in and day out to ask about the status of the project. The stakeholders will begin to trust you and automatically focus on your updates every time you complete another lap.

■ Repetition and receiving feedback result in a *learning process*. A steady rhythm in your project allows your team, the stakeholders and you to gradually grow into the project and find your flow in a comfortable manner.

■ A constant heartbeat helps you to *let go*, both when using situational leadership and when giving responsibilities to *self-organizing teams*. Clarity during the start will result in freedom during the rest of the lap.

Rhythm leads to progress without coercion.

Rhythm puts everyone into a trance

The project heartbeat creates a constant PDCA rhythm; it provides feedback to the team and makes the interim results visible - all without coming across as overbearing or patronizing. You will see that the team and the stakeholders, even if they do not ask for it at first, will quickly come to appreciate the rhythm. The heartbeat creates a natural cadence and puts the entire project environment into a kind of trance.

As a project manager, you are like a DJ: you decide on the project's beat and atmosphere, while the team still gets to feel autonomous as they dance. The project heartbeat is like a flywheel that gets the S-curve we discussed in section 7.4 going and can accelerate it. Action, structure and feedback not only lead to progress, but they can also improve motivation, stakeholder trust, teambuilding, etc.

Note that the project heartbeat has nothing in particular to do with Agile project management. Realizing a high PDCA rhythm is essential for both traditional and Agile projects. Of course, the Agile approach does offer an additional impulse: the rhythm is already there in the form of the sprint rhythm with interim results and the rhythm of the daily stand-up meetings to achieve coordination within the team.

8.2   Projecting your plan onto the heartbeat

We will cover the application of the heartbeat during the project execution phase in far more detail in the final chapter of this book, called *The Final Countdown*. For now, it is important to understand how you can make your detailed plan suitable for the execution phase; namely, by projecting the plan onto the heartbeat of your project. This will allow you to show the team, suppliers and stakeholders exactly which activities are planned during each heartbeat period. The result is that you can easily determine the project's status during a PDCA cycle and make any necessary adjustments. The description in this section also applies to Scrum, although the plan is automatically projected onto the heartbeat in Scrum by allocating the user stories to the different sprint periods.

Make the goal and performance per heartbeat visible

I hate it when I ask project employees what they have planned for tomorrow and they dodge the question, or when team leaders do not have a clear overview of the schedule for the upcoming week: what are the key activities, what deliverables from external parties are you depending on and what results must be realized? It is not that I want to exert control over their every move. The problem is that they can only respond reactively to anything that happens during the project if they work that way.

How great would it be if you could understand the requirements for each period that will lead to the realization of the project goals, just like during an ice-skating race? You would not have to worry so much about the total time and costs during the project execution. It would let you focus on the *now*, which motivates you and improves the quality of the execution. *If you are meeting your "lap times," that means you are on schedule.* Although this may sound restrictive, you will see that having a strict schedule does not limit your freedom, but

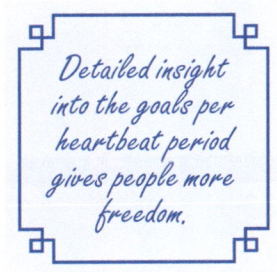

Detailed insight into the goals per heartbeat period gives people more freedom.

actually increases it. When you understand at all times what needs to be done to achieve the final goal, you have the opportunity to "play" with the plan. You are still in control of the execution and you are free to tailor it to the situation at hand. Flip back to the example of the TomTom in section 2.1, where the driver makes the call to take a different route. You can be more flexible when you understand what the consequences are and where there is room to move.

 Do you determine the project status by occasionally analyzing the entire project, or can you deduce this directly from the performance per week?

Knowing what you need to achieve during each heartbeat period results in discipline and helps prevent procrastination. It also helps with stakeholder and change management. When it is clear what you still have to do today or this week, it becomes easier to say "no." You and your environment can clearly see that the day or week is already filled with other activities. Just compare it with how hard it is to explain why you do not have time for a task when you don't know exactly what your schedule is like.

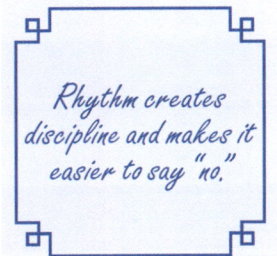

Rhythm creates discipline and makes it easier to say "no."

Making deliverables executable and measurable

Fortunately it is not hard to know what you have to do during each "lap" of the project – provided that you have a detailed plan, as discussed in section 6.4. All you have to do is project the elements of your plan onto the project heartbeat, as shown in figure 8.2: what do you have to do and deliver in week X? These elements are usually the deliverables, activities and input from others that you depend on (the intakes). By keeping these elements in your sight during the plan-do-check-act cycles with a sufficiently high frequency (often one week), it is virtually impossible for a project to stray off course without you realizing it.

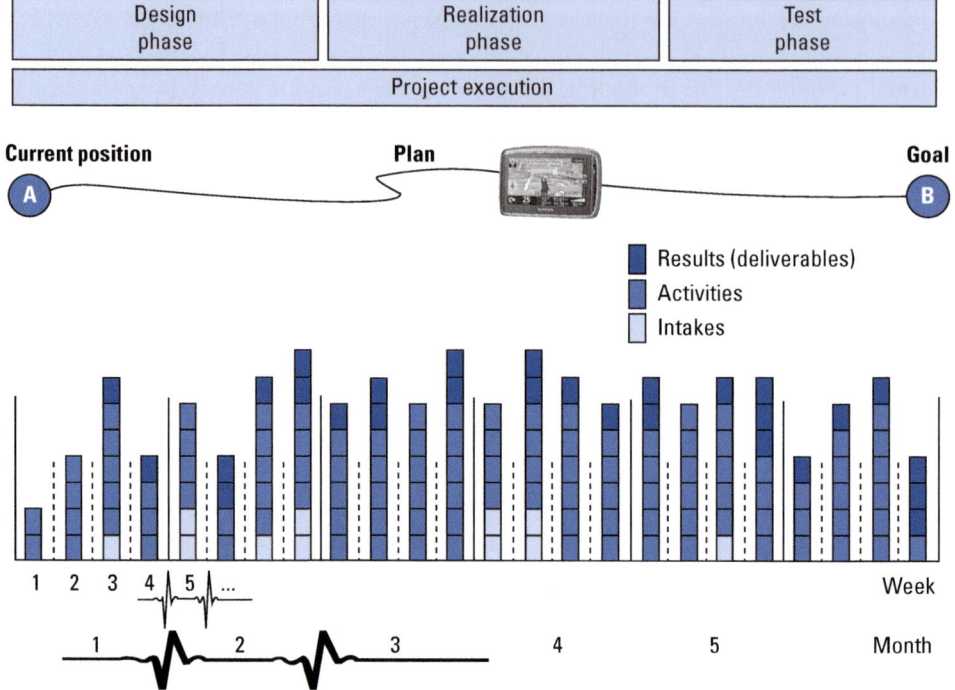

Figure 8.2   Intakes, activities and results from the plan projected onto the heartbeat

Create insight into the tasks and goals per heartbeat period.

The result of this projection is basically the same as the extraction we covered in figure 6.21 when we discussed the planning process. That extraction sorted activities and deliverables by their delivery moment on a week-by-week basis, i.e. the heartbeat period. Furthermore, you will notice that, in addition to the *weekly beat*, there is also a *monthly beat*. We will discuss this in more detail in the following section, where I will show you that there is often a heartbeat at the level of the individual (daily rhythm), the project (weekly rhythm) and the project board (monthly rhythm).

Making critical parameters executable and measurable

When you have a clear overview of your project's deliverables, activities and intakes and you evaluate and measure these regularly, you can assume that your project will be completed on time and on budget. That is, if your plan with its PBS and WBS is complete and correct. However, how can you really make sure that the project result will meet the goals when the project is done? Fortunately, you can do more to ensure that you are not entirely dependent on the correctness and comprehensiveness of your plan: by *measuring the critical parameters during the project execution.*

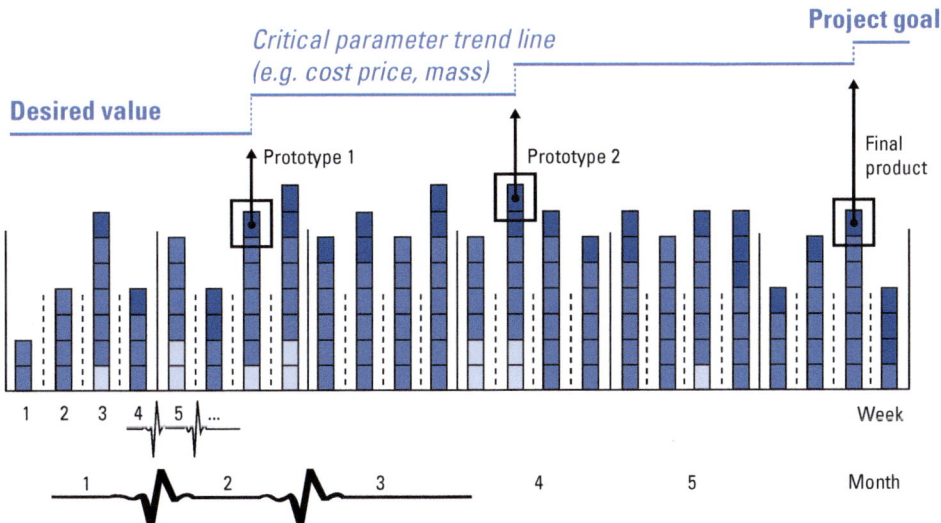

Figure 8.3   Projecting the trend line of a critical parameter onto the project heartbeat

Make sure to also project the expected development of the critical parameters during the project onto the heartbeat in advance. You can do this by identifying the interim products that will be tested and then predicting the expected values of the critical parameters for these deliverables. This creates a trend line as seen in figure 8.3. Later, during the project execution phase, you can compare the actual measurement outcomes of the critical parameters with your predictions. This lets you know if you are on schedule well before the final system tests are conducted. The figure shows how a critical parameter will develop from prototype 1 to prototype 2 to ensure that the final product will ultimately meet the project goal. Back when you developed the detailed plan and implemented Design for X (section 5.6), you should have already identified the deliverables that will be used to evaluate the critical parameters.

Project risk and change management as well
In addition to stimulating the PDCA cycle of the project execution with a constant heartbeat, it is advisable to also include other PDCA cycles in your project heartbeat, especially those of *risk management* and *change management*. These are both processes that can affect your path to the final goal in the short term (continuing to use the example of the TomTom, they are like traffic jams along the way and changes made by the driver). I will cover risk management in this section and we will return to change management in chapter 10.

The PDCA cycle of risk management usually consists of the same generic process steps:

Plan: *Risk identification*: what risks are there and what causes them?
Risk analyses: what is the probability of the risk occurring and what are its consequences (impact)?
Preventative measures: how can I reduce the probability of the risk occurring?
Corrective measures: what can I do if the risk does occur?

Do: *Execute* the preventative and (if necessary) corrective measures.

Check: *Evaluate* whether the measures are being executed correctly and how they affect the risk status.

Act: *Make adjustments* based on the Check stage, which then become part of the Plan stage of the next PDCA cycle.

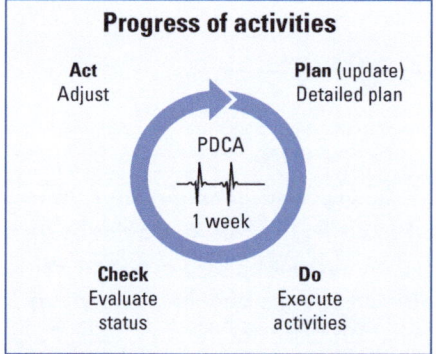

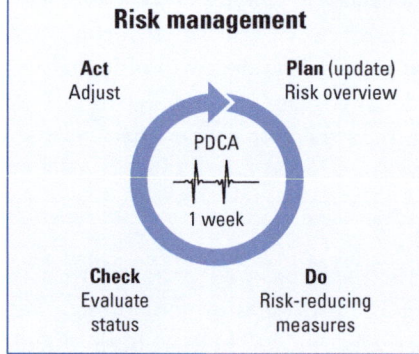
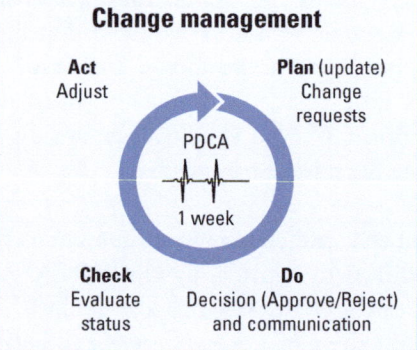

Figure 8.4   Include risk and change management in the heartbeat at the project level

If you use the *risk management table* from figure 8.5, this will help to ensure you do not overlook any element of the process. You should include the initial version of this table in your project management plan, while the updates are part of your weekly progress reports. In the table, the impact of a risk on the project's costs and lead time is estimated. By multiplying these numbers with the probability (P) of the risk, you get a weighted value that you can include in your project budget and time schedule. You must update this table during every PDCA cycle and include any preventative and corrective measures in your detailed plan. This ensures that the Do and Check of risk management become integral aspects of your regular project activities.

Do you actively apply risk and change management as part of the PDCA heartbeat or as ad-hoc processes?

Finally, remember that you can conduct opportunity management in a similar manner to risk management, using the approach we covered in section 4.2 on flip-thinking.

Risk name	Cause	Impact	Risk (= probability x impact)					Preventative measure	Corrective measure
			P (%)	Costs	P*Costs	Time	P*Time		
Resource problems	Reorganization: extensive changes	- Longer lead time - Extra costs	50%	50 kEuro	25 kEuro	8 weeks	4 weeks	- Extensive focus on knowledge assurance - Closely monitor progress	Deploy additional staff
Problems because of new technology	Technology is new for the organization	- Longer lead time - Extra costs - Problems for the client	25%	100 kEuro	25 kEuro	16 weeks	4 weeks	- Hiring external knowledge - Using DfX: early customer involvement	Using existing (old) technology and accepting reduced performance
New software has a lot of problems	Many changes in critical modules	- Longer lead time - Extra costs	50%	100 kEuro	50 kEuro	12 weeks	6 weeks	- Incremental integration: test early - Scrum iterations	Accept delay or reduce functionality
Missing requirements	Insufficient knowledge of the end user	- Longer lead time - Extra costs	25%	200 kEuro	50 kEuro	20 weeks	5 weeks	- Closely review requirements document with client - Evaluate interim results with end user	Accept delay or reduce functionality

Figure 8.5   The risk management table with an up-to-date overview of risks and measures

8.3   Heartbeat at different levels

In a project, you will encounter different heartbeat rhythms at different levels. This frequency is relatively low at the level of the project board and gradually increases as you move down to the project and individual levels. One thing will not change, however, the person responsible for establishing the rhythm is usually the project manager. That means you! In this section, I will discuss the heartbeat at the project, project board and individual levels. Its practical execution will be covered in chapter 10.

Driving the heartbeat

As mentioned previously, I believe that driving the heartbeat is one of the three elements for which a project manager should never require a stimulus from the environment to implement. The other two are developing the project charter and creating the PBS. These three elements together create the foundation for structure, early confrontation, communication and making adjustments. This makes them so important for the project's success that you only have yourself to blame if you neglect any or all of these factors.

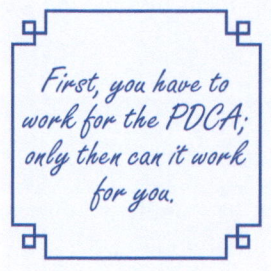

First, you have to work for the PDCA; only then can it work for you.

Driving the heartbeat requires initiative and perseverance because the flywheel rarely gets off to a great start. During the first few weeks, you will have to spend a lot of time communicating about approaches and activities, you will only receive input from your team members after asking for it several times and it will be difficult to draw up a report simply because there are so few results to report on at this stage. All this means that you have to truly understand the long-term benefits of driving the heartbeat to stick with it. That is probably why so many project managers only really start to focus on the PDCA cycle near the end of a project, when it becomes clear that the project goals are not being met. By that time, the heartbeat is no longer merely important, it is now truly urgent. That is a shame, because the flywheel could have been put in motion long before things got this far. They missed their chance to really reap the rewards of proactive and influencing behavior.

Heartbeat at the project level: weekly rhythm

The heartbeat at the project level is the cycle that a project manager needs in order to drive, evaluate and report on the execution of the project activities. This heartbeat typically has a weekly rhythm, but during a crisis (e.g. a production stoppage at the client's premises) it can also temporarily occur on a daily basis.

Heartbeat at the project board level: monthly rhythm

Meetings with the project board usually take place every month, although they can be more or less frequent than that. Of course, the seniority of the project team and the project board's ability to effectively delegate also factor into this. This heartbeat is mostly about reporting to the stakeholders. Project managers will not necessarily communicate about the status of the activities, but rather about the project's status compared to the final goal. They will cover aspects such as project timing, costs, risks, resource issues and changes that impact the project scope.

In organizations where multiple projects share more or less the same project board, e.g. R&D organizations, the project board meetings are often combined into a single monthly project review. This review session may take half or even a whole day, during which the project managers report on the progress of their project one by one. The advantage of this approach, besides the constant rhythm, is that it facilitates integral coordination and the setting of priorities across all projects.

Heartbeat at the individual level: daily rhythm

Lastly, there is the daily rhythm of the heartbeat at the individual level. This is about the execution of activities by the project employees. It is generally a process that all employees go through on their own, although with Scrum the activity level is coordinated with the entire team on a daily basis during the stand-up meetings.

The project employees make agreements about their activities and deliverables with the project manager or team leader. Depending on their maturity level (D1-D4), they will carry out their tasks on their own or under an appropriate level of supervision.

Heartbeat in a Scrum process
The Scrum process is, of course, characterized by its sprint rhythm. This is a constant rhythm that creates focus, "bans" all changes during a sprint and, in return, promises the guaranteed timely delivery of a working result at the end of a sprint period. In most cases, the sprint rhythm can easily be combined with the *monthly* heartbeat at the project board level. The sprint output consists of potentially shippable products, which are exceptionally relevant to the stakeholders in any case.

The Scrum process is made even more powerful by the daily stand-up meetings. This *daily* PDCA heartbeat leads to support for, and a shared understanding of, the tasks at hand, but it also ensures that the tasks are carried out by people with the appropriate skills. Who knows more about the competences that are required than the team members themselves? Because the status of the activities is updated on a daily basis, the project's overall progress is also clear. The daily heartbeat, therefore, also provides input for the *weekly* heartbeat at the project level.

8.4   EOS and OKR

How seriously would you take a TomTom if it took several minutes to update its route whenever something changed? You would probably stop using it if that were the case. The updates need to be done in less time than it takes you to reach the next intersection or turn. That means the heartbeat is determined by the dynamic of your environment, not by your own ability! Operating in a quick and flexible manner during the project execution is, therefore, an important condition for success. The PDCA cycle will only work for you if you are able to move through it at the desired pace. The same goes for projects, and also for change and operational processes within organizations. I will conclude this chapter with two examples of modern systems for business management that are built around a constant rhythm: *EOS, the Entrepreneurial Operating System*, by Gino Wickman and the *OKR system* that is used by such companies as Google, LinkedIn and Twitter.

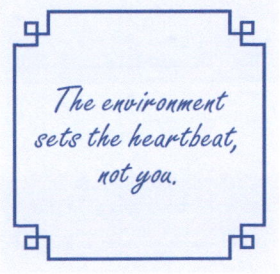
The environment sets the heartbeat, not you.

If you cannot complete the update during a heartbeat, your method is too complex!
Let's first look at your own project. As we have seen, you will have to structure your method in such a way that you can move through the PDCA cycle within a single project heartbeat, i.e. usually a week. If you cannot do that, your method is too complex and you will have to simplify it. Successful project managers simply do not hide behind the excuse of not having the time to update their plan. If you stop doing so, you will no longer have an up-to-date

path to the final goal and you run the risk of losing control of your project. Once you have experienced the benefits of having a constant rhythm during your project, you will always feel the need to restructure the process and ensure you have an up-to-date overview of the path to the final goal during each heartbeat.

As a project manager, I strive to spend no more than 25% of my time on the project's PDCA process. This includes discussing the activities with the project members, evaluating the project's status, conducting progress meetings, coming up with corrective measures and updating and communicating the detailed plan. That leaves me with 75% of the total time to do what project managers should do: be wherever they are needed most. In order to not exceed that 25%, it is essential to have a properly structured detailed plan as described in section 6.4. The other elements needed to realize this fast rhythm will be covered in the final chapter of this book.

Simplicity and results with EOS

What matters is the execution, yet that is exactly where the problem often lies. Organizations tend to make their processes overly complex, paralyze their employees by focusing on overcommitment and fail to translate goals into actions. That is what Gino Wickman explains in *Traction – Get a grip on your business* (Wickman, 2007). Now that we are using the heartbeat to move on to the actual project execution, it is interesting to note that successful systems for managing companies use those same elements: *simplicity, clarity, structure* and *rhythm*.

Translate the vision into executable goals that fit within the project heartbeat.

Wickman uses the principle of *less is more*, because taking action is the most important aspect of any change process. He states that *making* a decision is more important than *what* you decide. Action and especially repeated action lead to results, feedback and the ability to learn. You can only acquire "traction" by eliminating any unnecessary complexity, being clear about goals and responsibilities, and dividing the organizational objectives into small chunks that are easy to understand for the executors and fit well within the heartbeat rhythm. EOS is not about the umpteenth hype in the world of management; rather, it is about how to integrally apply existing and timeless principles to your organizational processes. This ties in perfectly with the core principles of project management and Agile leadership that are covered in this book.

The EOS model: the six key components

Wickman states that every successful business can be reduced to just six key components that each reflect the drive towards simplicity and results (figure 8.6):

1. **Vision**: successful entrepreneurs have a clear vision and are able to communicate this to every member of the organization. EOS makes this applicable in practice by asking eight questions that help you translate an appealing ten-year target into a three-year picture, then into one-year plans and finally into quarterly rocks. Like a kind of PBS, vision is

turned into small, executable goals at the individual level that fit well within the PDCA rhythm.

2. People: successful entrepreneurs surround themselves with the right people in the right seats. EOS views this as a factor 10 element and focuses on acquiring the right people and putting them in positions where they can do the most good. A lot of attention is given to clarifying roles and responsibilities (accountability).

3. Data: facts are needed in order to have productive discussions and make the right decisions. You can then use this data to adjust the plan and resolve problems quicker, driven by the rhythm of the heartbeat. In Wickman's words: "What gets measured, gets done." This is a perfect example of TomTom behavior. EOS focuses primarily on data that is predictive (leading indicators) and ties into the organizational goals and the quarterly rocks (individual execution). *You conduct measurements to learn, not just to control.*

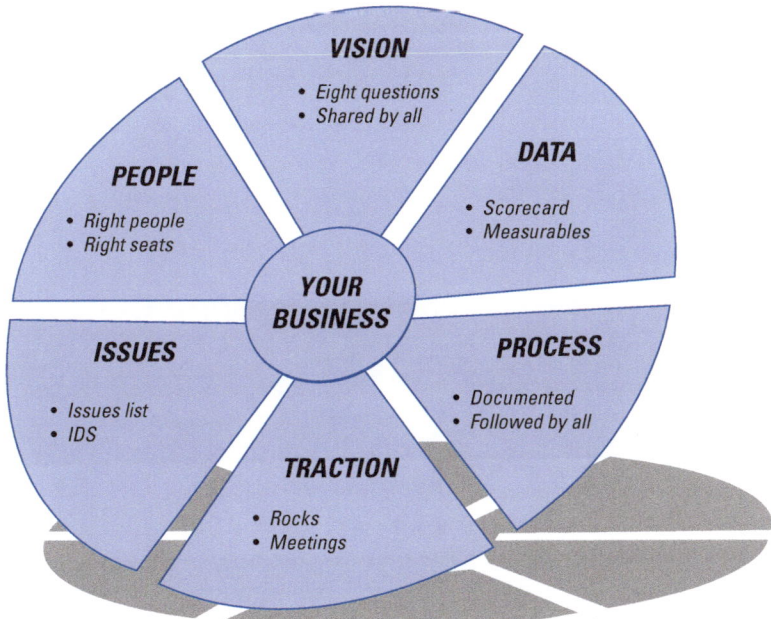

Figure 8.6   The six key components of EOS

4. Issues: in a practical manner EOS invests in issue management that should be part of the heartbeat. Firstly, by indicating that it is perfectly normal for issues to arise. The issue list does not have to be empty. It is important to foster an open and safe environment in which people can bring up issues. Furthermore, EOS covers how to work on the right problems in a structured manner using *identify, discuss and solve (IDS)*. This ties into the *8D method* that we will cover in chapter 10, which explains *how* to resolve these problems.

5. Process: EOS states that a process can only be fine-tuned when it is consistently applied throughout an organization. The organization's core processes will therefore have to be documented and followed by all employees. Only then will repetition, improvement, upscaling and growth become possible.

6. Traction: many organizations struggle with turning plans into concrete actions and results. Given that *Traction* is the name of the book, it should not surprise you that this is where everything comes together. The complex organizational goals have been divided up into concrete and measurable quarterly priorities (rocks, issues) and lead to traction through the application of a consistent PDCA cycle. EOS calls this the *Weekly and Quarterly Meeting Pulse*. Wickman agrees that translating vision into results calls for a constant rhythm, as seen in figure 8.7.

From goal to execution with OKR

OKR stands for *Objectives and Key Results*. This methodology was developed at Intel and it was given global renown in 1999 by John Doerr. When introducing OKR at Google, which was just a small company at the time, he said: "Ideas are precious, but they're relatively easy. It's execution that's everything."

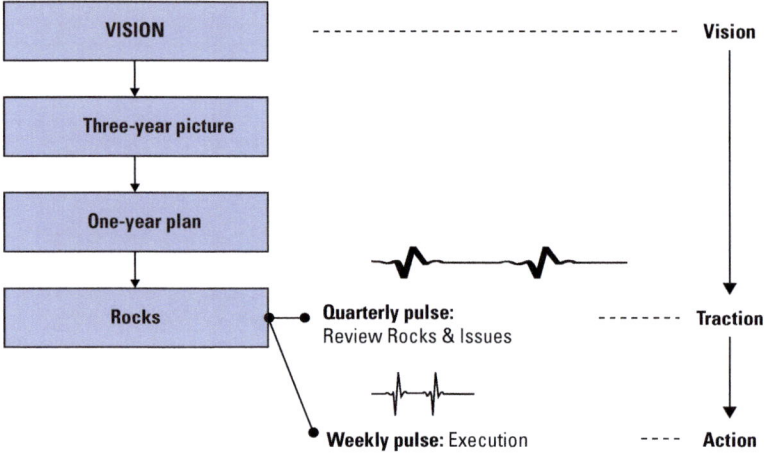

Figure 8.7   Traction through the decomposition of goals and rhythm

OKR is a relatively simple method with which to link business goals to employees' individual goals. This is not exactly rocket science, yet it is a highly effective method because it once again creates a link between vision and the employees' goals and because it only becomes valuable when the execution is also included in the system. That is why having a consistent heartbeat is such a major factor in OKR as well. This method is applied by many exponential organizations; companies that outperform the average business in their sector by a factor of ten.

OKR shares many similarities with EOS, as well as with other methods such as Robert Kaplan and David Norton's Balanced Scorecard. In 1992, they demonstrated how vision can be translated into action by connecting the objectives of four layered perspectives within the organization: the financial perspective, the customer perspective, the internal business processes perspective and the learning and growth perspective.

It is important to note that OKR distinguishes between *operational* and *aspirational* goals. The latter category differs from the former because it concerns higher goals that are usually less attainable. The bar is deliberately raised higher than what is achievable, which makes people strive to create more added value than the project calls for. Aspirational goals therefore result in creative tension, which we covered in the section on creativity in the previous chapter. Besides helping to realize goals, OKRs also improve employees' motivation and

Aspirational goals lead to results, motivation and innovation.

engagement and the organization's innovative power. *Challenging is more important than controlling!* John Doerr therefore recommends that OKRs are detached from the evaluation process of individual employees. They are intended to lead to coordination, focus and innovation.

Summary

- Creating a rhythm is an essential success factor in project management; without a heartbeat there is no PDCA cycle.
- If you know what needs to be delivered during each heartbeat period from the very start of the project, you can keep your team from only truly working hard when the end of the project (or the deadline) is in sight.
- Projects often have a different heartbeat at each level, for example:
  - Monthly rhythm: reporting to stakeholders/project board;
  - Weekly rhythm: coordinating the execution of activities and deliverables (with Scrum, this is a daily rhythm);
  - Daily rhythm: the execution of individual activities.
- Create a mapping on the heartbeat of your detailed plan and of the trend of the critical parameters and make sure you know what needs to be done during each period. This creates focus and a sequence of "small sprints" towards interim results. Remember the ten-kilometer speed skating race that is divided up into twenty-five 400-meter laps.
- The heartbeat and the PBS/WBS used in combination allow you to transition from deadline-driven direction to activity-driven direction.
- Heartbeat is a feedback and communication tool, *not* a control tool. Quite the opposite, it helps you let go of the reins of (self-organizing) professionals and teams in both Agile and traditional projects.
- All management activities from the PDCA cycle follow the project heartbeat, risk management and change management are no exception. Make sure your work method suits the desired update speed!
- Proactive project leaders know that it can take a while for the heartbeat to start up. They maintain an unwavering focus on their planning and control activities to get the flywheel going.
- In a change process rhythm is once again the key to translating goals into actions. Drive the project S-curve with the rhythm of the heartbeat and maintain a constant pressure on the entire process.
- Countless management books have been written on the subjects of mission and vision, but the EOS model and OKR demonstrate how you can also include the execution in operational business processes. Just as in this book, it is all about simplicity, clarity, structure and rhythm.

9   The blind check

- How our brain rewards us when we achieve results.
- Why the blind check leads to corrections after the fact.
- Avoiding the blind check is a mindset first and foremost. How can you utilize Fagan inspections, DfX and Agile to tackle the blind check?
- Why searching for defects requires a safe environment.
- Learn what techniques you can use to test "on the right side of the V" and, especially, proactively "on the left side of the V."

After projecting the activities and deliverables onto the project heartbeat, you end up with a weekly shopping list. If you follow it closely, it will ultimately lead to the desired project goal. But wait, wasn't having a shopping list a bad thing? It certainly is when you are first starting the planning process, because it could then result in a static to-do list without structure or dependencies. At the end of the planning process, however, it is a perfect tool to prepare the detailed plan (or scrum board) for the execution phase. That list is dynamic, not static, because you put together a new projection during every PDCA heartbeat using the updated detailed plan. With this overview, the project execution becomes a matter of *driving and checking off* weekly tasks.[13]

Checking these tasks off is highly useful, because it shows that you are productive, making progress and getting nearer to the final goal. It also has a mental effect on you. Every time you are challenged to achieve something and you reach that goal, your brain produces a substance as a reward, a hormone called *dopamine*. This neurotransmitter makes you feel relaxed and comfortable and drives you to experience the feeling again and again. In other words, dopamine helps you take action to earn even more rewards. The prospect of the next reward motivates

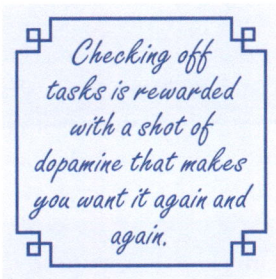

Checking off tasks is rewarded with a shot of dopamine that makes you want it again and again.

us to work harder and it gives our concentration levels a boost. To benefit from this chemical process, however, the deadline must be in sight. That is another explanation for the fact that focusing on deadlines that are far off in the future only results in procrastination, not action. It explains why dividing large tasks into smaller chunks improves our productivity. *A fast rhythm of small sprints to interim goals results in more reward moments and therefore a higher performance.*

---

13 This chapter ties into the following competences from IPMA's ICB4: Leadership, Results orientation, Quality, Procurement, Risk and opportunity.

9.1   Beware of the blind check

Checking tasks off in your detailed plan is a satisfying experience. However, it is important to only check items off your list if they are truly finished and have led to the desired result. Only then will the completed tasks and deliverables accurately reflect the status of the project, while the unchecked items represent the remaining path to the final goal. In other words, beware of the unwarranted checking off of a task, which I call the *blind check*.

The blind check gives an illusion of progress and leads to unexpected corrections later on.

Little more than a ceremony

The blind check can be a major problem during a project. No matter how good your preparation and detailed plan are, if the activities are executed incorrectly or if the quality of the results is insufficient, this will affect the final result. Worse still is that the checked-off activities suggest a project status that has not actually been achieved. It gives you the illusion of progress. Consequently, you will only discover at the end of the project, "in the top-right corner of the V," that you need to make a ton of corrections in order to reach the goal.

Unfortunately, people tend to "forget" the original purpose of activities when they complete them. Being able to say that something is done is more important than the question of what they have actually achieved. Consequently, the results are not critically evaluated. Many developers enjoy creating something new far more than testing what they have built. The pressure they feel as a deadline approaches will only exacerbate this problem. The client wants to move forward and the contractor wants to report good news, so it is tempting to simply push on without examining the results too closely. This makes reporting on the project's status little more than a ceremony, rather than a serious moment of evaluation during a PDCA cycle.

Check, check, double check

It is important that completed activities and delivered subresults are carefully evaluated. A critical evaluation does not have to take long and can save you a lot of problems further down the line. It is easier than you might think and having the right mindset goes a long way. For example, you can reduce the risk of the blind check when a test report is delivered by asking the author the following questions:

- Were you able to execute all test cases?
- How many test cases had a negative result?
- Did you notice anything that was not explicitly tested?
- How satisfied would you be with this product if you were its end user?
- Were your expectations met regarding which test cases are critical and which are not?
- Did the actual effort match the estimated time required?
- Do you have any new ideas regarding how to make the tests more productive next time?

Questions like these result in entirely different insights compared to remarks like: "Is it okay if I take the tests off the to-do list?", "It's good that we can move on now," and "Did that really have to take so long?" You will also see that questions that are relevant to the employee are generally not seen as overbearing, but rather as interested and helpful. That is because they concern the actual work itself, instead of being little more than fancy management jargon strung together. On top of that, they inspire improvement and growth. This means they fit well within all quadrants of situational leadership, as long as you realize that S1 and S2 call for a more controlling focus, while S3 and S4 require you to be a sparring partner and coach.

When is it deemed good enough? Carefully considering every delivered result and asking a few critical questions will go a long way. Consciously executing the plan-do-CHECK-act cycle allows you to add quality without investing a whole lot more time. Additionally, there are the review and inspection techniques that we will cover in the next section. Above all, the most important feeling that you as a project manager must have is that the delivered result will actually bring you one step closer to the project's final goal. That is when you are truly

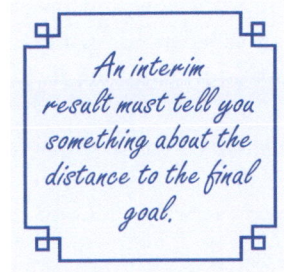

An interim result must tell you something about the distance to the final goal.

acting like your inspirator, the TomTom. *If you do not get that feeling strongly enough, keep asking more and more questions until you do.*

 Look around your project or your project environment. How many blind checks do you see?

9.2   Tackling the blind check with review and inspection techniques

First and foremost, avoiding the blind check is *a mindset.* Carefully execute the Check stage of the PDCA cycle, critically evaluate the delivered results and ask yourself how much closer they bring you to the final goal. *A task is only done when it is truly finished and its added value has been determined!*

Additionally, you can use certain review and inspection techniques to evaluate and improve the quality of a delivered result in a structured manner. The great thing about these techniques is that you can use them for virtually all completed deliverables on both the left- and right-hand sides of the V-model. Most other test techniques are based around testing physical results and are, therefore, primarily used during the test phase "on the right side of the V." Review and inspection techniques provide feedback during the early stages of your project and can therefore be seen as a DfX tool (section 3.3). We will cover four of these techniques, ranging from formal to informal:

1. Fagan inspections;
2. Peer reviews;
3. Walkthroughs;
4. Distribution for commentary.

The Fagan inspection process

While working at IBM in the 1970s, Michael Fagan was concerned by the amount of time that was wasted on repair activities during software development projects. These repair activities mostly occurred near the end of a project after the test phase. They even continued after the client had already started using the product. This made the lead time of projects unpredictable and had a negative impact on IBM's product quality and image. Fagan, an experienced quality engineer, decided to utilize quality assurance techniques from the world of hardware development. In addition to testing end results, he also had interim results inspected in a thorough and structured manner. After some exceptionally positive experiences with this approach, he introduced the Fagan inspection process in 1976 (Fagan, 1976). This inspection process is basically a test process for documents. Since you do not want to wait until you can test the final result, you will have to test its precursor. In many cases this is not a physical deliverable but a document.

A Fagan inspection is basically a test of a document.

Fagan was talking about the challenge that is represented in figure 9.1. Errors in project requirements and product designs are often only discovered when the whole system is tested. These are costly mistakes, because they require an entirely new round of design, implementation and testing. We have already covered this in detail back in chapter 3, when we discussed the V-model. *The Fagan inspection process was one of the first developments in the field of early confrontation.* These days, a project manager's arsenal has been expanded with many DfX methods and iterative development using the Agile approach.

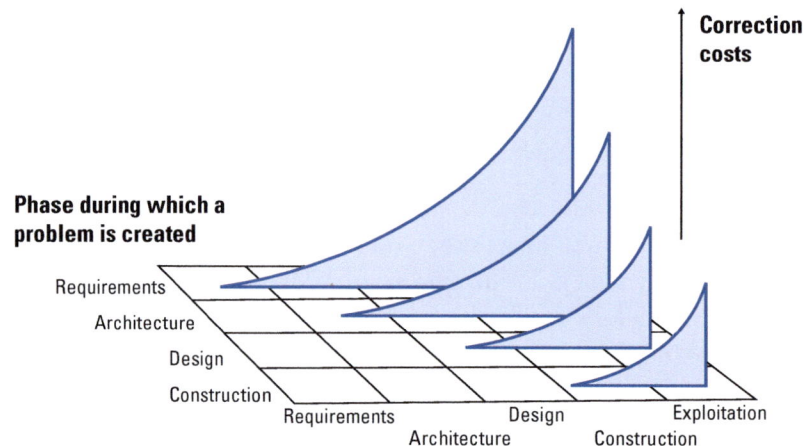

Figure 9.1   The correlation between the correction costs and the phase during which a problem is created and corrected

In addition to helping you discover errors sooner, the Fagan process also helps with creating support, and with your team members' growth and development processes. Last but not least, it is a highly efficient method that makes optimal use of your specialists' time!

 Do you have any experience with formal inspection techniques?

When I first took part in a Fagan process, the initial eye opener for me was the presence of a special *moderator*. This person's job is to make sure that all inspections are executed correctly. The moderator also serves as the chairperson during review sessions. Eye opener #2 was the *focus on teamwork*. When I scheduled the review, I had to choose the review members myself. I had to form a team of people who, taken together, possessed the right knowledge to inspect the document. Furthermore, the *role division* had to be explicit: who was to focus on what?

Next came eye opener #3: the importance of *preparation*. The review members received my document, in which line numbers had been added to the margins of every page. Prior to the review session, they were to study the document and list all their remarks, i.e. *defects*, in a defect list. Furthermore, they had to indicate the *severity* of these defects: major, minor, question or typo. Major defects affect the project result. Minor defects are undesirable, but they do not have any immediate consequences for the project. Questions speak for themselves and typos merely indicate typographical or grammatical errors in the document. Figure 9.2 shows an example of a defect list.

Page	Line	Description (defect)	Severity			
			M	m	?	t
6	7	Under scope, the subsystems for department X and Y are missing	x			
6	12	Create proper delineation. It is currently unclear that the maintenance phase is not part of the project.	x			
6	18	What do you mean by this remark?			x	
7	10	Add a diagram of the project organization		x		
7	15	interface = project interface				x
8	20	Two project results are missing: deliverable x and deliverable y	x			
9	15	Also include the reservation of test systems in the plan (resources)	x			

Figure 9.2   Fagan inspection defect list

This list was submitted to the moderator, who combined all lists into a single overview of all defects. This was a simple task, because each defect was accompanied by a specific page and line number. During the review session itself I experienced the biggest eye opener of all: *I had to shut up!* The process is set up to make the gathering of remarks as effective and efficient as possible. Collecting defects is the goal. That meant no discussions were allowed, we did not go over possible solutions and we did not point fingers and assign blame. At the end

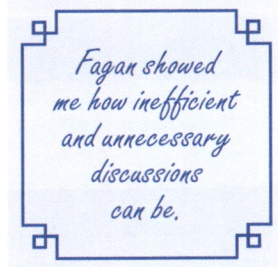
Fagan showed me how inefficient and unnecessary discussions can be.

of the session I was given the integral defect list and the reviewers decided together, based on exit criteria, whether the document would be approved after I had incorporated their remarks, or if it had to be rejected because it required more substantial modifications and a second round of reviews. In the former case, the document was officially released after the moderator had verified that I had correctly incorporated the submitted remarks. Figure 9.3 sums up the entire Fagan process.

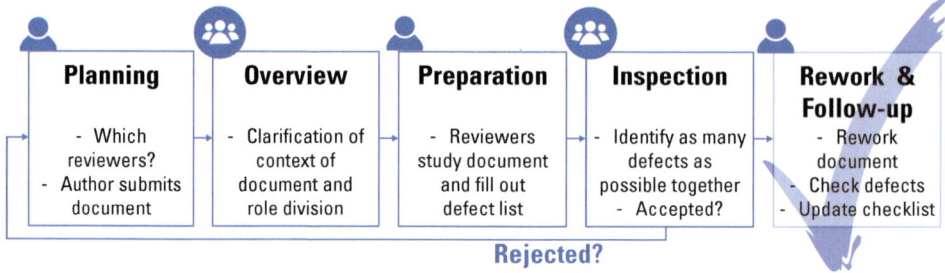

Figure 9.3   The steps of a Fagan inspection process

Motivation, learning curve and growth

Regardless of whether you closely follow the entire Fagan process or only utilize parts of it, it is interesting to experience for yourself the fact that processes become more effective when you *focus on the essence*. In this case, that involves finding as many defects as possible. It is a skill in its own right and it requires expertise and focus from everyone involved. On the other hand, you start to notice how often people act without a clear vision or process approach. *That opens the door for the blind check*. For example, without a proper role division reviewers may all focus on the same things, which means other major defects are overlooked.

 How hard do you try to organize activities in such a way that the focus is on their essence?

As a project manager with a focus on the final goal, you have the noble task of ensuring everyone is focused from the start of the project. This will not be easy. You will have to fight to get important things done "on the left side of the V," before they become urgent on "the right side of the V." After all, the reverse is usually our default behavior. As the American lieutenant general John W. Bergman aptly put it:

"There's never enough time to do it right, but there's always enough time to do it over."

Inspections are good for the document and even better for its author.

The following insight may help you when trying to motivate your environment to conduct proactive inspections. I believe that Fagan inspections are a good way to improve the quality of the document – but an even better way to allow the author to grow. Tom Gilb, the author of the standard work *Software Inspection* (Gilb, 1993), uses a study conducted at Ericsson in 1997 to demonstrate that an individual's learning curve is raised much higher through formal inspections than what could be otherwise achieved with training or process improvements in the organization itself.

Figure 9.4 shows that the number of major defects found during inspections drops from 28 to a mere 3-5 as a result of just four subsequent stages of learning. I have experienced this phenomenon for myself as the author of, for example, project management plans. After a few inspections (and after learning a whole lot from the concrete feedback you receive), you know for certain that your next plan will make it through the review session with minimal remarks. *Fagan inspections also give your self-confidence a serious boost!*

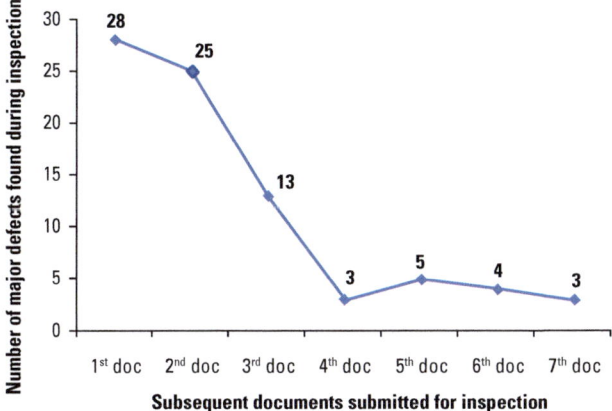

Figure 9.4   The learning curve of an Ericsson-Stockholm employee, measured by Tom Gilb (Gilb 1997)

Informal review techniques
In addition to formal Fagan inspections, there are other less formal ways to evaluate and improve documents. Below, you will find brief descriptions of some of the most common techniques.

Peer reviews
A peer review is a review undertaken by a colleague at the same level as the author. Peer reviews can occur at the author's own initiative or as part of a standard process. For example, you can set a rule that states new software code cannot be checked in to the system until it has passed a peer review. Personally, I believe it is highly useful to always conduct a peer review before a result is delivered or tested. Doing so benefits the project, it is a great way for people to learn from each other and it contributes to the quality of communication and collaboration within the team.

Walkthroughs
During a walkthrough, an author presents the contents of the document, the underlying thought processes, the deliberations and the decisions that have been made. Contrary to a Fagan inspection, the author plays an active role in a walkthrough. *The main goal is to inform others and learn from each other.* Finding defects is less important than acquiring support, although it is definitely a factor. As with a Fagan inspection, it is advisable to assign roles prior to a walkthrough.

Distribution for commentary

Your document is finished and you submit it to the parties involved with a request for feedback (also known as an email pass-around). This is an informal technique that we all use. It is an excellent way to inform others and acquire substantive feedback. Be aware that recipients may or may not read your document and give you feedback, depending on the document's importance and their available time. Of course, your way of asking and following up on the process are also important factors.

9.3 Tackling the blind check with DfX and Agile project management

We have already seen, back in chapter 3, how the critical parameter, Design for X and Agile project management all result in early feedback. This makes them excellent methods to avoid the blind check. In this section, I will give a few examples of how to do this.

Think from a perspective of the critical parameters

How can you know whether an interim result will bring you closer to the project's final goal? By asking critical questions upon its delivery, as discussed at the start of this chapter. A review or a formal inspection will also help you to eliminate defects from the deliverables. However, the only way to acquire direct information about the remaining path to the final goal is by measuring the interim status of the critical parameters and comparing this to the desired values, for which you use the trend line seen in figure 8.3.

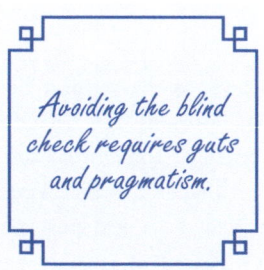

Avoiding the blind check requires guts and pragmatism.

Include Design for X activities

You often have to do something extra to evaluate the status of a critical parameter and avoid the blind check. You can do that by including DfX activities, as we saw during step 3.5 of the planning process (section 5.6). Methods such as Design for Six Sigma, Design for Testability, Design for Reliability, Design for Manufacturing, Design for Logistics and Design for Serviceability all provide enough examples of extra activities to evaluate the critical parameter at an early stage. However, do not go looking for the solution too far from home. It is ultimately about you and your team using your common sense and creativity to look for ways to proactively evaluate the critical parameter. You might come up with ideas similar to these:

Interim result to be evaluated	Extra evaluation activity
• user requirements	⇨ user survey
• system requirements	⇨ determine budget per subsystem and test feasibility
• system concept	⇨ create a model and conduct performance analysis
• design	⇨ develop test protocol to evaluate the testability
• supplier evaluation	⇨ conduct audit

Additional feedback helps you to avoid the blind check and allows you to take corrective measures early on. That is exactly what the TomTom would do. This calls for guts and a pragmatic attitude. *Guts* because you must sometimes acquire feedback in the customer environment or from your stakeholders during a vulnerable stage of the project. It is usually preferable to only do so once you have the final product in hand. This is similar to the guts it takes to apply the 10% confrontation rule.

You also need *pragmatism*. When developing a new system during my time at Assembléon, the people in the prototyping workshop proposed to develop a model of the system during the architecture phase in order to test the serviceability right away. They did not like having to wait until the 3D CAD models were finished. When I walked into the workshop one Friday afternoon, I discovered that the team had built a life-sized model of the contours of the entire system out of plywood. The people from the service department were learning how to conduct their service activities. This resulted in insights that were at least as valuable as performance calculations made using complicated dynamic models. *It also allowed disciplines that care less about writing and evaluating documents to take part in the decision-making process of the architecture phase.*

Design for X with the FMEA

"Having no problems is the biggest problem of all," is what Taiichi Ohno, the developer of the *Toyota Production System*, later known all over the world as the *Lean Manufacturing* methodology, once said. What he meant was that discovering a problem is not a bad thing, but rather a chance to make improvements or a *kaizen* (Japanese for "change for the better"). Ohno encouraged his people to adopt an open, transparent and interested attitude towards problems and to use the method of "ask 'why' five times" to keep asking questions until the cause was clear.

This open and hungry attitude when finding problems was also seen during the review and inspection process. Looking for defects instead of punishing the people responsible is an important aspect of avoiding the blind check. In that same vein, I will cover two DfX methodologies: the FMEA and the HALT methods. I will begin with the FMEA, or *failure mode and effect analysis*, which is used to identify the potential failure modes of a new product during the design phase. Next, I will cover HALT, or *highly accelerated life test*, which provides insight into the failure modes of a new product during the realization phase, making it possible to proactively tackle these weaknesses before the market launch.

The FMEA is basically a *risk management method*, which means it follows the steps outlined in section 8.2. Several steps have been added to ensure you use a *structured approach* and to help you *prioritize*. First of all, the product design to be investigated is systematically divided into modules to make the analysis easier and the coverage greater. Next, an FMEA meeting is held during which a multidisciplinary team identifies the potential failure modes and their respective causes. To do so,

The FMEA results in proactive actions during the design phase.

team members keep asking questions systematically according to the principle of *five times why* to uncover the true underlying cause(s). They then study the consequences (effects) of every potential failure mode. This often involves analyzing the situation "in a breakdown" until all details are fully understood (if this, then that, with such and such a consequence, etc.). Finally – and this is where the FMEA differs from a regular risk analysis – the team analyzes the possibilities of detecting the failure mode if it should occur. Failure modes that are visible before they have serious consequences have less of an impact than failure modes for which this is not the case. The multidisciplinary team then estimates the probability of failure (*occurrence*), the worst potential effect of the failure (*severity*) and the probability of failure discovery before the customer is affected (*detection*). Using these three factors, the total risk of the failure mode can be calculated: the *risk priority number* (RPN):

$RPN = O \times S \times D$

where:
O = Occurrence, the probability of the failure occurring (1 is low, 10 is high)
S = Severity, worst potential effect of the failure (1 is low, 10 is high)
D = Detection, probability of discovery if the failure occurs (10 is low, 1 is high)

The risk priority number is a value between 1 and 1,000. Sorted in a descending order, it indicates the priority with which each failure mode must be tackled. The FMEA results are listed in a table like the one in figure 9.5.

Module or function	Potential failure mode and cause		Potential effect		Current controls		RPN	Proactive action				
	Description	0	Description	S	Method of detection	D	O x S X D	Action	0	S	D	RPN
module 1	failure mode 1 and cause	5	effect...	10	detection...	4	200	action...	3	4	4	48
	failure mode 2 and cause	1	effect...	3	detection...	10	30	action...	1	3	4	12
	failure mode 3 and cause	2	effect...	8	detection...	6	96	action...	2	4	6	48
	failure mode 4 and cause	2	effect...	2	detection...	4	16	no action	2	2	4	16
	failure mode 5 and cause	6	effect...	10	detection...	5	300	action...	2	7	3	42
					detection...	2	10	no action	5	1	2	10

Figure 9.5   FMEA table with failure modes, RPN and proactive actions (with expected RPN reduction)

Design for X with HALT tests

Whereas the FMEA has you identify a product's failure modes using the design "on paper." HALT is about providing insight into failure modes by testing the (interim) product itself. Contrary to "normal" tests, *highly accelerated life testing* is not about demonstrating that the product meets the set requirements. Instead, it is about exposing the product to ever-increasing stress until it fails. It is, therefore, not a quality assessment used "on the right side of the V," but rather a Design for Reliability method that helps you *make the design as robust as possible* early on in the project.

Figure 9.6 illustrates the HALT methodology. It shows the limit at which the product will break down (the destruct limit) and the stress the product undergoes during regular use. Both are represented as a normal distribution around an average. During the HALT process, the product (or preferably an earlier prototype) is gradually subjected to increasing levels of stress, e.g. in the form of vibrations, high temperatures, etc. The stress level is increased until the two curves overlap and the product fails. The final stress level is, therefore, usually higher than what the product would be exposed to during normal operating conditions. The next step is improving the weak points, before continuing the test to uncover more weaknesses. *The HALT test is not a quality evaluation, but a method to identify failure modes and make the product more robust.*

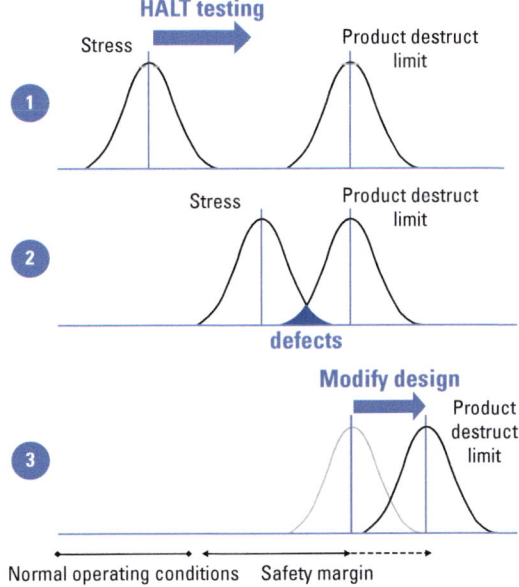

Figure 9.6   The HALT methodology: testing up to the point of failure to make the design more robust

HALT testing results in higher product quality and an improved predictability of the project course. During the project you create situations that would otherwise only occur during the test phase or even later, when the product is already in the hands of the end user. It is not only about constructions that break down, but also about hard-to-predict system behavior. I experienced this myself during a HALT test in which a system computer was booted up at ever-lower temperatures. Everything was fine at first, until the temperature was so low (10° Celsius, I believe) that the system would not boot up anymore and crashed. It turned out that the hard drive was taking more time to spin up and was not yet available when the motherboard tried to read data. By modifying the software and telling the system to wait for the hard drive to spin up, this problem was eliminated. As is often the case with HALT tests, a potentially major problem for end users was resolved with a few simple lines of software code. In

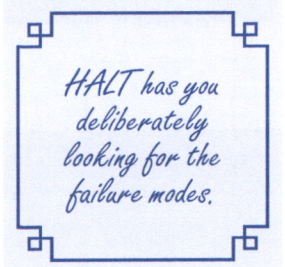

this manner, cheap modifications can massively improve the robustness of the system, as long as you implement these modifications before the project reaches – or completes – its final phase!

How Agile helps you avoid the blind check
Because the Agile process explicitly requires you to test subfunctionalities at an early stage, it is an excellent way to avoid the blind check. After every sprint, you will receive feedback that lets you know whether the delivered results meet the expectations of the client or end user. Nevertheless, this does not mean that Agile projects cannot benefit from inspections or, for example, a design FMEA. The methods complement each other and all lead to a critical evaluation of the (interim) results in their own way.

Agile helps to avoid the blind check, but it can also make people less attentive.

The Agile process itself includes a quality evaluation for each delivered sprint result during the *project execution*. On the other hand, the *definition phase* can benefit from additional inspections, because the flexibility of the project may make the client *less attentive when defining the wishes and goals*. The belief that "we can always adjust things later" may result in an attitude that opens the door for a multitude of blind checks during the project definition phase. Agile developers are not immune to this mentality either: the product is not robust / fool proof / 100% tested yet, but we will get to that during the next sprint. In that case, the advantage of flexibility in relation to the market has turned into flexibility to compensate for internal shortcomings. It is comparable to the risk of driving more recklessly just because you are in a safer car.

9.4   Testing on the right side of the V-model

By focusing so much on proactive leadership, I may have created the impression that the activities on the right side of the V are unimportant. Allow me to rectify this now. Test and verification activities are of the utmost importance. I merely want to keep them from being seen as a convenient safety net that leads to procrastination. *Quality is demonstrated – not realized – by testing.*

There are several methods you can use to demonstrate quality, depending on what level you have reached in the V-model. I will cover these methods briefly, starting at the point where we ended with HALT: the tests at the component level. From there, we "work our way up" until we get to the acceptance tests that lead to the client's approval and the closure of the project. This completes our overview of methods that can be used to avoid the blind check, as seen in figure 9.7. These test methods are also used in the example of the plan for project Roller Coaster at www.roelwessels.com.

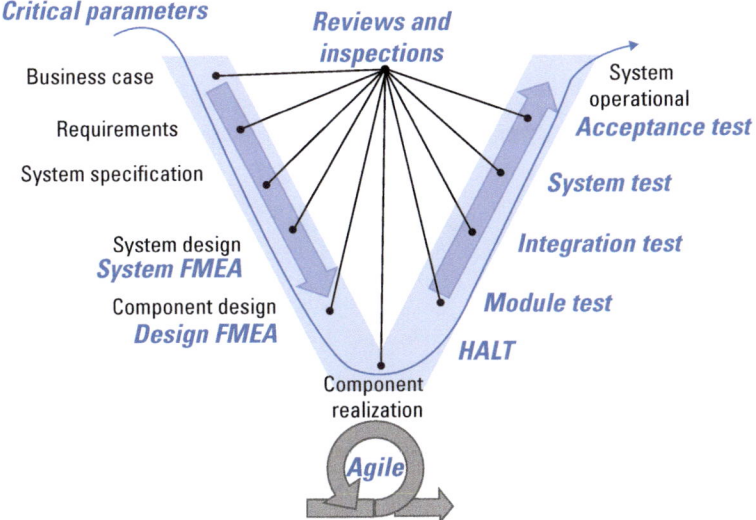

Figure 9.7   Methods to avoid the blind check

Testing at the component level

Testing at the *component level*, also known as a *module test* or *unit test*, is about testing the delivered components before they are integrated into the overall system. This allows you to verify the quality and behavior of individual components sooner and more effectively. Furthermore, it is a way to evaluate the results delivered by suppliers. A system developer's module test and an acceptance test of a component delivered by a supplier can, therefore, be one and the same. Testing at the component level is done based on the requirements of the subsystem, which were identified during the decomposition of the system requirements to the component level in accordance with the PBS (see section 5.4).

To test individual components, you usually require a test environment that creates the same conditions which would otherwise be provided by the system itself (inputs, interaction and feedback), see figure 9.8. You can create these conditions in a number of ways, e.g. with a mechanical or electrical test rig that is specifically designed for the module. When testing software modules, it is common to use *test stubs*: these are temporary software functions that simulate the behavior of the missing system environment. This makes it possible to test the software module on its own and in a replicable manner. A test environment for software also lets you automate the software tests. That is often a benefit, because the same tests will have to be repeated as part of the regression tests whenever the product is updated. We will discuss this further later in this section.

Stubs often have limited functionality and are used for an initial test of the *correctness and completeness of the interfaces*. Once that phase is complete, you can move on to testing specific behavior at the component level. You will need more extensive test tools for this, such as a *model* that *dynamically* simulates the rest of the system. This is also known as a *software-in-the-loop simulation* or *model-based testing*. Depending on the complexity of the model, this

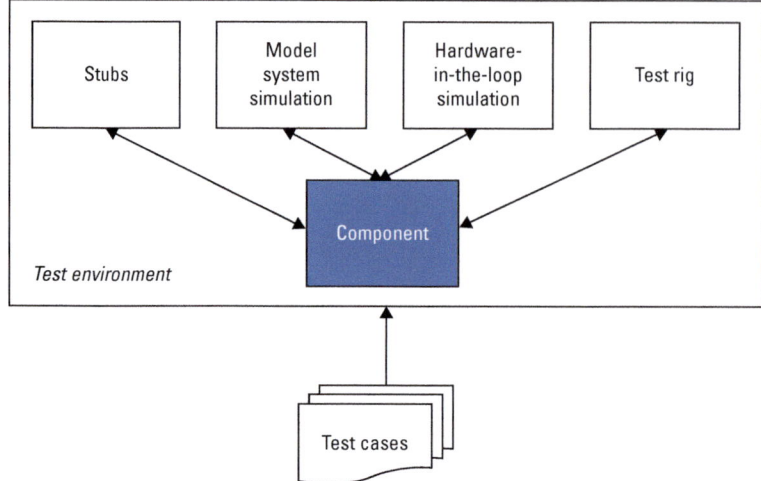

Figure 9.8   Testing at the component level often requires a specific test environment

lets you subject the component to a highly realistic verification long before the rest of the system is even available.

You should not underestimate the development of the model. This should be done "on the left side of the V," together with the design of the component itself. That means it requires a substantial investment. However, if you can afford to make this investment, you can expect to reap the rewards in multiple ways. You can subject components to tests that would be either too dangerous or outright impossible to conduct in real life. Furthermore, you can automate and reproduce the tests. When you develop such a test environment, you are automatically applying Design for Testability. Ultimately, it will also be possible to connect other (physical) modules to the model, which turns a software-in-the-loop simulation into a *hardware-in-the-loop* or HIL simulation. In this manner, the test environment is continuously expanded with sensors, actuators and other real components. In other words, you are already conducting basic integration tests.

Finally, I would like to briefly go over the key differences between *black box testing* and *white box testing*. This distinction is especially common in software tests. During a black box test, testers have no knowledge of the internal structure of the component they are testing. The component is a black box to them and they will mostly test at the (external) requirements level. During a white box test, however, the internal structure of the component is known and visible to the tester. That means you can also test the *internal behavior* of the component. Furthermore, you are allowed to modify the component to test specific functionality, e.g. by adding extra code that shows the value of certain parameters. White box tests must, therefore, be conducted by a software developer and they typically take place as part of the module test at the bottom of the V-model.

Integration tests

When I discussed the planning process in chapters 5 and 6, I emphasized then the importance of having an integration plan. If you want to prevent the system integration from becoming a confusing *big bang* plagued by problems that are hard to identify, it is important to build up and test the system one step at a time during integration testing. You start with module tests, before integrating more and more components from the bottom up. This results in testable interim steps and allows you to combine quality with quality. System integration requires a detailed integration plan, either as part of the project management plan or as a separate subproject plan.

System integration is about combining quality with quality.

Testing at the system level and the acceptance test

Now we reach the level we were aiming for all along: testing the behavior of the entire system. The system requirements serve as our guideline here and they must be tested one by one. System tests often consist of two steps, the FAT and the SAT. The FAT or *factory acceptance test* is the "in-house" system test that you conduct yourself before the system is delivered and installed at the client's location. After the FAT, the SAT or *site acceptance test* is conducted at the client's location. The FAT is commonly referred to as the *alpha test,* while the SAT is called the *beta test.*

In addition to testing the basic functionality, system tests often also include a safety test and a performance test. During the safety test, all safety functions are assessed. The performance test is designed to check and finetune the product's performance. This step is usually only possible after the system has been installed at the client's location. As you might expect, modifications can be made even during the system tests. Depending on the scope of the modifications, you may have to repeat certain component and integration tests (i.e. go through part of the V-model again). Of course, you want to minimize the number and impact of these changes by adopting a proactive mindset. However, you will always have to conduct *regression tests* when you implement a modification in order to check whether the other (non-modified) system components still function correctly.

Once all problems have been resolved and the tests indicate that the system meets the set requirements, the acceptance process can begin. During this process, the client verifies that all results and subresults have been delivered and conducts an *acceptance test* to check the entire system. The protocol for these tests, the *acceptance protocol*, is usually defined when the contract is drawn up at the start of the project. If all requirements are met, the client will accept the project result and make the final payments. The project team can now be disbanded. The project will enter the exploitation phase and you will only have to provide aftercare depending on the type of contract you have with the client (problem resolution, maintenance, updates, etc.).

Summary

- Projecting your detailed plan onto the project heartbeat results in a dynamic countdown list, which makes the project execution a matter of driving actions and checking them off the list.
- When you complete a task, your brain rewards you with a shot of dopamine. This continuously motivates you to go after the next result in line.
- Avoid the blind check. An activity is not done until it has led to the desired result and made the path to the final goal shorter.
- Avoid the blind check with:
  - The right mindset;
  - Review and inspection techniques;
  - Additional DfX activities (FMEA, HALT, etc.) and measuring the critical parameters;
  - The Agile approach and testing subfunctionality early on.
- Fagan inspections improve both a document and its author.
- Avoiding the blind check requires an open culture in which the discovery of defects is stimulated rather than penalized.
- You create quality on the left side of the V-model and demonstrate it by testing "on the right side of the V" using:
  - Tests at the component level (module tests);
  - Integration tests;
  - System tests (FAT, SAT);
  - Acceptance tests.

10 The Final Countdown

- How to integrate the activities from the heartbeat into your work processes.
- Why it is important that the Check and Act stages from the PDCA cycle take up no more than 25% of your time.
- How change management can be used as a basic process for controlling all deviations.
- How to visually communicate the project status and the remaining path to the goal to your team and stakeholders.
- Learn how to keep uncertainties from paralyzing you.

In this final chapter I will talk about the project execution. Isn't that a bit late, you might say? It would be if we had not discussed the techniques for the execution phase at all yet. However, you will see that many of these techniques have already been covered. Even better, you have applied them frequently during the definition phase. Although that phase is mostly about preparation and thinking, without combining it with action and execution you would not be where you are now: at the start of the project execution.[14]

A lot of what we have learned so far comes together in this chapter and I will show you how to put everything into practice. It is all about effectiveness, efficiency and pragmatism. Otherwise, all you have are good intentions. We will discuss how to execute planned activities, drive progress and evaluate results, with regard to the activities of both your own team and (external) suppliers. Furthermore, we will cover how you can determine the project status at any time and make it insightful for the project team and the stakeholders.

How do you deal with changes during the project? Change management, including tips to minimize the associated disruption, should of course be an integral part of the discussion of the execution phase. Finally, we will cover how you can do all this even if your project is rife with uncertainties. Particularly during difficult "expert slope" projects, it is important to make these uncertainties plannable and to stay in control of the path to the final goal.

The title of this chapter is *The Final Countdown*. During the execution phase, it is advisable to communicate in terms of time-to-go, costs-to-go, issues-to-go, etc. It is about checking off the remaining activities, after which the project result can be delivered – that is, if your PBS and plan are correct and complete. You can test the latter during the execution phase by measuring the critical parameters, because only these parameters offer an instant view on the project status compared to the final goal.

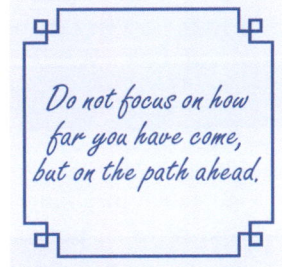

Do not focus on how far you have come, but on the path ahead.

---

14 This chapter ties into the following competences from IPMA's ICB4: Governance, structures and processes, Conflict and crisis, Results orientation, Scope, Time, Quality, Finance, Resources, Procurement, Plan and control, Risk and opportunity, Stakeholders, Change and transformation.

Viewing the project as a *countdown* ensures you maintain a constant focus on "the landing strip." The sooner you can switch to this "checking-off-tasks mode," the better. At the start of the project you run the biggest risk of falling behind without even recognizing it.

10.1 Summarizing the path to the execution phase

Before discussing the execution phase itself, I first want to summarize the previous chapters using four themes:
1. Your mindset throughout the entire project.
2. What you do right at the start (project preparation phase).
3. Proactive, influential and effective behavior.
4. How to develop the detailed plan (project initiation phase).

What have you done by the time the project execution phase starts?
Your mindset throughout the entire project:
- Learn from your TomTom. It is all about realizing the goal.
- The path to the goal is all that matters. The path behind is history.
- Think Agile: replanning is a fact of life. You should always actively look for the optimal path to the final goal. This is a core principle of Agile leadership.
- Make sure you always have a plan and understand the consequences for the project's end result, regardless of any uncertainties. Think in terms of different scenarios.
- Do not look at informing your stakeholders as an obligation, but rather as an opportunity to influence them.
- When communicating with your stakeholders, translate everything into consequences for the project's final result and goal (and the stakeholder's respective interests).
- You must take the initiative to realize three essential elements in your own interests, regardless of the attitude of your environment: the project charter (early coordination), the PBS (structure) and the heartbeat (communication and progress).
- Always look for early feedback opportunities, both at the project level and when executing the individual activities.
- If you focus solely on deadlines, this is little more than hoping everything will be okay in the end. Instead, focus on smaller chunks (intakes, activities and deliverables) that fit within the constant project heartbeat.
- Avoid the blind check and the illusion of progress when checking off activities and results.

What you do right at the start (project preparation phase):
- Immediately draw up a project charter and fill out every field. You should not spend more than two hours on this task. Do not allow yourself to be distracted or paralyzed by your drive for perfection. Surprise yourself with how much you already know and see how this initial step allows you to take control of the project from the start.
- Conduct a stakeholder analysis. Make sure to identify all stakeholders (not just the problem cases).
- Develop your relationships with stakeholders before any problems arise. For each stakeholder, come up with an initial proactive contact moment at the very start of the project.

- Maintain a clear role division between the project manager (contractor) and the client by distinguishing between the project result and the project goal.
- Map your project onto the V-model and consciously invest "on the left side of the V" for the purposes of "build the right product" and "build the product right."
- Develop a strategy and a project phasing structure, and decide for which project components you want to use the Agile approach.
- Identify the project's critical parameters and maintain a strong focus on them as you move through the V-model.
- Remember the project S-curve when starting up the project: motivation, stakeholder trust, insight, organization and collaboration have to grow over time. In addition to a project manager, you are also a change manager.
- Bear in mind that the start of a project offers the most influencing opportunities and carries a high risk of (unnoticed) delays. It is important to be focused from the very beginning and understand *you* are the driving force behind the project.
- Start driving the heartbeat as soon as possible, even if you have not developed a detailed plan as yet.

Proactive, influential and effective behavior:
- Instead of (reflexively) reacting, you should be acting (in a goal-oriented manner).
- Working hard is the factor 2, working smart is the factor 10.
- Always try to take the initiative, even when it is not obvious to do so (flip-thinking).
- Use the 10% confrontation rule for deliverables in order to acquire early feedback and avoid submarine behavior. This will automatically make you a proactive influencer.
- Apply the V-model to your own behavior and try to come up with proactive activities that guarantee results. Use these extra preparatory steps to also involve your environment in the process.
- Use Covey's seven habits of effective leadership, especially the circle of influence, Covey's quadrants (importance versus urgency), thinking win-win (emotional bank account), seeking first to understand and then to be understood, and synergizing (the whole is greater than the sum of the parts).
- Mix up your game by applying different leadership styles.
- Use situational leadership (S1-S4) to find the right balance between directive and supportive behavior, depending on the employee's maturity level (ability and willingness).
- Motivate your team members by satisfying their basic needs: competence, autonomy and relatedness. Start motivating before you encounter any resistance.
- Actively express your appreciation of your employees and celebrate successes.
- Stay in control without micromanaging by focusing on the critical parameters and correctly applying situational leadership.
- Communicate deliberately and attentively. Make sure that you can inform your stakeholders of the current project status and the consequences for the final goal during every project heartbeat. Do the same with regards to change and risk management. Be tactful about it, do not be more transparent than necessary and consider how you want to deliver your message.

How to develop the detailed plan (project initiation phase):

- The 10% confrontation rule first requires a project charter and a sketch with the team. Afterwards, you will have "plenty of time" to develop the detailed plan.
- Use the steps of the planning process to involve your team and the stakeholders in the development of the scope, approach, sketch with the team and detailed plan.
- Make a clear distinction during the planning process between *understanding the project size* (sketch with the team, product backlog) and *driving the execution* (detailed plan, scrum board) to combine early confrontation, agility, overview and detail at the activity level.
- Do not start with a "shopping list." Instead, use the PBS to develop a complete overview of subproducts (interim results) in a structured manner. When using Scrum, you can relate the user stories on the product backlog to the bottom row of the PBS.
- Rearrange the subproducts of the PBS until they match both the project content (e.g. architecture, technical aspects and finances) and the project organization.
- Improve the PBS with DfX deliverables to facilitate early feedback.
- Expand the PBS deliverables (the *what*) with the WBS activities (the *how*) and apply size and effort estimation. With Scrum, the team only determines the WBS activities during the execution phase prior to each sprint when drawing up the sprint backlog.
- Improve the WBS with risk-reducing activities and earlier interim results and turn individual buffers into a single project buffer.
- Integrate everything into the sketch with the team, a plan at the deliverables level. Only include the PBS deliverables so you can flexibly make changes. At this stage, the WBS activities are "only" used to determine the size of the PBS (with Scrum, you do so without the WBS by using Planning Poker). For Scrum (sub)projects, assign which user stories are realized in which sprint. Together with the team, improve the sketch with the team and coordinate the final result with your stakeholders.
- Expand the sketch with the team into a detailed plan that also includes all WBS activities (except when using Scrum). Be careful when making connections and create a smart project interface "at the top" of the detailed plan. This project interface is the dashboard with which you can maintain control and visualize results and problem areas.
- Make the plan suitable for the execution phase by projecting the intakes, activities and deliverables from the detailed plan onto the heartbeat.
- Also project the trend line of the critical parameters onto the heartbeat and use this to make the quality and status of the project results measurable.

Just do it

Once you have done all this, you will be in for a relaxing execution phase. Well, "relaxing" … let's just say that you will have done everything to avoid surprises. You will be able to maintain control, even during difficult projects. As I mentioned at the beginning of this book, you will be a project manager who actively seeks out difficult "expert slope" projects because you enjoy them and want to become even better at what you do. From this point on, the execution is a matter of just doing it. Proactive project management or *Design for Execution* has been taken care of. You are optimally prepared to move along with any events in the project environment in an Agile manner without ever losing sight of the project goal.

10.2 Heartbeat in practice

I covered the advantages of a constant project heartbeat in detail in chapter 8. We concluded that it is very useful for a project manager to take the lead in driving the PDCA cycle. Once the flywheel is in motion, it will start to work for you and your whole environment! A fast rhythm will give your direction and communication a boost and get people accustomed to *your* update moments. You will, therefore, no longer have to deal with one stakeholder after another asking you about the status of some aspect of the project. In this section I will explain how to start up the heartbeat of your project. First, however, I want to cover "*management by…*"

Management by objectives and by exception
Situational leadership (as shown in figure 4.8) is basically all you need to direct your employees and supervise their progress. Nevertheless, it is helpful to understand the relationship with a few other concepts that are part of "management by…" In this chapter I will particularly refer to *management by objectives* and *management by exception* when talking about the relationship of the project manager with the team members and the project board.

Management by objectives (MBO)
With management by objectives, the supervisor and the employee determine the objectives together (the *what*). Results are also discussed one on one. Employees have a certain degree of freedom to choose their own approach (the *how*), which improves their motivation and engagement. The emphasis is on coaching, teamwork, win-win and the employee taking responsibility. MBO is quite similar to S3 and S4 leadership and ties into the positive perception of a Theory-Y manager (McGregor's X-Y theory).

Management by exception (MBE)
Management by exception is also based on formulating objectives together. Contrary to MBO, however, progress is not monitored through regular feedback and coaching, but only if the project course is found to deviate from the plan. *"No news is good news."* It is about being given room to make decisions and escalating the situation if that boundary is crossed. As a result, employees will have a lot of freedom, while their supervisor does not have to spend as much time supervising them. This method does require a significant degree of task maturity from both parties, otherwise, it will lead to tardy interventions or the loss of support and trust. It ties into S4 leadership and, again, a positive perception of others.

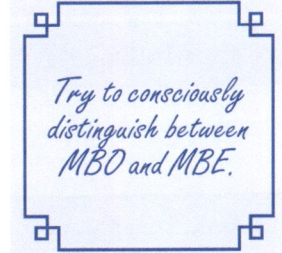

Try to consciously distinguish between MBO and MBE.

In addition to the above, there's also *Management by direction and control* (ties into S1 leadership), *Management by delegation* (ties into S4 leadership) and *Management by walking around* (ties into S3 and S4 leadership).

MBO and MBE are particularly interesting. Do you opt for regular meetings or do you only feel the need to discuss the situation in case of a deviation? Be careful not to slip into

MBE mode unintentionally, e.g. because you have no chemistry with the client or because you avoid each other for different reasons. There is nothing wrong with MBE, but it is not for the faint hearted! Only utilize it if both parties have achieved a sufficient degree of task maturity and mutual trust.

 Do you utilize MBE under the right conditions?

Other matters will also become more understandable when you distinguish between MBO and MBE. The PRINCE2 project management method, for example, uses MBE as its basic management principle and it is largely designed to facilitate its application. This is done by making strict agreements about the specifications of the deliverables, focusing extensively on the project organization and the structure of the project board, explicit authorization and acceptance of work packages and a clearly defined process for the initiation, execution and completion of project phases. S4 leadership is the standard in PRINCE2, which creates the necessary conditions for this leadership style through a highly structured process and organizational structure.

Choose how you want to manage
Should you manage the project board? Yes indeed: *manage yourself, manage your team, manage your environment.* Of course, you will not literally manage the project board, but you can take the lead during the reporting process and influence the communication within the project organization. You will soon start to see your circle of influence expand…

An oft-used approach is to use management by objectives for your team and suppliers, and management by exception for the project board. For your team, management by objectives facilitates a fast rhythm, extensive coordination and plenty of support. For your stakeholders, management by exception gives you the freedom to decide when and how to report to them. On top of that, it makes you less dependent on the leadership style of the stakeholders. You must, of course, ensure that your communication is effective in order to preserve your stakeholders' trust in both the project and yourself. If they desire more contact or a closer collaboration, you can always scale up to management by objectives. This basic approach is represented in figure 10.1.

A characteristic of the heartbeat is that the entire project has a fast rhythm during which the project activities and progress are coordinated. This is not only important for projects, but also when directing operational processes (see the EOS *meeting pulse* in section 8.4). Keep in mind that coordinating matters properly is not the same as having many and lengthy meetings. However, you cannot avoid having to coordinate closely with your team members at first, on top of any existing meetings. That is why it is important that people quickly realize the benefits of a constant heartbeat and discover that every minute spent coordinating with you results in a better understanding of their own activities and creates opportunities for feedback and coaching. This calls for an active and decisive approach.

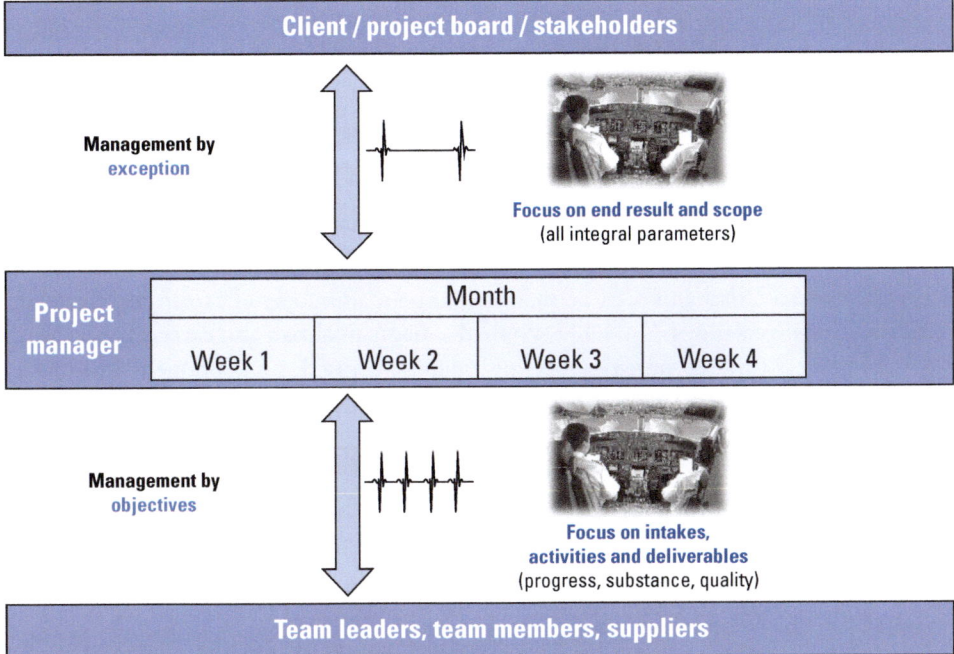

Figure 10.1   Coordination of the project manager with the team and stakeholders

Project managers have their work cut out as well, since the difficulty of proper coordination is often underestimated. They run the risk of working a little bit on a lot of things. During hectic projects, that is simply not good enough. You cannot afford to conclude at the end of the week that you don't actually know the status of several key aspects, or that you failed to initiate certain actions. Similarly, you should not receive an update from person X on Monday and wait until Thursday to coordinate with person Y. By that time so much

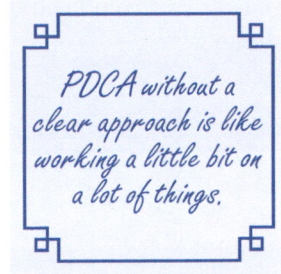

PDCA without a clear approach is like working a little bit on a lot of things.

will have happened that you will need to get back to person X to understand the situation. You have wasted a lot of time and still do not feel like you have a clear view of your project's status.

I have three tips to help you get the PDCA flywheel going:
- **REGULARITY:** it is better to coordinate frequently but briefly than to occasionally coordinate for a long time. Set up a regular pattern of coordination moments and ignore remarks such as: "We have nothing to discuss, let's cancel the meeting." In that case, tell the other party that the meeting will be short, but it will not be cancelled. You usually have more to discuss than you might think at first.
- **MOMENT:** try to complete the Check and Act steps from the PDCA cycle in as short a period of time as possible. Otherwise, the data will belong to different status moments and you will have to keep updating your information. Status is tied to a particular moment and it is constantly changing. Accept this fact and remember the interim measurements

conducted after every lap of a ten-kilometer race. Select a fixed moment during each heartbeat period at which you gather status information and coordinate the necessary corrections.

■ **INDIVIDUAL versus GROUP:** gathering, discussing and communicating project information is a process that usually cannot be done during a single *one-size-fits-all* meeting. Some elements require one-on-one contact with a specific team member, while others depend on the group dynamic. Be aware of this and avoid frustrating a group meeting by engaging in individual discussions or focusing on matters that should have been prepared beforehand. Vice versa, it is not a good idea to handle team coordination via individual conversations. You will become the team's mailman and carry all responsibility for the process (unless you enjoy playing a game of "divide and conquer," but that does not fit the spirit of this book).

PDCA in practice with your project team

How can you apply this in practice? The method I describe below is represented in figure 10.2. It consists of five steps and combines the aforementioned tips, which results in an efficient process. Executing it requires no more than 25% of a project manager's time. This is the PDCA approach I personally prefer to use, although you should feel free to put your own spin on it. Instead of copying it, be inspired by it and remember that every environment requires different choices. This method can be applied directly to traditional projects. Scrum projects also include elements of the five steps, although it should be noted that the weekly steps 1-3 are combined into a single team meeting that is held every day: the daily stand-up meeting.

(1) 15-minute individual meeting with each team member (or subproject leader)
(2) 1- to 1.5 hour progress meeting with all team members (or subproject leaders)
(3) Update detailed plan
(4) Draw up progress report and distribute it along with the detailed plan
(5) Rest of the week: be where you are needed most

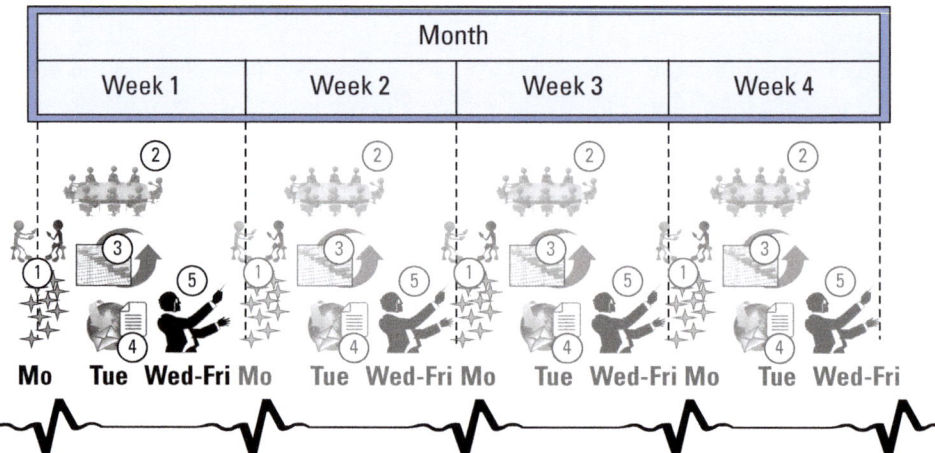

Figure 10.2   A PDCA cycle in practice with your project team and suppliers

1. *Individual meetings (Monday afternoon)*

The individual meetings serve several purposes. First of all, you discuss each team member's assigned tasks and realized progress. Secondly, these conversations provide the detailed information that you need to determine the project status. Finally, they help you prepare for the next day's progress meeting with the team. You have these individual meetings with your direct reports. If you are the project leader of a single team, those are all your team members (and the suppliers). If you are working on a larger project and have several subproject leaders

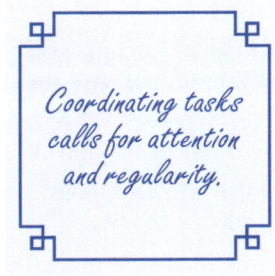

Coordinating tasks calls for attention and regularity.

below you, you have individual meetings with said subproject leaders (and the suppliers). The subproject leaders will have their own individual meetings with the members of their respective team. Of course, you do not need to have these meetings with the members of a Scrum team because of the daily stand-up meetings.

During the individual meetings, you look back on the previous heartbeat period and ahead to the next one while utilizing situational leadership. For D1 employees, you devote more attention to their activities (WBS) and task execution. For D4 employees, you focus mainly on work and progress based on the deliverables (PBS) and project goals. It is, therefore, important to also involve people with a high degree of task maturity in this process; do not make the mistake of believing that you have nothing to discuss with self-managing employees! With suppliers, you coordinate the delivery of their deliverables – which you use as intakes – using S3 and S4 leadership.

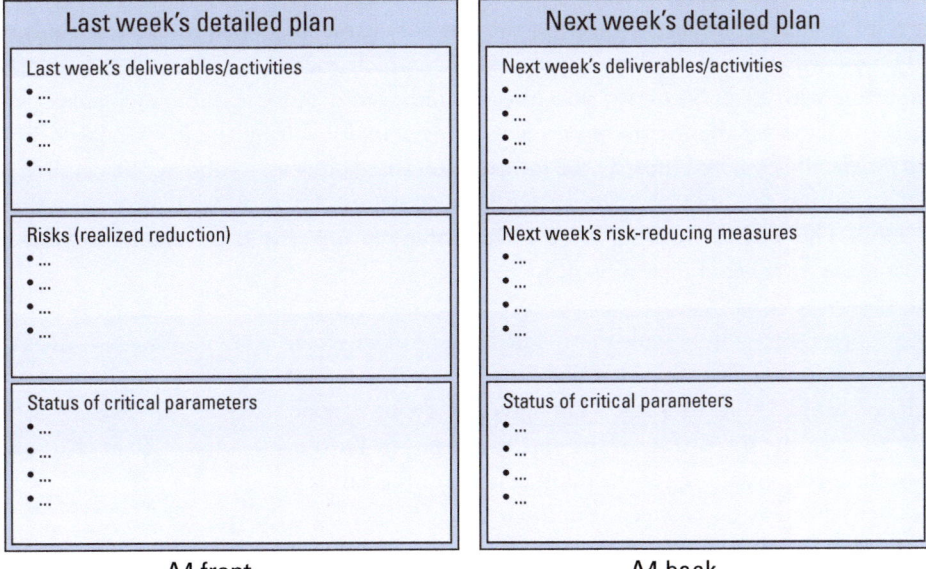

Figure 10.3   Management by objectives: discuss progress together

During the paper age, I used a two-sided A4 page as a reporting tool (figure 10.3). These days, I recommend automating the process using the to-do list generated from the detailed plan as seen in figure 6.21 in chapter 6. You are free to choose, as long as you take the detailed plan projected onto the heartbeat periods as a starting point. Afterwards, you can copy the page so you and your employee both know the plan for the next period. Furthermore, this gives you all the information you need to update the detailed plan later on. This allows you to perfectly coordinate the work and progress together, based on management by objectives. You avoid the blind check by asking critical questions.

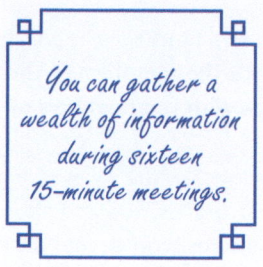

How long should these meetings be? That all depends on your own schedule and the levels of experience of both you and your team members. In any case, a well-structured process will often lead to surprising results. For example, I initially had four team members and spent an hour on each meeting. That was a bit long, though, and it made each meeting far more comprehensive than necessary. Next, the project scope expanded and I had eight team members. I strived to spend no more than half a day on these meetings and it turned out thirty minutes per meeting was also enough. Finally, I was in charge of projects with around sixteen direct reports, which is close to the limit. It was hard work and I was very tired by Monday evening, but I learned that it was possible to have sixteen 15-minute meetings that combined into a perfect weekly overview of the project's status!

2. Progress meeting with the team (Tuesday morning)

There are several advantages to having the individual meetings before the team meeting. Firstly, you will be very well prepared yourself, which means you can play your role as chairperson with ease. Secondly, you already understand most of the main issues, which gives you a clear agenda for the progress meeting. Finally, during the individual meetings, you have already gathered most of the information that you need to update the detailed plan later on. During the progress meeting you can, therefore, focus on what is most useful for the group. This way of working is a great example of "applying the V-model to your own behavior," as we covered in section 3.5.

The progress meeting should not take any longer than necessary. It is a good idea to schedule the meeting before lunch, say from 11:00 to 12:30. This gives everyone a good reason to keep the discussions short and to the point. During the meeting you should cover the main issues and the subjects with interdependencies between team members. Furthermore, this meeting is the perfect opportunity to discuss corrective measures, so you can make optimal use of your team members' knowledge and be assured of their proper coordination. Use

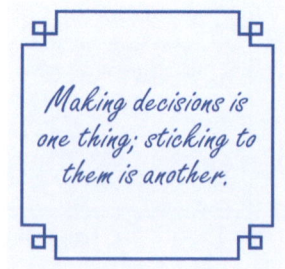

the team's diversity also to avoid the blind check and discuss the impact of delivered results on the critical parameters. Next, update the risk management table (figure 8.5) so *risk management* is also part of the PDCA cycle. Finally, it is a good idea to end with the topic of *change management*. This eliminates the need to schedule a separate (weekly) meeting for this aspect. It also ensures that all decisions and actions can be included in your update to the detailed plan. We will cover change management in detail in section 10.3. In the "What about Scrum?" element of this section, I will explain how the daily team meeting works in Scrum.

3. Update the detailed plan

Tuesday afternoon is all about updating the detailed plan in the planning tool, drawing up brief minutes and communicating both documents to the parties involved. In doing so, Check, Act and the next Plan of the PDCA cycle have all been taken care of in as little time as possible. You successfully completed another "lap" of your project and everyone understands the project status and has instructions for the subsequent lap. During the rest of the week, you and your team can focus on executing the tasks scheduled for this lap, i.e. the Do stage of the PDCA cycle.

If you have developed the detailed plan using the tips from section 6.4, updating it should be a relatively simple affair. Furthermore, you have all the information you need after completing step one and two: you know which activities have been completed, which subresults have been delivered, when the intakes are scheduled, how unfinished matters will be corrected and what activities need to be added to the detailed plan. This makes updating the plan in the planning tool more of an administrative task that you can complete in just one or two hours: checking off, replanning and adding deliverables and activities. Figure 10.4 shows the process of rescheduling unfinished tasks, with the intakes, activities and deliverables vertically stacked per week (as previously explained in figure 8.2).

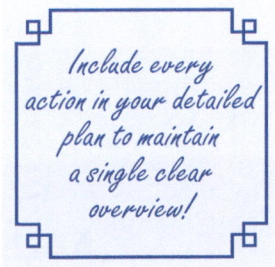

Include every action in your detailed plan to maintain a single clear overview!

When asked what actions should be included in the detailed plan, my answer is clear: all of them! I think it is essential to maintain a single clear overview. *I therefore also add the actions derived from risk management, change management and the list of action points from the progress meeting to the detailed plan.* As a result, they will automatically end up on the employees' exported to-do lists and be covered during the individual progress meetings held on Monday afternoon.

4. Communicate the progress report and the detailed plan

After updating the detailed plan, you should immediately draw up your progress report as well so you can actually end the "lap." Your report can be concise, because the updated detailed plan already contains most of the information that must be communicated. Figure 10.5 contains an example of the contents of a progress report. Start with a summary of the completed activities and delivered results. Next, explain how these affect the project status. It is often best to do so in a graphical format. Section 10.4 contains some examples of graphical status reports for activities, results, time, money, risk management and change management. Of course, it is important that the activities that have to be executed during the next period are clear. You can make sure of this by attaching the updated detailed plan (e.g. an MS Project file) and the extraction of activities (usually an Excel file) to your report. Finally, show the updated status of the risk management table (figure 8.5), an overview of the remaining issues and the decisions made regarding change management. You can present the latter two as tables, although they will often come in the form of references to a database for large-scale projects.

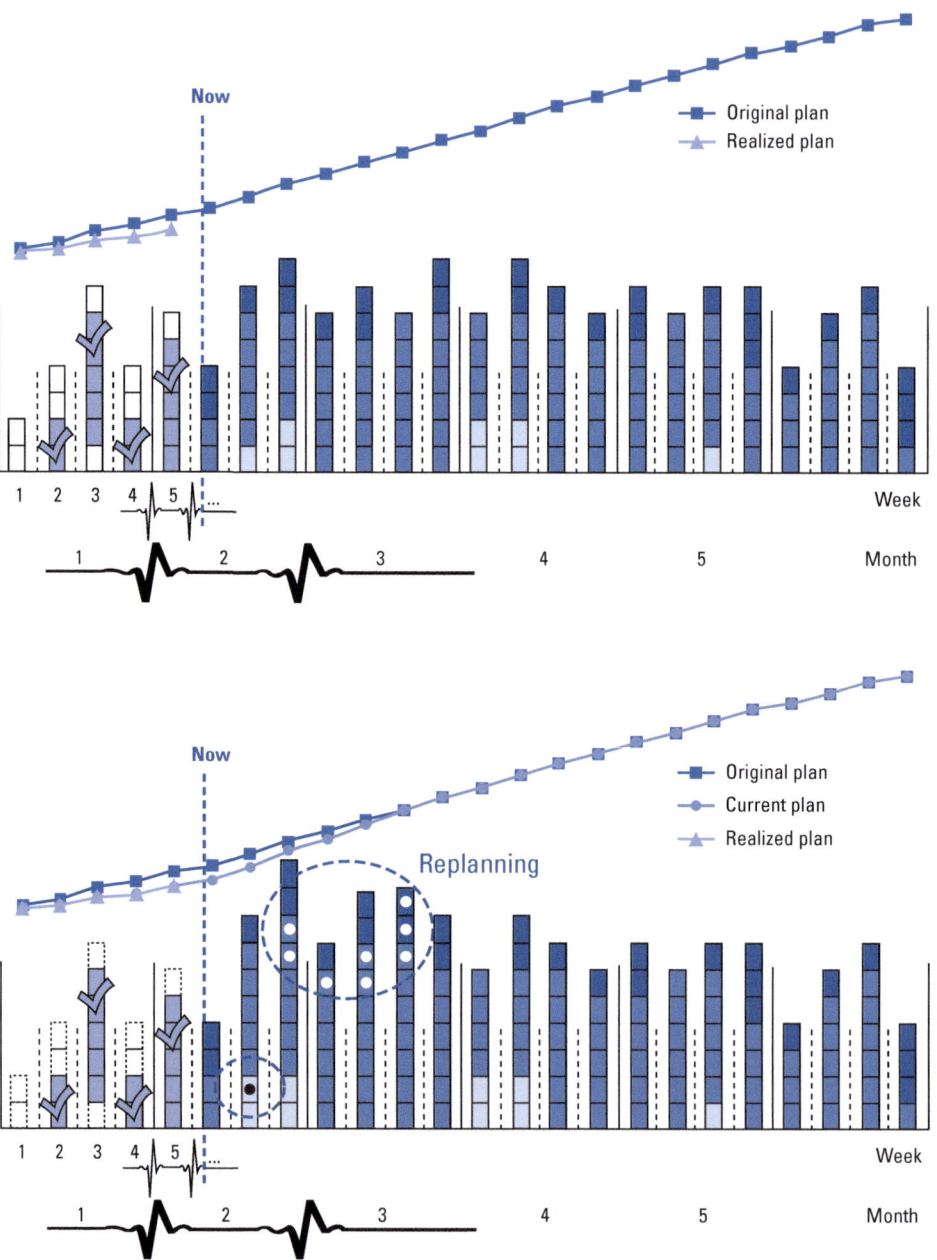

Figure 10.4   The process of determining a project's status and updating the detailed plan

Lastly, I want to briefly cover the *list of decisions*. It is a powerful tool with which to communicate decisions and it can help you stick to them later. Contrary to the action list, from which tasks are taken off after completion, all decisions will remain visible throughout the entire project. It will help you quickly distinguish between useful and useless discussions later on. Simply refer to the decision list and ask what has changed since then. You will quickly see how adding a simple overview like the one in figure 10.6 to your progress report benefits your communication and helps you avoid unrest and confusion down the line.

- ☐ Executed (key) activities last period
- ☐ Delivered results (deliverables) last period
- ☐ Status plan: status activities and results versus plan
- ☐ Status time and money versus plan
- ☐ Update detailed plan (attachment): activities to be executed next period
- ☐ Update risk table
- ☐ Update status issues: test issues, design issues, etc.
- ☐ Update status change management: requests, impact, decisions
- ☐ List of action points
- ☐ List of decisions

Figure 10.5   The contents of the weekly progress report

Date (year.wk.no)	Decision details
2019.02.1	...
2019.15.1	...
2019.15.2	...
2019.17.1	...
2019.18.1	...

Figure 10.6   The list of decisions as part of the progress report

By communicating the progress report, the updated detailed plan and the exported to-do lists, you complete this project heartbeat's PDCA cycle and lay a solid foundation for a successful next round.

5. The rest of the week: execute activities
I have already mentioned that you should strive to complete the entire PDCA cycle, from acquiring insight into the project status to communicating the updated plan, in circa 25% of your time. Note that this takes some practice and it requires you to take charge. Once you can do that, *you will be just as flexible and effective as the TomTom*. You can then use the rest of your week to carry out the activities from the plan and offer support where needed; you can spend enough time on *important* matters and will only be involved in *urgent* matters that were truly unforeseen. This is a practical example of the application of Covey's third habit.

What about Scrum?
The aforementioned steps are virtually the same for Scrum. However, the Scrum process will help you give substance to REGULARITY, MOMENT and INDIVIDUAL versus GROUP with its daily stand-up meetings. This means that the items we covered in steps 1-3

are handled on a daily basis at the team level. During the daily Scrum, each team member answers the following questions (Sutherland, 2014):

■ What did I do yesterday to help the team finish the sprint?
■ What will I do today to help the team finish the sprint?
■ What obstacles prevent the team or me from completing the sprint?

The Scrum team meeting even offers daily status updates (steps 1-3).

The daily stand-up meeting instantly provides an update of the status of the Scrum (sub)project, using visual aids such as a Scrum whiteboard and magnetic Scrum cards to represent the user stories and tasks (instead of the tools illustrated in figure 10.3). The meeting is facilitated by the scrum master, which means project managers can afford to focus on the project level, rather than the activity level. They can, for example, devote their attention to preparing sprints (from product backlog to sprint backlog), evaluating the process (the sprint retrospective) and creating the right conditions to allow the team to perform optimally. So, should project managers attend the daily stand-up meetings? It is often preferable that they don't, because they can damage the team's ability to direct itself by taking charge of the meeting. This choice depends on considerations such as the team's capacities and the project manager's ability to act as a listener rather than a director (see also Robert Quinn's competing leadership styles in section 4.4).

Although the team members themselves already communicate on a daily basis, it is still necessary to communicate with other parties involved in the project. That means the project manager still has to communicate the status report (step 4) to ensure the success of the weekly "lap." The main challenge for project managers is to avoid getting caught up in the daily updates. Instead, they should save everything for that one weekly communication opportunity.

PDCA in practice with the project board

Once you have established a proper (weekly) heartbeat at the project level, you are in control of the key part of the execution phase: the realization of the (sub)results. What remains is the communication with your stakeholders. This is such an important aspect that it is advisable to set some time aside every day to conduct stakeholder management. Note, however, that this is not the same as (reactively) reporting every single day…

When dealing with your stakeholders, it is particularly important to develop a rhythm. The goal is to protect yourself against constant unwanted interruptions and make people patiently wait for your next status update instead. This heartbeat is often a monthly one, although it is not uncommon to use a bi-weekly heartbeat in a highly dynamic environment. Figure 10.7 presents a possible structure for the PDCA cycle with the project board.

When reporting to the project board, you are dealing with different information than in your reports to your own team. It is less about the path and more about the consequences for the final goal. That is what stakeholders care about most. *If you play your cards right the balance in your stakeholders' emotional bank account will grow and they will trust you more.* You will be given the freedom to manage the process as you see fit. It is far more efficient and effective to present a proper integral status update once a month than to provide a variety of fragmented status information throughout the month.

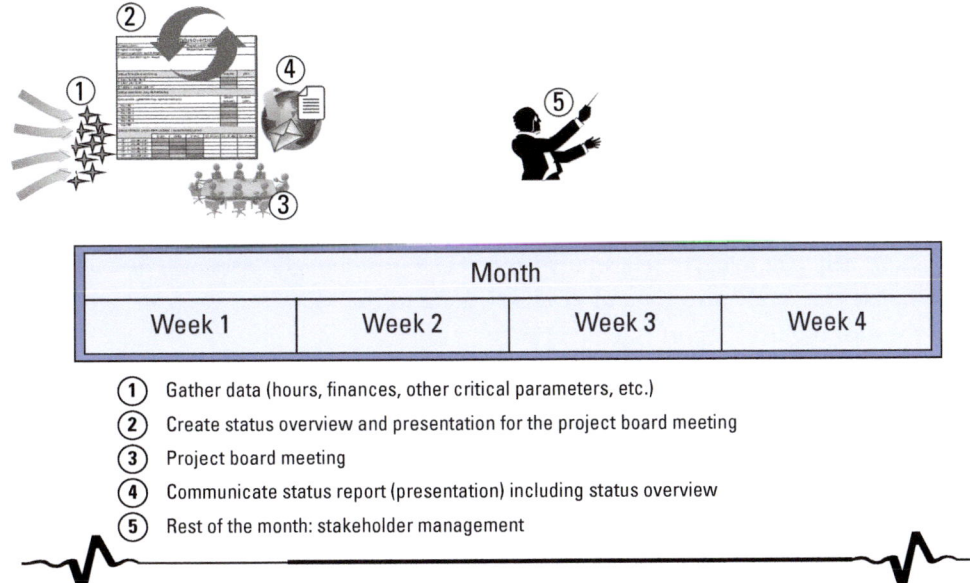

Month			
Week 1	Week 2	Week 3	Week 4

1. Gather data (hours, finances, other critical parameters, etc.)
2. Create status overview and presentation for the project board meeting
3. Project board meeting
4. Communicate status report (presentation) including status overview
5. Rest of the month: stakeholder management

Figure 10.7   PDCA activities for communication with the project board in practice

1. Gather data

Gather the data you need once per period and in as short a time as possible. This will often be at the end of the month, because that is when (official) figures become available from other processes, e.g. the monthly financial statement. It is advisable to use (formal) data from official channels: you do not have to look for the information yourself and you can make sure that the data in your report matches the official figures. You would not be the first person to work hard to calculate the project's financial status yourself, only to get into a discussion with the

Foster good relationships with data providers.

financial controller or CFO during the project board meeting because their financial figures are different from yours. Instead, be "lazy" and use the results of others to your advantage. *Taking control does not necessarily mean you have to be the one who takes action. On the contrary!*

You will often have to make an effort to receive the data you need in the right manner and at the right time. If the data becomes available on the fourth day of the month and you have to produce your report on the third day, this is obviously a problem. However, do not try to reinvent the wheel. Talk to the controller and explain that you would like to use the official data in your report, but that it is released a day late. Chances are that the controller

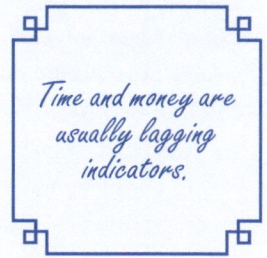

Time and money are usually lagging indicators.

is able to send you a preliminary version of the data two days earlier, which you can then use for your report. Why? Because it is often refreshing and motivating for a controller to work with project managers who do their best to benefit from the information systems instead of complaining about them. The financial controller is, therefore, an important stakeholder to include in your stakeholder management efforts. A good relationship will offer you many benefits as a project manager. This is yet another example of factor 10 behavior!

Of course, financial data and updates on milestones are very important. Nevertheless, you should also include updates on the other critical parameters in your monthly reports. These leading indicators can provide valuable information about the real status of the project results and help you make timely adjustments. Having an integral data overview allows you to complete the "lap" properly and gives you a status overview that you can refer back to until the next monthly report is drawn up.

2. Develop a status overview and presentation for the project board

Collect the data you have gathered into a single status overview and clarify how the values compare to the plan and what this means for the final result. You can use the format shown in figure 10.8. This status overview is derived from the project charter and expanded to be used during the execution phase. It contains all the information you need to clarify the project scope and status compared to the final result: time, money, key deliverables and the status of the critical parameters. For the latter category, the goal (original plan) and the realized value (current status) are represented in time. This ensures a constant focus on the trend throughout the course of the V-model. Of course, you can also use colors in your status overview: make the fields with the current values green, orange or red, depending on how they compare to the (original) plan.

When your project status overview is in order, you can face virtually any project board. You are well prepared, you understand the status of the project at a quantitative level as well and you know the optimal path to the final goal. All that you have to do now is succinctly present all this information in a status report, often in the form of a presentation that you show during the project board meeting. In this presentation, you cover the data from the status overview and you communicate with the project board members about

Change yourself from a reporter to an influencer.

changes, risk management and other decisions that have to be made. For example, you might want to hear their opinion on your proposal for an "alternate path" or would like the board members to make certain urgent decisions. Figure 10.9 shows some common subjects for the status report. Try to keep the structure of your presentation the same from one month to the next, preferably using one slide per topic. This allows your audience to grow accustomed to your fast rhythm and your powerful "laps" and it ensures the project board stays out of your way for the rest of the month. I will provide examples of the graphical presentation of the status report in section 10.4.

3. Project board meeting

Back in section 2.3, we had already concluded that informing your stakeholders is an opportunity, not an obligation. You now have this opportunity when you report to the project board. Experience for yourself how a thorough preparation will make you an influencer. You do that by drawing up a proper project status overview in advance, but also by utilizing *stakeholder management prior to* and *during* the meeting! Make sure that the project board members are not caught off guard by your presentation. Talking things over for fifteen minutes or so with an important project board member prior to the actual meeting will do wonders and turn an opponent into an ally. Prepare people for what you have to say and the decisions they have to make. You should also remember that being right is not the same as getting your way and make use of Quinn's competing leadership styles. Alternate between the roles of director, producer, broker, innovator, facilitator, coordinator and monitor.

Project status overview					
Project name:		**Project number:**			
Project manager:		**Report week: 2019.xx**			
Client:					
Project goal and scope					

Financial status and timing				**Current**	**Plan**
Project budget [euros]					
Project hours [hours]					
Project end date (year.wk)					

Status results (key deliverables)					
Deliverable (sorted by delivery moment):				**Date (current)**	**Date (plan)**
- Result 1					
- Result 2					
- Result 3					
- Result 4					
- Result 5					
- Result …					

Status of critical parameters (current status /original plan)						
	31-Jan	28-Feb	31-Mar	Q2 (30-Jun)	Q3 (30-Sep)	Q4 (31-Dec)
- KPI 1 (current/plan)	(.../...)	(.../...)	(.../...)	(.../...)	(.../...)	(.../...)
- KPI 2 (current/plan)	(.../...)	(.../...)	(.../...)	(.../...)	(.../...)	(.../...)
- KPI 3 (current/plan)	(.../...)	(.../...)	(.../...)	(.../...)	(.../...)	(.../...)
- KPI 4 (current/plan)	(.../...)	(.../...)	(.../...)	(.../...)	(.../...)	(.../...)
- KPI … (current/plan)	(.../...)	(.../...)	(.../...)	(.../...)	(.../...)	(.../...)
- KPI … (current/plan)	(.../...)	(.../...)	(.../...)	(.../...)	(.../...)	(.../...)
- KPI … (current/plan)	(.../...)	(.../...)	(.../...)	(.../...)	(.../...)	(.../...)
- KPI … (current/plan)	(.../...)	(.../...)	(.../...)	(.../...)	(.../...)	(.../...)

Figure 10.8   Monthly status overview for communication at the project board level

- ☐ Status phases and timing (current versus plan)
- ☐ Status key deliverables (current versus plan)
- ☐ Status financial data (current versus plan)
- ☐ Status critical parameters (current versus plan)
- ☐ Status resources (current versus plan)
- ☐ Status project risks
- ☐ Change management and other decisions to be made

Figure 10.9   Contents of the status report (presentation) for the project board

4. Communicate status report and status overview

After the project board meeting you can end the "lap" on a high note by communicating the presentation with the decisions that were made and the project status overview to the project board members and the other stakeholders. With this, you complete the PDCA cycle and are ready for the next heartbeat period.

5. The rest of the month: stakeholder management

By completing the status analysis, reporting and communicating steps in a short period of time, you have cleared the rest of the month for important matters: namely proactive stakeholder management. The quality of your project status overview and your own leadership skills will determine whether you can successfully avoid having to conduct any analyses in the interim. Will you resolutely refer back to last period's status overview halfway through the month or will you be tempted to produce a "half-time update" that does not really offer any new information yet takes a lot of time to put together? This will definitely be a learning process, but you have already laid the foundation needed to change from a project reporter to a project influencer.

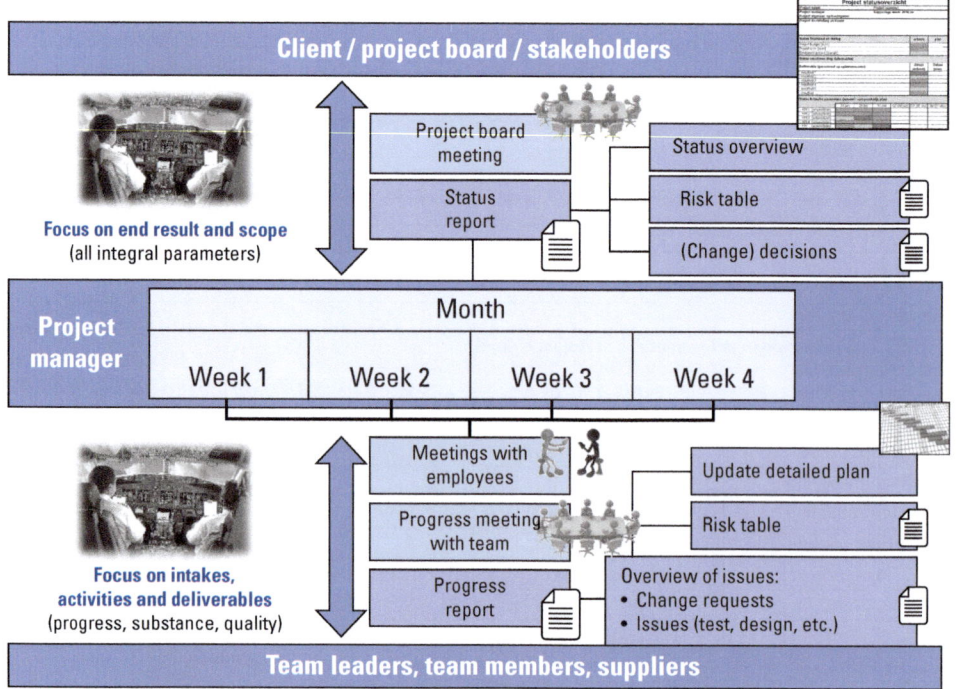

Figure 10.10   Complete overview of activities and reports for the project team and stakeholders

10.3 Change management

In projects, as in life, *the only constant is change.* That is why no matter how good your detailed plan is, you will not be able to realize the desired project goals unless you recognize and address scope changes. The project scope is initially recorded in the project charter and later formalized in the project management plan, which serves as the contract between the project manager and the client. *Change management* is the process that ensures you deal with changes responsibly.

Even if changes do not affect the project scope, they still have to be managed effectively; if an employee is available on a different day than originally planned, this will likely not affect the project result. However, it is still important to communicate the change. Another example is the update of a completed project result in order to implement improvements: the change does not have to be front-page news, but it still has to be properly coordinated and documented.

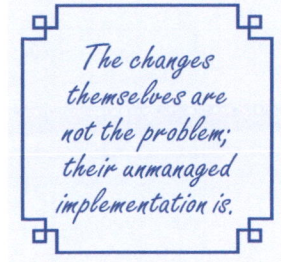

The changes themselves are not the problem; their unmanaged implementation is.

All this goes to show that changes are not necessarily a bad thing, they are simply part of (project) life. Some changes even benefit your project. It is, therefore, not advisable to act defensively right from the off when changes threaten the project scope or your detailed plan. Doing so is protective, yes, but it is often also inflexible and not in the best interests of the client or the project goal. Modern project managers are characterized by the professional way in which they deal with changes or even initiate them if that benefits the project result. In doing so, they integrally protect their own and their stakeholders' interests in line with Covey's win-win – not only in Agile projects, but also in traditional ones.

The change process and the change control board
In order to deal with changes in a structured manner, it is advisable to apply the change process shown in figure 10.11. This process contains a lot of common sense. The challenge, therefore, mainly lies in its execution: identifying, analyzing, making decisions, ensuring the right communication and, especially, actively implementing this process from the very start of the project! If you neglect to do the latter, change management will be about reactive damage control instead of proactive management. If we return to the example of the TomTom from chapter 2, it would mean only starting when the arrival time has already moved up to 10:03, instead of doing so as soon as it first moves from 09:48 to 09:51 because of a traffic jam up ahead. Make sure to identify all changes right away and take appropriate action during that same heartbeat period.

 Do you respond to changes in an ad-hoc manner or do you actively look out for them?

The change process is actually a standard cycle, or *change life cycle,* that every change has to go through: submission, evaluation, decision and implementation. Giving names to these moments in the life cycle makes it possible to monitor status and progress. You should, therefore, make sure that all change requests are recorded separately in an overview or database and keep their status up-to-date. Before the weekly progress meeting, check what changes are new, which have been evaluated and are in need of a decision and which have been implemented. *By doing so, you make an inherently disruptive and hard-to-plan process insightful and manageable.*

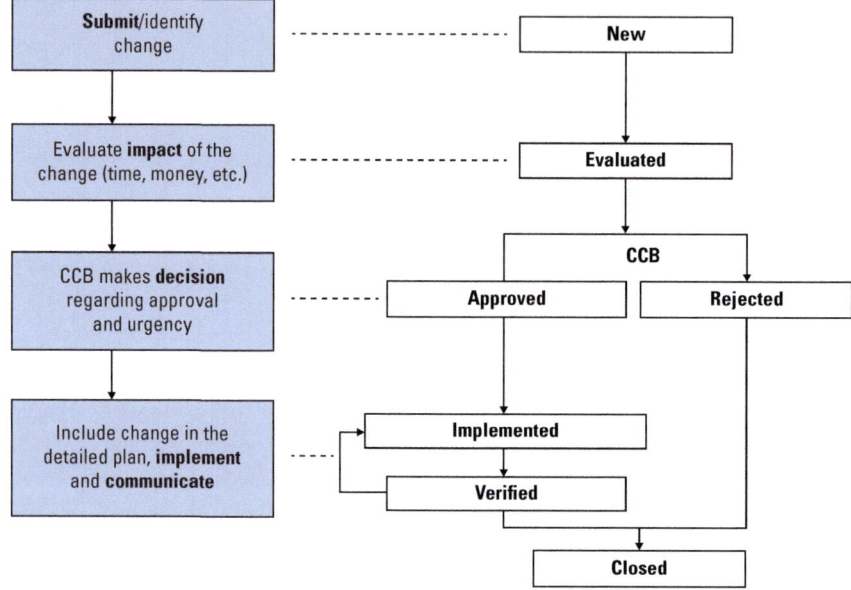

Figure 10.11   The change process (left) and the respective status names (right)

Appoint the CCB as early as possible and see how this saves time and money and offers peace of mind.

Who is in charge of the change process? That's you, the project manager – although you are not alone. This is what the *change control board (CCB)* – also known as the *Change Authority* in PRINCE2 – is for. The change control board makes decisions, sets priorities and manages the database (or list) of changes. The composition of the CCB must be such that it is able to execute its tasks. To deal with changes that fall within the project scope, there is the *project CCB*. You are a member of that board and you will have to appoint others who understand the impact of changes on a substantive level (e.g. an architect) and those who understand what the consequences are for the final result (e.g. a product manager). It is practical to schedule the project CCB meeting prior to, or after, the progress meeting to ensure you have the team's support and all items are up-to-date when you update the detailed plan. In Scrum, this is usually done during the daily stand-up meetings. The CCB determines whether newly submitted items must be evaluated and makes a decision regarding their approval, implementation and urgency. Although this may look like more overhead, the project CCB is actually an effective and efficient mechanism. It keeps changes from being made without proper coordination or communication and team members from deviating from the plan without fully understanding the situation at hand – no matter how good their intentions are. It is also important for the technical check - does the change have any unforeseen negative side effects? The CCB lets you clarify the roles and responsibilities and integrate change management into the project's PDCA cycle.

For changes that affect the project scope, there is the *CCB at the project board level*. This CCB is often made up of the same people as the project board itself, which means change decisions are usually made during your monthly reports to the project board.

Change management in practice

When I ask project managers why their project does not have a CCB, they often reply: "We hardly receive any change requests from the client, so we use an ad-hoc approach." Apparently, many people think that formal change management reeks of bureaucracy and should only be applied when absolutely necessary. That is a missed opportunity because, if you look carefully, you will see that every project is teeming with changes – although they are often unintentional or go unnoticed. A seemingly small change made by the client can lead to an avalanche of modifications to subcomponents. Even if a change does not affect the project scope, it can certainly impact the plan!

Think of, for instance, team members who fail to complete their activities every week because they immediately resolve any problems found during testing. Although this is a great example of people taking the initiative, is it really necessary to solve all problems? If so, should that be a top priority? Similarly, team members may passionately strive to make the product better than required. This is also laudable, but the question remains whether they are ignoring other, more important matters and whether the client will even appreciate these changes 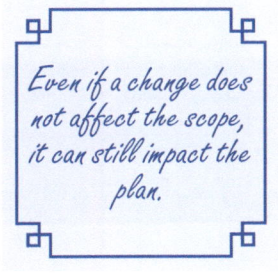 or perhaps should be charged extra for them. *Better is the enemy of good!* In other words, your team members' autonomy is valuable, but project managers are in trouble when they lose control of the *what* of their project. By not only viewing change requests made by the client as changes, but also all other extra tasks and deliverables that pop up, change management and the project CCB suddenly assume an entirely different position within the project. You end up with not only a detailed plan that addresses all existing agreements, but also a change process that, driven by the heartbeat, ensures that changes are added to the detailed plan in a transparent and controlled manner. In Scrum, these agreements are recorded in the product backlog (user stories and defects) and the corresponding tasks are coordinated during the sprint planning meeting and the daily stand-up meetings by means of the scrum board (sprint backlog).

To make all this more concrete, I have illustrated four types of changes in figure 10.12. Two of these always impact the project scope (extra work and delivering more than required), while the other two occur within the project scope. The project CCB focuses on all items on a weekly basis. By asking who or what caused the change, whether it will require extra work and whether it will offer the client any added value, you can determine whether decisions have to be made at the project or project board level and how you can protect the interests of the client and, especially, your own project.

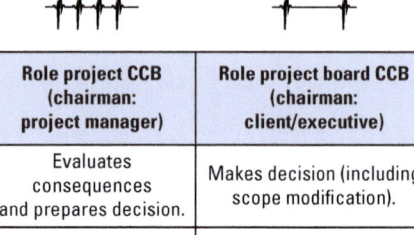

Type of change	Cause	Impact on plan	Impact on value for client	Role project CCB (chairman: project manager)	Role project board CCB (chairman: client/executive)
Conduct **extra work**	Request from the client	Workload usually increases	Increases	Evaluates consequences and prepares decision.	Makes decision (including scope modification).
Dealing with a (technical or organizational) **setback**	Various	Workload increases or execution is disrupted	Unchanged (provided that the setback is resolved)	Makes decision and resolves the problem within the project. (no scope change)	None. Only involve the project board if the client caused the change or if the setback has a major impact on the final result. Seize any opportunity to inform the project board about successful corrections.
Software bugs, test problems and other **issues**	Test results, inspections, etc.	None, accounted for in budget (to a certain extent)	Unchanged (provided that the issue is resolved)	Makes decision and resolves the problem within the project. (no scope change)	None. Only involve the project board if the size of the issues far exceeds what was budgeted for.
Deliver **more than required**	Seize opportunity or "gold plating"	Workload usually increases	Increases (but not at the client's request)	Prepares decision and avoids doing extra work "for free."	Decides whether a modification of the scope (extra time or money) is acceptable.

Figure 10.12   Types of changes and their consequences for follow-up by the project CCB (within scope) and project board CCB (outside scope)

Staying in control when unexpected events occur

A proper change process keeps you from chasing your own tail. By accounting for changes instead of resisting them, you can stay in control even in a dynamic environment. Figure 10.13 illustrates the advantages of taking control. Instead of allowing all changes to disrupt your team's daily activities, you can also significantly reduce their impact by filtering, assessing their urgency and planning *modification phases* in advance. *You can plan for changes, even if you do not know what they will be.* Estimate the size, set aside a "change budget" and plan modification phases. By only resolving critical problems right away (and allowing them to disrupt the plan), you can keep other corrections from doing the same – provided that their size does not exceed the predicted change budget. This is a great factor 10 tool that proves you can be Agile even in a traditional project environment!

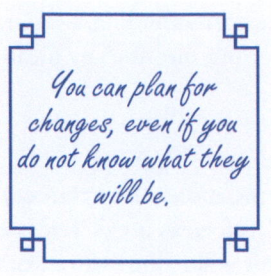

You can plan for changes, even if you do not know what they will be.

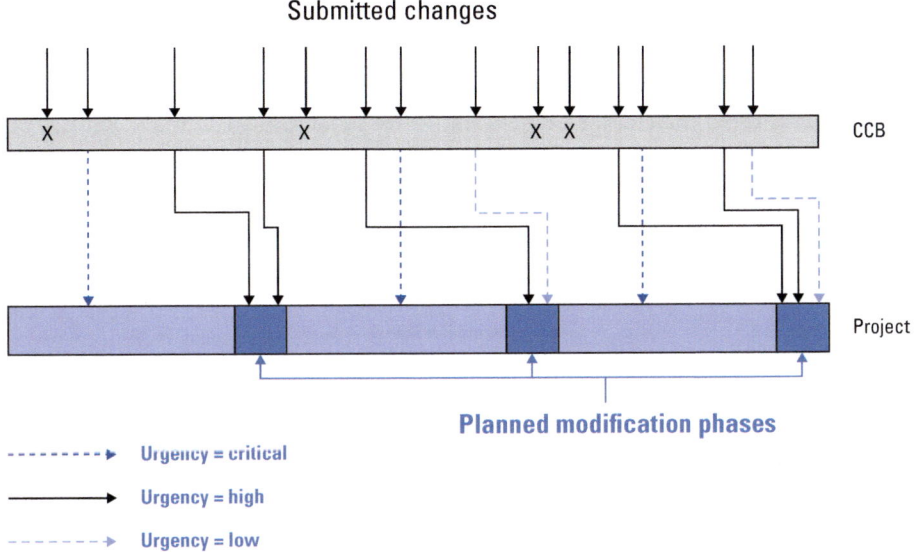

Figure 10.13   Minimizing disruptions by accounting for changes in advance

Flip-thinking: a development process is a series of changes

Finally, I want to raise the bar a bit. If you use flip-thinking, you could say that the life cycle of a function to be developed is also a change process leading from the moment that

it is still a requirement through to the final acceptance by the client (see figure 10.14). There is nothing unexpected about any of this, because it has all been planned for. Nevertheless, this way of thinking could be useful to provide insight into the status and progress, and to authorize activities. If you create a single overview of all functions to be developed, list the status of each item and update this after each progress meeting, you will have an overview that you can easily use to illustrate the project status and the activities that still have to be completed.

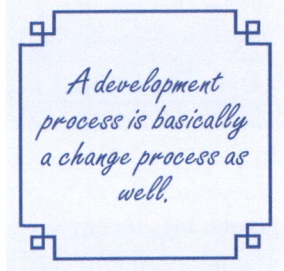

This approach is particularly effective for software development projects, because of the large number of functions that have to be independently implemented. It can also be used for activities such as the purchase and assembly of a prototype. By adding status moments such as *defined, ordered, received, built in* and *tested*, you can see what has not yet been delivered or tested at the component level. Of course, you do not need a CCB for these kinds of changes, because the activities were already authorized when the project management plan was approved. The team members can, therefore, change the status themselves whenever they complete an item (e.g. on a scrum board-like overview with status columns) and you can discuss their progress during the weekly individual meetings. This is another example of being Agile in a traditional environment.

There are many tools available on the market that let you define life cycles and which automate this entire process (status change, status analysis and communication via email to stakeholders in the event of a status modification). Furthermore, you may have noticed that this kind of change management ties in directly with *configuration management*. You know the status and therefore the content (configuration) of all sub-deliverables and end products. That means the change process can easily be expanded into a *configuration and version management process*.

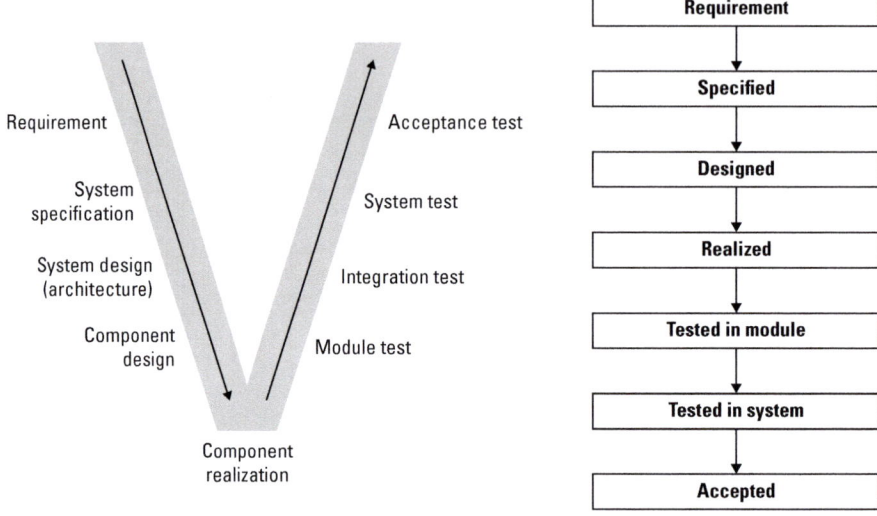

Figure 10.14   The development life cycle from requirement to end result

10.4 Providing insight into status and remaining path

In section 10.2, I explained how you can execute the PDCA cycle with your team and the project board in practice. In this section I will give you several examples of ways to graphically present the status and remaining activities. Let yourself be inspired by these examples and think about how they can help you direct your team and communicate with your stakeholders.

It requires some effort, but it is important to *translate data into information*. How can you show the project status? How can you make sure that the stakeholders understand your report? How can you illustrate both causes and effects? How can you show the effects of scope changes? How can you act in a service-oriented manner towards your stakeholders, while also making sure they do what you want?

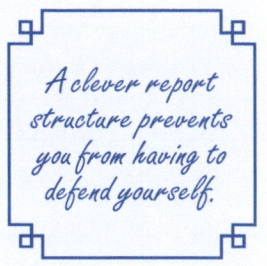

A clever report structure prevents you from having to defend yourself.

Producing good and useful reports is a skill in its own right. Always providing the right insight that answers stakeholders' questions while also motivating them to take the appropriate follow-up actions requires both judgment and presentation skills. Although there is no single comprehensive method,

I want to give you the following tip: *make sure you can convey your message with a single image*. One image for the project timing, one for the financial aspects, one for unresolved issues, etc. This image may certainly contain details, but above all it must be understandable and leave no room for confusion about the conclusions. This will allow you to get your point across in the least amount of time and stay in control during meetings. After all, if the project board takes control, you will be pushed into a defensive role that you do not want. Choosing the correct format for your reports is yet another example of factor 10 behavior.

Reporting to the project team

It should not come as any surprise that my preferred method for status analysis and reporting is by projecting the PBS/WBS onto the heartbeat. Only then are you talking about the activities that have truly been completed and those that remain. Many other analysis methods are based on the budget, how much of it has been spent and what is left. If you do not have a WBS, you have little choice but to use this approach, although it tells you nothing about whether the remaining work will fit within the remaining budget. This was also

covered in section 8.1 when we discussed milestone-driven direction. The foundation for the graphical report to your team members is therefore similar to the foundation for the individual meetings, as discussed in section 10.2. The heartbeat-driven extraction of intakes, activities and deliverables in the form of a table can easily be turned into a graphical version like the one in figure 10.15.

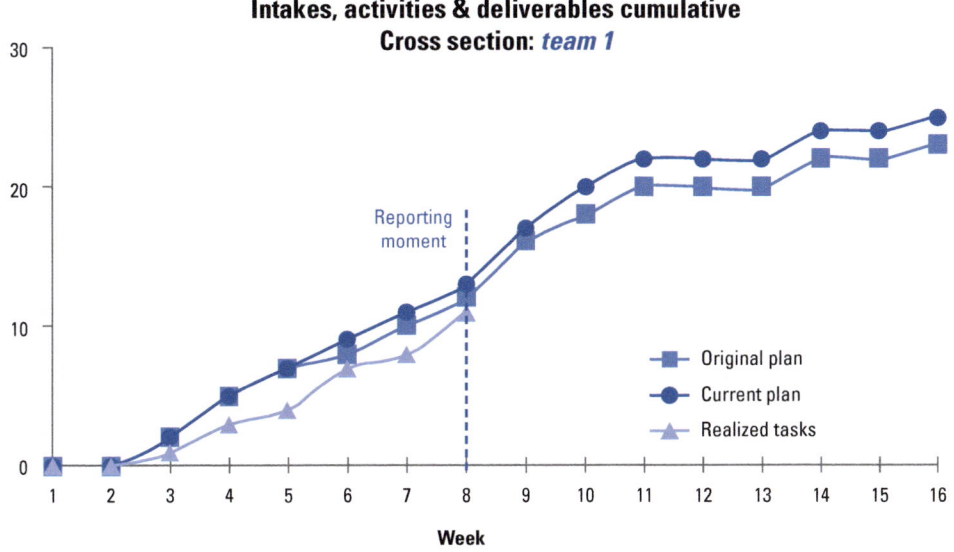

Figure 10.15   Cumulative weekly overview of planned and realized tasks

You are free to decide which elements from the detailed plan to use. Add a *tracking* column to your MS Project file (or other application) and indicate per task (yes/no) whether you want to include it in the extraction (figure 6.21) and the graphical report (figure 10.15). Similarly, you can create different overviews, e.g. of the status of a given subteam's tasks or of the tasks needed to realize the prototype (figure 10.16). Experience the power of tailoring your report to the audience. The more specific it is, the easier it will be to identify with and accept it as a tool. Furthermore, the report also reveals whether the number of tasks (the scope) has increased since the start of the project (current plan versus original plan).

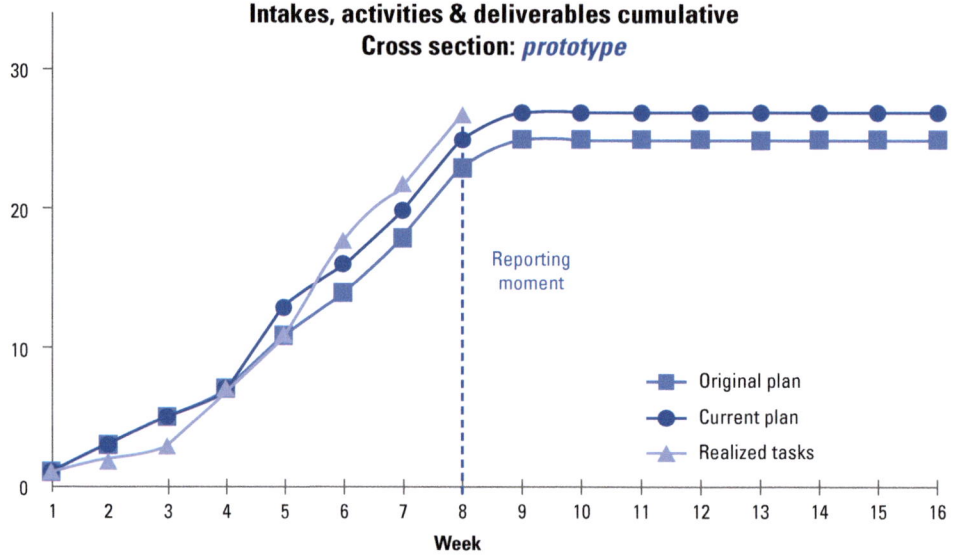

Figure 10.16   Report with tasks needed to realize the prototype

Experience the power of a countdown process.

In addition to this cumulative weekly report, other useful reports are those that show the status *during the execution of a specific subresult*, e.g. a Scrum sprint or a test process. Figure 10.17 shows a *Sprint burndown chart*. It indicates the daily progress of the sprint process and is updated during every daily stand-up meeting. It tells you when tasks are completed and how this affects the sprint backlog. It also shows the team's remaining available hours. A sprint burndown is great input for your weekly progress report. In a similar manner, you can create other reports using the *countdown principle*, for example on how the availability of materials needed to start an assembly process is progressing or on the progress of a test process (figure 10.18).

I want to end this section on reporting to the project team by explaining how you can provide insight into the status and the necessary actions for those processes that are hard to plan. Figure 10.19 shows a so-called *maturity grid*. This overview instantly shows the status of twenty-one unresolved problems and tells you which of these have priority (first the dark fields, then the lighter ones). On the vertical axis, you see the progress

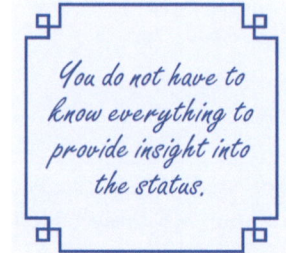

You do not have to know everything to provide insight into the status.

of the problem based on the 8D method (more on that in section 10.5), while the horizontal axis shows the problem's impact for the client. The maturity grid demonstrates that you can provide insight into the status even if there are uncertainties and indicates how you can show what people should focus on and do first.

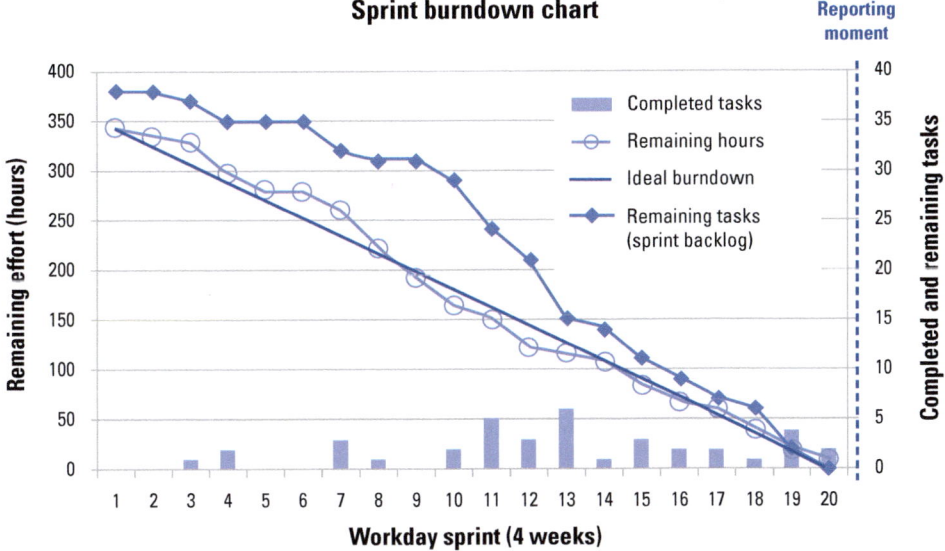

Figure 10.17   Scrum burndown report with sprint backlog and available hours

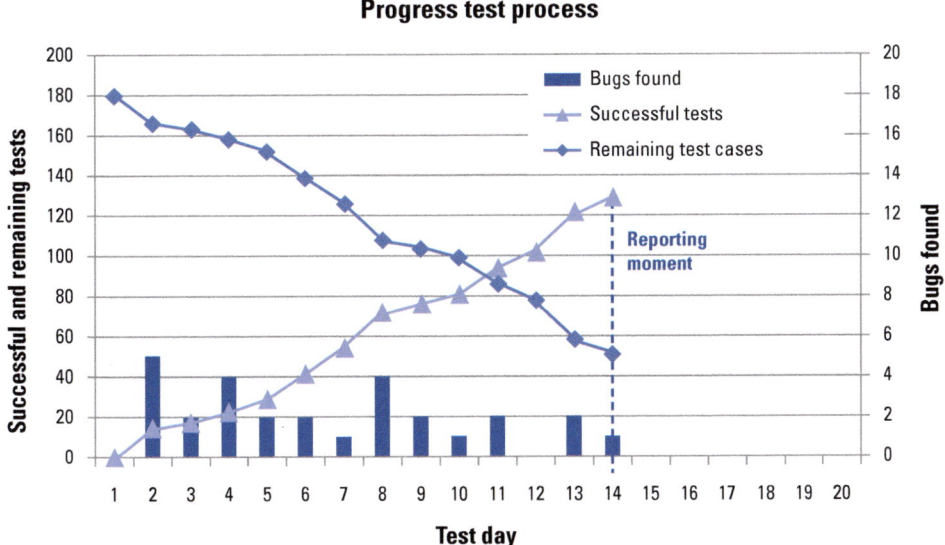

Figure 10.18   The progress of a test process presented as a countdown process

Reporting to the project board

When reporting to the project board, you can of course utilize the same overviews that you used when reporting to the project team. However, the focus will be different, namely on the status in relation to the final goal and on managing the project scope. There are several additional overviews you can use for this.

Maturity grid

8D progress ⬇ Severity of the problem ➡	Safety problem	System out of order	Severe interruption of production	Moderate interruption of production	No effect on production	Total
1D-2D No temporary solution		2		1	1	4
3D Cause unknown	1	1	1	2		5
4D Solution unknown			1		2	3
5D Solution not yet implemented	1	1	1	2		5
6D Re-occurrence of the problem still possible		2	2			4
Total	2	6	5	5	3	**21**

Figure 10.19   Reporting and prioritizing when resolving problems with the maturity grid

The first overview I want to cover is an obvious one, yet one that is often underestimated, the project overview shown in figure 10.20. This overview is based on the project strategy from the planning process, which we discussed in chapter 5 (figure 5.16). By using colors and extending delayed activities, you can create an instant overview of the entire project and its timeframe. You can also add the milestones if you wish. This representation is really suitable for use as an introductory summary that provides a clear overview and identifies the problem areas.

To zoom in further on the project, you can use the cumulative status overview of the project deliverables, just as you also do at the team level (figures 10.15 and 10.16). Be sure to choose other cross sections, however, such as *all* project deliverables or the deliverables that have to be completed in order to finish an important interim result for the client.

If you use Scrum for (parts of) the project, it is important to provide insight into the status of the product backlog. You can do so on a monthly basis with the backlog overview seen in figure 10.21. This overview shows how the product backlog shrinks during the sprints and whether the project is on schedule in terms of the delivery of results. It also reveals whether the project scope is changing. In this case, twenty functions have been added to the product backlog in August.

Even if you do not use an iterative development method, you can still present the project status in this manner. In this case, all functions to be developed have to be defined separately and each function must have its own development status as seen in figure 10.14. When you create a monthly overview like the one in figure 10.22 and indicate what functions have a

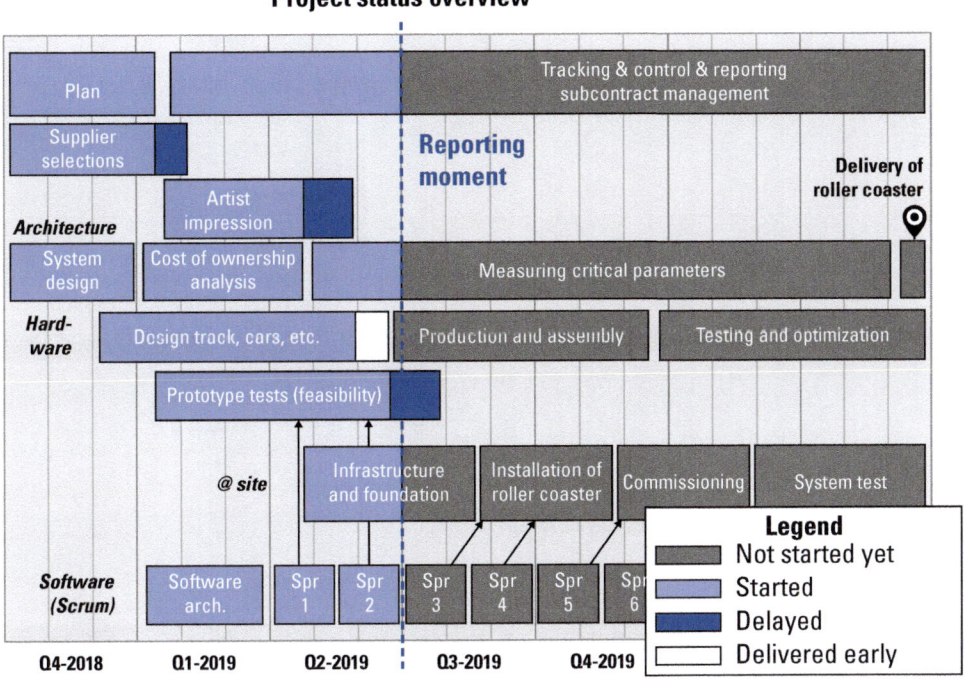

Figure 10.20   Graphical overview of the project status of project Roller Coaster

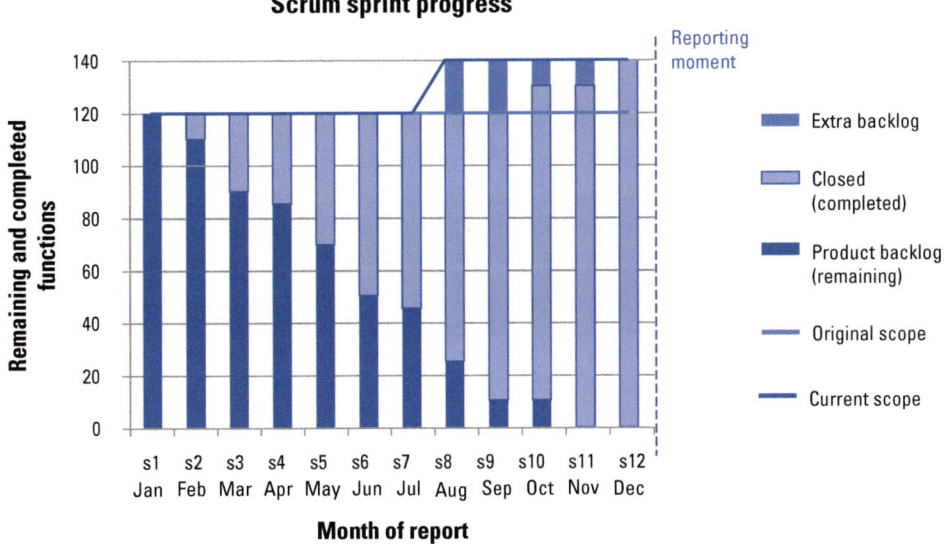

Figure 10.21   Scrum sprint overview with the status of the product backlog per month (and per sprint)

certain development status, it becomes clear what phase your project is in (specification, design, test, etc.) and whether any functions are being overlooked.

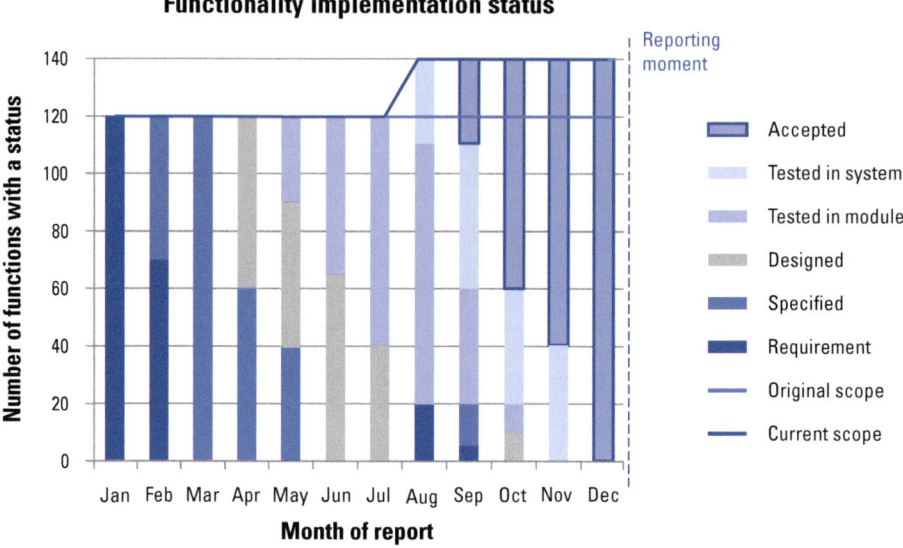

Figure 10.22   Status overview per function reported on a monthly basis

Insight into the status of the functions to be developed is certainly useful, but we have already concluded that the only way to get a reliable prediction of the future end result is by measuring the critical parameters in the interim. Figure 10.23 is a logical addition to the projection of the critical parameters onto the project heartbeat that we discussed earlier. Any deviation of the measured data from the predicted trend line serves as a clear and early indicator that the plan has to be modified. In this case, a deviation was detected while testing the first prototype.

Perhaps the lack of any sexy financial overviews has given you the impression that the project's finances are of secondary importance. That is definitely not the case: a project's financial performance is crucially important to its success and it is rightfully given a prominent position on the project charter and the project manager's monthly status overviews. The problem is that there is not much you can do about it. The project finances are often *lagging indicators*, resulting from the substantive progress of the intakes, activities, deliverables and critical parameters. Nevertheless, a clear report detailing the budget and hours spent is an essential part of your report to the project board.

You can use figure 10.24 for inspiration on how to report the project's financial status. This figure shows the monthly project expenses from different categories (people, materials, purchased services, etc.) and the budget required to achieve the final result (costs-to-go). By comparing the current plan to the original budget, you can also see exactly when the budget was exceeded (or the scope was changed). In this case, that happened in April.

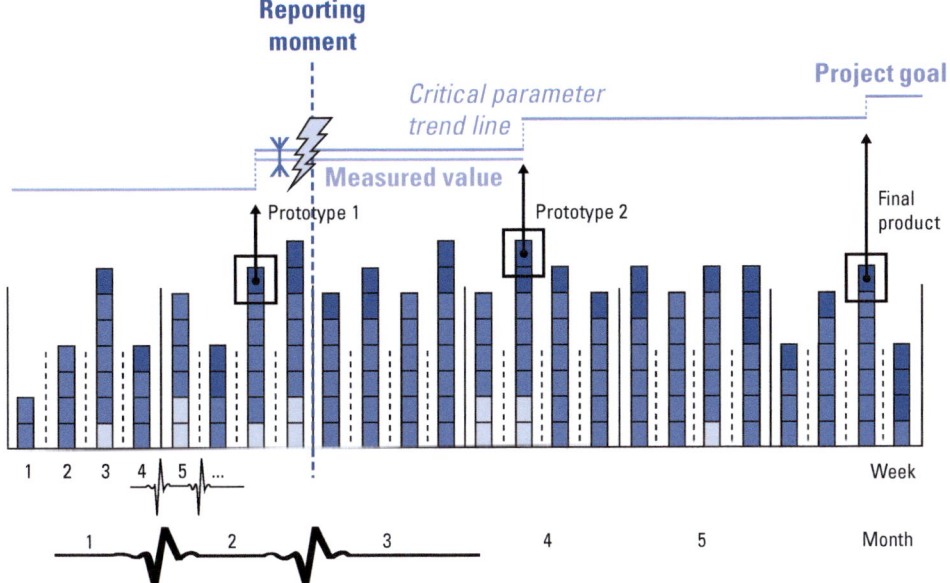

Figure 10.23   The predicted trend line and measured values of the critical parameter

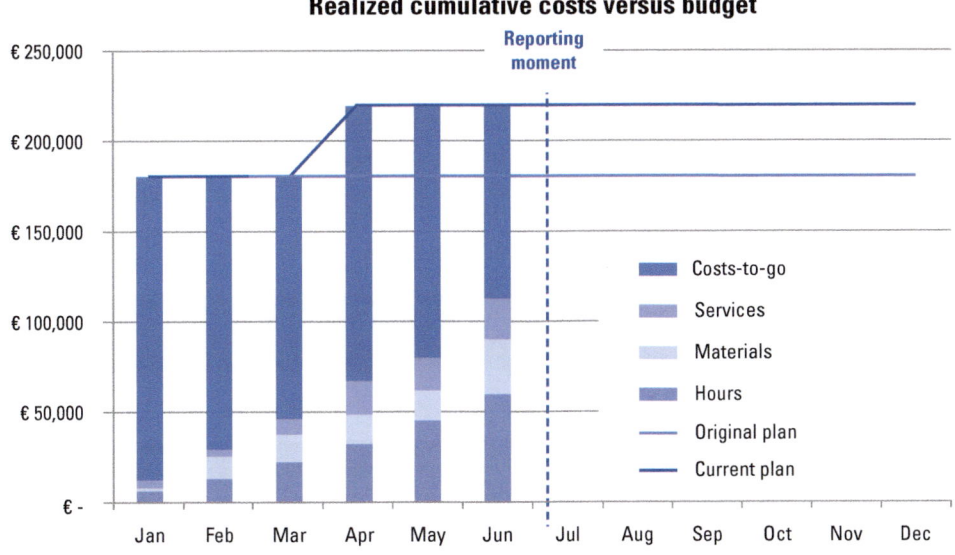

Figure 10.24   Monthly report on the project expenses versus the expected costs

For larger projects, the hour overview from figure 10.25 is also useful. It shows both the monthly planned project staffing per department (to the right of the "reporting moment" line) and the actual hours logged (to the left of this line). You get an instant overview of both the agreements for the future and the actual number of hours used in the past.

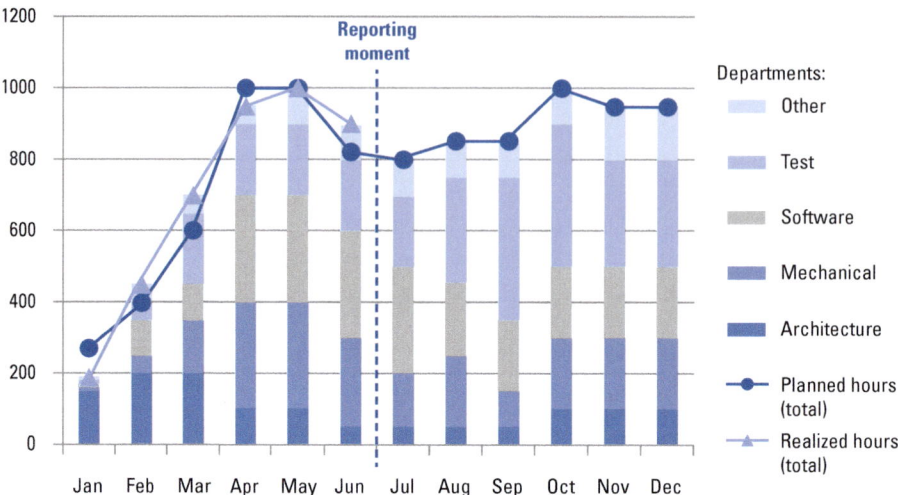

Figure 10.25   Overview of planned (to the right of the reporting moment) and spent hours (to the left of the reporting moment)

If you work with a project buffer, you can use the report shown in figure 10.26. The trend of the project buffer usage provides an insight into the expected end date of the project. If the project buffer is used in its entirety, the project will be completed right on time. If you have some of the buffer left at the end, the project will be done "too early." For three possible scenarios, the figure shows how the used project buffer offers a prediction of the project completion date.

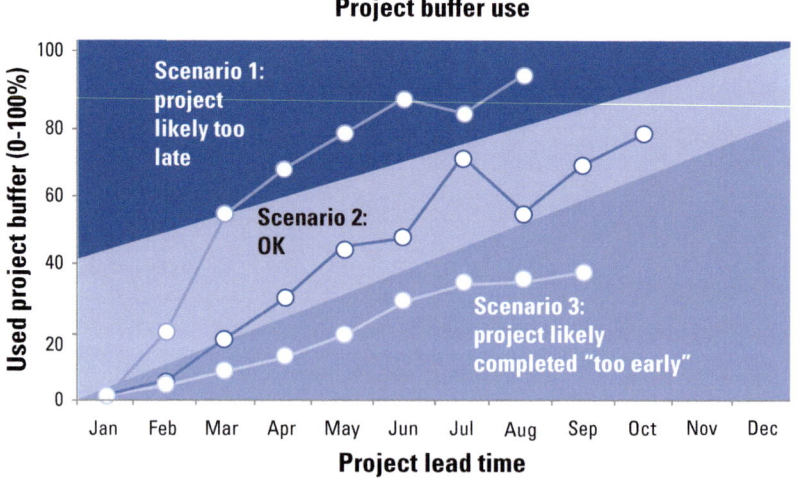

Figure 10.26   Monthly report on the use of the project buffer

As mentioned in section 6.2, the project board and the other stakeholders must understand the mechanism and there must be a degree of mutual trust in order for you to present the project buffer in a transparent manner. As a project manager, you should not be overly naïve by allowing your project buffer to be taken away from you too soon or by having the expected earlier completion date (scenario 3) turned into a new commitment. If the project board is not ready to deal with this, you can still use project buffers with your team, but it is advisable to avoid explicitly mentioning them in your external reports. Your stakeholders can still enjoy the fact that their project manager is realizing the goals and may exceed their expectations, but they will only discover that once it is actually true.

10.5 Making uncertainties plannable

Officially, this final section is unnecessary. We have already discussed everything you need to know to successfully complete your project. Nevertheless, there is still a chance that you become paralyzed by everything you do not yet know when making your plans. Although some people are more susceptible to this fear than others, everyone will surely recognize the feeling: you lose your way while exploring uncertainties and you can no longer see the wood for the trees, which keeps you from taking any action at all.

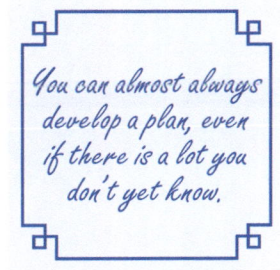

You can almost always develop a plan, even if there is a lot you don't yet know.

Earlier in this book, I discussed several ways to deal with this situation, such as dividing the project into smaller chunks with the PBS and using the 10% confrontation rule that keeps you from procrastinating by deliberately planning early confrontation moments. We also learned that Agile iterations help if there are any uncertainties in the project scope. Nevertheless, there are several additional planning tips that can help you deal with uncertainties and get rid of *the excuse that you cannot develop a plan yet because you do not have enough information.*

Consequences for the end point

The planning tips to deal with uncertainties are all based on the principle that was introduced in chapter 5: *determining the size of the project execution is not the same as knowing all detailed activities.* You must determine the size early on during the definition phase, while the detailed plan is only needed when the execution actually begins. With PRINCE2, for example, you first develop a high-level project plan that contains the size of all phases until the project end point. Prior to each phase, you create a detailed stage plan with which you manage the execution. This distinction between understanding the project size and the detailed activities was also mentioned when we talked about the sketch with the team and the detailed plan in chapter 6. People often become paralyzed when developing a plan because they confuse the two elements and try to present both at the same time. As a result, they are far too late in communicating the project size and the stakeholders probably already have the wrong expectations. In this section I will provide some tips to help you develop a plan despite the following uncertainties:

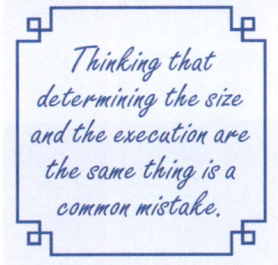

Thinking that determining the size and the execution are the same thing is a common mistake.

1. The size and details of certain project components are not available yet;
2. The stakeholders are indecisive;
3. There are several project scenarios.

1 – If the details are not available yet

Situations in which a lot is already clear, despite part of the project not being so, are quite common. As mentioned, it is not advisable to ignore this part in your communication with the client, unless it can easily be excluded from the project scope. However, waiting for more information is not usually an option, either. A possible solution would be to make a best-guess estimate of the size of the project part and use this as a provisional estimate in your plan and reports (figure 10.27). You can do this for the project's hours, costs, lead time or other requirements and consequences.

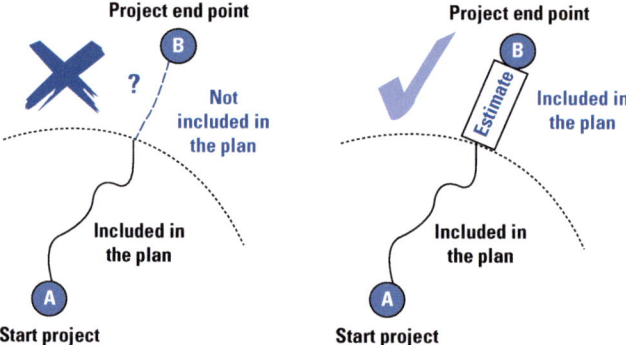

Figure 10.27   Using a provisional estimate to delineate and manage the project size

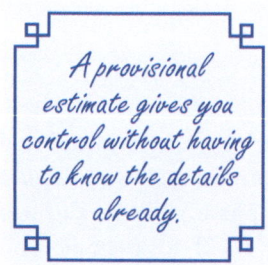

A provisional estimate gives you control without having to know the details already.

I covered this method back in section 2.4 when I gave the example of outsourcing the remodeling of the ground floor of a house. In the example, the contractor drew up a detailed quote without knowing which radiators would be used. By including the radiators as a provisional sum of €3,500, it was possible to sign the contract and begin the execution. It is important that the provisional estimate is included in the PDCA cycle for the client throughout the entire project. During each reporting moment, you check whether the actual costs or time required will fall within the estimated budget (see figure 10.28). The advantage of this method is that you can begin the project execution without having to personally bear the consequences of poor specifications. In short, you delineate any uncertainties and treat them separately as reserved budgets. That part of the project is then given its own treatment, while the project manager and the client take their responsibility *together*.

Of course, you can also use this mechanism in other situations. You can define all kinds of provisional estimates in order to deal with uncertainties without writing a blank check. One example is a buffer with which to accommodate extra wishes from the client. Resolving the problems found during testing in a correction phase is a similar process, as are the modification buffers we discussed in the section on change management. Budgeting for the correction phase in such a way that you can resolve, for instance, forty problems, means you can monitor during the test phase whether the number of problems found is too large to be solved without project delay. This allows you to *anticipate* in the project, long before the planned correction phase actually begins.

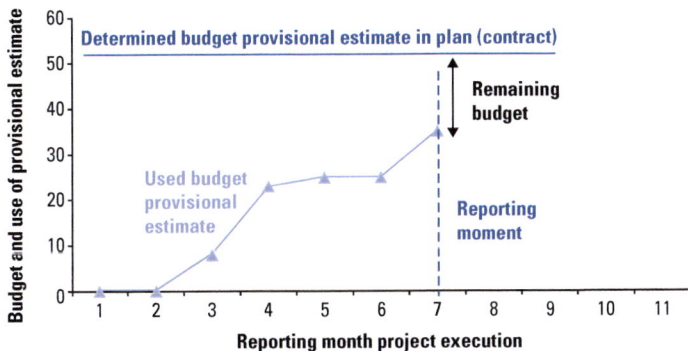

Figure 10.28 Status report on the part of the provisional sum that was used up during the project execution

2 – If the client is indecisive

You probably recognize this situation. The timeframe is critical, you want to move ahead, but the client is holding you back by not offering the clarity you need or making the necessary decisions. The worst thing you can do is accept the client's uncertainties like a kind of Trojan Horse and allow them to upset the scope of your project later on. However, waiting around is usually not an option either. Once again you could use provisional estimates, but there is often an easier way: instead of giving indecisive clients a choice, present them

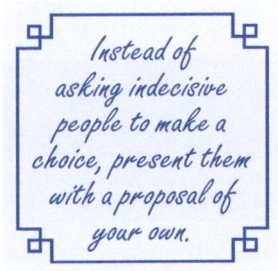

Instead of asking indecisive people to make a choice, present them with a proposal of your own.

with your own proposal. You will be surprised to find how many of your proposals are accepted with minimal fuss. Of course, this does mean that you, as the project manager, have to take charge resolutely and put yourself in the client's position (Covey's fifth habit). My experience is that, when having to make a choice, people tend to be sure of the 10% they really want and the 10% they definitely do not want. However, they do not really have an opinion about the remaining 80%. Ensure you know about the 10% of dos and don'ts and propose an approach that you prefer, taking into account the remaining 80%. *This gives you an important factor 10 element!*

3 – When faced with various project scenarios

What do you do if no decision has yet been made about whether to invest in risk reduction on the left side of the V? The solution is often straightforward: in addition to presenting the scenario with the *investment*, you should also address the scenario covering the *consequences* of not making the investment, i.e. the risks. However, this is often where the problem lies, project managers do not always know what those consequences are. No wonder they cannot convince the client to invest in risk-reducing measures!

Clients will only make an investment if you show them the advantages it offers.

I try to explain this in figure 10.29. To summarize: if you cannot explain what problems (in this case €42,000 worth) a risk-reducing measure that costs €5,000 will solve, you are not *persuasive* enough. It is no surprise that clients hope to follow the dotted path that does not include either expense. Instead, you should take the time to estimate the consequences. You do not have to provide a ton of detail; just the size will be sufficient. You can learn a lot about that by talking to the right people for an hour or so. Only when clients have to choose between the €5,000 scenario and the €42,000 scenario can you expect them to make a wise decision. If they refuse to make the investment, you have no choice but to include an expense of €42,000 in your plan. That will not be easy, but it will likely lead to a discussion for which you will be well prepared. This is another example of the benefits of factor 10 behavior.

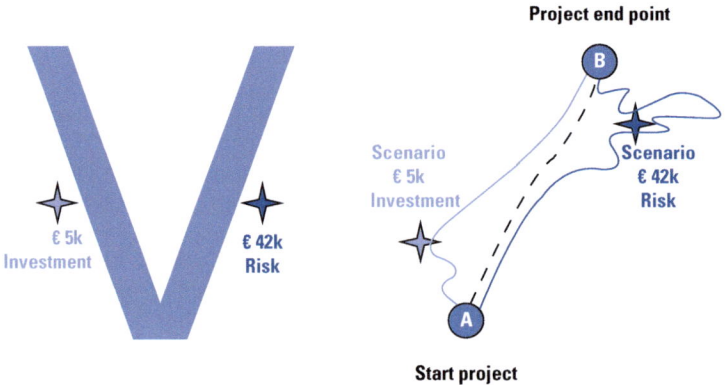

Figure 10.29   Show both scenarios with their consequences for the project's final result

The 8D method

Solving problems is a process that is often plagued by uncertainties, which makes it hard to plan or control. Depending on the scope and context of your project, you may have to deal with dozens or even hundreds of such problems with varying sizes and degrees of importance. Some problems occur with the end user (often called *field problems*), some affect the production or logistical process and some are found during the project itself (e.g. during testing). Resolving problems can have a major impact on your project; because of the capacity it requires, because it disrupts your existing plan and because the progression of a problem-resolution process can be difficult to predict.

The 8D method helps you structure your problem resolution efforts and make your progress measurable. The method was made popular by Ford and consists of the eight logical steps seen in figure 10.30. These steps provide structure and peace of mind at times when you face a lot of external pressure and have to rely largely on your gut feelings.

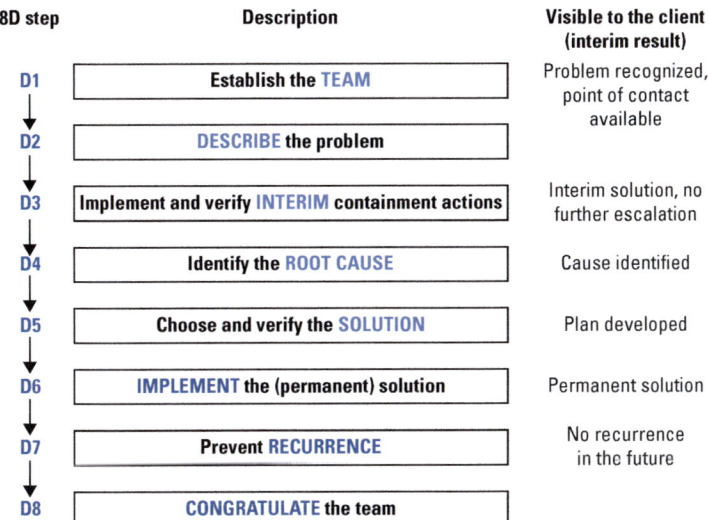

8D step	Description	Visible to the client (interim result)
D1	Establish the **TEAM**	Problem recognized, point of contact available
D2	**DESCRIBE** the problem	
D3	Implement and verify **INTERIM** containment actions	Interim solution, no further escalation
D4	Identify the **ROOT CAUSE**	Cause identified
D5	Choose and verify the **SOLUTION**	Plan developed
D6	**IMPLEMENT** the (permanent) solution	Permanent solution
D7	Prevent **RECURRENCE**	No recurrence in the future
D8	**CONGRATULATE** the team	

Figure 10.30   A structured approach to problem resolution with the 8D method

As you can see, the 8D method not only offers a series of steps to follow, it also provides substantive and strategic direction. *Jumping to conclusions*, the tendency to think in solutions right away, is avoided by first bringing the right people on board and properly understanding the problem (D1 and D2). Next is the D3 step that every crisis needs: "implementing interim containment actions" to prevent further escalation. The process up to and including D3 is urgent and leads to a visible interim result. However, as long as the cause of the problem

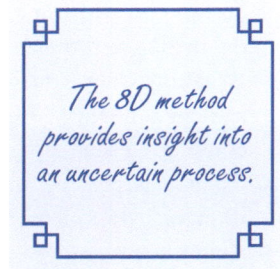

The 8D method provides insight into an uncertain process.

has not been identified – not to mention the solution – it is impossible to predict when the problem will actually be resolved. The D4 and D5 phases are, therefore, positioned along the tipping point of "we have no idea how long it will take" and "we have a plan." This point is essential for your communication with the client and your management of the project size. After the implementation of the final solution at the client's, there is another important step that is often overlooked: understanding how the problem was caused and preventing it from happening again. That makes the D7 step a true *process-improvement step* with which you can structurally improve the quality of your organization. The process ends with the D8 step: congratulating the team and celebrating the success. The 8D process, therefore, also contributes to motivating and rewarding the team.

In addition to effectively and efficiently resolving problems, this method makes the murky area between "we have a problem" and "the problem has been solved" transparent. Moving on to the next 8D status and being able to show the interim results that go with it gives your client peace of mind and your team direction: *there is no final solution yet, but we are making progress!* Furthermore, you can provide insight into how the progress of the entire set of problems in the project develops using the *maturity grid*, as seen in figure 10.19. Like the PBS, the 8D method is about creating structure, except instead of cutting a large project into smaller pieces, you divide the uncertain problem-resolution process into clear and easy-to-understand steps.

Summary

- Deliberately choose how to direct your team in the heartbeat and how to report to your stakeholders:
  - Team (and suppliers): focus on activities and results, often based on *management by objectives;*
  - Project board: focus on status in relation to the final goal and on the project scope, often based on *management by exception.*
- Get the PDCA flywheel in motion by providing:
  - Regularity: it is better to frequently coordinate briefly than to occasionally coordinate for a long time;
  - Moment: conduct the Check and Act steps in as short a time as possible;
  - Individual versus group: some forms of coordination require individual attention, while other forms rely on the group process.
- Coordination calls for rhythm. Make sure that all changes (including risk and change management) are included in the updated detailed plan (and the Scrum product and sprint backlogs).
- Scrum also features a daily rhythm at the team level. This allows the team to be self-organizing and makes the weekly meetings largely unnecessary.
- By taking charge during your reports to your stakeholders, you change from a reporter into an influencer. Keep the project board off your back for the rest of the month by completing each lap with a thorough reporting moment.
- Change is part of any project. The changes themselves are not the problem; their unmanaged implementation is.
- Appoint the change control board members as early in the project as possible. Also use change management for changes that do not affect the project scope!
- A smart report format ensures you will not have to defend yourself during project board meetings. With a single overview, provide insight into the project's status compared to the final result and the remaining path.
- You can almost always develop a plan, even if there is a lot you don't yet know. Avoid paralysis and do not wait for uncertainties to be resolved. Instead, use provisional estimates, make your own proposals or present alternate scenarios. Having a plan (up to the end point!) will give you and your environment peace of mind and help you do the right things.
- Use the 8D method to structure the problem-resolution efforts and to provide insight into the progress before the solution has been found or implemented.

Afterword

After reading this book, you will have a more thorough understanding of the core principles of project management. This will help you combine the most useful elements of various project management methods and link them to highly effective factor 10 behavior. It is not the methods that make the difference, but the way *you* apply them! Now that you understand the essence, you can even be Agile in a traditional environment, get teams to take responsibility in top-down-controlled organizations and turn coordination with the client from a contractual negotiation into a co-production.

The word *complete* in the book's title is not meant to suggest that it is a comprehensive overview of project management. Instead, it is intended to stimulate you and make you realize that the profile of a successful project manager is quite broad. You can achieve more by truly understanding your environment, internalizing the many project management tools without prejudices, and integrating them into your personal style. Remember that you do not have to wait until you have fully mastered each of the methods covered in this book. Quite the opposite: the best way to learn is by doing. Do not let your desire to be complete paralyze you and lead to procrastination. Consciously applying the techniques is more important than doing so perfectly! Start today and use this book's descriptions of *how* to help you out.

Discover the skills you already possessed, but did not always utilize until now. Much of what you have learned while reading this book can be applied right away: for example, automatically influencing others with the 10% confrontation rule, always taking the initiative with factor 10 behavior, translating project goals into subresults with the PBS, enforcing progress and learning ability with the project heartbeat and, of course, exhibiting flexible TomTom behavior by always showing the path to the final goal. Visit my website at www.roelwessels.com for even more tips and tools, or to share your experiences in using this book during your projects.

I truly hope that you will be able to let go of the feeling of "I will do better next time!" Instead, you can start doing better today! I want you to enjoy the many wonderful aspects of the project management business. Putting everything you have learned from this book into practice will certainly help you get there. Good luck!

Roel Wessels

Acknowledgements

I want to take a moment to thank everyone who helped with the development of this book.

Firstly, thanks to my wife Sonja and my children Joeri and Fleur for their understanding when "the writer" was caught up in his work again and for all their valuable lessons. Family life is perhaps the most wonderful project of all.

Thanks to the hosts, hostesses and fellow guests of Castle Slangenburg in Doetinchem, where much of this book was written. The Benedictine rules we lived by at Slangenburg helped me with my writing and provided substantive inspiration for this book.

Thanks to my employer Holland Innovative and especially to Hans Meeske for making the many writing hours available and to Joke van den Dool and Hans Pieter van den Berg for enthusiastically looking over my shoulder. Thanks also to the reviewers who offered their substantive feedback and helped make this book even more readable for a wide audience. And thanks to Vivian de Corti for the valuable support during the English translation process.

Thanks to everyone with whom I had the privilege of collaborating over the years. Colleagues, supervisors, team members and course participants: thank you for everything you have taught me.

Finally, thanks to both my parents, who gave me the opportunity to become the project manager, physicist and musician that I am today.

Appendix 1: Examples of the application of the project model

1. When an IT company accepts a new project and executes it for a client: the development of a new website.

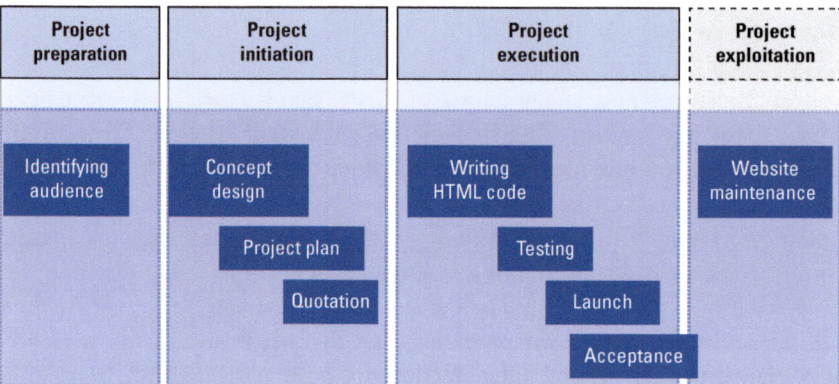

2. Increasing the productivity in a factory up to a predefined performance level (94%) as an external specialist.

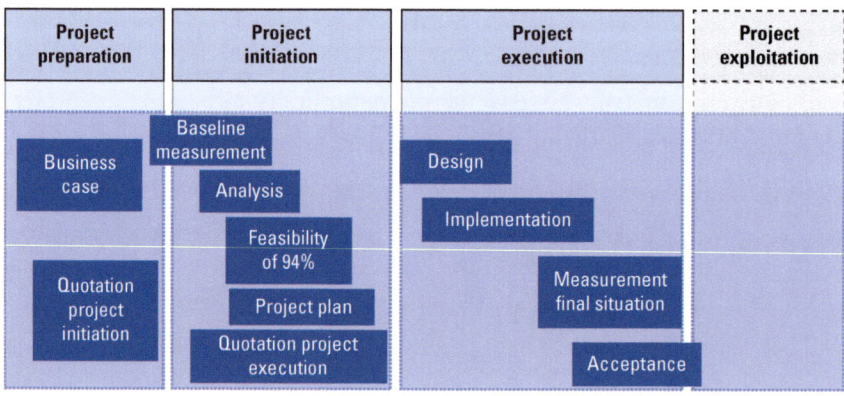

3. Supervising the merger of two organizations.

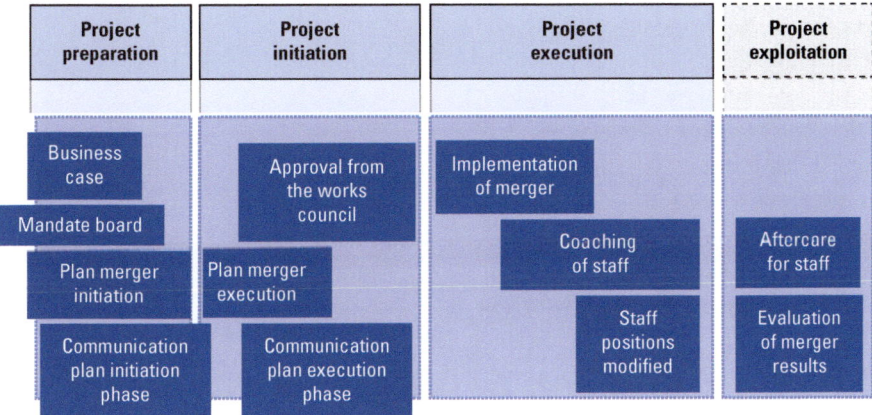

4. Internal change process: improving employee satisfaction.

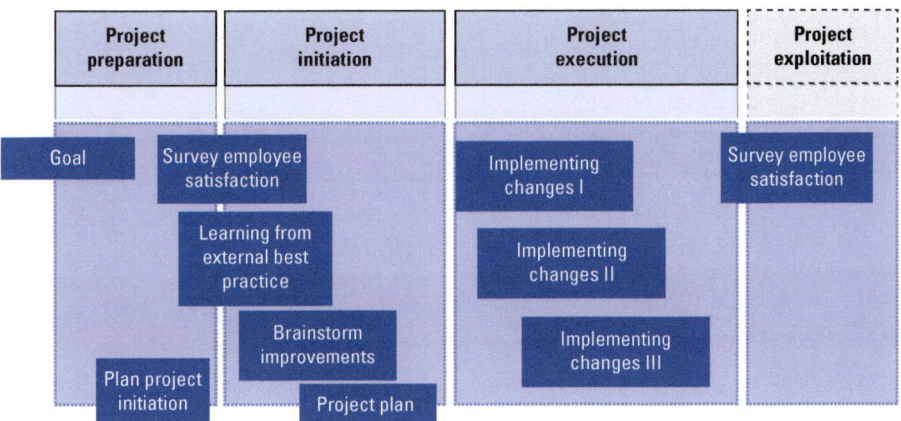

Appendix 2: The complete project manager toolkit

The complete project manager (CPM) toolkit:

CPM-Project model (traditional and Agile)
CPM-Stakeholder analysis
CPM-Project organization model
CPM-Decision enforcement matrix
CPM-Factor 10 inspirator
CPM-Planning process checklist
CPM-Project charter
CPM-Product breakdown structure
CPM-DfX and critical parameter implementer
CPM-Robust estimation tool
CPM-Scrum implementer
CPM-Sketch with the team
CPM-Detailed plan
CPM-Project motivator
CPM-Directing creativity inspirator
CPM-Risk matrix (project and FMEA)
CPM-Blind check prevention tool
CPM-Heartbeat & PDCA implementer
CPM-Change management implementer
CPM-Reporting inspirator

Download the tools from the CPM toolkit at www.roelwessels.com

Bibliography

Blake, R., Mouton, J., *The Managerial Grid: The Key to Leadership Excellence*, Gulf Publishing Co., 1964

Block, P., The empowered manager, Jossey-Bass, 1986

Cialdini, R., *Influence*, William Morrow & Co, 1984

Covey, S., *The Seven Habits of Highly Effective People,* Free Press 1989

Dalkey, N., Helmer, O., *An Experimental Application of the Delphi Method to the use of experts*, 1963

Deci, E., Ryan, R., *The Handbook of Self-Determination Research*, University of Rochester Press, 2002

Fagan, M., *Design and Code Inspections to Reduce Errors in Program Development*, in: IBM Systems Journal 15, 3 (1976): 182-211

Gaspersz, J., *Compete with Creativity, available at: SSRN: https://ssrn.com/abstract=983934 or http://dx.doi.org/10.2139/ssrn.983934*

Gilb, T., Graham, D., *Software inspection.* Addison-Wesley Longman, 1993

Goldratt, E., *Critical Chain,* North River Press, 1997

Guilford, J., *Creativity*, in: American Psychologist, Volume 5, Issue 9, p. 444–454, 1950

Gunster, B., *Omdenken - the Dutch art of flip-thinking*, A.W. Bruna, 2016

Harnish, V., *Mastering the Rockefeller Habits: What You Must Do to Increase the Value of Your Fast-Growth Firm*, Gazelles Publishing, 2002

Hayes, J., *Cognitive processes in creativity*, Dorsey Press, 1989

Hersey P., Blanchard, K., *Management of Organizational Behavior*, 3rd edition Prentice-Hall, 1977

Herzberg, F., Mausner, B., Snyderman, B., *The Motivation to Work*, 2nd edition, John Wiley & Sons Inc., 1959

Kaplan R., Norton D., *The Balanced Scorecard*, Harvard Business Review Press, 1996

Kurzweil, R., *The Age of Spiritual Machines*, Penguin Books, 1999

Lammers, M., *Yes! a crisis*, Tirion Sport, 2010

McGregor, D., *The Human Side of Enterprise*, McGraw-Hill, 1960

Mendelow, A.L., *Stakeholder Mapping*, in: Proceedings of the 2nd International Conference on Information Systems, Cambridge, MA, 1991

Newell, A., Simon, S., *Human problem solving*, Prentice Hall, 1972

Poincaré, H., *The foundations of science*, The Science Press, 1913

Quinn, R. a.o., *Becoming a Master Manager*, 6th edition, John Wiley & Sons Inc., 2015

Rook, P., Rook, E., 'Controlling software projects', *IEEE Software Engineering Journal* 1(1), 1986, pp. 7-16

Snowden D., Boone M., *A Leader's Framework for Decision Making*, in: Harvard Business Review, 2007

Sutherland, J., *Scrum*, Crown, 2014

Tuckman, B., Developmental sequence in small groups. In *Psychological Bulletin*, Vol 63 (6), Jun 1965

Wertheimer, M., *Productive thinking*, University of Chicago Press, 1982

Wickman, G., *Traction*, BenBella Books, 2007

Wiseman L., McKeown G., *Multipliers*, HarperCollins Publishers Inc., 2010

About Roel Wessels

Roel Wessels (1969) is married and a father of two. He is employed at Holland Innovative as Senior Director Project Management and Technology. Prior to this, he worked as Senior Director Innovation at Assembléon (currently Kulicke & Soffa), a high-tech equipment manufacturer, where he was responsible for product development.

Roel has a sharp eye for detail. Above all, he strives to create overview and facilitate out-of-the-box thinking to bring people, processes and goals together. He learned the ins and outs of project management and product development at such organizations as DAF Trucks, Ordina, Vanderlande Industries, Philips and Assembléon.

He combines his work as a board member at Holland Innovative with his training sessions, master classes and coaching in project management and leadership development, and the execution of projects for clients in the high-tech, healthcare and agro & food sectors.

Roel is a physicist, but music also played a major role in his development. With his motto "I am the project manager in the band and the artist in the development team," he passionately strives to unite two fascinating worlds. In this book, the world of project management is covered from the perspective of a project manager, a physicist and a musician.

Visit www.roelwessels.com for more information, the details of project Roller Coaster and other extras.

Index